Driving Democracy

Do Power-Sharing Institutions Work?

Proposals for power-sharing constitutions remain controversial, as highlighted by contemporary debates in Iraq, Afghanistan, Nepal, and Sudan. This book updates and refines the theory of consociationalism, taking account of the flood of contemporary innovations in power-sharing institutions that has occurred worldwide. The book classifies and compares four types of political institutions: the electoral system, parliamentary or presidential executives, unitary or federal states, and the structure and independence of the mass media. The study tests the potential advantages and disadvantages of each of these arrangements for democratic governance. Trends in democracy are analyzed for all countries worldwide since the early 1970s. Chapters are enriched by comparing detailed case studies. The mixed-method research design illuminates historical developments within particular nations and regions. The Conclusions draw together the practical lessons for policymakers.

Pippa Norris is the McGuire Lecturer in Comparative Politics at the John F. Kennedy School of Government, Harvard University, and she has recently served as Director, Democratic Governance, United Nations Development Programme. Her work compares elections and public opinion, gender politics, and political communications. Companion volumes by this author, also published by Cambridge University Press, include *A Virtuous Circle* (2000), *Digital Divide* (2001), *Democratic Phoenix* (2002), *Rising Tide* (2003), *Electoral Engineering* (2004), *Sacred and Secular* (2004), and *Radical Right* (2005).

D1418269

Also by Pippa Norris

Political Recruitment: Gender, Race and Class in the British Parliament, with Joni Lovenduski (1995)

Passages to Power: Legislative Recruitment in Advanced Democracies (1997)

A Virtuous Circle: Political Communications in Post-Industrial Democracies (2000)
>   Awarded the 2006 Doris Graber award by APSA's political communications section

Digital Divide: Civic Engagement, Information Poverty, and the Internet Worldwide (2001)

Democratic Phoenix: Reinventing Political Activism (2002)

Rising Tide: Gender Equality and Cultural Change Around the World, with Ronald Inglehart (2003)

Sacred and Secular: Politics and Religion Worldwide, with Ronald Inglehart (2004)
>   Awarded the 2005 Virginia A. Hodgkinson prize by the Independent Sector

Electoral Engineering: Voting Rules and Political Behavior (2004)

Radical Right: Voters and Parties in the Electoral Market (2005)

Driving Democracy

Do Power-Sharing Institutions Work?

PIPPA NORRIS
Harvard University

CAMBRIDGE
UNIVERSITY PRESS

CAMBRIDGE UNIVERSITY PRESS
Cambridge, New York, Melbourne, Madrid, Cape Town, Singapore, São Paulo, Delhi

Cambridge University Press
32 Avenue of the Americas, New York, NY 10013–2473, USA

www.cambridge.org
Information on this title: www.cambridge.org/9780521694803

First published 2008

Printed in the United States of America

A catalog record for this publication is available from the British Library.

Library of Congress Cataloging in Publication Data

Norris, Pippa.
Driving democracy : do power-sharing institutions work? / Pippa Norris.
    p. cm.
Includes bibliographical references and index.
ISBN 978-0-521-87319-2 (hardback) – ISBN 978-0-521-69480-3 (pbk.)
1. Democracy. 2. Comparative government. 3. Public administration.
I. Title.
JC423.N67 2008
321.8–dc22   2007044303

ISBN   978-0-521-87319-2 hardback
ISBN   978-0-521-69480-3 paperback

Contents

Tables

Figures

Preface and Acknowledgments

Worldwide more electoral democracies exist today than at any time in history. Almost half of all governments can be considered democratic, according to one of the most widely used comparisons developed by Freedom House. Nevertheless most of the surge in democratization occurred during the late-1980s and early-1990s, following the fall of the Berlin wall. During the early twenty-first century, global progress has stagnated and there are also signs of an incipient backlash in some parts of the world, threatening fragile gains. It is therefore time to look anew at the capacity of institutional reforms to facilitate sustainable democratic regimes and to generate lasting peace settlements in multiethnic states, especially those emerging from deep-rooted civil wars.

Social scientists and policymakers remain divided about whether constitutional reforms designed to share power can reduce political instability in states experiencing internal conflict, or whether these arrangements may prove counterproductive by unintentionally reinforcing ethnic hatred or even fueling a strong resurgence of intercommunal violence. Despite decades of heated debate, this issue remains unresolved. Cases of both apparent success and failure of power-sharing institutions can be quoted by proponents on both sides. To look afresh at these issues, this book uses global comparisons from 1972 to 2004 and 10 selected case studies to reexamine classic questions about the potential impact of political institutions in fostering sustainable democracy. Building upon ideas that consociational theory first developed many decades ago, the study analyzes a new body of systematic evidence for understanding how the process of democratization is strengthened by proportional electoral systems, federal and decentralized forms of government, parliamentary executives, and freedom of the press. The paired case studies illustrate the divergent historical pathways taken by democracies and autocracies with different institutions, even among neighboring countries sharing a broadly similar cultural history, social structure, and level of economic development. This analysis builds on my previous book *Electoral Engineering: Voting Rules and Political Behavior* (2004), which examined the role of electoral systems in explaining patterns of voting behavior and political representation. I hope that this study will contribute toward informing the debate about the role of power-sharing institutions, and their importance for reformers, in the contemporary world.

This book owes multiple debts to many friends and colleagues. The theme of the book received encouragement in many conversations over the years with colleagues in the John F. Kennedy School of Government, Harvard University, and in the Democratic Governance practice, United Nations Development Programme. The book expresses the personal views of the author, however, and it does not necessarily reflect the views of the United Nations or its Member States. I am also most grateful to all of those who went out of their way to provide feedback on initial ideas, or to read through draft chapters and provide detailed comments. The research also received generous financial support with grants received from the Ash Institute for Democratic Governance and Innovation, the Kuwait Program Research Fund Middle East Initiative, and the Women and Public Policy Program, all at the John F. Kennedy School of Government, and the Weatherhead Center for International Affairs at Harvard. The collaboration with Cambridge University Press has been invaluable, particularly the patience and continuous enthusiasm of the editor, Lew Bateman, as well as the comments and encouragement of the reviewers.

Cambridge, Massachusetts

PART I

DO POWER-SHARING REGIMES WORK?

I

What Drives Democracy?

Why do some regime transitions generate effective and successful democratic states which persist over many decades while other autocracies persist unreformed? This process can be illustrated during the last decade by developments in two neighboring states in West Africa, Benin and Togo, which took divergent pathways on the road traveled to democracy. Both Benin and Togo inherited the legacy of French colonial rule. Both are poor. Both are multiethnic societies. Both states gained national independence in 1960, and after a few short years as fragile parliamentary democracies, both became military dictatorships. Yet in the early-1990s, under a new constitution, one made the transition to a relatively successful democratic regime, experiencing a succession of elections during the last decade which observers have rated as free and fair, and a peaceful and orderly transition of power from governing to opposition parties. The other remains today an unreconstructed and corrupt military-backed autocracy.[1]

What caused the contrast? In particular, did the power-sharing constitution adopted in Benin during the early-1990s facilitate the development of a sustainable democracy? Proponents of power-sharing arrangements make strong claims that regimes which include elite leaders drawn from rival communities encourage moderate and cooperative behavior in divided societies.[2] Power-sharing regimes are widely believed to be valuable for democracy in all states, but to be vital for containing and managing intercommunal tensions in multiethnic societies emerging from civil conflict, thereby helping to sustain fragile democracies. Similar assumptions have influenced the outcome of many recent peace settlements and treaties in deeply divided societies, for example in Bosnia-Herzegovina in 1995, Kosovo in 2001, and Northern Ireland in 1998.[3] Theories about the virtues of power-sharing regimes for multiethnic societies have been developed in the work of Arendt Lijphart, Eric Nordlinger, Gerhard Lehmbruch, Klaus Armingeon, and others, conceptualized alternatively as 'consociational democracy', 'consensus democracy', 'proportional democracy', or 'negotiation democracy'.[4] Today the more common concept is a focus upon 'power-sharing regimes', a term which is used here since it has been widely adapted in international relations and political science. Despite important differences embedded in these notions and arguments, the primary idea is that in multiethnic societies divided into different linguistic, religious, or national communities, power-sharing institutions and procedures turn political opponents into cooperative partners, by providing communal leaders with a guaranteed stake in the democratic process. By contrast, power-concentrating regimes offer rival communities a zero-sum game, where losers have fewer incentives to work within the conventional political rules.

These claims have always proved controversial, however, generating heated debates about the core concept and its consequences and the classification of cases. A chorus of skeptics have expressed serious doubts about the assumed virtues of power-sharing regimes and emphasized the breakdown and failure of these arrangements, drawing upon historical examples concerning the outbreak of armed conflict in Cyprus in 1963, Lebanon in 1975, Northern Ireland in 1974, and Czechoslovakia in 1993.[5] Controversy has rumbled on in the research literature for almost 40 years. Contemporary debates focus upon the difficult cases of Bosnia-Herzegovina and Iraq, and despite a wealth of case studies cited by both proponents and critics, many questions remain. Most importantly, do power-sharing regimes generally serve to dampen armed conflicts in deeply divided multiethnic societies and thereby produce a durable peace settlement, political stability, and the conditions under which sustainable democracy flourishes? Or may they instead, as critics charge, freeze group boundaries, heighten latent ethnic identities, hinder rebuilding the state in the early stages of recovery from violent internal conflict, and thereby fail to facilitate sustainable multiethnic democracies?[6] This unresolved debate raises critical issues both for academic researchers seeking to understand the underlying drivers of democratization and the causes of civil conflict and for policymakers concerned with negotiating effective peace treaties, supporting practical institutional reforms and constitutional settlements, and promoting sustainable democratic regimes.

Drawing upon this long-standing controversy, the aims of this book are twofold. The first is to update and refine theories of power-sharing regimes to take account of the flood of contemporary developments in state-building and institutional reforms which have occurred worldwide. The theory of consociationalism originally developed in the late-1960s to emphasize the importance of certain institutional arrangements which helped to maintain democratic stability in divided societies, including the existence of coalition governments, minority veto rights, proportional representation in public offices, and self-governing autonomy for territorial communities. Processes of regime change worldwide since the early-1970s and many recent negotiated constitutional settlements provide a wealth of natural experiments, operating under widely varying conditions. In a revision of the classic framework provided by the original theory of consociationalism to take account of contemporary developments, types of power-sharing or power-concentrating regimes are defined and conceptualized in this study in terms of four formal institutional features:

- The basic type of *electoral system* (shaping patterns of party competition and coalition governments);
- The horizontal concentration of powers in the type of *executive*;
- The vertical centralization of power in *unitary or federal states*; and
- The structure and independence of the *mass media*.

Constitutions commonly lay down many other normative principles and institutional characteristics of regimes, by establishing the basic structure and rules governing the state, but these four aspects represent some of the most fundamental building blocks. Other formal institutions in civil society also play a vital role in sustaining democratic governance by linking citizens and the state, notably competition and bargaining among multiple interest groups, parties, voluntary organizations, and community associations, but these organizations exist outside the state and, other than the guarantee of freedom of association, regulations of parties, and the establishment of basic civil liberties, beyond the core principles established in most formal constitutions.

Building on this conceptual foundation, the book tests the impact of power-sharing institutions on patterns of democratization in all societies worldwide, as well as in multiethnic societies, using a wider range of evidence and indicators than previous studies, covering more countries and a longer time period. The book adopts a mixed research design blending quantitative breadth with qualitative depth.[7] A large-N pooled dataset establishes the big picture. The study systematically analyzes patterns of regime change for three decades since the early 1970s in 191 contemporary nation-states worldwide (excluding independent territories). Time-series cross-sectional data is invaluable for testing how far theoretical generalizations about the impact of power-sharing institutions hold across diverse conditions and types of society. It facilitates formal models with multiple controls which can be tested using standard econometric techniques suitable for cross-national time-series data. The broad-brush perspective facilitates comprehensive comparisons across nation-states and over time. Nevertheless, alternative interpretations of panel data are possible since the test results remain particularly sensitive to specification issues, such as the use of lagged variables. This global picture is therefore combined with autopsies of 10 particularly dramatic cases of success and failure in democratic consolidation, to poke about among the underlying blood and guts. The technique of focusing upon comparable societies which took divergent political pathways – with cases such as Benin and Togo, South Korea and Singapore, Uzbekistan and Ukraine, the United Kingdom and New Zealand, as well as India and Bangladesh – facilitates more fine-grained examination of the causal mechanisms and political processes underlying the statistical patterns. Cases drawn from different regions, eras, cultures, and contexts, including both relatively homogeneous and multiethnic societies, help us to understand historical developments and processes of institutional changes within particular states, thereby adding a richer texture to the theory. Anomalies to general patterns also suggest possible revisions and extensions to the formal model. Before setting out the core argument and evidence in more detail, a brief comparison of the divergent West African cases serves to illustrate the classic issues at the heart of this study.

SUSTAINABLE DEMOCRACY IN BENIN VERSUS ELECTORAL AUTOCRACY IN TOGO

In 1960, after gaining independence, the French-administered section of Togoland became the nation of Togo. Although starting as a parliamentary democracy, Togo soon fell victim to a military coup. In 1963, when the army came out of its barracks, Togo saw the assassination of its first president, Sylvanus Olympio, a period of short-lived interim governments, and in 1967 the seizure of power in a military coup by Gnassingbe Eyadema, head of the armed forces. For subsequent decades, with the support of the security forces, Eyadema maintained his grip on power, banning all opposition parties and dissident movements. In the early-1990s, however, in line with the global wave of democratization, the international community put pressures on Togo to improve its human rights record, leading to the legalization of political parties in 1991. The following year, a new constitution established a presidential republic. In the presidential elections which followed, Eyadema won under the banner of the Rally of the Togolese People party (RPT), but only after the security forces suppressed the opposition and cheated in the polls. Democratic activists who mobilized with general strikes were met by armed troops, killing many protestors. Periodic clashes occurred between dissidents and the military, with an outbreak in 1994 causing an estimated 300,000 Togolese to flee to neighboring countries. The leadership of the opposition was hounded into exile abroad. In the 1998 presidential contest, when the possibility of a landslide victory for the opposition became apparent, the security forces halted the count and members of the Electoral Commission were forced to resign. Eyedema's main rival was banned from standing in the 2003 contest. The security forces maintained control through human rights violations, terror, and repression; Amnesty International reported many cases of political 'disappearances', arbitrary arrest, torture, and deaths in detention.[8] The National Assembly remains overwhelmingly dominated by the ruling party, providing no effective check on the executive: in 2002, the ruling Rally of the Togolese People party won 72 of the 81 seats.

In early-2005, after 38 years in power, when President Eyadema died in office, he was the longest serving ruler on the continent. His passing presented Togo with a short-lived opportunity for regime change but it was lost overnight. Bypassing the constitutional succession, the military immediately appointed his son, Faure Gnassingbe, as president. After an international outcry, a presidential election was held in April 2005, but the poll, which confirmed Faure Gnassingbe's grip on power with 60% of the vote, was widely regarded as

TABLE 1.1. *Key Indicators in Benin and Togo*

	Benin	Togo
SOCIAL AND ECONOMIC INDICATORS		
Area	116,622 sq km	56,785 sq km
Pop., 2007	8.1m	5.7m
Pop. below poverty line (%)	33%	32%
GDP per capita (PPP US$), 2006	$1,100	$1,700
Life expectancy at birth, 2003	53 years	58 years
Human Development Index, 2003	0.431	0.512
Adult literacy (% of pop. 15+), 2001	34%	61%
Ethnic fractionalization (Alesina), 2002	.787	.709
POLITICAL INDICATORS		
Year of independence (from)	1960 (France)	1960 (France)
Liberal democracy, Freedom House Index, 1973	6.5	6.5
Freedom House classification, 1973	Not free	Not free
Liberal democracy Freedom House Index, 2007	2	5.5
Freedom House classification, 2007	Free	Not free
Control of corruption (Kaufmann), 2005	16	30
Government effectiveness (Kaufmann), 2005	31	6
Political stability (Kaufmann), 2005	57	12
Rule of law (Kaufmann), 2005	36	14
Voice and accountability (Kaufmann), 2005	55	13
Regulatory quality (Kaufmann), 2005	30	21

Note: See the Technical Appendix for details of these indices and sources of data. Freedom House Index 7-point scale (where 1 = high, 7 = low). The Kaufmann indices rank each country on 0–100 point scales where higher = better governance ratings.

Source: Daniel Kaufmann, A. Kraay, and M. Mastruzzi. 2006. *Governance Matters V: Governance Indicators for 1996–2005*. Washington, DC: World Bank. www.worldbank.org

rigged in favor of the ruling party. West African observers reported irregularities in voter registration, limited information available during the campaign with a censored media, and prohibition of independent electoral monitors.[9] To maintain control, the president subsequently appointed his brother as the defense minister. Protests were met by tear gas and live ammunition from the security forces; about 500 deaths were recorded following the contest, according to UN estimates; and around 40,000 Togolese fled to neighboring Benin and Ghana. Several radio and TV stations critical of the military-backed succession were closed and Web sites were blocked. Togo is categorized among the 45 states worldwide rated as 'not free' by the 2006 Freedom House index, with ratings of political rights and civil liberties which are similar to those of Qatar, Tajikistan, and Rwanda (see Table 1.1 and Figure 1.1). It also performs weakly among African nation-states by the 2002 Kaufmann/World Bank indicators of voice and accountability (ranking 39th out of 49 in African states) and government effectiveness (ranking 40th), while being in the middle ranks of African nation-states for levels of corruption, regulatory quality, and rule of

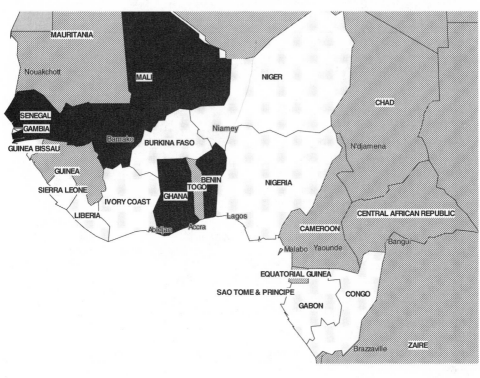

Key

Free   ■

Partly free   □

Not free   ▨

FIGURE 1.1. West Africa by Type of Regime, Freedom House, 2004. *Source:* Freedom House. 2004. *Freedom in the World.* www.freedomhouse.org

law. It is characterized by official corruption, a weak judiciary and lack of rule of law, and abusive powers exercised by the security services.

Togo is not among the most repressive one-party regimes and military dictatorships around the world, and it has avoided the most extreme abuses found in Equatorial Guinea, Eritrea, Zimbabwe, and Sudan – but neither has it registered sustained progress in human rights. It falls into the category of an 'electoral autocracy'. This important type of regime, which is neither fully autocratic not fully democratic, exists in an ambiguous gray zone which has been conceptualized by different authors alternatively as either 'electoral autocracies' (Diamond, Schedler), 'illiberal democracies' (Fareed), or 'competitive authoritarian regimes' (Levitsky).[10] Other common terms include 'hybrid' regimes, 'competitive authoritarianism', 'transitional democracies' (implicitly assuming that these regimes will eventually adopt broader institutional and political reforms in a progressive trend), or else as 'semi-free' states (Freedom House). These types of regime adopt some of the formal trappings of liberal democracy, notably holding flawed elections for legislative bodies which often function as powerless rubber-stamps, or rigged plebiscites to legitimate elite rule, but where in practice genuinely free and fair multiparty competition is restricted and basic human rights are widely abused.

After gaining independence from France, the neighboring state of Dahomey (which was renamed 'Benin' in 1975) started down a similar political road. In 1963, President Hubert Maga was deposed in an army coup led by Colonel Christophe Soglo. The country subsequently experienced a succession of half a dozen short-lived military and civilian regimes with a period of political instability which lasted until 1972, when Mathieu Kérékou seized power. The Parti de la Revolution Populaire du Benin (PRPB) established a one-party state in 1975, under an official Marxist-Leninist ideology, and appointed Kérékou president in 1980. The Kérékou government had a poor record on human rights although they started to liberalize the economy from state control, and in 1989 Marxism was abandoned as the official ideology. Under pressures from the international community and the opposition movement, in 1990 the government agreed to a new constitution and multiparty elections, with these changes approved in a popular referendum. Under the new arrangements, the president was to be directly elected for a five-year term, renewable only once, using a second ballot majoritarian system. The unicameral national legislature (Assemblée Nationale) was to be directly elected by party list proportional representation, using the largest remainder-Hare formula in multimember districts. An independent Constitutional Court, Supreme Court, and High Court of Justice were established. Local areas were governed by 12 départements and 77 communes (with municipal elections introduced in 2002). The national conference established a transitional government headed by the prime minister, Mr. Nicéphore Soglo, an ex–World Bank official. After passage of the new constitution, 70 political parties officially registered, rising to more than 100 by 1998. The result of February 1991 legislative elections was that the opposition party, the Union for the Triumph of Democratic Renewal (UTRD), gained a plurality of seats. After the presidential elections of March 1991, organized in a multiparty system, the main opposition UTRD candidate, Nicéphore Soglo, was elected president of the republic with over 67% of the vote.[11] In 1996, presidential elections returned the former president, Mathieu Kérékou, to the presidency of the republic, and in 2002 he was reelected, against a field of 17 candidates, for his final term in office. By the time of the March 2006 presidential elections, however, President Kérékou had to retire as he was over 70, and thus disqualified from restanding by the constitutional age-limit. Mr. Soglo was also too old, leaving the field open to younger contenders. In total, more than two-dozen candidates stood in the first round before the field was narrowed to Thomas Yayi Boni (an Independent, former banker, and newcomer to politics), who won with an overwhelming three-quarters of the vote in the second round, with Adrien Houngbedji (vereran leader of the Democratic Renewal Party) in second place. The presidential election represents another critical milestone in Benin's history. In April 2007, President Yayi Boni's coalition won control of parliament. Following this contest, the legislature contains a dozen parties, with 64 members of parliament acting as a seven-party coalition supporting the Presidential Movement while 19 members from five parties are on the opposition benches. The largest parliamentary party, the Cauri Forces for an Emerging Benin, gained 35 out of 83 seats (42%).

For more than a decade now Benin has experienced a series of legislative and presidential elections which domestic and international observers have reported as free, peaceful, and fair, including the transition bringing the opposition party into power. Today Benin is widely regarded as a successful African democracy with constitutional checks and balances, multiple parties, a high degree of judicial independence and respect for human rights, and a lively partisan press which is often critical of the government. The country is categorized as 'free' by the 2006 Freedom House index, comparable to Argentina, Mexico, and Romania in its record of civil liberties and political rights (see Table 1.1 and Figure 1.2). It also performs strongly against other African nation-states according to the Kaufmann/World Bank indicators of voice and accountability (ranking 10th out of 49 states in Africa), political stability (ranking 5th), and rule of law (ranking 14th). Benin still faces endemic poverty and many problems of governance common in African states, including corruption in the public sector, but several high-profile cases of malfeasance have been pursued by the courts. Benin has contributed toward peacekeeping in Cote d'Ivoire and helped to mediate political crisis in neighboring Liberia, Guinea-Bissau, and Togo. In short, from the 1991 transition onward, Benin has been widely regarded as a model country in sub-Saharan Africa for having successfully achieved a durable democratic transition without bloodshed and military coups. Will democracy eventually break down in Benin? The danger continues, as in any poor developing society, the future remains unforeseen, and the history of regime change in the continent suggests that democracy remains a fluid situation with steps forward and back. But a democratic regime has persisted in Benin since the early-1990s in the face of the odds.

EXPLAINING REGIMES IN THE CASES OF TOGO AND BENIN

So what caused the divergent political pathways taken by Togo and Benin, and what does this suggest more generally about the drivers of regime change and the conditions most favorable to building sustainable democracies and lasting peace?

Individual Leaders

Many historical accounts of the breakdown of autocracies emphasize the decisive contribution made by individual leaders in government or opposition who

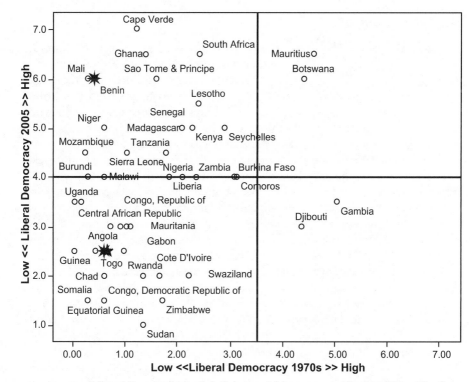

FIGURE 1.2. Liberal Democracy in Sub-Saharan Africa, 1970s and 2005. *Note:* The figures are the mean score of each country on the 7-point liberal democracy scale by Freedom House. *Source:* Freedom House. *Freedom in the World.* www.freedomhouse.org (various years).

were committed to political liberalization and human rights, while unsuccessful democratic transitions have been blamed on the failure of ruling elites to adjust successfully to political change.[12] Without the role of particular leaders, it is often argued, countries would have followed a different track, as exemplified by the impact of Adolfo Suarez in post-Franco Spain, Constantine Karamanlis's position after rule by the military junta in Greece, Lech Walesa's leadership of Solidarity in Poland, and Nelson Mandela's statesmanship in post-apartheid South Africa, to name just a few key historical figures. From this perspective, the routes followed by Benin and Togo could possibly be explained by the contrasting actions and decisions of particular presidents: Kérékou, who obeyed the constitution by standing down as president in 1991, and Eyadema, who flouted any limitation on his power until he eventually died in office. Individual actors can obviously play an important role in historical processes of regime change, but if the Benin transition flowed simply from an idiosyncratic leadership decision, this would not explain why the ruling party elite retired to the opposition bench after the 1991 elections in Benin, while by contrast the Rally of the Togolese People party, backed by the security forces, continues to rule in Togo, even after Eyadema's demise.

Economic Development

What of alternative structural explanations, discussed in detail in Chapter 4, emphasizing the underlying developmental, international, and cultural drivers of regime change? The classic developmental thesis associated with the work of Seymour Martin Lipset suggests that democracies flourish most in affluent societies with conditions of widespread literacy and education, and with a substantial middle class.[13] Both Benin and Togo remain among the poorest countries in the world, with domestic economies based on subsistence agriculture, employing about two-thirds of their workforce. Benin ranks 161st lowest out of 177 states in the 2003 United Nations Development Programme (UNDP) Human Development Index, with a per capita GDP (in purchasing power parity [PPP]) of $1,115. One-third of the population lives with incomes below the poverty level and two-thirds of the adult population is illiterate. Togo's economy is heavily dependent upon cocoa, coffee, cotton, and phosphate for exports, currently ranking slightly better than Benin (143rd lowest) in the 2003 UNDP Human Development Index, with a $1,700 per capita GDP (PPP). Living standards have deteriorated in Togo since the 1980s and the country remains heavily in debt. Life expectancy is around 54 years in both countries. Agrarian economies lack a propertied middle class, as well as organized labor unions among urban workers, both of which are often thought to provide the underlying conditions for civil society organizations connecting citizens and the state. Lack of development may contribute toward Togo's autocracy. But if so, this explanation fails to account for the successful political liberalization evident in even poorer Benin.

Natural Resources

The well-known 'resource curse' is another related economic explanation, suggesting that countries with abundant reserves of non-renewable mineral resources, such as Nigerian oil, Democratic Republic of the Congo (DRC) gold, or Sierra Leone diamonds, produce less diversified and less competitive economies, more income inequality with lower investment in building human capital, and heightened danger of state capture and rent-seeking by ruling elites.[14] Lootable resources, in particular, are thought to make a country particularly vulnerable to civil war, insurgency, and rebellion.[15] Togo's economy was concentrated more narrowly on natural resources (phosphorus exports) than Benin's, but after prices for this commodity plummeted during the 1980s, this potential explanation cannot account satisfactorily for divergent developments which occurred during the following decade. In general, the resource thesis also needs to explain how oil-rich extractive industries can be an apparent blessing for the Norwegian state but a curse in Saudi Arabia, and how diamonds can contribute toward tensions in Sierra Leone and yet remain a valuable source of national revenue for peaceful Botswana.[16] In these cases, the institutional arrangements that govern the distribution of revenue streams derived from natural resources and which promote political accountability and state responsiveness, as much as the existence and concentration of natural resources, seem important to the role of natural resources in conflict.[17]

Ethnic Divisions

Ethnic hatred is widely regarded as the root of much civil conflict.[18] Deeply divided societies with a high level of ethnic fractionalization among distinct religious, linguistic, nationalistic, or racial communities are often thought to be most vulnerable to armed internal conflict.[19] Multiethnic societies are widely assumed to face particularly serious challenges in holding democratic elections, maintaining political stability, and accommodating rival communities. For example, Mansfield and Snyder argue that holding early elections as part of any peace settlement in poor and conflict-ridden states can exacerbate tensions, by generating populist leaders seeking to heighten latent ethnic identities to maximize their popular support.[20] In this view, it is important to follow a sequential process in this context, first reconstructing the core functions of the state to maintain security and manage the delivery of basic public services before subsequently moving toward elections. Tensions among different ethnic communities are generally thought to undermine government legitimacy, social tolerance, and interpersonal trust, all of which are believed to lubricate the give-and-take of political bargaining and compromise which characterize democratic processes. In the worst cases, ethnic conflict may lead to deep-rooted and prolonged civil wars, and occasional cases of outright state failure, as exemplified by developments in Bosnia-Herzegovina, Rwanda, Sudan, Azerbaijan, Chechnya, and Sri Lanka.[21]

But the degree of ethnic fractionalization alone also fails to explain divergent developments in the particular cases under comparison. Both Benin and Togo are multiethnic plural societies, with tensions between groups, although they have escaped some of the severe ethnic conflict common in sub-Saharan Africa, and the sort of civil wars that have produced state collapse in Angola, Sierre Leone, Congo-Kinshasa, and Somalia. The Togolese population contains Ewe, Mina, and Kabre tribes and languages. The main cleavages follow a north-south division, with an estimated 70%–80% of the military forces drawn from the north. The multiethnic population in Benin is divided among an estimated 42 ethnic groups, distributed in different regions, with two main linguistic groups each with dialect variations, as well as divisions between those practicing different animist religions as well as the minority Christian and Muslim groups. Parties in Benin are largely structured along ethno-regional lines, facilitating group mobilization and interest representation in the political system.[22] The way that ethnic groups are represented in any political system is a complex process, discussed later, depending in part upon the type of electoral system used and the geographical distribution of ethnic groups within and across electoral districts, as well as the mobilization and heightening of ethnic identities through party politics, and the presence of cross-cutting cleavages (for example, regional, linguistic, and religious ties).[23] It may well be the case that ethnicity functions differently for politics in Benin and Togo, as a result of the way that communal grievances are mobilized, the accommodation of group interests, or the historical legacy of communal tensions. Ethnic diversity is widely recognized as not equivalent to ethnic conflict.[24] But simple measures estimating the degree of ethno-linguistic and ethno-political fractionalization suggest considerable similarities between both societies.[25]

Popular Demands from Radical Movements

The politics of economic inequality, and the way that this can generate radical demands for political change, is emphasized by other accounts, notably in a sophisticated rational game theoretic model developed by Acemoglu and Robinson.[26] According to this view, the story of democracy is one in which, faced with serious social unrest and the threat of revolution from below, the affluent ruling elite faces three options. They can decide to grant redistributive policy concessions to ameliorate popular discontent. They may choose to expand voting rights to poorer sectors of society, thereby conceding power. Or they can engage in repression by actively putting down rebellions. Acemoglu and Robinson argue that in many European countries, such as Britain, France, and Sweden, the extension of the universal male franchise during the nineteenth century took place as a result of pressure from the credible threat of popular violence, social turbulence, and chaos, arising from the radicalization and organization of urban workers.[27] Affluent elites conceded the voting suffrage to men, in this view, because they calculated that this option was less costly than letting loose the grapeshot on the streets of London, Paris, and Stockholm. One can argue whether this theory fitted the timing and sequence of historical developments which occurred with the expansion of the franchise in European democracies.[28] In Britain, for example, the threat of revolutionary action appeared stronger and more credible during the radical Chartist movement mass protests, which peaked with the 1848 petition signed by 6 million, at a time when Louis Philippe had been removed from the French throne and revolutions were soon to convulse other European capitals. By contrast although there were mass rallies, British politics were more quiescent around 1867 or 1884, when the Second and Third Reform Acts were passed expanding the franchise to adult male citizens living in urban and rural areas, respectively.[29] The account by Acemoglu and Robinson does not seek to explain the expansion of the universal franchise to the majority of the British population, when there was no revolutionary threat, with passage of votes for women in 1918 and 1928.

Without pursuing the accuracy of the historical argument in more detail, the 'revolutionary threat' thesis also fits most uneasily in the particular cases under comparison. Regimes in both Benin and Togo faced internal and external pressure for change during the early-1990s, including street protests and mobilization by the opposition movement. In the Togolese case, the security forces did not hesitate to suppress protest by using brute force and armed repression. Opposition activists were killed or fled to neighboring states. This led to some financial loss of development aid but the financial penalty was insufficient to force concessions from the military. In Benin, by contrast, the constitutional concessions agreed in the early-1990s stabilized and, upon losing the 1991 election, the ruling party conceded power to the opposition. In short, the game theoretic model of regime transition does not take us very far unless we know why rulers choose either to concede power or to employ repression.

International Pressures

Another possible factor for the growth of democracy in Benin could lie in the role of the international community, which has invested growing resources involving a wide range of actors and initiatives in promoting and facilitating democratic governance, where this has come to be understood as a vital component of human development.[30] This includes multilateral agencies such as the United Nations, the United Nations Development Programme, and the Bretton Woods institutions, which have become increasingly active during the last decade.[31] Regional organizations have also served an important function, such as the European Union, the Organization of American States, and African Union, as well as international agencies and nongovernmental organizations (NGOs) such as the International Institute for Democracy and Electoral Assistance (IDEA), the Inter-Parliamentary Union, and IFES (formerly the International Foundation for Election Systems).[32] Since the early-1980s, significant bilateral development aid offered by the United States has been devoted to democracy promotion, primarily channeled through the activities of the United States Agency for International Development (USAID), the National Endowment for Democracy, and the sister bodies, the National Democratic Institute for International Affairs (NDI) and the National Republican Institute for International Affairs.[33] Under the Bush administration, after 9/11, the rhetoric of US foreign policy also gave increased emphasis to linking democracy promotion with American interests, understood as a new doctrine of 'democratic realism'. Hence at a presidential speech on the 20th anniversary of the National Endowment for Democracy in November 2003, the Bush administration directly related the global expansion of freedom to American security. "As in Europe, as in Asia, as in every region of the world, the advance of freedom leads to peace."[34] In his second inaugural address, on 20 January 2005, President Bush went further in expanding this instrumental or pragmatic claim into a full-blown vision which the administration hoped would be capable of guiding US foreign policy for many generations.[35] Although the role of the United States has perhaps attracted the most attention and controversy, especially after interventions attempting state-building in Afghanistan and Iraq, in fact many other advanced industrialized countries have also channeled increasing resources into the promotion of democracy, 'good governance', and human rights, notably by development agencies such as Norway's Norwegian Agency for Development Cooperation (NORAD), Canada's Canadian International Development Agency (CIDA), and UK's Department for International Development (Dfid).[36]

Development aid has been invested in programs seeking to foster inclusive forms of participation, including elections as the most dramatic symbol of democratic progress, but also multiple projects designed to strengthen civil society associations and the independence of the news media. Other programs have sought to build state capacity, notably by carrying out public administration reforms designed to improve the transparency, accountability, and efficiency of the executive branch at national and subnational levels; by strengthening the power of elected legislatures; and by reinforcing rule of law through the judiciary. Decentralization has proved a popular strategy, seeking to develop the capacity of local communities to determine their own lives.[37] Programs have also emphasized the need to monitor and protect human rights, as well as integrating principles of gender equality into the heart of democratic governance.[38] It remains difficult to measure the precise impact of these diverse types of programs through standard econometric techniques, since any effects are often gradual, indirect, and long-term. Levels of aid expenditure are also a crude gauge of effectiveness; for example, the DRC transitional presidential election in 2006 cost $248 million, a staggering expenditure compared with the cost of a program directed at parliamentary strengthening in the same country. The empirical comparative evidence based on cross-national development aid has generated mixed results; for example, a study for the World Bank examined the impact of spending on democratization in a large sample of recipient nations over the 1975–2000 period and found no evidence that aid promotes democracy.[39] Nevertheless one of the most detailed studies analyzing trends in patterns of USAID expenditure on democracy promotion indicates that this was capable of generating tangible benefits in subsequent levels of democratization.[40]

There are also many case studies of specific programs and countries assessing the most effective strategies which the international community has used to respond to challenges in democratic transitions.[41] Cases suggest that these activities can help to sustain democratic regimes, where the international community provides financial resources, capacity-building, and technical assistance to support agencies and policies within each country seeking to promote human rights, strengthen civil societies, and reform governance. This process is exemplified by the role of the European Union in contributing to the dramatic political transformation of many post-Communist nation-states in Central Europe, notably in Hungary, Poland, and the Czech Republic, where democratic governance was required as a condition of entry into the European Union.[42] But there are also many conflicting pressures in foreign policy, and international pressures can also prove negative for democracy, for example, where the foreign policies of Western countries have served to support oil-rich autocracies or ruling elites which serve their own strategic interests.[43] Carothers has emphasized the inherent dualistic tensions within the Bush administration; the campaign against Al Qaeda means that the United States needs friendly allies, military cooperation, and diplomatic ties with states such as Pakistan, Saudi Arabia, Russia, and Uzbekistan, in contrast with the more idealistic desire to support opposition reform movements and human rights campaigners seeking to overturn autocratic regimes.[44]

How do these factors influence the two cases under comparison? In terms of international relations, both West African states are relatively minor players. Neither serves a vital strategic role, whether for external military bases or foreign investors, or as trading partners with major industrialized nation-states. As regional powers, in multilateral organizations, both are clearly outweighed by Nigeria and Ghana. Benin and Togo could therefore differ today because of the distribution of support from the international community. In particular, lack of democratic reforms has halted aid flows to Togo from the European Union and the United States. By contrast, with a more favorable human rights record, Benin receives about six times the total official development assistance from the international community. Nevertheless it is difficult to attribute Benin's success to international aid as the financial rewards have largely followed the shifts toward democracy in the early-1990s, reinforcing developments in each country and perhaps acting as an incentive for ruling elites. Other than functioning as a potential incentive, the timing of intervention and patterns of democratic aid assistance cannot be used as a cause to explain satisfactorily the initial regime transition which occurred in Benin during the early-1990s.

Regional Diffusion

Regional diffusion is another popular argument for processes of regime change, for example, the dramatic toppling of Communist states throughout Central Europe after the collapse of the Soviet Union.[45] Diffusion is not simply developments spreading accidentally in lagged fashion within a region; instead it requires that knowledge of innovation in one state spreads to others where similar strategies or tactics are adopted, as illustrated by the electoral revolutions which swept illiberal regimes from power since the mid-1990s in Bulgaria and Romania and then moved to Slovakia, Croatia, Serbia-Montenegro, Georgia, Ukraine, and Kyrgyzstan.[46] Other types of regional neighborhood effects are suggested by the striking predominance of autocratic regimes throughout the Arab world, where the third wave transition to democracy experienced in many parts of the world bypassed political regimes.[47] As noted earlier, regional organizations have also played an important role by shaping political developments within their sphere of influence, notably the European Union's impact over states both in the Mediterranean and in Central Europe, as well as the Organization of American States's impact in Latin America.[48] In recent years the African Union (AU) has given growing emphasis to human rights and democratic governance, at least in official declarations, treaties, and conventions.[49] Hence at a meeting in Addis Ababa in January 2007, the AU endorsed the *African Charter on Democracy, Elections, and Governance,* signed by 10 countries, including Benin.[50] Nevertheless these developments are relatively recent and the geographical explanation of regional diffusion remains unsatisfactory in the West African cases, as patterns of regime change within neighboring states remain checkered (see Figure 1.2); Togo and Benin are surrounded on their borders both by autocracies (Burkina Faso, Niger, Cote d'Ivoire) and by growing democracies (Mali, Ghana), as well as states which veer uncertainly between the two (Nigeria). Both countries have a common French colonial background, so this also rules out path-dependent historical explanations focused on different colonial legacies. Togo is slightly smaller than Benin in both size and population, so the relative advantages of governance and public administration which are often enjoyed by small and compact nation-states are also implausible as a possible reason for Benin's success.[51]

In short, several popular explanations of the underlying conditions leading toward processes of regime change – emphasizing the role of individual actors, levels of economic development, the resource curse, the existence of ethnic tensions, pressures derived from revolutionary threats and from the international community, and geographic patterns of regional diffusion – leave us with a continuing puzzle as these factors fail to account satisfactorily for these cases. Within the last decade, while initial attempts at liberalization stalled under military rule in Togo, the neighboring state of Benin progressed a long way down the road toward becoming a peaceful democratic regime with alternating parties in power, where the military stayed in the barracks. At this stage, having eliminated some of the usual suspects in the democratization literature as unconvincing, we may be tempted to conclude that the divergent developments in each country were simply accidental, explained by a particular configuration of specific circumstances and contingent events which are not repeatable elsewhere. Yet such a conclusion would be ultimately unsatisfactory and indeed if Benin's democracy is simply a one-off 'accident', how do we account for similar political developments in equally poor democracies on the continent, exemplified by Mali, Mauritius, Lesotho, Senegal, Namibia, and Ghana, as well as the well-known case of South Africa? Regime change may be triggered by many proximate catalysts, whether the death of a long-standing dictator, a failed military coup d'etat, an upsurge of 'people power' deposing a discredited regime, an external military invasion, or a sudden economic crisis or outbreak of internal conflict which generated state collapse. Each transition can be treated as sui generis, but the challenge for social scientists and for policymakers is to distinguish the factors which are common in the simultaneous breakdown of autocratic regimes and the consolidation of sustainable democratic regimes across many countries worldwide during the third wave.

Institutional Arrangements

The primary suspect, which has not yet been considered, concerns the type of institutional arrangements created by the new constitutions introduced in each country in the early-1990s. Togo opted for a strong presidency, with only weak legislative and judicial checks to counterbalance executive power. The Togolese constitution specified majoritarian elections, following France in using the second ballot electoral system (also known as the 'two-round' or 'runoff' system) for both presidential and legislative contests.[52] This requires 50% of the vote or more to win, raising the threshold facing minor parties. The ruling party holds 89% of the seats in the Togolese legislature, providing a rubber-stamping body with no effective restriction on the president. In other divided African states, the second ballot system has been blamed for the break-down of the electoral process and renewed outbreaks of civil war, including in Angola and in Algeria in 1992, and in the Republic of Congo in 1993.[53] Benin also adopted a presidential form of executive with a majoritarian second ballot system, but with multiple contestants; for example, the first round election saw 13 candidates in 1991 and 7 in 1996. Moreover the country opted for a pro-portional representation electoral system for the legislature, using closed party lists, the Hare quota, and greatest average, with no minimum legal threshold, producing a more competitive multiparty system. The judiciary also enjoys greater independence with the Constitutional Court responsible for the final announcement and validation of the election results, and an independent Elec-toral Commission that organizes parliamentary and presidential contests since 1995. Both are unitary rather than federal states, but Benin also decentralized more decision-making powers to regional and local elected bodies. Constitu-tional guarantees of press freedom are also far more extensive in Benin, where there are more than 50 newspapers, state and commercial TV channels, and over 30 state or commercial radio stations. Reporters without Borders's 2005 *Index of Press Freedom* ranked Benin as 25th worldwide, comparable to the United Kingdom, and higher than France, Australia, and the United States.[54] In Togo, by contrast, the government owns and controls the only significant television station; the only regular daily newspaper, the *Togo Presse*; and many of the radio stations.

The question – which is explored at the heart of this book – is whether the constitutional structures established in the early-1990s can be credited as the key element which led the countries down divergent political paths, par-ticularly contrasts between power-concentrating regimes with few checks on executive autonomy, exemplified by Togo, and the greater degree of power-sharing among multiple stakeholders found in Benin. Of course, there are many reasons to be cautious, and indeed skeptical, before accepting this poten-tial explanation. In regarding institutions as providing durable constraints on political actors, the precise timing of any rule changes must be carefully mon-itored. The adoption and effective workings of power-sharing regimes can be the product of a more democratic culture and society, as well as its endogenous cause. Political elites make constitutional rules which then bind their hands.[55] Some constitutional rules prove sticky; others prove malleable. Disentangling the direction of causality needs close attention to tracing step-by-step devel-opments and 'before-and-after' natural experiments in regime change. Issues of effective implementation are also fundamental, since de jure constitutional restrictions on executive power can exist as parchment barriers which are widely flouted in practice. We need to understand how power-sharing constitutions arise and what process of bargaining and pact-making leads to their acceptance and implementation among elites, especially in negotiated and imposed peace settlements. It would be premature to rule out other potential explanations for democratization which have not yet been considered, or to confirm at this stage that constitutional rules do indeed matter for regime change, in these particular countries and across a wide range of other cases. But certainly an initial comparison of Benin and Togo suggests that the institutional choices made in the early-1990s remain a prime suspect in any search for the reasons for the different type of regimes existing today. If so, Benin's power-sharing constitution may hold important lessons for democracy promotion strategies in other poor and divided societies, both in Africa and elsewhere in the world.

TRENDS IN DEMOCRACY WORLDWIDE

The timing of the breakdown of military rule in Benin in the early-1990s and the subsequent development of a sustainable democratic regime over successive elections were far from accidental. Events in this country illustrate broader trends, as the growing popularity of democratic regimes represents one of the most striking and dramatic political transformations experienced worldwide during our lifetimes. The broader phenomenon, popularly known as the 'third wave' of democratization as Huntington termed it, is conventionally understood to have commenced with the toppling of dictatorships in Portugal, Spain, and Greece during the early-to-mid-1970s.[56] Spreading from Mediterranean Europe, the movement toward democracy surged rapidly worldwide during the late-1980s and early-1990s, after the fall of the Berlin Wall and the collapse of Communist Party control throughout Central and Eastern Europe. Autocracies lost their grip over governments in many Asian states, and a series of elections in Latin America saw the end of military regimes in the region. The Middle East remains the global region least affected by these developments, although even here there have been growing pressures and some liberalization of the regimes, for example, multiparty national elections held in Algeria, Iraq, Palestine, and Egypt, and municipal elections held in Saudi Arabia; the expansion of political information from independent television news channels in the region; the formation of Human Rights Commissions in Egypt and Qatar; and the moves toward women's empowerment in Oman, Iraq, Afghanistan, and Morocco.[57]

The net impact of the third wave of democracy has transformed the global political map. There are many complex issues about how best to classify, measure, and categorize types of regimes, as discussed in Chapter 3. One of the most common approaches uses the estimates provided by Freedom House, a think-tank monitoring civil liberties and political rights worldwide. This organization classifies three-quarters of all countries as 'electoral democracies'

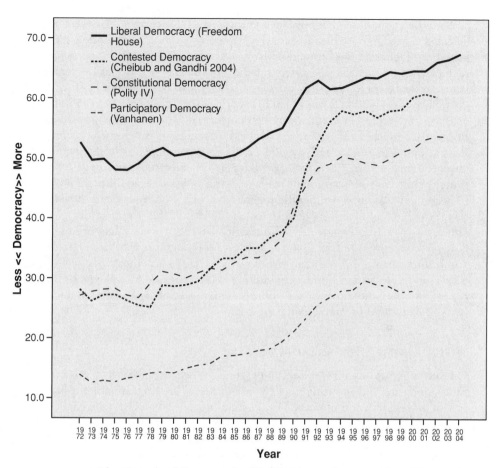

FIGURE 1.3. The Growth of Democracies Worldwide, 1972–2004. *Note:* The graph shows the growth in the proportion of democratic regimes worldwide as monitored using standardized 100-point scales by Freedom House, Cheibub and Gandhi, Vanhanen, and Polity IV. See Chapter 2 for a discussion of these measures and trends.

today, compared with less than half before the start of the third wave.[58] Nor is this simply a product of the measure and typology employed; as Figure 1.3 illustrates, both Polity IV and Vanhanen report a similar surge in levels of democratization, despite using different indicators and methodologies, as discussed fully in subsequent chapters.

During the early-1990s, stunned by developments, Francis Fukiyama anticipated 'the end of history' or at least the collapse of most authoritarian regimes and the triumph of Western political values and liberal democracy.[59] Subsequent events have made commentators, rightly, more cautious. After a few heady years in the late-1980s and early-1990s, indicators suggest that the tide of regime change lost momentum, despite the 'color revolutions', and the pace of sustained progress in democratization slowed in the early twenty-first century. Indeed, although it remains too early to tell for certain, observers have detected signs of a possible third reverse wave since 2000.[60] Any backlash may have been fueled by the Bush administration's rhetorical emphasis on democracy promotion while supporting strategic allies in the 'war on terror' such as Pakistan, Uzbekistan, and Egypt.[61] Trends may also have been influenced by the failure of the Maliki government in Iraq to achieve political progress, reduce conflict, and achieve a stable peace-settlement; as well as by the global price of oil; the threat of terrorism; the new assertiveness of states such as China, Russia, and Venezuela; and specific events undermining fragile democracies in places such as Fiji, Thailand, and Bangladesh. Electoral autocracies, illustrated by the case of Togo, have stagnated and failed to make the 'transition' to becoming sustained democratic regimes, as earlier observers had hoped. In this regard, many observers have detected the rise of the new type of regime, although this category has proved difficult to pin down as it has been alternatively conceptualized as 'hybrid regimes', 'semidemocracies', 'competitive authoritarianism', 'illiberal democracies', or 'elected autocracies'.[62] Overall it is apparent that despite subsequent striking and important breakthroughs since the early-1970s, the third wave revolution remains limited in its depth, uneven in its breadth, and incomplete in its impact.

THEORIES OF POWER-SHARING REGIMES

Questions about processes generating regime change, at the heart of this book, raise significant and enduring intellectual puzzles, attracting an immense literature in the research community.[63] Understanding these issues is a core challenge for scholarship in the social sciences and it is also vital for establishing what policy initiatives taken by the international community and by domestic reformers will prove most effective in promoting and sustaining democratic reforms. After more than three decades, like a complex series of natural scientific experiments, global developments in regime change since the early-1970s present major opportunities to understand and shape this important phenomenon. This preliminary and brief comparison of recent developments in Togo and Benin leads us to suspect, although these cases do not yet establish, that the institutional rules may matter for this process, allowing flourishing of liberal reforms and a reduction in conflict and instability, even in poor and divided societies. At some level it is obvious that formal institutional rules matter for regime change. Nevertheless reliable, systematic, and precise estimates of the effects of different types of institutions on democracy are often lacking. It is likely that societies that differ for a variety of reasons, such as geography, natural resources, and culture, will differ both in their political institutions and in their level of democracy. If this initial hunch that formal institutions matter is indeed correct, what specific institutions count, and what theories provide insights to help understand and explore these issues more systematically beyond these particular African cases?

This book builds upon, and updates, the theory of consociationalism, which has dominated scholarly debates about the most appropriate regime for democratic transition and consolidation, especially in deeply divided postconflict societies.[64] Consociational theory addresses the essential contrasts found between power-sharing and power-concentrating regimes.

Power-sharing regimes are understood in this study most generally as those states which are characterized by formal institutional rules which give multiple political elites a stake in the decision-making process. Such arrangements are most relevant for multiethnic societies, where each ethnic, linguistic, religious, or national community acquires a stake in the political process, but they are also potentially important for countries deeply divided by types of deep-rooted civil conflict which are not ethnically based, such as the Nepalese peace-settlement with the Maoist rebellion or an end to violence in Colombia between the state and outlawed armed groups and drug cartels. By contrast, *power-concentrating regimes* are characterized most broadly by more restrictive formal institutional rules which limit office to a smaller range of actors. This study focuses upon the formal institutional rules, notably the basic type of electoral system, the type of presidential or parliamentary executive, and the division of powers between the central state and regions, as well as freedom of the independent media, which are at the heart of any regime.

These institutional rules are also referred to collectively in this study as the 'constitutional arrangements' characterizing the regime, although the rules are not necessarily embodied in a written 'constitution', a 'fundamental law', or the 'basic laws' of a country.[65] This usage echoes the view of Dicey: "Constitutional law, as the term is used in England, appears to include all rules which directly or indirectly affect the distribution or the exercise of the sovereign power in the state."[66] The focus in this study is on the formal institutional rules governing the regime, in part because in a few countries such as the United Kingdom there is no single document representing the written constitution, but also, more importantly, because in others the formal rules governing the electoral system or the role of the independent media are determined by a range of secondary laws, administrative practices, and judicial decisions, with only the most general principles contained in the formal written constitution. Moreover in the case of freedom of the press, the practical constraints and legal restrictions which exist are sometimes totally at odds with the grand rhetoric embodied in the official state constitution.

The book draws upon but then updates the classic theory of consociationalism, which was originally developed in the late-1960s and early-1970s to explain stability in a few deeply divided European societies, including Austria, Belgium, and the Netherlands. The scope of this idea was subsequently widened considerably to cover several developing societies, such as Lebanon, South Africa, and Malaysia. The concept was developed by several writers, including Gerhard Lehmbruch, Jorg Steiner, and Hans Daalder.[67] The seminal political scientist, however, and the scholar who has continued to be most closely associated with developing and advocating the concept throughout his lifetime is Arend Lijphart.[68]

In 1968, Lijphart published *The Politics of Accommodation: Pluralism and Democracy in the Netherlands*. The book reflected upon the way that the Netherlands was a stable European parliamentary democracy despite being a deeply divided society with multiple cleavages or 'pillars' of religion and class. At the time, this phenomenon was considered puzzling, because it was widely assumed that the most stable representative democracies required the type of institutions which characterized the British political system during this era. Westminster was characterized by a two-party system in parliament, with the regular electoral swing of the pendulum producing a rotation of the major parties between government and opposition. The largest party with a parliamentary majority was empowered to govern without coalition partners, with the prime minister heading a collective cabinet and a well-disciplined parliamentary party. Westminster was centralized with a strong unitary state across the United Kingdom, although local governments administered parishes, counties, and municipalities. The British political system rested on the foundation of single member plurality elections, a relatively homogeneous society with the primary class cleavage reflected in the main parties, and a strong civic culture. Lijphart theorized that the Netherlands had nevertheless developed a stable democracy, despite social segmentation or 'pillarization', mainly due to the power-sharing structures, which encouraged elite cooperation. Proportional representation elections, multiparty parliament, and coalition cabinets generated multiple stakeholders in the political system, where community leaders learned to work together to bargain and compromise and, in turn, this situation encouraged tolerance and accommodation at mass levels. Consociational theory takes for granted the existence of social cleavages and rivalry among distinct communities for economic, social, and political goods and suggests that stable political systems overcome these rivalries by encouraging consensus, negotiation, and compromise among community elites.

Broadening the theory beyond the specific case of the Netherlands, Lijphart's consociationalism emphasizes the importance of governing incentives which work through a 'top-down' two-stage process. First, power-sharing arrangements are thought to mitigate conflict among leadership elites. "Consociational democracy means government by elite cartel designed to turn a democracy with a fragmented political culture into a stable democracy."[69] These arrangements are designed to maximize the number of 'stakeholders' who share an interest in playing by the rules of the game. This process is exemplified by proportional electoral systems with low vote thresholds which usually produce multiparty parliaments, with many minor parties each representing distinct segmented communities. In this context, party leaders have an incentive to bargain and collaborate with other factions in parliament in order to gain office in governing coalitions. Executive power-sharing is theorized to temper extreme demands and dampen expressions of ethnic intolerance among elites. In segmented societies, the leaders of all significant factions at the time of the settlement are guaranteed a stake in national or regional governments. This is thought to provide a strong enticement for politicians to accept the legitimacy of the rules of the game, to moderate their demands, and to collaborate with rivals. By making all significant players stakeholders, it is hoped that they will not walk away from constitutional agreements. In turn, to preserve their position in government, in the second stage of the process, community leaders are thought to promote conciliation among their followers and to encourage acceptance of the settlement. Under these arrangements, each distinct religious, linguistic, or nationalistic community, it is argued, will feel that their voice counts and the rules of the game are fair and legitimate, as their leaders are in a position to express their concerns and protect their interests within the legislature and within government.

Lijphart identified four characteristics of 'consociational' constitutions as an ideal-type: *executive power-sharing* among a 'grand coalition' of political leaders drawn from all significant segments of society; a *minority veto* in government decision-making, requiring mutual agreement among all parties in the executive; *proportional representation* of major groups in elected and appointed office; and considerable *cultural autonomy* for groups.[70] These arrangements, Lijphart suggested, have several benefits over majority rule in any society, generating 'kinder, gentler' governance with more inclusive processes of decision-making, more egalitarian policy outcomes, and better economic performance.[71] But the potential advantages of power-sharing institutions are nowhere more important for democracy and good governance, it is suggested, than in segmented societies which lack cross-cutting cleavages. In the most heterogeneous societies, Lijphart argues, "Majority rule spells majority dictatorship and civil strife rather than democracy. What such regimes need is a democratic regime that emphasizes consensus instead of opposition, that includes rather than excludes, and that tries to maximize the size of the ruling majority instead of being satisfied with a bare majority."[72] Lijphart argues that power-sharing regimes encourage group cooperation (at best) and avoid outright ethnic rebellion (at worst), in plural societies divided into distinct linguistic, religious, nationalistic, and/or cultural communities. If true, this represents an important claim that may have significant consequences. Power-sharing regimes can be regarded as, at minimum, a realistic initial settlement achieving the widest consensus among all factions engaged in postconflict negotiations. Proponents suggest that such regimes are also the most effective institutions for establishing democracy and good governance.

In subsequent work, Lijphart amended the core concept to draw a line between 'consensus' and 'majoritarian' democracies, extending the comparative framework to include 10 institutions divided into two dimensions. The 'executive-parties' dimension compared the concentration of executive power in single party or coalition cabinets, the use of dominant or balanced executive-legislative relations, two-party versus multiparty systems, majoritarian or proportional electoral systems, and pluralist or corporatist interest group systems. The federal-unitary dimension included unitary or federal systems, unicameral or bicameral legislatures, flexible or rigid constitutions, judicial review, and central bank independence. On the basis of this conceptual map and the comparison of 36 democracies, Lijphart argues that consensus democracies have many advantages. Where parties and politicians representing diverse ethnic communities are included in the governing process, Lijphart theorizes that segmented societies will more peacefully coexist within the common borders of a single nation-state, reducing pressures for succession. In this claim, Lijphart cites the conclusions drawn from early work by W. Arthur Lewis on the failure of 'Westminster'-style democracy when it was exported to post-colonial West African states.[73] For more systematic evidence, Lijphart shows that, with any prior controls, significantly fewer violent riots and political deaths were recorded in consensus rather than majoritarian democracies (measured by the executive-parties dimension).[74] Consensus democracies, Lijphart suggests, also have many other benefits, notably in the quality of democracy (for example, by generating a larger proportion of women in elected office, greater party competition, higher voting turnout, and stronger public satisfaction with democracy), as well as by producing more successful macroeconomic management (in terms of the record of inflation, unemployment, and economic inequality). As Bogaards notes, in making this argument, the description and classification of consociational institutions evolve in Lijphart's work into normative prescriptions of the best type of regime for divided societies.[75]

The power-sharing model was originally established as an alternative to 'Westminster'-style majoritarian or power-concentrating regimes, characterized by unitary states and majoritarian-plurality elections. Consociationalism claims that winner-take-all regimes are more prone to generate adversarial politics in a zero-sum power game. Even critics would not dispute that majoritarian democracies can work well under certain conditions: in relatively homogeneous societies, as well as in cultures characterized by deep reservoirs of interpersonal trust and social tolerance, and in stable democracies with regular alternation among the main parties in government and opposition. In this context, losing factions in one contest will accept the outcome of any single election as fair and reasonable because they trust that, in due course, a regular swing of the pendulum will eventually return them to power in subsequent elections. But these conditions may well be absent in societies with a legacy of bitter and bloody civil wars, factional strife, or intercommunity violence, and in transitional post-authoritarian states, such as Benin, with little or no experience of electoral democracy. Where minority groups are persistently excluded from office in the legislature or in executive government, majoritarian systems dilute the incentives for community leaders to compromise their demands, to adopt conciliatory tactics, and to accept the legitimacy of the outcome. These problems can be exemplified by sporadic outbreaks of sectarian violence and the lack of sustained progress toward democracy evident in Kenya, Nigeria, and Zimbabwe.[76] The worst-case scenario of civil war, ultimately leading to genocide, is illustrated by Burundi's 1993 election held under majoritarian rules, where Sisk suggests that the fears of the minority Tutsi were exacerbated by the ascendance to power of a party representing the more populous Hutu.[77]

Majoritarian regimes fail to incorporate minorities into government, encouraging excluded communities to resort to alternative channels to express their demands, ranging from violent protest to outright rebellion and state failure.

Lijphart emphasizes that power-sharing regimes are not only best for creating a durable long-term accommodation of cultural differences; in reality these are the only conditions which are broadly acceptable when negotiating any postconflict settlement. Consociationalism can be regarded as, at minimum, the most realistic perspective, representing the necessary conditions to secure peace-agreements among all parties.[78] Lijphart reasons that considerable uncertainty surrounds the implementation and outcome of any new constitutional agreement. Groups may have partial information about the strength of their support and thus the outcome of any contest. Political actors are also assumed to be relatively risk-averse. Majoritarian rules of the game raise the stakes of any negotiated peace-settlement: some parties will win more; others will lose more. The risks are therefore higher; if one faction temporarily gains all the reins of government power, few or no effective safeguards may prevent them from manipulating the rules to exclude rivals from power on a permanent basis. Established democracies have developed deep reservoirs of social trust and tolerance which facilitate the give-and-take bargaining, compromise, and conciliation characteristic of normal party politics. Yet trust is one of the first casualties of societal wars. Under majoritarian rules, without any guarantees of a regular swing of the electoral pendulum between government and opposition parties, losing factions face (at best) certain limits to their power, potential threats to their security, and (at worst), possible risks to their existence. For all these reasons, Lijphart argues that the only realistic type of settlement capable of attracting agreement among all factions in postconflict divided societies are power-sharing regimes which avoid the dangers of winner-take-all outcomes. More inclusive power-sharing regimes are likely to develop stronger support from stakeholders and thus to generate stable institutional equilibrium. Empirical evidence supporting this argument is presented by Linder and Baechtiger, who compared 62 developing countries in Asia and Africa and report that a summary index of power-sharing is a significant predictor of democratization.[79] Nevertheless in the longer term power-sharing institutions may also produce certain undesirable consequences for good governance, including the potential dangers of policy-stalemate, immobility, and deadlock between the executive and legislature; the lack of an effective opposition holding the government to account and providing voters with a clear-cut electoral choice; a loss of transparency in government decision-making; and the fragmentation of party competition in the legislature, while federalism is accompanied by the dangers of secession.

CRITICS OF POWER-SHARING REGIMES

Despite the popularity of the theory that power-sharing regimes are the most effective for sustaining democracy, especially in divided multiethnic societies, critics have challenged the core assumptions and claims.

The strongest charges are that power-sharing regimes which recognize exist-ing community boundaries assume that ethnic divisions in mass society, such as those between rival communities in Northern Ireland, are intractable and persistent. Understood in this light, the major challenge becomes how best to reflect and accommodate such social cleavages within the political system. An alternative constructive perspective emphasizes instead that ethnic identities are not fixed and immutable; instead they have social meanings which can be rein-forced or diluted through political structures and through elite leadership.[80] Donald Horowitz articulated perhaps the most influential critique by argu-ing that power-sharing regimes may in fact serve to institutionalize ethnic cleavages, deepening rather than ameliorating social identities. In particular, he suggests, the lower vote thresholds characteristic of proportional represen-tation electoral systems provide parties and politicians representing minority groups with minimal motivation to appeal for voting support outside their own community.[81] In this context, in deeply divided societies, leaders may use populist rhetoric to exploit, and thereby heighten, social tensions, ethnic hatred, and the politics of fear. Indeed, moderate leaders who seek to coop-erate across ethnic lines may find that they lose power to counter-elites who regard any compromise as a 'sellout'. By failing to provide leaders with an effective electoral incentive for cross-group cooperation, Horowitz suggests that in the longer term proportional representation (PR) may serve to institu-tionalize and thereby reinforce ethnic tensions in society, generating greater political instability, rather than managing and accommodating communal differences.

The clearest illustration of these dangers can be found in the case of the post-Dayton power-sharing arrangements introduced to govern Bosnia and Herze-govina. The division of government among the Bosnians, Croats, and Serbs was implemented with an intricate set of constitutional arrangements balanced at every level. Proportional elections for the lower house were held in 1996 when the major leaders of each community mobilized support within each of the three national areas by emphasizing radical sectarian appeals, and electors cast ballots strictly along ethnic lines. Studies suggest that after Dayton, subsequent population shifts led to fewer multiethnic communities, not more.[82] In this perspective, power-sharing regimes based on formal recognition of linguistic or religious groups may magnify the political salience of communal identities, by institutionalizing these cleavages and by providing electoral incentives for politicians and parties to heighten appeals based on distinct ethnic identities. Snyder presents a strong argument that in the early stages of democratization, weak politicians may decide to fan the flames of ethnic hatred and nation-alism to build popular support: "Purported solutions to ethnic conflict that take predemocratic identities as fixed, such as partition, ethno-federalism, eth-nic power-sharing, and the granting of group rights, may needlessly lock in mutually exclusive, inimical national identities. In contrast, creating an institu-tional setting for democratization that de-emphasizes ethnicity might turn these identities towards more inclusive, civic self-conceptions."[83] In this perspective, explicit recognition of ethnic rights may make it more difficult, not easier, to generate cross-cutting cooperation in society, by reducing the electoral incentives for elite compromise.[84] PR electoral systems, in particular, lower the vote threshold to electoral office; as a result parties and politicians may be returned to power on the basis of electoral support from one religious or linguistic minority community, rather than having to appeal to many segments of the broader electorate.

By contrast, Horowitz theorizes that the higher vote thresholds characteristic of electoral rules where the winner needs to gain an absolute majority of the vote (50% + 1) give politicians and parties a strong incentive to seek popular support (vote-pooling) across groups. Both the alternative vote (also known as the preferential vote or 'instant runoff', used for the Australian House of Representatives) and the second ballot (used for many presidential elections, such as in France) require parties and candidates to win an absolute majority of the votes, so politicians must seek support among a broad cross section of the electorate. Majoritarian electoral systems are thought to encourage 'bridging' cross-identity appeals, targeting rich and poor, women and men, as well as diverse ethnic communities.[85] More moderate electoral appeals should thereby foster and encourage the cultural values of social tolerance, accommodation, and cooperation in society. Along similar lines, Ben Reilly argues that the alternative vote electoral system is more effective at providing incentives for parties and politicians to seek multiethnic votes, generating moderating compromises with members of other communities for the sake of electoral success.[86] Nevertheless few countries have adopted an alternative vote electoral system, and when this system was used in Fiji it failed spectacularly in the May 2000 coup led by George Speight.[87] Barkan also suggests that in agrarian African societies, PR often does not produce electoral results that are significantly more inclusive than majoritarian elections with single-member districts.[88] Moreover, he suggests that under PR multimember constituencies, the weaker links connecting citizens with elected members and the loss of constituency service and public accountability of elected officials reduce the prospects for long-term democratic consolidation in Africa.

Another challenge arises from Lijphart's claim that power-sharing regimes are the only realistic way to achieve a voluntary peace settlement and a consensus about the constitutional rules among rival factions in divided societies. This is not necessarily the case, however, because of the trade-off values involved in the choice of any new institutional framework and the need to balance competing demands.[89] This is shown, for example, by the contrasts between the new constitutions in Iraq and Afghanistan. Both countries have differed in their priorities; Afghanistan selected a majoritarian electoral system (single nontransferable vote) with provincial constituencies for the lower house (Wolesi Jirga) and the second ballot system for the presidential election (second ballot). By contrast, the Iraqi parliament uses proportional representation elections (regional party lists with a Hare quota) plus compensatory seats for minority parties. In Iraq, PR elections generated a multiparty legislature and a multiparty coalition government was established with a mixed type of executive, where powers were divided between the prime minister, Nuri al-Maliki, and an indirectly elected three-person presidential council, headed by Jalal Talabani. By contrast, in Afghanistan the constitutional agreement following the Loya Jirga concentrated considerable decision-making power in the presidency and executive, checked by a weak legislature.

Another important issue in postconflict agreements, such as in Bosnia, East Timor, Kosovo, and Sudan, is how power-sharing arrangements are brokered, and in particular whether they arise from negotiated pacts among all major parties, from one side achieving a decisive victory and seizing control of the state following an armed struggle, or from a peace settlement generated by the international community and external forces. Power-sharing constitutions which are imposed by external powers on a country after intense ethnic conflict seem least likely to survive and to provide durable peace-settlements, particularly once the outside powers withdraw and cease to enforce the arrangement.[90] The chances of a durable peace remain relatively poor; for example, Collier estimates that 40% of civil wars recur within a decade and thus, on average, a country that has terminated civil war can expect the outbreak of a new round of fighting within six years.[91] The civil wars that end with an outright victory – as compared to a peace agreement or a ceasefire – are three times less likely to recur, possibly because one party is sufficiently subdued or deterred from fighting again.[92] Furthermore, in civil wars where third parties intervene by economic, diplomatic, or military means, conflict persists, except when the intervention clearly supports the stronger party, in which case it mainly shortens conflict.

Given these estimates, consociational theory may underestimate certain practical realities about achieving durable power-sharing agreements in societies such as Sri Lanka, Rwanda, Timor Leste, or Iraq, which are emerging from years of violent rebellion, prolonged militant hostilities, and armed uprisings. The initial period of peace-building in such a society is one fraught with considerable uncertainties and risks, where a few spoilers may use violent tactics to block full implementation of any constitutional settlement. In the immediate aftermath of conflict, the public is likely to place considerable priority upon restoring security, repairing the basic infrastructure, and encouraging the conditions for economic regeneration. Newly elected legislatures and governments engaging in lengthy periods of internal negotiation and partisan squabbling in the allocation of government portfolios may prove incapable of achieving a consensus and taking effective action in a timely fashion, for example, in determining national priorities about restoring basic services. In these circumstances, the public may well become impatient and blame the constitutional settlement for the perceived lack of progress. In this context, constitutional settlements which generate power-concentrating regimes may be preferable, by strengthening the capacity of elected government leaders to take difficult but necessary actions to improve security and rebuild the state.

In a related argument, both Roeder and Rothschild and Mansfield and Snyder suggest that a sequencing process is necessary for the peaceful consolidation of democracy.[93] In the early stages of the initial transition from autocracy, when political institutions remain weak, states remain highly unstable and vulnerable to increased likelihood of violence and war. Power-sharing is one of the easiest ways to arrive at a multiparty negotiated peace-settlement but nevertheless this arrangement may tend to freeze in the divisions already present in a country. The peaceful transition to democracy, Mansfield and Snyder argue, requires that states first need to establish national boundaries, administrative capacity, and rule of law, concentrating power in strong central state institutions, for example, in the public sector and police force, before taking the step of encouraging mass political participation and elections. The strength of domestic institutions is measured by the degree to which domestic authority is concentrated in the state's central government, or the antithesis of power-sharing. If this sequence is not followed, the authors argue, the danger is that rising populist pressures, and lack of state capacity to mediate conflicting pressures from different interests, may fuel internal conflict and a bellicose nationalism which triggers war. There may also be a contagion effect at work; Tull and Mehler suggest that Western efforts to solve violent conflict in African states through power-sharing peace-settlements may encourage rebel leaders elsewhere across the continent to embark upon the insurgent path, challenging the state through violent uprisings, in the hope of gaining power.[94] Overall in failed states, where basic services have broken down, the public may prioritize government effectiveness in the delivery of basic public services, such as security, housing, and electricity, rather than constitutions requiring lengthy debate, negotiation, and bargaining among multiple parties, bodies, and agencies to arrive at decisions. Power-sharing may thereby reduce confidence in the new constitution and undermine the long-term process of democratic consolidation. By contrast, power-concentrating regimes may prove more effective at taking decisive and timely actions to prevent war or to restore the infrastructure devastated by conflict.

THE PLAN OF THE BOOK

To summarize, given the divergent theoretical perspectives and empirical findings in the research and policymaking communities, it is important to reexamine the arguments put forward by consociational theorists about the suitability of power-sharing constitutional arrangements for successful democratic consolidation, especially in divided societies. Many claims are based upon specific case studies, exemplifying both the success and the failure of these arrangements, but it remains difficult to generalize from these systematically to broader patterns found elsewhere. We also need to analyze the relative importance of political institutions compared with alternative explanations for democratic consolidation, and how institutions work under different social and cultural conditions.

The book therefore sets out to reexamine whether political institutions, particularly power-sharing arrangements, explain the divergent pathways taken by autocratic and democratic regimes.

Part I of the book lays the foundations for the study by considering the most appropriate research design, comparing alternative measures of democracy, and examining the social and cultural conditions which underpin and reinforce the impact of institutions on democratic consolidation. *Chapter 2* summarizes and critiques the methods and approaches which have been used to examine consociational theory in the previous literature and then describes the research design adopted by this study. One reason why the debate remains unresolved is the difficulty of operationalizing many of the core concepts in consociational theory. This study seeks to clarify the argument by establishing consistent and reliable comparative evidence about power-sharing arrangements used in a wide range of countries. Lijphart's theory of power-sharing suggests that these arrangements provide more stable democracies, which benefit in terms of a number of social and economic outcomes, for example, in terms of gender equality and social welfare. He emphasizes that these arrangements are generally desirable for *all* states but that they are also vital for those seeking accommodation in multiethnic societies, where linguistic, religious, or national communities coexist within the borders of a single nation-state.

This study therefore adopts a large-N approach by comparing time-series cross-sectional data (CSTS) covering 191 contemporary countries around the globe, including both ethnically heterogeneous and relatively homogeneous nation-states. This strategy is also important because in this study ethnicity is not treated as 'given' and immutable; instead it is understood as at least partially politically constructed, so that focusing upon only the contemporary multiethnic or divided societies would distort the results of the analysis by introducing a systematic bias. The analysis covers political developments occurring from 1972 to 2004, years that are widely recognized as the period of the 'third wave' of democratization. The cross-sectional time-series data analysis compares institutions across all societies and then runs the models again for multiethnic (plural) societies, measured by the Alesina index of ethnic fractionalization. The models for all societies also control for ethnic fractionalization.

In addition, the specific case studies explore these relationships in more depth by examining how ethnic minorities are accommodated under power-sharing arrangements, for example, for the Maoris in New Zealand, along with the multiple linguistic and religious communities in India. No single approach is wholly persuasive by itself, however, and there are limits to the analysis of panel data, so this quantitative analysis is supplemented by qualitative paired case studies illustrating processes of historical development within particular nation-states. The research design does not make any assumptions using the conventional distinction made between indigenous (homeland) minorities and immigrant minorities, and the political consequences of each, because it is not self-evident that this is the most important aspect of ethnicity which leads toward demands for self-government. In addition, this conventional dichotomy fails to capture the complexity of ethnic identities in many parts of the world. Hence some cases under comparison examine the politics of indigenous minorities (for example, in New Zealand), while others examine multiple dimensions of ethnicity.

Chapter 3 considers the most suitable indicators of democracy. Four measures are compared: Freedom House's index of liberal democracy, the Polity IV project's measure of constitutional democracy, Vanhanen's indicator of participatory democracy, and Przeworski and colleagues' classification based on notions of contested democracy. These represent the most widely cited standard indicators of democracy which are commonly used by scholars and policy analysts in comparative research. Each has several strengths and weaknesses. The pragmatic strategy, adopted by this book, is to compare the results of analytical models using alternative indicators, to see whether the findings remain robust and consistent irrespective of the specific measure of democracy which is employed for analysis. If so, then this generates greater confidence in the reliability of the results. Comparison of these indicators also identifies major trends in the democratization process during the third wave period. These indicators are distinct from notions of 'good governance' which are also widely used, for example, measuring levels of corruption or rule of law, and the concluding chapters explore the relationships of democracy, indicators of the quality of governance, and broader issues of human development.

Before testing the impact of any constitutional arrangements, the study first needs to consider the most appropriate controls for properly specified multivariate models, since institutions represent only part of any comprehensive explanation of the process of democratization. *Chapter 4* examines the underlying social conditions believed to sustain democracy, notably the impact of wealth and poverty. An extensive literature, following the seminal work of Seymour Martin Lipset, has emphasized the overwhelming importance of economic development for democratic consolidation. Economic accounts are probabilistic; it is not claimed that democracies can *never* be established in poor states, such as Benin, but it is implied that this type of regime rarely flourishes for long in inhospitable environments. Despite the extensive literature, the precise reasons for the relationship between wealth and democracy remain poorly understood. Moreover previous studies often do not examine political developments occurring since the early-1990s in many poorer African, Asian, and Latin American nation-states. To reexamine the evidence, to update the literature, and to establish suitable controls for subsequent models, this study analyzes how far patterns of democracy are systematically related to economic development. Building upon a range of studies in the literature, other structural conditions which are also analyzed in this chapter include the extent to which democracy is related to the size of nation-states, the role of colonial legacies, patterns of regional diffusion, and the degree of ethnic heterogeneity. The East Asian cases of South Korea and Singapore help to illustrate the strengths and limitations of economic explanations alone.

Having laid the preliminary groundwork, *Part II* analyzes the evidence for the consociational claim that power-sharing regimes are more effective than power-concentrating regimes for sustaining democracy. Successive chapters in this section focus upon four central aspects of power-sharing arrangements which have widely featured in contemporary constitutional debates, each of which provides potential checks on the autonomy and power of the single-party executive, namely, the type of electoral system, presidential versus parliamentary executives, federalism and decentralization, and regulation of political communications.

Chapter 5 considers the most appropriate typology of *electoral systems*, how these rules generate patterns of party competition which are important for power-sharing within legislatures and coalition governments, and whether the type of electoral system is systematically related, as consociational theory claims, to democratic consolidation. Multiple rules shape electoral systems and scholars have focused on several major aspects: the basic type of electoral system, the vote-seats allocation formula, the mean district magnitude, the ballot structure, the use of legal minimal vote thresholds for parties qualifying for seats, the existence of positive action strategies for women and minorities, and the regulation of state funding and campaign communications for political parties. In established democracies electoral rules are often regarded as endogenous, but elsewhere these institutions have sometimes proved far less sticky, and, as Colomer emphasizes, it is usually politicians who make the rules.[95] Where electoral reforms are introduced, in order to disentangle the direction of causality, studies need to pay careful attention to the 'before' and 'after' temporal sequence, for example, the effective number of parliamentary parties in the elections immediately preceding and succeeding the implementation of any reform. Established democracies have also sometimes experienced pressures for major revisions to their electoral systems, and Britain and New Zealand provide illustrative cases here. Both these nation-states once exemplified classic majoritarian or 'Westminster' parliamentary democracies, sharing strong cultural bonds and historical ties, yet with different experiences of electoral reform since the early-1990s.

Beyond elections, the type of executive, determining horizontal linkages in government decision-making, is often regarded as important for democratic consolidation. *Chapter 6* analyzes the systematic contrasts found between presidential and parliamentary executives. Parliamentary systems headed by a prime minister are commonly regarded as more effective for political stability, through binding together the executive and legislature. Cabinet governments are collegial bodies where the classical notion suggests that the prime minister is 'first among equals' (primus inter pares). By including representatives from minority parties in cabinet office, coalition governments facilitate bargaining and compromise among parties within the executive. Presidential systems, by contrast, are winner take all as executive power is concentrated in the hands of a single leader. Some evidence supports the notion that parliamentary systems are superior for strengthening democratic regimes. Stepan and Skach compared types of executives during the early-1990s and concluded that parliamentary executives were more effective for democratic consolidation than presidential systems. The reasons, they suggest, are that parliamentary democracies are more likely to allow the largest party to implement their program, even in multiparty systems. Moreover unpopular prime ministers can be replaced without destabilizing the whole administration through the impeachment process or through calling fresh elections. By facilitating leadership turnover and thereby providing an outlet for popular disaffection, a parliamentary system is also thought less susceptible to military coups.[96] And parliamentary democracy also encourages long-term party-government careers, strengthening the partisan bonds and legislative experience of political leaders.[97]

Still no scholarly consensus exists about the supposed virtues of parliamentary executives for sustaining democracy, in large part because much of the previous evidence was limited to comparing presidential systems in Latin America with parliamentary systems in Western Europe, making it difficult to compare like with like.[98] Presidential systems used to be relatively rare, although these arrangements have now been adopted in a wide range of newer democracies. Moreover research on post-Communist states suggests that what matters may be less the formal structure of a presidential or parliamentary executive than the strength or weakness of the legislature, and thus the ability of this body to check the executive.[99] Rather than simple dichotomies of parliamentary versus presidential systems, there are many different types of checks on the power of presidential executives, so we need to consider the impact of these institutional variations. In the light of this debate, this chapter reexamines the global evidence for the relationship between types of executives and the democracy indicators.

Another institutional feature, influencing vertical channels of decision-making, concerns how far power is concentrated in the nation's central government and how far it is devolved downward to subnational and local levels. *Chapter 7* examines federalism and decentralized structures of decision-making. The second half of the twentieth century saw a proliferation of federations, and a variety of related forms of decentralization designed for multicultural societies, most recently in the constitutional reforms occurring in Belgium (1993), South Africa (1997), and Spain (since 1978) and devolution in Britain (in 1999).[100] These arrangements are often believed to be critical for democratic consolidation, especially in divided societies, by allowing ethnic minorities considerable self-determination over their own affairs on culturally sensitive matters, such as linguistic and educational policy. Partition which separates groups and redistributes populations into distinct regions, allowing each minority group to exercise self-government and gain security in the areas where it forms the majority, has been argued to be the only realistic solution to intense civil wars where ethnic loyalties have calcified into ethnic hatreds.[101] Yet critics of federalism fear that this process can result in succession and the breakup of nation-states, such as in the shattered former-Czechoslovakia and Yugoslavia, especially if boundaries are drawn to reinforce ethnic identities and regional parties.[102] Treisman examines a range of empirical evidence and suggests that decentralizing powers from central to local governments does not necessarily produce more effective and responsive rule, as advocates claim.[103]

Chapter 8 turns to the role of the fourth estate, as independent journalism can provide another vital check by reporting the abuse of power by the executive, as well as providing a channel of expression for dissident forces and opposition movements, strengthening the transparency of government decision-making, and revealing problems of corruption in the public sector. Commonly regarded as part of the public sphere, rather than a classic institution of government, nevertheless the regulation of the primary channels of political communications, particularly the independent news media, should be seen as an important part of the institutional reforms for strengthening and consolidating democratic regimes. For example, Besley and Burgess found that in the Indian case, governments proved more responsive to shocks, such as falls in crop production and crop flood damage, in states where newspaper circulation was higher and electoral accountability greater.[104] Cases examining the role of the press are selected from post-Communist Eurasia, a region which has registered some important gains for electoral democracy following the fall of the Berlin Wall, but which also contains some strongman autocracies, such as Belarus and Turkmenistan, where practices such as censorship, persecution and intimidation of independent journalists, and disinformation campaigns by the state remain common. Ukraine and Uzbekistan are selected for in-depth comparison.

Part III concludes by focusing upon the consequences of institutional choices for development and for public policy, with important lessons both for domestic reformers as well as for the international community. If power-sharing regimes are important for sustaining democracy, as the evidence indicates, how can they be developed? The conclusion in *Chapter 9* summarizes the main findings of the book, reflects upon challenges to the argument, considers the broader policy implications for reducing conflict and for developing sustainable democracies worldwide, and discusses the lessons both for domestic actors as well as for the international community.

2

Evidence and Methods

Establishing systematic evidence to assess the impact of power-sharing arrangements is important, both theoretically and politically. Whether these arrangements serve the long-term interests of peace-building, durable conflict management, and democratic consolidation in multiethnic societies remains an open question. Despite the desirability of establishing practical guidelines for crafting new constitutions, and the extensive literature which has developed, the evidence available to compare the performance of power-sharing on democracy and the management of ethnic conflict remains limited. Several approaches have been used in previous research, including in-depth treatment of selected national case studies, historical-institutional accounts of political development within particular countries, comparative cross-sectional approaches based on analyzing a subset of democracies (Lijphart) or minorities at risk (Gurr), and analogies drawn between the experience of the legislative underrepresentation of women with that of ethnic minorities. Unfortunately this literature remains inconclusive as a result of inconsistent results, with certain limitations in each approach. Given the inherent flaws of any single method taken in isolation, this study opts for a mixed research design, combining the virtues of rich and detailed studies of contrasting paired cases with the advantages of comparing large-N time-series cross-sectional data.[1] Understanding both the methodology and its limitations is important in order to evaluate the results, but those wishing to focus upon the meat-and-potatoes findings may wish to skip ahead to Chapter 4.

Small-N Case Studies

Small-N national case studies have often been discussed to illustrate the pros and cons of power-sharing regimes. This approach is invaluable as a way to explore the complex processes of regime change, using historical narrative to examine detailed changes within each nation-state.[2] Cases allow researchers to develop theories, to derive hypotheses, and to explore causal mechanisms. This approach is particularly useful with outliers, such as the wealthy autocracy of Singapore and the poor democracy of Benin, which deviate from the generally observed pattern. This method fails to resolve the debate between proponents and critics of power-sharing, however, since the danger of potential selection bias means that different cases can be cited on both sides. There are also arguments about which cases best fit the consociational ideal type. The classic exemplars among established democracies are generally agreed to include the Netherlands, Belgium, and Austria (and possibly Switzerland),[3] all plural societies containing distinct ethnic communities divided by language, religion, and region, with constitutions characterized by multiple veto-points and extensive power-sharing. Lijphart also highlights equivalent cases in many developing societies which are deeply segmented, including South Africa since 1994, India since 1947, Lebanon from 1943 to 1975, and Malaysia from 1955 to 1969. Colombia, Czechoslovakia (1989–1993), and Cyprus (1960–1963) are other potential cases, along with the European Union and Northern Ireland. These cases provide successful examples of ethnic power-sharing in plural societies as diverse as Belgium, India, Switzerland, and South Africa but there are also many well-known 'failed' cases.[4] The breakdown of consociational democracy is exemplified most clearly in Lebanon, where the 1943 National Pact divided power among the major religious communities, a system which collapsed in 1975 when civil war erupted. Other notable cases of malfunction include the consociational system in Cyprus, before civil war in 1963 and subsequent partition between the Greek and Turkish communities disrupted these arrangements. Another case which can be regarded as a potential failure concerns the intricate consociational arrangements for power-sharing along ethnic lines developed in the new constitution for Bosnia and Herzegovina set up by the Dayton Agreement, which seem to have reinforced ethnic homogeneity within each area, although also eliminating bloodshed.[5] Czechoslovakia also experimented with these arrangements briefly in 1989–1993, before the 'velvet revolution' produced succession into two separate states. Studies have compared countries as diverse as Afghanistan, Cyprus, Kosovo, Macedonia, and South Africa, where these arrangements have been proposed or implemented.[6] What often remains unclear from selected case study comparisons which focus upon states which have experienced power-sharing institutions or those which focus upon recent peace-building settlements, however, are the counterfactual cases which may have adopted majoritarian institutions decades or even centuries ago and thereby generated greater contemporary social cohesion. Consensus democracy may not be the root cause of the political problems experienced by societies such as Cyprus and Lebanon; nevertheless examples which have clearly failed temper strong claims that these arrangements, by themselves, are *sufficient* for managing ethnic conflict. Moreover it is also not clear whether consensus democracy is *necessary* for political stability in divided societies; we can also identify certain contemporary cases of newer democracies in multi-ethnic societies with majoritarian arrangements, including Mali and Botswana, which are classified by Freedom House as relatively successful at consolidating political rights and civil liberties, compared with many equivalent African nation-states.[7]

Constitutional Reforms as 'Natural Experiments'

An extension of the case study method uses historical explanations of constitutional reforms occurring within particular countries to provide an alternative way to examine changes in regimes, patterns of democratic consolidation, and the degree of conflict in multiethnic states. This is perhaps most effective with occasional 'natural experiments' allowing researchers to utilize 'before' and 'after' studies of the longitudinal impact within particular societies when political institutions change. The breakdown of regimes and the wholesale construction of new constitutional settlements, such as those which occurred in contemporary Iraq and Afghanistan, provide the most dramatic cases. But this approach is also illustrated in older democracies which have altered some fundamental aspects of their political arrangements, with a narrower reform which makes it easier to isolate specific institutional effects, as exemplified by comparison of the representation of the Maori community in New Zealand when the electoral system moved from majoritarian single-member districts to a combined system (mixed member proportional).[8] Other natural experiments include monitoring the impact of varying degrees of regional autonomy on conflict in the Basque region, for example, whether this prompted ETA to renounce terrorist violence and end their bombing campaign in March 2006.[9] Other cases include evaluating the impact of constitutional reforms on the linguistic communities and nationalist feelings in Belgium.[10] Studies have also monitored changes in national identity in the United Kingdom and attitudes toward separatism following the establishment of the Scottish Parliament and Welsh Assembly.[11]

The most common approach here has examined changes over time to electoral systems. These institutions used to be regarded as fairly stable, with only minor adjustments in the basic electoral formula translating votes into seats. In recent years, however, a range of minor and major reforms to electoral systems and processes have been more widely recognized. Hence Reynolds, Reilly, and Ellis noted that 27 countries worldwide changed the basic electoral formula used for their national parliamentary elections over the decade 1993–2004; for example, South Africa switched from first-past-the-post to list proportional representation (PR), Venezuela moved from list PR to a combined-dependent system, while Japan changed from single nontransferable vote to a combined-independent system.[12] During a far longer period, Colomer's study of electoral systems in democracies in 94 countries since the early nineteenth century monitored no fewer than 82 major changes in the electoral system used for legislative contests (for example, from majoritarian to mixed or from mixed to proportional formula).[13] Considerable instability was evident in some countries; for example, Colomer reported that Greece experienced nine major changes in the electoral system, France had seven, and Italy and Portugal each had six changes.

A comparison by Goldner suggests that more than half the 125 countries that have held democratic elections since 1946 have experienced a change in their electoral system, based on a broader definition of what counts in this regard, including any shifts in district magnitude or assembly size of 20% of more, the introduction of presidential elections, alterations to electoral tiers or electoral formula, or the breakdown or reintroduction of democratic regimes.[14] The estimated total number of reforms would rise even further if changes to the nomination and campaigning process were added to this list, including the widespread introduction of gender quotas into candidate recruitment processes or the use of new regulations governing party finance.

Electoral reforms represent natural experiments which are invaluable for understanding processes of political change in any one society over time. One important problem facing analysts, however, is that historically much else often alters simultaneously alongside these institutional reforms; for example, successive contests often produce shifts in patterns of party competition and in the composition of the governing coalition. These simultaneous changes make it difficult to isolate the specific impact of constitutional reforms, for example, on levels of democracy, the strength of ethnic identities, the degree of political stability, or patterns of multiethnic cooperation at community level. In addition, there are also problems in disentangling the direction of causality; negotiated peace-settlements which are the result of reduced intercommunal violence may also generate proportional electoral systems.[15]

Understanding particular case studies, and processes of constitutional reform occurring within each nation, is therefore unlikely to provide definitive answers and more systematic analysis is required to generalize causal inferences across nation-states and over time. Even in large-N comparisons, however, involving multiple cases, the reliability and meaning of the results are heavily dependent upon the selection of the most appropriate sample of nation-states. Potential bias arises where the observations are restricted to a nonrandom set of observations. For example, Lijphart's work provides the most extensive attempt to operationalize and measure 'consensus' democracies – defined in terms of their institutional characteristics.[16] Lijphart classified three dozen 'long-term democracies', defined as those states which had been democratic from 1977 to 1996, in terms of 10 institutions and then compared their performance. Unfortunately by committing the sin of 'selecting cases on the dependent variable', this comparative framework is inherently flawed for any analysis of patterns of political stability and democratic consolidation. The universe excludes comparison of unstable states, whether they subsequently failed in violent internal wars (Lebanon, Yugoslavia, Cyprus), experienced a coup d'etat (Gambia, Fiji), split with peaceful succession (Czechoslovakia), or simply gradually became more repressive and authoritarian (Russia, the Maldives, Bhutan, Egypt, Liberia).[17] Similar systematic sampling biases are often found in many other attempts to generalize about the institutions common in democracies, for example, Goldner's and Colomer's studies of electoral reform, which exclude any comparison of autocracies.

Minorities at Risk

Another common approach utilizes the comparative dataset derived from the Minorities at Risk (MAR) project. Initiated by Ted Robert Gurr, this project compares politically active communal groups.[18] The evidence has been widely used in the literature on ethnic conflict, including incidents of nonviolent protest, violent protest, and political rebellion (the latter ranging from sporadic acts of terrorism to cases of protracted civil war). For example, Frank Cohen employed this data to compare patterns of behavior among 233 ethnic groups in 100 countries. The study concluded that both federalism and PR electoral systems were significantly related to lower levels of rebellion by ethnic groups, confirming that consensus democracies are more effective at managing ethnic conflict. Nevertheless, the comparison of 'minorities at risk' remains problematic for this task mainly because sample bias is also inherent in the methodology employed in selecting cases for observation. A 'minority at risk' is defined by the codebook as an ethno-political group that (i) "collectively suffers, or benefits from, systematic discriminatory treatment vis-à-vis other groups in a society" and/or (ii) "collectively mobilizes in defense or promotion of its self-defined interests."[19] Religious, linguistic, and regional minorities are therefore systematically excluded from the dataset if they are successfully integrated or assimilated into society so that they do not organize separately as a political association. Multiple cleavages exist in society, but MAR only recognizes those which become and remain politically salient. The traditional deep division between Catholics and Protestants remains critical to the Good Friday Peace Agreement in Northern Ireland, for example, and the imprint of this cleavage continues to mark party politics in many nation-states in continental Europe. In Britain, by contrast, although many people continue to express a religious affiliation, the political difference between Protestants and Catholics, which was critical to British politics from the Reformation until the late-nineteenth century, gradually faded as a salient party cleavage and electoral cue during the early twentieth century.[20] Unfortunately, therefore, the MAR data also suffers from serious problems of systematic selection bias, by monitoring contemporary cases of ethno-political conflict but excluding the most successful cases of ethnic accommodation, where minorities have been politically integrated or assimilated into the majority population.

Gender and Ethnicity

Rather than examining direct indicators, an alternative strategy for studying ethnic minority representation seeks to generalize by analogies with the experience of the role of women in elected office, where this is regarded as a proxy indicator of 'minority' representation in general.[21] Certainly both women and ethnic minorities are commonly some of the most underrepresented groups in legislative office in most established democracies.[22] A considerable body of evidence has also now accumulated suggesting that female representation is commonly greater under PR party lists compared with majoritarian electoral systems.[23] But is it legitimate to generalize from the experience of women to the representation of ethnic minorities? In fact, there are many reasons why this strategy may prove seriously flawed. After reviewing the literature, Bird concludes that substantial differences exist in the reasons underlying the under-representation of women and ethnic minorities.[24] In particular, concentrated ethnic communities are clustered geographically within certain areas, allow-ing territorial groups to make local gains in particular minority constituen-cies within majoritarian electoral systems, even in heterogeneous plural soci-eties; for example, African-American representatives are elected to Congress in minority-majority districts in New York City, Detroit, and Los Angeles.[25] By contrast, the male-to-female ratio in the population is usually fairly uni-formly distributed across different electoral constituencies. Htun also points out that positive action strategies often differ substantially in the opportuni-ties they provide for women and ethnic minorities.[26] Statutory gender quotas mandating the minimal proportion of women that parties adopt as legisla-tive candidates are common in many established democracies, for example, although none of these nation-states have adopted similar quota laws to com-pensate for the underrepresentation of ethnic minority candidates. By contrast, reserved seats in parliament are used for ethnic, racial, national, linguistic, or religious communities in more than two dozen countries, including guaran-teeing the inclusion of specified minorities in legislatures through the creation of separate electoral rolls, the allocation of special electoral districts, or provi-sions for direct appointment to the legislature.[27] Most countries adopting these mechanisms have majoritarian electoral systems which are unable to guarantee adequate minority representation through other means. For all these reasons, direct comparisons of women and ethnic minority representation are a flawed research strategy, and alternative approaches are needed to explore the cross-national evidence on a more systematic basis.

Cross-Sectional Large-N Comparisons

Another common large-N approach within the quantitative tradition has sought to classify political institutions in many countries worldwide, developing typologies of electoral systems, public sector bureaucracies, patterns of interest group politics, party systems, or presidential and parliamentary executives, and then comparing how far the contemporary performance of democracy varies systematically by institutional types. Ever since Aristotle, analytical typologies have always been a vital part of comparative politics, with recent attempts to classify membership of each type using the logic of fuzzy sets.[28] By selecting a larger range of cases using a random sample of countries, or the universe of independent nation-states worldwide, the cross-sectional comparative strategy overcomes many of the potential problems of selection bias which limit case-study approaches, but it also raises important methodological questions. The next chapter discusses the challenge of establishing appropriate operational measures of core concepts, notably how we develop indicators of democracy which are generally regarded as valid and reliable, and which are genuinely independent from the variables thought to explain democracy. Serious difficulties also relate to many other aspects which are central to comparative studies of the relationship between institutions and democratization, including measures of ethnic fractionalization, federalism, and corruption. In addition, cross-sectional comparisons taken at one point in time face the challenge of establishing the endogeneity of political institutions.

Political institutions can be understood as the formal rules and the informal social norms which structure the workings of any regime. Formal rules include the legislative framework governing constitutions, as embodied in official documents, constitutional conventions, legal statutes, codes of conduct, and administrative procedures, authorized by law and enforceable by courts. Institutions provide incentives and sanctions which constrain human behavior. It is neither necessary nor sufficient for rules to be embodied in the legal system to be effective; social norms, informal patterns of behavior, and social sanctions also create shared mutual expectations among political actors. Nevertheless this study focuses most attention upon the formal rules as these represent the core instruments of public policy.[29] These rules are open to reform and amendment by the political process, whether by legislation, executive order, constitutional revision, administrative decision, judicial judgment, or bureaucratic decree. Although there is a 'gray' overlapping area, by contrast most social norms are altered gradually by informal processes such as social pressures, media campaigns, and cultural value shifts located outside the formal political arena. Drawing upon the distinction first suggested by Duverger, institutional changes to the formal rules can be understood to exert both mechanical effects, including those brought about by the legal system, as well as psychological effects, shaping social norms and beliefs.[30] In societies characterized by rule of law, the impact of mechanical effects can be expected to be manifested relatively fast, for example, the introduction of a lower formal vote threshold for elections to the legislature. By contrast, the psychological effects of such a legal change may only become evident over a long-term process, as people gradually learn to adapt their behavior to the new rules, for example, in their perceptions about whether casting a ballot for a minor party represents a wasted vote.

If institutions are regarded as relatively durable, exemplified by the basic division of powers between the executive and legislative branches established in the US Constitution, then the formal rules governing the political system can be understood as shaping the incentives governing the behavior of lawmakers and presidents. Nevertheless there are also complex issues of reciprocal causality; political actors make the rules which then tie their hands. The problem of institutional endogeneity is least serious in established democracies which have not altered their basic constitutional arrangements for many decades, perhaps for more than a century, even if there are a series of more minor adjustments in administrative procedures and political roles.[31] In this regard, institutions can be regarded as persistent constraints influencing subsequent patterns of political behavior and social norms. The difficulty of disentangling cause and effect arises with greater urgency in established democracies which have experienced more fundamental reforms, such as devolution in Scotland and Wales, decentralization in Catalonia and Galicia, and electoral reform toward combined systems in New Zealand and Italy. Here the conventional story suggests, for example, in Scotland, that growing nationalist identities in the postwar era led gradually toward the creation of the Scottish Parliament in 1999, but that in a reciprocal effect, devolution has also served to slightly strengthen Scottish identities.[32] Similarly, the standard account emphasizes that discontent with the power of the executive generated pressures for electoral reform in New Zealand, and, once the electoral system altered from first-past-the-post (FPTP) to mixed member proportional (MMP), this facilitated fragmentation in the party system.[33] Attention to developments over time is critical to understanding the causal process under analysis.

The problem of treating political institutions as endogenous factors causing democratization is most acute in countries which have undergone fundamental constitutional changes where institutions are not sticky, including in many newer democracies. As Colomer emphasizes, parties make electoral rules.[34] It follows that plural societies engaging multiple parties and factions in peace-negotiations, for example, are probably more likely to adopt PR electoral systems and federal power-sharing, since this arrangement makes establishing agreement easier among many participants and minor parties. If we assume that political actors are risk-averse, and that new rules are established under conditions of considerable uncertainly about their outcome, power-sharing agreements reduce the risks of losing.[35] Given their recent history and experience of internal conflict, some countries using power-sharing institutions may therefore have a far worse historical legacy of political stability and internal conflict, a pattern which spills over into contemporary politics, in comparison with homogeneous societies which may have adopted power-concentrating rules. Although there is a growing literature on the causes of electoral system change, the reasons why countries select one or another constitutional arrangement remain poorly understood. Rational calculations about the potential consequences of these choices are hampered by the limited information and uncertainty surrounding the consequences of each constitutional option. A 'mixed scanning' approach may be adopted, where policymakers consider a limited range of constitutional options, based on past histories and comparisons with neighboring states. Countries continue to reflect an imprint from their colonial legacies; for example, about 60% of ex-British countries adopted first-past-the-post for the lower house of parliament, while about the same proportion of ex-Spanish colonies adopted PR.[36] Cultural proximity, influential regional models, and learning across national borders are also part of the process, as illustrated by the way that many Latin American countries adopted presidential executives, while by contrast Central European states were more likely to adopt parliamentary systems.

Problems of establishing the direction of causality are equally severe when understanding the relationship between ethnic identities and political institutions. On the one hand, essentialist perspectives assume that ethnic identities reflect fixed and stable psychological orientations.[37] These assumptions lie at the heart of the consociational thesis that political institutions will reduce ethnic tensions most effectively by incorporating stakeholders from rival communities into decision-making processes. Ethnic identities and separate communal boundaries are regarded in consociational arguments as the enduring social base upon which political institutions arise to form the superstructure. The boundaries drawn between Protestant and Catholic communities in Belfast, black-white racial tensions in Los Angeles, or violent conflict between Arab militias and black African farmers in Darfur, for example, are seen to reflect long-standing cultural dissimilarities which precede the construction of the modern nation-state, making them difficult to alter and manipulate, for example, through assimilation policies. Hence the logic of the post-Dayton peace agreement which sought to balance the interests of the Bosniak, Serbian, and Croatian communities by a careful allocation of seats in the new parliament governing Bosnia and Herzegovina, for example, with the office of the speaker rotating among members drawn from each community.[38]

By contrast, constructivist perspectives challenge the basic assumption that ethnic identities and community boundaries are fixed and stable. This view emphasizes that the design of political institutions and public policies can either heighten or weaken latent ethnic identities, so that social cleavages based on language, religion, race, or nationality should not be regarded as endogenous to the political system.[39] In Serbia, for example, Gagnon shows how Slobodan Milosevic was elected to office on a public platform which deepened ethnic hatred and intercommunity rivalry, manipulating symbols and myths to maximize popular support.[40] Snyder argues that elites in democratizing states have incentives to manipulate and exploit nationalist conflict, a process exacerbated by electoral pressures.[41] Colonial powers have drawn boundaries creating nation-states and provinces which cut across or which reflect existing community boundaries.[42] Byman argues that policies of assimilation are capable of breaking down communal boundaries, although they also conflict with recognition of minority rights, for example, when Turkey attempts to repress the Kurdish language in all schools and mass media, or where states attempt to encourage more positive opportunities for minority integration into the majority culture.[43] Given the constructivist perspective, studies examining the relationship between ethnic identities and constitutional arrangements therefore need acknowledge the potential problem of treating the former as endogenous to the political system. To disentangle the direction of causality involved in this relationship, ideally time-series data is needed, as well as historical case studies tracing the dynamics of the process of democratization, institutional change, and the waxing and waning strength of ethnic identities within particular countries.

THE MIXED RESEARCH DESIGN

The unresolved debate between consociationalism and its critics has therefore received widespread attention in the extensive body of scholarly research, as well as within the policymaking community. The cases of Benin and Togo suggest the need to explore these issues further. Subsequent chapters go on to compare countries around the globe more systematically to see whether institutions matter for democracy, controlling for a wide range of social and cultural factors which may also contribute toward democratization. To overcome the shortcomings of each of the methods already discussed, this study supplements large-N quantitative comparisons with in-depth paired case studies.

Time-Series Cross-Section (CSTS) Data

The period of analysis focuses upon patterns of regime change occurring during the third wave of democratization, for 30 years from 1973 to 2004 (or the end point of the series, if slightly earlier). The research design relies on cross-sectional time-series (CSTS) data facilitating comparison over space and time. This sort of data consists of repeated observations on a series of fixed (nonsampled) units (all contemporary nation-states worldwide), where the units are of interest in themselves. The country-year is the basic unit of analysis, generating 5,680 observations across the whole period. This produces a large enough time-series to model the dynamics for each unit. The comparison covers 191 contemporary nation-states (excluding dependent territories and states which dissolved during this period).

   The analysis of cross-sectional longitudinal data needs to address certain important challenges and analysis of any panel datasets raises complex issues.[44] Ordinary least squares regression estimates assume that errors are independent, normally distributed, and with constant variance. This type of data violates these assumptions and raises potential problems of heteroskedasticity, autocorrelation, robustness, and missing data. Heteroskedasticity is produced if the range of variations in the scatter of nation-states around the regression line is not uniform across different levels of democracy. Autocorrelations are generated because, with time-series data, the same countries are being counted repeatedly and the additional observations do not provide substantially new information. The danger is that the study will fail to identify the lack of independence between cases and will subsequently reach false conclusions. The beta coefficients in any regression analysis will remain unbiased but the disturbance terms from the errors (i.e., omitted variables) are likely to be correlated. The use of ordinary least squares regression models leads to estimates of standard errors, used for evaluating the significance of the relationship, which are less accurately measured than they appear. In other words, the significance of any coefficients will be inflated, suggesting that significant relationships exist when they do not. Various options are available to overcome the problem of both autocorrelated and heteroskedastic disturbances found in cross-sectional time-series datasets, such as feasible generalized least squares that estimate errors with an ARH1 model, or the use of robust regression.

Following the advice of Betz and Katz, when comparing relationships across countries, the study uses ordinary least squares (OLS) linear regression with panel-corrected standard errors (PCSE) to measure the impact of the independent variables on levels of democratization across each nation.[45] This approach is particularly suited to the dataset as the number of countries under comparison (N = 191) is far greater than the number of years (T = 30). Nevertheless this form of data analysis needs considerable care to double-check the robustness of the results given different specification issues, alternative models, and diagnostic tests.[46] When computing the standard errors and the variance-covariance estimates, OLS regression analysis models with PCSE assume that disturbances are, by default, heteroskedastic and contemporaneously correlated across panels. One important advantage of this approach is that the results are relatively easily interpretable, as OLS regression is the most widely familiar statistical technique in the social sciences. The use of panel-corrected standard errors is the most appropriate approach where the data contains all contemporary countries worldwide, rather than a sample of countries drawn from a larger universe, where estimating the random effects may be more suitable.[47] Moreover with a large time-series, the results of fixed and random effects models usually converge, so there is no substantial difference in the use of either approach. The use of fixed effects has its costs, however, since it forces us to drop any independent variables from the model that are unchanging attributes of each country, such as region. Fixed effects models also make it hard for any slowly changing variables to appear substantively or statistically significant, making a rigorous test for estimating the impact of any institutional reforms.[48]

To check the robustness of the results under different specifications, the regression analysis models are presented for the Freedom House data. The results are then replicated using the other three standard indicators of democracy discussed in the next chapter, provided by Polity IV, Vanhanen, and Cheibub and Gandhi, to examine whether the key findings are confirmed and the results hold irrespective of the particular measure selected for analysis. The large-N comparison produces systematic patterns which hold across many instances but this process loses the depth which is derived from examining the process of democratization through intensive case studies. Nevertheless all regression analysis is subject to certain well-established pitfalls, such as unit heterogeneity, autocorrelation, and the use of different time lags, and conclusions relying solely upon this method would not be wholly satisfactory or convincing.

Case Studies

To put more flesh on the bones, the large-scale econometric analysis is supplemented by selected case-study narratives, illuminating the dynamics of regime change from a more qualitative perspective. No single method or technique can be regarded as wholly convincing but the combination of approaches provides a more plausible story. To illustrate the theory and analysis with more concrete examples, paired cases are selected within each region to compare leaders and laggards in the process of democratization during the third wave. This process is exemplified by the West African cases already described briefly, including the contrasts between the end of military rule and the transition to stable multiparty democracy and a free press experienced in Benin, compared with persistent repression found in Togo. Beninese and Togolese shared a common history for many centuries and both countries remain among the poorest nation-states in the world. Both societies are divided ethnically by cleavages of religion and language. Despite all that these neighboring states share, during the last decade Benin has established the conditions for the peaceful rotation of governing power, while Togo remains an unreconstructed autocracy. Similar paired case-study comparisons are discussed to illustrate contrasting political developments in other regions, including contrasts among Costa Rica and Venezuela, Taiwan and Singapore, Hungary and Belarus, and Turkey and Egypt.

Classifying Institutions

The comparison also needs to classify the core institutions at the heart of consociationalism. In practice, executive power-sharing can take many institutional forms, making the ideal type notoriously difficult to test empirically; for example, it may involve a coalition of ethnic parties in cabinet (as in South Africa), the allocation of ministerial portfolios based on explicit recognition of major religious or linguistic groups (as in Belgium), a presidency made up of a committee of three representing each nation, with a rotating chair (as in Bosnia and Herzegovina), or (as in Lebanon) the division of the presidency (Maronite Christian), prime minister (Sunni Muslim), and speaker (Shi'a Muslim). Other arrangements used to secure the election of minorities to the legislature, even within majoritarian electoral systems, include reserved seats (used in New Zealand), overrepresentation of minority districts (such as smaller electoral quota used for Scottish constituencies at Westminster), and minority redistricting (exemplified in the United States). Territorial autonomy can also take multiple complex forms, with the powers and responsibilities for services such as education, taxation, and domestic security divided among multiple layers of government and administrative units.

In *Democracies* and *Patterns of Democracy*, Lijphart refined and built upon his earlier work in the attempt to operationalize consociationalism as an ideal type and to classify established democracies into two categories: 'consensus' (power-sharing) or 'majoritarian' (power-concentrating) democracies.[49] The major institutions are understood to cluster into two main dimensions. The 'parties-executive' dimension for consensus democracies rests on the existence of proportional representation elections, multiparty competition, coalition governments, executive-legislative balance, and interest group corporatism. The 'federal-unitary' dimension for consensus democracies includes federalism and decentralization, balanced bicameralism, constitutional rigidity, judicial review, and central bank independence. Rather than attempting to test the impact of all the institutions of consensus democracy, this study focuses upon comparing the role of four important pillars, namely, proportional representation electoral systems (leading, in turn, toward multiparty legislatures and coalition governments), the type of parliamentary or presidential executive (leading toward horizontal patterns of unified or divided government), federalism and decentralization (leading toward vertical patterns of regional autonomy and the protection of minority rights for territorial groups), and the regulation of channels of political communication (as one of the primary channels available for opposition movements in civil society). Many other institutional reforms have been associated with strengthening democracy; for example, beyond the electoral process, Carothers notes that the standard democracy assistance template usually includes improving the integrity of governance and reducing corruption; expanding the capacity of public sector management; strengthening the rule of law, human rights, and the role of an independent judiciary; and building an active range of civil society organizations and NGOs.[50] These are all potentially important reforms which are worth exploring in a broader study of the full impact of democracy assistance, but this study focuses upon a narrower set of institutions. Reforms designed to achieve power-sharing in executive-legislative relations and in the decentralization of decision-making are likely to have a strong impact on promoting democratic consolidation in divided societies. The conceptualization, classification, and measurement of each of the main types of institutions compared in this study are discussed in subsequent chapters.

Some have sought to examine the impact of power-sharing arrangements by constructing single indicators. The concept of 'veto points', developed most fully by Tsebelis, is an attempt to identify the functionally equivalent checks and balances within any political system and to aggregate these into a single index.[51] Linder and Bachtiger adopt a similar measure, the power-sharing index, which includes a horizontal dimension through the use of proportional representation electoral systems as well as institutional veto points (such as a strong separation of powers and multiparty governing coalitions) and a vertical dimension based on the degree of federalism.[52] The study found that the horizontal dimension of power-sharing, but not the vertical dimension, was more strongly related to democratization in Africa and Asia than economic development. These combined measures may be useful for some analytic objectives, but they can be problematic from a policymaking perspective, since any analysis of the impact of power-sharing arrangements on democracy will be unable to identify the specific institutions which produced these effects. The measure may be particularly sensitive to the aggregation process and it is not at all obvious how best to proceed in this regard, for example, whether a political system with a strict division between the judiciary and executive is functionally equivalent in power-sharing terms to another system which has minority vetoes guaranteed in the constitution. Both provide a form of power-sharing but how should these rules be counted? Another potential problem is that the veto point indicators may be measuring some of the same components that are used for the construction of certain indicators of democracy, such as the criteria used by Polity IV, contaminating the independent and dependent variables. By contrast, examining the separate effects of the types of electoral systems, executives, federalism, and the mass media on democracy provides a cleaner and more policy-relevant interpretation of the results of the analysis. These institutions are also independent of the selected indicators of democracy. For example, as discussed in the next chapter, although Polity IV incorporates the use of elite competition or direct elections as part of its measure of limitations on executive authority, the project does not monitor the particular type of electoral system used for this purpose. In the same way, Cheibub and Gandhi define regimes as democratic if those who govern are selected through contested elections, but the type of electoral rules, whether majoritarian or proportional, is not part of their measure.

Measuring Ethnic Fractionalization

One of the most complex issues facing empirical research on consociationalism concerns the most appropriate concept and measurement of ethnic fractionalization. Cross-national studies of the evidence have been hindered by the difficulties of establishing robust and consistent measures of ethnic identities that are applicable across many different types of societies. States often contain multiple cultural cleavages and forms of social identity, some overlapping, and studies need to choose the one that is most salient politically and most relevant theoretically to the issue under consideration. Ethnic groups are defined here as a community bound by a belief in common ancestry and cultural practices, whether based on religion, language, history, or other cultural customs and ties. Debate continues to surround the origins and nature of ethnic identities. The essentialist perspective regards ethnic identities as largely fixed at birth or in early childhood, due to the physical characteristics of groups, such as their racial skin color or facial features, or based on enduring social conventions and cultural norms. By contrast, as discussed earlier, the constructivist perspective regards ethnic identities as socially created, where the salience of alternative identities is open to manipulation. In this view, community differences can be exacerbated (for example, where politicians preach the heated rhetoric of ethnic hatred and nationalism to maintain their popularity) or ameliorated (where there are successful attempts to assimilate groups). In practice, there are substantial difficulties in comparing ethnic identities across nation-states. Nigeria, for example, contains an estimated 250 tribal groups, as well as sharp regional divisions between northern Muslims and southern Christians. Language is important in Switzerland, which splits into the predominant German and the minority French- and minority Italian-speaking regions. Belgium divides into the Fleming and Walloon segments. By contrast, the United Kingdom divides by nationalist identities into England, Scotland, Wales, and Northern Ireland (the latter subdivided into Protestant and Catholic communities), while the United States uses the idea of racial characteristics and language as the defining basis of the major ethnic cleavages. Given that the meaning and form of identities are so culturally diverse, it remains unclear whether cross-national studies can compare like with like, or whether they can even compare functionally equivalent groups, across societies.

Moreover the available data to estimate ethnic identities is often limited and unreliable. Aggregate sources drawn from official population censuses, household surveys, and general social surveys facilitate analysis of the distribution of religious, linguistic, national origin, or racial groups in each country. But not all surveys seek to incorporate these items, in part because of their cultural sensitivity, and, unlike measures of occupational class and socioeconomic status, no standard international practices maintain consistency across sources. Where religious, linguistic, racial, national, or other forms of ethnic identities are systematically monitored in official surveys, the data usually allows us to monitor the distribution of these populations, but far fewer survey questions seek to measure the salience or meaning of these identities. What may matter is less ethnic fractionalization, as commonly measured, than ethnic polarization, meaning the distance between groups. Clearly, given these limitations, the measurement of ethnic diversity needs further research.[53] Many previous studies of linguistic cleavages have also had to rely upon badly flawed aggregate sources, exemplified by the Soviet-era *Atlas Narodov Mira* (1964), the original dataset used to construct the ethno-linguistic fractionalization (ELF) index.[54] The index has been widely employed by economists, following Easterly and Levine's study showing that economic growth was negatively related to ethno-linguistic fractionalization.[55] ELF is computed as 1 minus the Herfindahl index of ethno-linguistic group shares, and it estimates the probability that two randomly selected individuals from a population belong to different groups. Nevertheless it is now recognized that the atlas contains some basic coding inaccuracies, the material is also badly dated, and the linguistic cleavage represents only one dimension of ethnic identities, and not necessarily the most important one.[56]

This project compares systematic cross-national evidence worldwide to classify nation-states according to the degree of ethno-linguistic fractionalization, based on a global dataset created by Alesina and his colleagues.[57] This study classifies 201 countries or dependencies on the basis of the share of the population speaking each language as their 'mother tongues'. The dataset was usually derived from census data, as collated in most cases by the *Encyclopaedia Britannica*, with a few cases of missing data supplemented by the *CIA World Factbook*. Religious fractionalization is also calculated for 215 nation-states and dependencies, drawing upon the same sources. The relationship between these indicators, and the distribution of countries under comparison, is illustrated by the scatter-plot in Figure 2.1. As expected, certain societies in the top-right quadrant emerge as highly heterogeneous on both measures, notably many

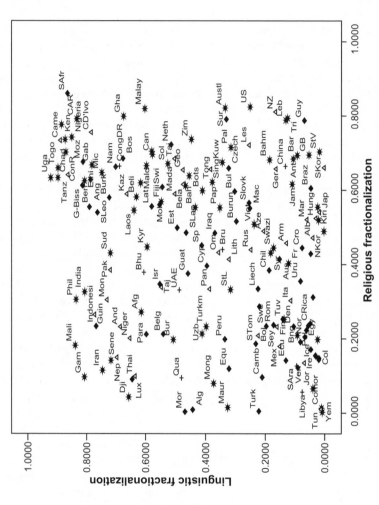

Electoral system
✳ Majoritarian
△ Combined
◆ Proportional
+ No elections

FIGURE 2.1. Linguistic and Religious Fractionalization. *Note:* For the linguistic and religious fractionalization indices, see Alesina et al. 2003. For the classification of the major type of electoral system, see Norris 2004.

sub-Saharan African nation-states (such as South Africa, Uganda, Kenya, and Nigeria). At the same time, many Arab states such as Saudi Arabia, Libya, and Jordan, located in the bottom-left quadrant, are very homogeneous according to these indicators. Because the underlying data sources used for constructing these indicators are fairly imprecise, and they depend heavily upon the categorization scheme used and the underlying population estimates, modest differences in the position of countries on the ethnic fractionalization indices are probably unreliable. Nevertheless the indices can be used to make broad classifications and each is therefore dichotomized, with scores from 50 and above on the 100-point scales defined as plural societies.

It should be noted that this index estimates the objective distribution of different linguistic and religious groups in the population, but it does not seek to measure the subjective meaning or societal importance of these forms of identity. In this regard, analogies can be drawn between the 'objective' indicators of occupation and income used to gauge socioeconomic status and the 'subjective' identifications which respondents offer when asked in surveys where they feel that they belong in terms of social class. In the same way, 'objective' and 'subjective' indicators of ethnic identities may coincide or they may differ sharply. For example, Canada is classified as relatively heterogeneous in religion, divided between Protestants and Catholics, but as this society has become fairly secular, these forms of formal religious identity may carry few significant consequences beyond the completion of official forms for the government census or birth certificates. On the other hand, France is classified as fairly homogeneous in religious identities, as it remains predominantly Catholic, although the expression of religious identities has aroused heated debate in recent years, exemplified by legal bans passed against the wearing of Muslim headscarves in schools. The evidence within this study only seeks to compare the existence of objective indicators of religious and linguistic cleavages, not their subjective salience. A constructivist perspective emphasizes that people possess multiple social identities, and the salience of these latent characteristics may rise or fall in response to situational factors, including the role of parties and politicians competing for power, and how far they 'play the ethnic card' in whipping up ethnic hatred through manipulating symbols and myths.[58] These are important insights but nevertheless the strength of ethnic identities remains extremely difficult to measure and compare with any degree of accuracy in the absence of representative surveys, especially any changes occurring over time in response to the cues provided by political elites, and hence beyond the limitations of this study. On this basis, we can go on to consider the alternative indicators of democracy and what these reveal about trends in democratization during the third wave.

3

Democratic Indicators and Trends

Before proceeding to examine the evidence, the notion of democracy and the most appropriate measure of this concept need to be considered.[1] In particular, what philosophical concepts of 'democracy' underline alternative empirical indicators? Is it best to adopt a minimalist approach toward measurement by selecting a few key indicators, or is it preferable to provide a more comprehensive set of benchmarks? When operationalizing the concept of democracy, should indicators be continuous, implying subtle gradations in levels of democratization? Or should they be categorical, suggesting that regimes cross a specific threshold, such as holding a competitive multiparty election, after which they can then be considered democratic? Should the evidence rest on observable regularities from 'objective' data, such as official levels of voter turnout, the frequency of national elections, or the number of parties contesting legislative seats? Or should such benchmarks be supplemented by subjective evaluations, exemplified by expert judgments used by Freedom House to evaluate conditions of political rights and civil liberties in each country, or the Polity IV project's coding of institutional restrictions on the executive? What are the major sources of random and nonrandom measurement error arising from these decisions that could potentially bias estimates of effects and generate misleading comparisons? What are the problems of missing data limiting these measures and how does this restrict the country coverage and comparative framework? What is the relationship between notions of democracy and of 'good governance', a concept which has become increasingly common in the developmental literature.[2]

To explore these issues, four measures of democracy are compared, each with a different focus and measure: Freedom House's index of liberal democracy, the Polity IV project's assessment of constitutional democracy, Vanhanen's indicator of participatory democracy, and Przeworski and colleagues' classification based on the notion of contested democracy. These represent the most widely cited standard indicators commonly used by scholars and policy analysts in comparative research. They each have broad cross-national scope and a lengthy time-series, with data based on annual observations classifying regimes worldwide.[3] After reviewing their pros and cons, the chapter concludes, agnostically, that no single best measure of democracy exists for all purposes; instead, as Collier and Adcock suggest, specific choices are best justified pragmatically by the theoretical framework and analytical goals used in any study.[4] The most prudent strategy, adopted by this book, is to compare the results of analytical models using alternative indicators, to see whether the findings remain robust and consistent irrespective of the specific measures of democracy employed for analysis. If so, then this generates greater confidence in the reliability of the results since the main generalizations hold irrespective of the particular measures which are used. If not, then we need to consider how far any differences in the results can be attributed to the underlying concepts which differ among these measures. The chapter concludes by summarizing the research design, comparative framework, and cross-sectional time-series dataset used in this book.

MEASURING DEMOCRACY

Two criteria – validity and reliability – are particularly important for evaluating the construction of any empirical indicators in the social sciences.[5] *Valid* empirical measures accurately reflect the analytical concepts to which they relate. The study of the origin and stability of democratic regimes requires attention to normative concepts in democratic theory, as well as to the construction of appropriate operational empirical indicators. Invalid measures miss the mark by producing unconvincing inferences, for example, if the operational indicators fail to capture important aspects of the underlying concept. *Reliable* empirical measures prove consistent across time and place, using data sources which can be easily replicated to allow scholars to build a cumulative body of research. Scientific research makes its procedures public and transparent, including the steps involved in selecting cases, gathering data, and performing analysis. For Karl Popper, the classic hallmark of the scientific inquiry is the process which subjects bold conjectures to rigorous testing, allowing strong claims to be refuted, if not supported by the evidence.[6] While repeated confirmations cannot prove inductive probabilities, attempts to refute findings can advance the body of scientific knowledge. Scientific progress arises from successive attempts to prove ourselves wrong. This process requires reliable empirical measures which are easily open to replication in cumulative studies conducted by the scientific community.

Multiple approaches to measuring democracy exist in the literature and these broadly divide into either minimalist or maximalist conceptualizations, each with certain strengths and weaknesses (see Table 3.1). Indeed, it can be argued that trade-offs often exist, with minimalist approaches usually strongest in terms of their reliability, and maximalist indicators commonly more satisfactory in terms of their measurement validity. Much debate in the literature therefore revolves around which criteria should be regarded as more important,

TABLE 3.1. *Indicators and Measures*

	Liberal Democracy	Constitutional Democracy	Participatory Democracy	Contested Democracy
Source	Freedom House	Polity IV	Vanhanen	Przeworski et al./ Cheibub and Gandhi
Core attributes	Political rights and civil liberties	Democracy and autocracy	Electoral competition and electoral participation	Contestation of executive and legislature
Measurement of attributes	Continuous 7-point scales for each	Continuous 20-point scale	100-point scales	Dichotomous classification
Annual observations	1972 to date	1800 to 1999	1810 to 2000	1946 to 2002
Main strengths	Comprehensive scope	Extended time period	Replicable data sources	Clear coding rules
Main weaknesses	Problems of conflation and measurement	Exclusion of mass participation; aggregation problems	Inappropriate indicators	Exclusion of mass participation; weakly related to state repression

with theorists employing econometric models often preferring the elegance and parsimony of replication, and more policy-oriented and qualitative approaches usually giving greater priority to comprehensive if less easily replicated measures.

Minimalist measures of democracy focus attention upon just one or two key benchmarks, notably by concentrating on the rules governing party competition for government office. Reflecting Schumpeterian conceptions, where democracy is seen to exist in the competitive struggle for the people's vote, this type of regime is commonly defined procedurally as a political system where two or more parties or candidates contest executive office through popular elections.[7] The advantage of minimalist definitions, proponents argue, is that this process helps to develop clear and unambiguous empirical indicators, precise operational definitions, and reliable and consistent classification procedures. This facilitates scientific replication, to test whether key findings reported by one study hold true in other contexts, leading toward well-founded general theories in the social sciences. Minimalist approaches emphasize that coding decisions need to be transparent, leaving little room for the subjective judgments of individual researchers or the personal evaluations of independent observers and national experts. By focusing upon a narrow range of benchmarks, this approach reduces the risks of including theoretically irrelevant attributes and redundant elements in composite measures.

The advantages of reducing the potential errors which arise from inconsistency and misclassification of cases are thought to outweigh the potential limitations of minimalist definitions. The most commonly acknowledged danger is leaving out certain important dimensions of the concept of liberal democracy which are included in more comprehensive measures. For example, minimalist definitions may not attempt to measure the quality of democratic performance, such as how far states achieve inclusive representation, accountable leaders, freedom of expression, and equality of participation, on the grounds that these factors are difficult or even impossible to gauge systematically with any degree of reliability and consistency. Yet stripping the concept of democracy down to its bare essentials may thereby neglect certain vital aspects; for example, Cheibub and Gandhi focus on electoral competition for executive office but thereby leave out any consideration of mass participation as a central characteristic of democratic regimes.[8] Marshall and Jaggers acknowledge the importance of civil liberties for all citizens in their conception of democracies, and the rule of law, systems of checks and balances, and freedom of the press, but in practice Polity IV never attempts to code data on any of these aspects.[9] The primary danger of minimalist procedural approaches is that certain critical aspects of democracy may thereby be excluded from consideration. In particular, many countries have multiparty competition for the executive and legislature, with processes of election contested by more than one party or candidate which observers report are conducted under conditions which are reasonably free and fair. Nevertheless the quality of democracy in these states often varies greatly in many other important regards, such as in the treatment of dissident minorities and opposition reform movements, restrictions on basic human rights, respect for the rule of law and judicial independence, or accountability of the executive to the legislature.

These problems are particularly dangerous in categorizing regimes such as Togo, Belarus, Egypt, Malaysia, Uzbekistan, or Zimbabwe, which use multiparty competitive elections for the legislative and executive office as a façade to legitimate autocratic regimes. This important type of regime which is neither fully autocratic not fully democratic exists in an ambiguous gray zone which has been conceptualized by different authors alternatively as either 'electoral autocracies' (Diamond), 'illiberal democracies' (Fareed), or 'competitive authoritarian regimes' (Levitsky).[10] Other common terms include 'hybrid' regimes, 'competitive authoritarianism', 'transitional democracies' (implicitly assuming that these regimes will eventually adopt broader institutional and political reforms in a progressive trend), or 'semi-free' states (Freedom House). Unfortunately the expansion in alternative typologies has added confusion rather than clarity.[11] Electoral autocracies are characterized by some of the formal trappings of liberal democracy, but genuinely free and fair multiparty competition, human rights, and civil liberties are restricted in practice by the ruling elites. Traditional autocracies usually maintain their grip on power through different means, such as one-party states (Cuba, North Korea), military dictators (Burma, Thailand), or traditional monarchies (Saudi Arabia, Qatar). By contrast, electoral autocracies bow to pressures to hold elections but use more subtle and complex techniques to stifle dissent and deter opposition. Common techniques which limit genuine electoral competition, often reported by observer missions, include coercion, intimidation, and fraud in the attempt to ensure electoral victory; major restrictions on access to the ballot for opposition parties and legal or physical threats used against challengers; widespread use of intimidation, coercion, or bribery of voters by security forces at the polling station; and strong pro-government bias and limits on independent journalism in campaign coverage in the media airwaves.[12] The number of these regimes has expanded in recent years, where elections have been adopted as a result of international or domestic pressures but where this has not been accompanied by any subsequent effective change in autocratic rule. If a single criterion is adopted as a benchmark to classify regimes by minimalist definitions, then the danger is that regimes in the gray zone can be easily misclassified. This is most common where holding the first multiparty competitive elections in postconflict peace-settlements is widely regarded by journalists, popular commentators, and the international community as indicative that a regime is transitioning to becoming more stable and on the road to becoming democratic, irrespective of subsequent developments and ineffective institutional checks and balances on elite power.

By contrast, maximalist or 'thicker' approaches to defining and measuring liberal democracy as a regime type have been strongly influenced by Robert Dahl's body of work published in *Politics, Economics, and Welfare* (1953), in *A Preface to Democratic Theory* (1956), and in *Polyarchy* (1971).[13] Dahl argued that liberal democracies are characterized by two main attributes – contestation and participation. In practice, Dahl suggested that democratic regimes or 'polyarchies' can be identified by the presence of certain key political institutions: (1) elected officials, (2) free and fair elections, (3) inclusive suffrage, (4) the right to run for office, (5) freedom of expression, (6) alternative information, and (7) associational autonomy.[14] Polyarchies use competitive multiparty elections to fill offices for the national legislature and the chief executive. Contests in this type of regime are free and fair, with an inclusive suffrage allowing widespread voting participation among all citizens, and citizens have the unrestricted right to compete for elected offices. For electoral competition to be meaningful, polyarchies allow freedom of expression, availability of alternative sources of information (freedom of the media), and associational autonomy (freedom to organize parties, interest groups, and social movements).

Dahl's approach attracted widespread acclaim but empirical indicators which attempt to measure polyarchy have employed alternative indicators of participation and contestation, and not all studies have treated both components with equal weight. For example, Freedom House's approach to regime classification monitors, among other indicators, self-determination for ethnic minorities, freedom of religious expression, academic freedom, freedom of assembly and association, equal opportunities and gender equality, and rights to private property.[15] Polity IV's measure of democracy emphasizes the existence of constraints on the powers of the executive, the openness of executive recruitment, and the regulation of participation.[16] By contrast, Hadenius's specification focuses upon freedom of organization and freedom from coercion.[17] Foweraker and Krznaric go even further in seeking to integrate 21 measures of liberal democratic performance, although for a smaller range of 40 nation-states as a result of constraints in data availability.[18] What these 'thicker' conceptualizations of liberal democracy share is the attempt to develop comprehensive scales which facilitate fine-grained distinctions across diverse regimes and subtle gradations of states classified by levels of democratization. For example, levels of democracy can be gauged by monitoring equal opportunities for political participation, the channels of expression available through a free press, freedom of organization and assembly for opposition movements, a universal franchise for all adult citizens, as well as the institutions of the rule of law and an independent judiciary, a functioning and effective bureaucracy, and the protection of civil liberties. The aim is to include all the relevant aspects of contestation and participation.

Therefore tensions exist in the literature. Minimalist approaches emphasize the values of reliability and consistency, but at the expense of potentially omitting vital components of democratic regimes and thus misclassifying types of regimes. Maximalist approaches prioritize using richer and more comprehensive multiple indicators, but with the danger of relying upon softer data and less rigorous categories. Both these approaches are common in the research, where there have been multiple attempts to measure democracy; indeed a recent review noted almost four dozen separate indicators of democratic performance, differing in their geographic and temporal scope.[19] Many of these, however, are restricted in the number of states they cover, the frequency of the measures, or the years to which they apply. Time-series which end prior to the early-1990s cannot fully capture the dynamics of the third wave democracies in Central Europe, nor more recent developments occurring elsewhere. We can also set aside for our purposes those datasets which only concern advanced industrialized societies, indicators applying to particular regions such as Latin America, those which arbitrarily exclude smaller states falling below a certain population minimum (thereby skewing the results with a systematic bias), or measures where data limitations exclude important periods or many nation-states (including autocratic states) worldwide. Publicly available indicators which are widely used in the comparative literature are also those which reflect the prevailing consensus among researchers, excluding more idiosyncratic approaches. Using these criteria reduces the longer list to four measures, each reflecting differing conceptions of the essential features of democracy. Table 3.1 summarizes the key dimensions of each. Let us consider the construction and meaning of each of the main indicators that are selected for detailed comparison – by Freedom House, Polity IV, Vanhanen, and Przeworski et al. – to consider the strengths and limitations of each.

Freedom House: Liberal Democracy

One of the best-known measures of liberal democracy, and one of the most widely used in the comparative literature, is the Gastil index of civil liberties and political rights produced annually by Freedom House. The measure has been widely employed by practitioners; for example, its results are incorporated into the benchmark data employed by the US Millennium Challenge Account to assess the quality of governance and award aid in poorer societies. It has also been employed by many comparative scholars, such as in recent publications by Diamond, Barro, and Inglehart and Welzel.[20] Freedom House, an independent think tank based in the United States, first began to assess political trends in the 1950s with the results published as the Balance Sheet of Freedom. In 1972, Freedom House launched a new, more comprehensive annual study called *Freedom in the World*. Raymond Gastil developed the survey's methodology, which assigned ratings of their political rights and civil liberties for each independent nation-state (as well as for dependent territories) and then categorized them as free, partly free, or not free. The survey continued to be produced by Gastil until 1989, when a larger team of in-house survey analysts was established. Subsequent editions of the survey have followed essentially the same format although more details have recently been released about the coding framework used for each assessment.

The index monitors the existence of political rights in terms of electoral processes, political pluralism, and the functioning of government. Civil liberties are defined by the existence of freedom of speech and association, rule of law, and personal rights. The research team draws upon multiple sources of information to develop their classifications, which are based on a checklist of questions, including 10 separate items monitoring the existence of political rights and 15 on civil liberties. These items assess the presence of institutional checks and balances constraining the executive through the existence of a representative and inclusive legislature, an independent judiciary implementing the rule of law, and the existence of political rights and civil liberties, including to reasonable self-determination and participation by minorities, and the presence of free and fair election laws.[21] Each item is allocated a score from 0 to 4 and all are given equal weight when aggregated. The raw scores for each country are then converted into a 7-point scale of political rights and a 7-point scale for civil liberties, and in turn these are collapsed to categorize each regime worldwide as either 'free', 'partly free', or 'not free'. As a result of this process, Freedom House estimate that out of 193 nation-states, roughly two-thirds or 123 (64%) could be classified as electoral democracies in 2007 (defined as 'free' or 'partly free').[22] This represents a remarkable advance during the third wave, but nevertheless they estimate that the balance of regime types has largely stabilized during the last decade; for example, Freedom House reported that in 1995 there were 117 electoral democracies around the globe (around 61%).

The emphasis of this measure on a wide range of civil liberties, rights, and freedoms means that this most closely reflects notions of liberal democracy.

The index has the advantage of providing comprehensive coverage of nation-states and independent territories worldwide, as well as establishing a long time-series of observations conducted annually since 1972. The measure is also comprehensive in its conceptualization and it is particularly appropriate for those seeking an indicator of liberal democracy.

Despite these virtues, the index has been subject to considerable criticism on a number of methodological grounds.[23] The procedures used by the team of researchers employed by Freedom House lack transparency, so that scholars cannot double-check the reliability and consistency of the coding decisions; nor can the results be replicated. The questions used for constructing the index often involve two or three separate items within each subcategory, allowing ambiguous measurement and aggregation across these items. The process of compositing the separate items is not subject to systematic factor analysis, so it remains unclear whether the items do indeed cluster together into consistent scales of political rights and civil liberties. The multiple dimensions included in the index provide a broad-ranging attempt to monitor human rights, for example, concerning owning property, freedom of religious expression, choice of marriage partners, and absence of economic exploitation. These are all widely regarded as important dimensions of human rights, with intrinsic value, but it is not clear that these are necessarily essential components or valid measures of democracy per se. The concepts of freedom and democracy are not equivalent. It remains an empirical question whether democratic regimes promote these sorts of values, for example, whether they are associated with free market capitalist economies or whether some prefer protectionist economic policies and a greater role for the government in economic planning and the welfare state.[24] If the separate scores for the individual components of the Gastil index were publicly released, then researchers could construct narrower measures reflecting their chosen specification of democracy, but unfortunately only composite scores are available. Moreover since the index contains such a broad range of indicators, this also makes it less valuable as an analytical tool useful for policymakers; for example, if it is established that the Freedom House measure of democracy is consistently linked to the protection of human rights, economic growth, peace, or the provision of more generous welfare services, it remains unclear what particular aspect of the index is driving this relationship.[25] The construction of the measure therefore suffers from certain problems of conflation and redundancy, and although it is widely used, it essentially reflects liberal notions of democracy, and other approaches emphasize alternative concepts.

Polity IV: Constitutional Democracy

Another approach commonly used in the comparative and international relations literature is the classification of constitutional democracy provided by the Polity project.[26] This project was initiated by Ted Robert Gurr in the 1970s and it has evolved over the past three decades. The latest version, Polity IV, provides annual time-series data in country-year format covering 161 countries from 1800 to 1999.[27] Coders working on the Polity IV project classify democracy and autocracy in each nation-year as a composite score of different characteristics relating to authority structures. Democracy is conceived of conceptually as reflecting three essential elements: the presence of institutions and procedures through which citizens can express preferences about alternative policies and leaders, the existence of institutionalized constraints on the power of the executive, and the guarantee of civil liberties to all citizens (although not actually measured). The classification emphasizes the existence or absence of institutional features of the nation-state. For example, competitive executive recruitment is measured by leadership selection through popular elections contested by two or more parties or candidates. The openness of recruitment for the chief executive is measured by the opportunity for all citizens to attain the position through a regularized process, excluding hereditary succession, forceful seizure of power, or military coups. By contrast, autocracies are seen as regimes which restrict or suppress competitive political participation, in which the chief executive is chosen from within the political elite, and, once in office, leaders face few institutional constraints on their power. The dataset constructs a 10-point democracy scale by coding the competitiveness of political participation (1–3), the competitiveness of executive recruitment (1–2), the openness of executive recruitment (1), and the constraints on the chief executive (1–4). Autocracy is measured by negative versions of the same indices. The two scales are combined into a single democracy-autocracy score varying from −10 to +10. Polity has also been used to monitor and identify processes of major regime change and democratic transitions, classified as a positive change in the democracy-autocracy score of more than 3 points.

The Polity IV scores have the virtue of providing an exceptionally long series of observations stretching over two centuries, as well as covering most nation-states worldwide. The provision of separate indices for each of the main dimensions allows scholars to disaggregate the components. The emphasis on constitutional rules restricting the executive may be particularly valuable for distinguishing the initial downfall of autocratic regimes and the transition to multiparty elections. Unfortunately the democracy-autocracy score also suffers from certain important limitations. Polity IV emphasizes the existence of constraints upon the chief executive as a central part of their measure. As Munck and Verkulian point out, however, there is a world of difference between those restrictions on the executive which arise from democratic checks and balances, such as the power of the elected legislature or an independent judiciary, and those which arise from other actors, such as the power of the military or economic elites.[28] Although more information is now released in the user's codebook, the processes which the Polity team uses to classify regimes continue to lack a degree of transparency and therefore replicability by independent scholars. Moreover although acknowledging the importance of civil liberties as part of their overall conceptualization of democracy, Polity IV does not actually attempt to code or measure this dimension. The Polity IV index was originally conceived by Gurr for very different purposes, to monitor notions of political stability and regime change, and the growing use of this measure to assess constitutional forms of democracy represents a newer development.

Vanhanen: Participatory Democracy

A more minimalist approach is exemplified by Tatu Vanhanen, who developed a scaled measure of democracy in each country according to two criteria: the degree of *electoral competition* (measured by the share of the vote won by the largest party in the national legislature) and the degree of *electoral participation* (the proportion of the total population who voted in national legislative elections), which he combines to yield an index of democratization.[29] Both these indicators use measures which are straightforward to calculate and the empirical data can be compiled from various publicly available sources. These criteria reflect both of Dahl's key dimensions of polyarchy, namely, contestation and participation. In a series of publications, Vanhanen develops this scale to classify levels of democracy in 187 nation-states worldwide on an annual basis from 1810 to 2000. The author argues that the level of electoral turnout in each country, gauged by the total valid votes cast in an election as a proportion of the voting-age population (Vote/VAP), is usually regarded as an important indicator of democratic health, hence the widespread popular concern about any indication of falling electoral participation. Moreover the measure of Vote/VAP also provides an indirect indicator of the extent of universal adult suffrage, highlighting states where major sectors of the adult population are denied the franchise on the basis of citizenship requirements, literacy qualifications, social class, sex, race, ethnicity, religion, mental capacity, imprisonment, or other related characteristics which disqualify residents from voting rights.[30]

It is true that the universal suffrage is an important component of democracy and a major part of the historical fight for equal rights. Official data on voter turnout is readily available from standard reference sources, for example, from International IDEA; hence this provides a reliable empirical indicator.[31] Nevertheless the question is whether this measure is a valid indicator of democracy, and there are several reasons to doubt this. If isolated from other conditions which are important for meaningful and fair electoral contests, by itself the comparison of voter turnout statistics may prove a highly misleading measure of democratization. In plebiscitary elections held to legitimize authoritarian rule, even in one-party states, voters may be successfully mobilized through intimidation and manipulation by government forces, rigged voting, ballot stuffing, vote buying, pressures on opposition politicians, and state control of the media. In such cases, turnout may be far higher than in elections held under free and fair conditions; for example, voter turnout in national elections was usually greater in the one-party Soviet Union than in countries such as the United States, India, and Switzerland. International IDEA's worldwide comparison of countries ranked by levels of turnout (measured by the average ratio of votes cast to registered voters in national elections to the lower house held from 1945 to 2001), ranks Singapore second and Uzbekistan third (both with

93.5% turnout). This suggests that levels of voter turnout are meaningless by themselves as indicators of democracy unless the prior conditions of multiparty competition and civil liberties are specified, requiring other indicators. Moreover turnout is produced by multiple factors which are only loosely related to democracy per se; for example, if we just compare postindustrial nation-states, it would seem odd to argue that high turnout generated by the strict use of compulsory voting laws meant that Australia (with an average Vote/VAP since 1945 of 84.2%) should be regarded as automatically more democratic than the United Kingdom (73.8%), or, for the same reasons, that Italy (92%) should be seen as more democratic than France (67.3%). Indeed certain aspects of democratization are inversely related to patterns of turnout, such as holding more frequent elections and broadening the voting franchise to younger age groups, which both expand opportunities and yet also usually dampen levels of participation.[32]

Party contestation has been operationalized in the literature in different ways. In countries holding multiparty national legislative elections, Vanhanen assesses competition by the share of the votes won by the largest party, arguing that if the combined share of the vote for all the other smaller parties is very low (for example, less than 30%), then the dominance of the largest party is so overpowering that it is doubtful whether such a country could be regarded as a democracy.[33] This measure is based on objective data which is transparent and easily replicable by cross-referencing various standard compilations of election results. Nevertheless the proposed procedure introduces a systematic bias from the electoral system, because the winning party may be predominant over successive contests as a result of the exaggerative quality of majoritarian electoral rules, even if they receive only a relatively modest share of the popular vote. Moreover there are also difficult cases under this rule where there are many parties, and the conditions of elections free of manipulation, fraud, and intimidation, and yet one party attracts overwhelming popular support, exemplified by the 70% share of the vote received by the African National Congress party in April 2004 elections to the National Assembly. It would have been preferable to gauge party competition using standard indicators such as the Laakso and Taagepera measure of the '*effective* number of parliamentary parties' (ENPP), and the '*effective* number of electoral parties' (ENEP), both of which take account of not only the number of parties but also the relative size of each.[34] Finally, the degree of party competition in the legislature does not tell us anything about the frequency with which parties alternate between government and opposition over a certain period. Indeed in pluralist societies with very fragmented party systems, with a high ENEP, multiple opposition parties exist but for this very reason, through 'divide and rule', the governing party can continue in power for decades.

Przeworski, Alvarez, Cheibub, and Limongi: Competitive Democracy

The fourth alternative measure under comparison, which is the most minimalist, was originally developed by Przeworski, Alvarez, Cheibub, and Limongi and subsequently extended by Cheibub and Gandhi.[35] This approach defines democratic states as those regimes where citizens have the power to replace their government through contested elections. This conception reflects the long tradition established by Joseph Schumpeter, followed by many subsequent commentators, which regards the presence of competitive multiparty elections as the key feature of representative democracy.[36] There is a broad consensus that at a minimum all democratic regimes require regular elections providing alternative party choices at the ballot box. Contestation is one of the essential aspects of Dahl's notion of polyarchy, alongside participation.[37] Regular free elections for all major government offices provide opportunities for citizens to discipline their leaders. The credible threat of losing power compels elected representatives to pay attention to citizens' interests. For the threat of electoral defeat to be credible, effective party competition is essential to facilitate opposition scrutiny of the government during interelectoral periods and party choice among citizens at the ballot box. Countries are clearly recognized as autocratic if they fill national legislative offices and the chief executive office through appointment, patronage, or inheritance, rather than by popular elections. One-party states which hold elections for the national legislature, but which ban any other party from organizing and from contesting elections, such as Cuba, also fall unambiguously into the autocratic category. In some cases a limited degree of electoral choice is maintained where individual candidates from within the same party run for office, as exemplified by local elections among alternative Communist Party candidates in China or among Movement candidates in Uganda. But in general the presence of competition from alternative parties is widely regarded as essential for genuine electoral choices and democratic contestation. Only parties can present voters with a choice of leadership teams and programs representing a coherent set of policies, and thus allow collective responsibility. As Schattschneider claimed, modern representative democracy is unworkable without parties.[38] Parties are necessary to build and aggregate support among a broad coalition of citizens' organizations and interest groups; to integrate multiple conflicting demands into a coherent policy program; to select and train legislative candidates and political leaders; to provide voters with a choice of governing teams and policies; and, if elected to office, to organize the process of government and to stand collectively accountable for their actions in subsequent contests. For all these reasons, political parties thereby form the cornerstone of a democratic society and serve a function unlike that of any other institution.

But how can party competition and contestation for government offices best be measured? The essential feature of democratic states, Przeworski et al. argue, is that they provide regular electoral opportunities for removing those in power. More than one party has to compete in regular elections for the lower house of the national legislature and for executive office in presidential systems. An opposition party has to have some chance of winning elected office as a result of popular elections, and there must be some uncertainty about the outcome, so that the incumbent party may lose power. If the incumbent party loses, there has to be the assurance that they will leave office and the winning party will succeed them.[39] Through this mechanism, governing parties can be held accountable for their actions, and, if they fail to prove responsive to public concerns, they face a realistic chance of being replaced by the opposition in a regular and orderly constitutional process. Following this conceptualization, Przeworksi et al. classify all states as either a democracy or an autocracy according to certain institutional rules, namely:

1. The lower house of the legislature must be elected.
2. The chief executive must be elected (directly in presidential systems and indirectly by members of the elected legislature in parliamentary systems).
3. There must be more than one party.
4. And (if states pass all these rules), if the incumbent party subsequently held, but never lost an election, such regimes are regarded by default as authoritarian. Regimes which fail any of these rules are classified as autocratic.

They therefore examine whether government offices (both for the chief executive officer and the legislative body) are filled as a consequence of contested elections. Contestation is understood to occur where there are at least two parties and an opposition party has some chance of winning office as a result of elections. If the incumbent party loses an election, democracies require that they leave office. If no alternation occurs, then regimes are classified as autocratic. On the basis of this series of rules, Przeworski, Alvarez, Cheibub, and Limogi categorize all regimes every year from 1950 to 1990, supplemented with data by Cheibub and Ghandi which updates the series to 2000. This dataset represents a major advance in the literature by clearly specifying a limited set of decision rules defining party contestation and proposing a transparent process of applying these procedures to develop a typology of regimes. This process is also easily replicable from published sources, allowing the dataset to be extended by other scholars to test their key findings in other contexts and periods.

The main limitation of this approach, however, is that, while parsimonious, this stripped-down measure is open to the charge of neglecting certain important dimensions which are integral to the conception of liberal democracy. The most notable omission from the Przeworski et al. definition is any consideration of mass participation; in particular, they do not seek to code whether elections are held under conditions of a universal adult suffrage. Yet most would regard any state as undemocratic if it held elections which systematically excluded certain major categories of its adult population from voting rights. All countries have some categories of the population who are disqualified from exercising the franchise, for example, resident noncitizens, citizens living overseas, those declared mentally disabled, or people convicted of certain criminal offenses or undergoing a sentence of imprisonment. The conditions for citizenship and any residency requirements for voting also vary cross-nationally.[40] In principle, however, universal adult suffrage is necessary for democracy, although it is not sufficient by itself. Contestation without universal adult suffrage can be confined to a coterie of competitive oligarchies and their band of followers.[41] If we simply rely upon Przeworski et al.'s rules, for example, Britain would qualify as a democracy after the Glorious Revolution of 1688, which established the rule of law, parliamentary sovereignty, and limited power for the monarchy, after which the Whig and Tory parliamentary parties rotated in government and opposition, despite the fact that opportunities to vote in many corrupt boroughs were restricted to a small group of property-owning middle-class men, prior to the Reform Acts of 1832, 1867 and 1884, 1919, and 1927. In the same way, the United States would be classified as democratic from the era of the Jacksonian party system, when the competition from Democrats and the Whig opposition emerged around 1828, well before the enfranchisement of slaves in 1870, the passage of female suffrage in 1919, and the Voting Rights Act of 1965, which swept away restrictive practices for African-American citizens. Przeworski et al. argue that they are only seeking to monitor contemporary democracies since 1945, when most states had established the universal adult franchise. But nevertheless some major omissions remained in this period, notably in Switzerland, which only introduced the female suffrage for national elections in 1971, while South Africa retained apartheid until 1994, and the franchise continues to be withheld from women in contemporary Saudi Arabia.

The lack of attention to mass participation is a major problem with the validity of the Przeworski et al. approach, but, along similar lines, concern is also raised by the way that party competition is measured in a minimal way without taking account of other conditions which may make it meaningful. For example, without the protection of human rights, freedom of the press, free and fair elections, and civil liberties, parties cannot compete effectively for electoral support, and citizens cannot evaluate government performance and party policies to arrive at an informed choice at the ballot box. These problems are exemplified by pro-state bias in the campaign television news and limits on the independent media, reported by Organization for Security and Cooperation in Europe (OSCE) observers as occurring in Belarus. Elsewhere there are problems of overt censorship and severe repression of journalists, noted by the Committee to Protect Journalists as occurring in Algeria, Iraq, Colombia, and Russia.[42] As noted earlier, the cases of 'electoral autocracies' are particularly difficult regimes to classify, for example, Russia, which classified as continuously 'democratic' since 1992, according to the Przeworski rules, yet which has seen a subsequent progressive deterioration in civil liberties, according to Freedom House and Polity IV. One way to test how far the Przeworski measure taps any broader indication of civil liberties is to examine the correlation between this measure and the Cingranelli-Richards (CIRI) Database monitoring a range of human rights, including civil liberties (the extent of freedom of association, movement, speech, religion, and participation), women's rights (in the economic, political, and social spheres), and the worst abuses arising from state repression (through the use of extrajudicial killings, political imprisonment, torture, and disappearance).[43] The Przeworski et al. measure of competitive democracy was fairly strongly related to civil liberties (R = .75***) but was far more weakly linked to indicators of state repression (R = .36***). For example, among the regimes classified by Przeworski as democratic, torture was found to be practiced frequently by 31% and extrajudicial killings were frequently employed by 15%. In this regard, the measure of competitive democracy is far more generous in its interpretation of a democratic regime than the stricter monitoring of human rights provided by the Freedom House index.

Another potential difficulty with this measure is that contested multiparty elections appear relatively straightforward and unambiguous to code from public sources because of the presence of more than one party on the ballot. In practice, however, degrees of party competition in the process of nomination, campaigning, and election vary substantially from one country to another. The fact that more than one party contests an election does not imply, by any means, the existence of a level playing field so that all parties stand an equal chance of winning seats, let alone government. This is most problematic in the cases of 'electoral democracies' or 'competitive authoritarian regimes', such as Zimbabwe and Belarus. Even among the clearer cases of established democracies, few ban any parties outright, but some party organizations are occasionally declared illegal, for example, radical right parties are restricted by the German constitution and limited by Belgian laws against hate speech. Parties associated with violent terrorist tactics have been banned in Spain (Batasuna, the political wing of ETA in the Basque region) and France. The Turkish Constitutional Court shut down the Welfare Party, a radical Muslim organization with considerable popular support. More commonly, most democracies have a range of regulations restricting candidate and party access to the ballot, sources of campaign funds, and the media. In every nation, the type of electoral system, notably the effective threshold, limits which candidates win seats. All of these rules make party systems more or less competitive. Although free and fair elections are contested, where the opposition remains divided, predominant parties may be returned with a plurality of the vote for decades, such as the Liberal Democrats in Japan. The fact that multiple parties campaign in Japanese elections does not mean that the allocation of government offices rotates regularly between government and opposition parties. While accepted limits on multiparty competition do not raise major concern in categorizing long-established democratic states such as Germany, Belgium, and Japan, legal restrictions on the ability of opposition parties and reform movements to campaign and challenge the ruling elites pose far more difficulty in classifying regimes such as Russia.

Last, Przeworski et al. classify all regimes as either democracies or autocracies, yet in reality regimes do not shift from autocracies one year to democracies the next, as dichotomous measures suggest. Mexico, for example, did not automatically become democratic the day after Vincente Fox was elected president by defeating the Institutional Revolutionary Party (PRI) candidate; instead the country experienced a series of steps which allowed opposition parties to make gains on some local states, which allowed the Electoral Institute to clean up political bribery and ballot stuffing, and which generated freer criticism of the governing PRI in the mass media. Recognizing that important distinctions may be lost by the idea of a strict dichotomy dividing the world into democracies and autocracies, there have been numerous attempts to introduce categories in the gray zone which have been conceptualized as, alternatively, 'semidemocracies', 'competitive authoritarianism' (Levitsky and Way), and 'illiberal democracies' (Zacharia). Each of these qualifying terms suffers from certain ambiguities, implying subcategories. The democratization process refers to the stages which regimes go through in order to become democratic. The process can be progressive (where regimes become more democratic) or degenerative (where states become more autocratic).

Good Governance. The last decade has seen a proliferation of alternative initiatives which have sought to operationalize the related notion of 'good governance'. The World Bank has used assessments of government performance in allocating resources since the mid-1970s. Focusing at first on macroeconomic management, the assessment criteria have expanded to include trade and financial policies, business regulation, social sector policies, effectiveness of the public sector, and transparency, accountability, and corruption. These criteria are assessed annually for all World Bank borrowers. Among these, the issue of corruption has moved toward the center of the World Bank's governance strategy, as this is regarded as a fundamental impediment to reducing poverty.[44]

The most ambitious attempt to measure all the dimensions of 'good governance' are the indices generated by Kaufmann and colleagues for the World Bank Institute. The Kaufmann-Kray indicators (also known as 'The Worldwide Governance Indicators') are some of the most widely used measures of good governance. Compiled since 1996, these composite indices measure the perceived quality of six dimensions of governance for 213 countries, based on 31 data sources produced by 25 organizations. The underlying data is based on hundreds of variables and reflects the perceptions and views of experts, firm survey respondents, and citizens on various dimensions of governance. The World Bank does not generate these separate assessments; rather it integrates them into composite indices. The measures specify the margins of error associated with each estimate, allowing users to identify a range of statistically likely ratings for each country. The Worldwide Governance Indicators measure the quality of six dimensions of governance: *voice and accountability:* the extent to which a country's citizens are able to participate in selecting their government, as well as freedom of expression, freedom of association, and free media; *political stability and absence of violence:* perceptions of the likelihood that the government will be destabilized or overthrown by unconstitutional or violent means, including political violence and terrorism; *government effectiveness:* the quality of public services, the quality of the civil service and the degree of its independence from political pressures, the quality of policy formulation and implementation, and the credibility of the government's commitment to such policies; *regulatory quality*: the ability of the government to formulate and implement sound policies and regulations that permit and promote private sector development; *rule of law*: the extent to which agents have confidence in and abide by the rules of society, and in particular the quality of contract enforcement, the police, and the courts, as well as the likelihood of crime and violence; *control of corruption*: the extent to which public power is exercised for private gain, including both petty and grand forms of corruption, as well as 'capture' of the state by elites and private interests.

Related well-known attempts to monitor several aspects of 'good governance' include the Corruption Perception Index generated annually since 1995 by Transparency International. The International Country Risk Guide is another measure, which has been assessing financial, economic, and political risks since 1980 for about 140 countries. Global Integrity, based in Washington, DC, assesses the existence and effectiveness of anticorruption mechanisms that promote public integrity, using more than 290 indicators to generate the Global Integrity Index for more than 40 countries. The Cingranelli-Richards (CIRI) Database monitoring a range of human rights, such as civil liberties, women's rights, and state repression, has already been discussed.[45] Perceptual assessments using expert surveys and subjective judgments may prove unreliable for several reasons, including reliance upon a small number of national 'experts', the use of business leaders and academic scholars as the basis of the judgments, variations in country coverage by different indices, and possible bias toward more favorable evaluations of countries with good economic outcomes. Nevertheless in the absence of other reliable indicators covering a wide range of nation-states, such as representative surveys of public opinion, these measures provide some of the best available gauges of good governance.

These and many associated projects have greatly expanded the number of political indicators which are now widely available and often used by analysts and policymakers. This study integrates selected Kaufmann-Kray good governance indicators as part of the analysis. Nevertheless the primary focus of this book rests on the four indicators of democratic governance which have already been discussed. The reasons are that the core concept of 'good governance' contains a number of distinct dimensions, it is often overloaded and conflated with multiple meanings and measures, and it remains undertheorized compared with the work on democratic governance.[46] As Grindle has argued, the 'good governance' agenda is poorly focused, overlong, and growing ever longer, depending upon the emphasis given to nostrums for reform.[47] Moreover, equally importantly, the Kaufmann-Kray indicators started in the mid-1990s and so observations are simply unavailable for the longitudinal study, which examines trends since the start of the third wave in the early-1970s. For all these reasons, this study emphasizes understanding the primary drivers of democratic governance, not good governance.

TABLE 3.2. *Correlation among Democratic Indicators*

		Liberal Democracy	Participatory Democracy	Constitutional Democracy
		Freedom House	Vanhanen	Polity IV
Participatory democracy (Vanhanen)	Correlation	.730(***)		
	Sig. (2-tailed)	.000		
	N	3006		
Constitutional democracy (Polity)	Correlation	.904(***)	.751(***)	
	Sig. (2-tailed)	.000	.000	
	N	4382	4051	
Contested democracy (Cheibub and Gandhi)	Correlation	.826(***)	.681(***)	.856(***)
	Sig. (2-tailed)	.000	.000	.000
	N	5076	4661	6784

Notes: N = Number of cases. *** All correlations are significant at the 0.01 level (2-tailed).

THE PRAGMATIC CHOICE AND COMPARISON OF INDICATORS

To summarize the debate about measures and indicators, prominent scholars continue to disagree about the merits of the main minimalist and maximalist concepts of democracy most commonly used in the literature, as well as the value of adopting either dichotomous classifications (such as the Przeworski categorization) or graded measures (such as the 20-point Polity index). There is no consensus about the most appropriate criteria used to measure democratic regimes, the weighting which should be given to separate components, the reliability of the coding procedures used by different researchers, and the way that these indicators should be translated into regime typologies.

In practice, however, despite all the differences in the construction of democratic indices, it is striking that the four alternative measures most commonly used in the comparative literature correlate strongly with each other.[48] For comparison, the Polity IV scale of democracy-autocracy was recoded to a positive 20-point scale, and the Freedom House index was recoded so that a score of 1 represented the least democratic regimes, while a score of 7 represented the most democratic. Table 3.2 shows that the Freedom House rating was strongly and significantly related to the Polity IV score (R = .904**), the Cheibub classification of the type of democratic-autocratic regime (R = .826**), and the Vanhanen index of democratization (R = .730**).

A visual examination of the trends since 1972 documented by each of these indicators also shows considerable agreement among the series, despite differences in their conceptualization, measurement, and periods (see Figures 3.1 to 3.5). This suggests that there is an underlying consensus about

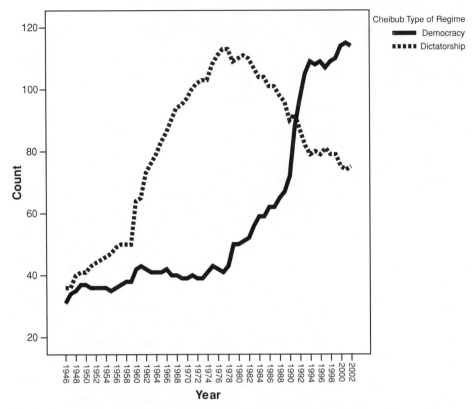

FIGURE 3.1. Trends in Cheibub and Gandhi's Classification of Regime Types, 1945–2002. *Source:* José Cheibub and Jennifer Gandhi. 2004. 'Classifying political regimes: A six-fold measure of democracies and dictatorships.' Presented at the American Political Science Association Annual Meeting. Chicago, September 2–5.

historical developments, generating confidence about the reliability and robustness of measures. The trends monitored in each series differ in their starting points, with Polity IV presenting the longest period, from 1800 onward. As shown in Figure 3.1, the Cheibub and Gandhi series since the end of the Second World War suggests a steady and substantial rise in the number of dictatorships worldwide from 1960 until the late-1970s (the period identified by Huntington as the second reverse wave of democratization), then demonstrates a fairly steady fall which continues to their most recent observation. The parallel rise in the number of democratic regimes appears to occur in this series from the early-1980s onward (later than the Huntington periodization of the third wave) and continues to the end of their series in 2002.

The Freedom House series monitoring political rights and civil liberties in liberal democracy starts in 1972. Their tripartite classification of regime

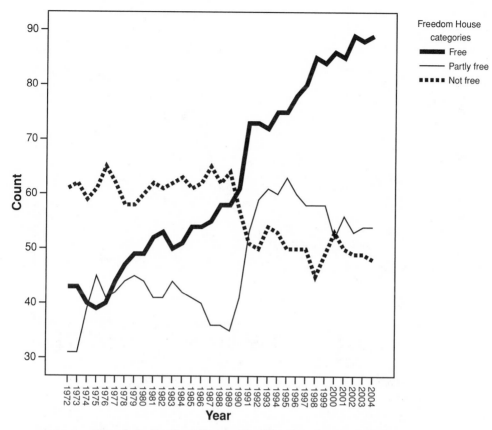

FIGURE 3.2. Trends in Freedom House Classification of Regime Types, 1972–2004.
Source: Freedom House. *Freedom in the World.* www.freedomhouse.org (various years).

types, shown in Figure 3.2, also suggests that a gradual rise in free nation-states occurs from the mid- to late-1970s, experiencing a sharp surge in the 1989–1991 period, then registers a continuous more steady growth to date. The number of 'not free' nation-states remains steady throughout the 1970s and 1980s, only dropping precipitously in the 1989–1990 period (with the fall of the Berlin Wall) and then hitting an erratic plateau at a lower level. In this series, the number of 'partly free' states rises sharply in the period 1989–1990. The mean Freedom House rating on the Gastil index, shown in Figure 3.3, shows a steadier picture of developments with rising levels of liberal democracy in countries around the world.

The mean Polity IV autocracy-democracy 20-point score of constitutional democracy provides the longest time-series, extending over two centuries. Figure 3.4 shows a steady erosion of autocracy from roughly 1820 until the first peak reached a century later. In Europe this era saw multiple developments with the growth of parliamentary democracies independent of the monarchy,

FIGURE 3.3. Trends in Freedom House's Measure of Liberal Democracy, 1972–2004.
Source: Freedom House. *Freedom in the World.* www.freedomhouse.org (various years).

the evolution of competitive party systems, the expansion of the universal franchise to broader sectors of society, including the working class and eventually
to women as well. After the initial advance, according to Polity IV, the interwar
era saw the first substantial reverse wave, with the rise of Hitler and Mussolini,
but also a reversal of democracy in many Latin American nation-states. The end
of the Second World War registered a second sharp wave of democratization,
notably the new constitutions established in Germany and Poland, and fragile
democratic constitutions established in many ex-colonies which were achieving independence. The era from 1950 to 1980 displayed the sharp erosion in
democratic states worldwide which Huntington terms the second reverse wave.
It is only from the early- to mid-1970s, with the end of dictatorships in Spain,
Portugal, and Greece, that democracy expands again around the globe in the
Polity IV series, with the sharpest rise registered during the 1989–1991 period
following the fall of the Berlin Wall.

Finally, trends in the Vanhanen index of participatory democracy, illustrated
in Figure 3.5, also extend from 1810 onward. The series suggests a slow rise
in participatory democracy during the nineteenth century, with a sharp expansion in the 1920s, in large part because of the expansion of the franchise to the
working class and women in many countries. The interwar years register strong

FIGURE 3.4. Trends in Polity IV Measure of Constitutional Democracy, 1800–2000. *Source:* Monty Marshall and Keith Jaggers. 2003. *Polity IV Project: Political Regime Characteristics and Transitions, 1800–2003.* http://www.cidcm.umd.edu/inscr/polity/

setbacks for democracy, which is sharply reversed in the late 1950s, creating a more volatile picture during these years than the other indicators under comparison. The Vanhanen series also confirms the rise in democratization which occurs during the third wave, registering here from the mid-1970s onward.

It remains possible that systematic bias may affect all these measures, where similar data sources and reference works are used to construct these scales, or if subjective evaluations of each country are influenced by the published results derived from other indices. Yet despite the important differences in the conceptualization and measurement used in each of these scales, which might have been expected to produce considerable inconsistencies, in fact there appears to be considerable consensus about the overall classification of regime types. The most sensible approach to the analysis in this book, therefore, is not to pick any one of these indicators arbitrarily as the core way to measure democracy, but rather to test whether the results of the different models used for analysis remain consistent using each measure. If there are similar results – as we would expect, given the strong correlation among measures – then this suggests that the generalizations derived from the analysis remain robust irrespective of the particular measure which is adopted. If there are important differences,

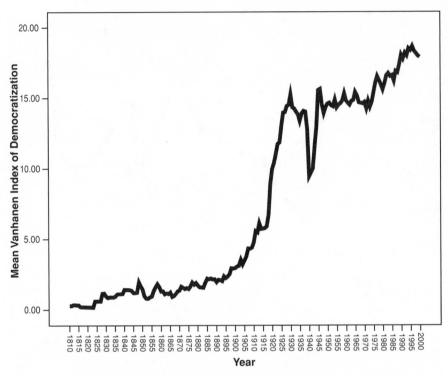

FIGURE 3.5. Trends in Vanhanen's Measure of Participatory Democracy, 1810–1998.
Source: Tatu Vanhanen. 2000. 'A new dataset for measuring democracy, 1810–1998.'
Journal of Peace Research 37 (2): 251–265.

however, then we need to consider the reason for such inconsistencies and
whether they arise from the differing underlying meanings associated with
each measure.

METHODS AND RESEARCH DESIGN

Research on democratization draws on a mélange of intellectual disciplines
derived from development economics, political sociology, contemporary history, international relations, area studies, and political science. Ideally general
theories about the process of democratization should meet multiple criteria.[49]
They need to achieve comprehensiveness to apply across a wide range of conditions, nation-states, eras, and contexts. Integration with the previous literature is important to build cumulative knowledge rather than attempting to
start de novo. Thick depth is valuable to penetrate beyond truisms and over-
simple banalities. Relevance to the policy community allows research to be
utilized in the real world. Rigor, accuracy, and precision let theories generate a series of specific hypotheses which are potentially falsifiable when tested

against a body of empirical evidence. Awareness of the extent to which analytical theories are rooted in a broader set of normative assumptions enriches
and deepens research. Parsimony facilitates intellectual elegance and logical
clarity. And creative innovation provides insights which go beyond previous
knowledge.

Inevitably in practice research involves trade-offs from these ideals, with
individual scholars and disciplines prioritizing different approaches. Contemporary historians and scholars of area studies, for example, commonly opt for
thick and detailed narrative case studies, utilizing descriptions of sequential
developments in countries which experienced regime change. Such accounts
often provide persuasive and comprehensive explanations of specific events in
each nation; for example, Nancy Bermeo used compelling narratives of the
breakdown of 13 parliamentary democracies in the interwar years to examine
the role that ordinary citizens and elites played in this process.[50] The in-depth
case study approach is valuable, but it can limit our ability to generalize across
different countries and regions, political systems, and cultural contexts; for
example, Guillermo O'Donnell drew heavily upon the experience of Argentina
in developing his influential account of bureaucratic authoritarianism, but with
the benefit of hindsight it appears that the experience of this country was an
outlier compared with that in many others throughout Latin America.[51] As
the literature has broadened the comparative framework, so this has generated
greater challenges of generalizing across diverse regions such as Latin America,
post-Communist Europe, Asia, and Africa. Studies have often used evidence
drawn from a small sample of cases, or from a narrow set of explanatory variables, raising doubts about the validity of causal general theories when attempts
have been made to apply these explanations elsewhere.[52]

By contrast, scholars from disciplines such as developmental economy, political economy, and comparative politics typically prefer large-N statistical comparisons, testing empirical regularities statistically using multiple observations
drawn from cross-sectional or time-series data to examine simple propositions
which are more narrowly conceived and more easily measured. This process,
exemplified most recently in a series of publications by Adam Przeworski, José
Antonio Cheibub, and their colleagues, prioritizes rigor and replicability in
empirical generalizations, but at the loss of the richness and depth derived
from national or regional case studies.[53] The range of causal factors which
could potentially contribute to democratization is also so great that rather
than generating robust generalizations, any results remain heavily dependent
upon the specific choice of control variables, time periods, and cross-national
frameworks. The emphasis upon analytical clarity, parsimony, and theoretical elegance is also shared with formal rational choice and game theoretic
approaches, building a sophisticated series of logical propositions, for example, about the preferences for key actors engaged in regime transition, based on
a few core axioms. As Green and Shapiro suggest, however, many of the core
theoretical conjectures generated by rational choice accounts have not been

tested empirically, or else they generate testable propositions which may prove banal and irrelevant to real world problems.[54]

No single approach is entirely satisfactory, but a combination of methodologies holds great promise for adopting the best features, and ideally avoiding the limitations, of each. As discussed in the previous chapter, the research design in this book therefore seeks to combine large-N quantitative studies with a series of selected case studies. To generalize across the conditions leading toward durable democracies, as mentioned earlier, the study draws upon cross-sectional time-series (CSTS) data, consisting of annual observations of each regime worldwide, from 1973 to 2005, in 191 independent nation-states. The research examines trends since the early-1970s, understood as the conventional start of the third wave. Following the approach of Betz and Katz, multivariate ordinary least squares regression analysis is employed with panel-corrected errors.[55] In this dataset, the 'regime-year' is the primary unit of the comparison, providing over 5,000 observations. Data is derived from a wide variety of sources, including aggregate indicators collected from official government statistics by international agencies such as the UNDP and World Bank, and cross-national survey data based on representative samples of the general public, for example, from the World Values Study. The Technical Appendix provides details of the core variables used in the analysis, described in more detail in each chapter. On this basis, the next section of the book goes on to examine whether institutions are related to trends in democratization, considering the cross-sectional time-series analysis as well as particular case studies of leaders and laggards in each region, providing thicker descriptive narratives of the process of regime change.

4

Wealth and Democracy

Can formal democratic institutions succeed if they are built in societies with inhospitable social and economic conditions? In particular, will attempts to hold competitive elections fail to strengthen democracy in poor and divided nation-states, as well as in regions such as the Middle East which are dominated by autocracy? Skeptics point to an earlier wave of institution building, when European-style parliaments were transplanted to many African societies during the era of decolonization, including in Benin and Togo, only to collapse as the military usurped their powers.[1] We first need to establish the influence of certain underlying economic and social conditions on democratic consolidation before proceeding to examine the impact of power-sharing institutions in subsequent chapters. As Dahl points out, where the underlying conditions are highly unfavorable, then it is improbable that democracy could be preserved by any constitutional design. By contrast, if the underlying conditions are highly favorable, then democratic consolidation is likely with almost any constitution.[2] But many cases fall into the muddy middle ground. The analysis of cross-sectional time-series data illuminates the general patterns and which conditions count, focusing upon examining the role of wealth, the size of nation-states, colonial legacies, regional diffusion, and the degree of ethnic heterogeneity. All of these factors can be regarded as 'structural' constraints on political development, meaning that it is difficult for domestic policymakers or the international community to alter these conditions in the medium to short term, if at all; for example, countries cannot change their histories or choose their neighboring states, although they can attempt to grow their economy. The East Asian cases of South Korea and Singapore provide further insights into how certain structural factors facilitate, but do not determine, democratic consolidation. Both Asian societies have experienced rapid economic transformation in recent decades, yet South Korea has adopted multiparty elections and strengthened human rights, with the regimes rated by Freedom House as equivalent to Greece or Israel, while Singapore is rated only 'partly free' by

Freedom House. The contrasts help to explain the strengths – and limits – of socioeconomic explanations of democratization.

THEORIES OF WEALTH AND DEMOCRACY

The proposition that wealthy societies are usually also more democratic has a long lineage. Political philosophers have suggested this proposition; for example, John Stuart Mill, reflecting upon the British colonies, theorized that democracy was not suitable for all nation-states.[3] Exactly a century later, the political sociologist Seymour Martin Lipset laid the groundwork for the systematic empirical analysis of the complex relationship between wealth and democracy.[4] The original claim, subsequently referred to as the Lipset hypothesis, specified that "The more well-to-do a nation, the greater the chances that it will sustain democracy."[5] Development consolidates democracy, Lipset theorized, by expanding levels of literacy and schooling and media access; broadening the middle classes; reducing the extremes of poverty; facilitating intermediary organizations such as labor unions and voluntary organizations; and promoting the values of legitimacy and social tolerance. The shift from agrarian to industrial capitalist production was thought to weaken the power of the traditional landed estates. Newly unionized urban workers and the middle-class professional groups each mobilized around parties reflecting their interests and demanded access to the voting franchise. Lipset emphasized that extreme social inequality maintained oligarchy or tyranny, but more egalitarian conditions, and in particular the expansion of the educated middle class, facilitated moderation and mass participation: "Only in a wealthy society in which relatively few citizens lived in real poverty could a situation exist in which the mass of the population could intelligently participate in politics and could develop the self-restraint necessary to avoid succumbing to the appeals of irresponsible demagogues."[6] Dankwart Rustow reinforced the argument that the transition to democracy could be attributed to a predictable series of social changes accompanying economic development and societal modernization, as predicted by measures such as per capita energy consumption, literacy, school enrollments, urbanization, life expectancy, infant mortality, the size of the industrial workforce, newspaper circulation, and radio and television ownership.[7]

Following in the footsteps of Lipset and Rustow, the relationship between wealth and democracy has been subject to rigorous empirical inquiry. For more than half a century the association has withstood repeated empirical tests under a variety of different conditions, using cross-sectional and time-series data with a large sample of countries and years, and with increasingly sophisticated statistical tests, as well as in many historical accounts of political developments within particular nation-states. Many have reported that wealth is associated with the standard indicators of democratization, although the precise estimates of effects are sensitive to each study's choice of period, the selection of control variables specified in causal models, and the basic measurement of both democracy and economic growth.[8] The Lipset hypothesis has been confirmed by studies conducted by Jackman (1973); Bollen (1979, 1983); Bollen and Jackman (1985); Brunk, Caldeira, and Lewis-Beck (1987); Buckhart and Lewis-Beck (1994); Vanhanen (1997); Barro (1999); and Przeworski, Alvarez, Cheibub, and Limongi (2000), among others, as well as more recent work by Lipset (1993, 2004).[9]

Adam Przeworski, Michael Alvarez, José Antonio Cheibub, and Fernando Limongi provide the most thorough recent analysis, which compared the experience of economic and political development in 141 countries from 1950 to 1990, in a pooled sample where the unit of analysis was the country-year.[10] Democratic and autocratic regimes were classified by electoral contestation, based on the Schumpeterian rules discussed in Chapter 2.[11] Przeworski et al. confirmed the conventional empirical observation that wealthier countries were more likely to sustain democracy. But the authors emphasized that this relationship operated through a threshold effect, rather than as a linear process. Above a certain minimal level of economic development (estimated at a GDP per capita of around $4,000), they argue, democracies are impregnable and endure. Below this level, the study found that democracies may prosper or they may falter and die. Wealth remained strongly related to democracy even after controlling for levels of ethnic fractionalization, the predominant type of religion, the type of colonial legacy in each society, and the type of presidential or parliamentary executive. Przeworski et al. also found that the reverse relationship did not hold: that is, democracies were no better (and no worse) than dictatorships at generating economic growth.[12] Przeworski et al. concluded that wealth therefore helps to sustain and consolidate democracy, but gradual economic growth does not create a transition from autocracy. Indeed the authors remain strictly agnostic about the multiple contingent reasons why autocracies may fail, whether triggered by the death of a dictator, external military intervention, regional contagions, domestic economic crisis, a military coup, people power uprising, or many other particular events. This is an equifinal event, they imply, where the same result can be produced by various causes. Despite establishing the strong correlation between wealth and democracy, the authors remain agnostic about the precise causal mechanisms underlying this relationship, as well as the policy implications.

The claim that wealth sustains democracy has therefore become one of the most widely recognized generalizations in the social sciences, but nevertheless it is important to test whether this relationship is confirmed by the dataset used in this study because, although often replicated, certain issues remain unresolved in the previous literature. In particular, the relationship between wealth and democracy is probabilistic and even a casual glance at the standard indicators reveals many important outliers. Affluent autocracies are exemplified by Singapore, Saudi Arabia, and Kuwait, with high per capita GDP, and today there are also many poor democracies such as Benin, Ghana, Costa Rica, Nepal, Hungary, and Turkey, plus the classic case of India. These outliers suggest that economic development is neither necessary nor sufficient for democratization. The exceptions to the rule can provide important insights, both for scholars and for policymakers, into the precise conditions under which this relationship fails to operate. As well as highlighting and scrutinizing cases which do not fit the Lipset hypotheses, the analysis needs to be updated to take account of dramatic developments occurring in the post–cold war world. Most previous research has only examined the evidence in the period prior to the early-1990s, so the contemporary pattern needs analyzing to see whether the correlation has weakened during recent years, particularly if many low-income nation-states in Africa and Asia have managed to sustain substantial gains in human rights and civil liberties during the last decade, as some suggest.[13] The Latin American experience since World War II is also thought to undermine the claim that economic development is a determinant cause of democratic change.[14]

Equally important, for those interested in political institutions, previous econometric models are also commonly underspecified. Many fail to consider the impact of a wide range of institutional variations in democratic and autocratic regimes, central to the consociational thesis; for example, Przeworski et al. do not control for the effects of the type of electoral system or federal arrangements. Questions also remain about the most appropriate interpretation of the direction of causality in any relationship between wealth and political institutions and democratic consolidation. In the standard view, economic factors are usually regarded as endogenous, the foundation upon which democratic regimes arise as superstructure. But it is equally plausible to assume, as Persson and Tabellini argue, that constitutional arrangements such as electoral systems and the incidence of coalition government have the capacity to influence economic policies and economic performance, for example, patterns of government spending, budget deficits, and labor productivity, and thus patterns of socioeconomic development.[15] This argument reverses the assumed direction of causality, as certain types of democratic institutions may impact upon a country's stock of wealth, as well as its level of democracy. For all these reasons, we need to unpack the correlation between wealth and democracy to understand the conditions under which the relationship does, and does not, hold.

EVIDENCE OF THE RELATIONSHIP BETWEEN WEALTH AND DEMOCRACY

Before considering the evidence, we first need to determine the best way to model the association between wealth and democracy. Scholars differ as to whether this should be understood as a linear pattern (implying that progressive economic development gradually leads eventually to growing democratization), a logarithmic relationship (suggesting that the early stages of industrial development are the most important for democracy), a stepped-shift (a threshold effect, where democracy is stabilized above a certain level of income), or a more complex 'N' curve (related to stages of agricultural and industrial development, exemplified by O'Donnell's argument that democracies in South America are most common in societies at intermediate levels of development).[16] A curve-fit regression model was used to explore the best way to model the relationship between wealth (measured by per capita GDP in current US$) and the Freedom House measure of liberal democracy, comparing the results of alternative linear, logarithmic, quadratic, cubic, and power transformations.

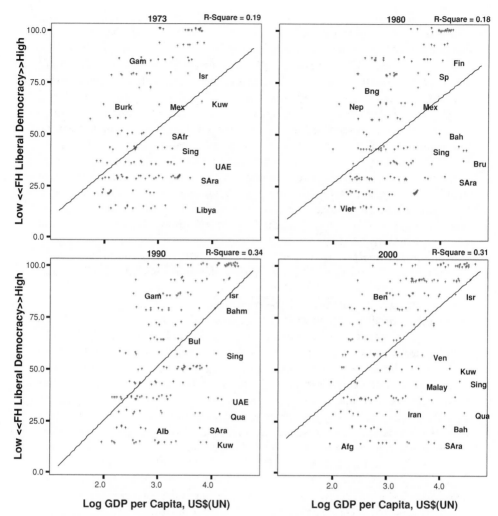

FIGURE 4.1. Wealth and Liberal Democracy, 1973–2000. *Note:* The figure shows the mean standardized liberal democracy 100-point scale by Freedom House, and the logged per capita GDP in current prices (United Nations), for the selected years, 1973, 1980, 1990, and 2000. The R² summarizes the strength of the relationship in each year. *Source:* Freedom House. *Freedom in the World.* www.freedomhouse.org (various years).

The curve-fit results suggested that a logarithmic relationship provided the best fit of the data, and accordingly a natural log transformation of per capita GDP was selected for subsequent analysis.

Wealth and Democracy

As a first visual eyeballing of the evidence, Figure 4.1 illustrates the relationship between wealth (measured by logged per capita GDP in purchasing power parity) and democracy (measured by the standardized 100-point Freedom House measure of liberal democracy, ranging from low [0] to high [100]). For comparison of the strength of the relationship over time, the correlations are shown in selected years every decade, namely, in 1973, 1980, 1990, and 2000. The simple correlations, without any prior controls, show that the relationship remains moderately strong and significant in each year. Far from weakening, the relationship between wealth and democracy (measured by the R^2) strengthened in more recent years. Many countries cluster on the diagonal, meaning that greater wealth is associated with stronger political rights and civil liberties. But there are also clear groups of outliers, notably the rich Arab autocracies in the bottom-right corner, as exemplified by the United Arab Emirates, Saudi Arabia, and Bahrain. At the same time a scatter of poor democracies are located in the top-left corner, for example, Jamaica, Costa Rica, and Gambia in 1973; Nigeria and Nepal in 1980; Senegal and the Solomon Islands in 1990; and Benin and Malawi in 2000.

Multivariate analysis is needed, including a series of structural controls, for more reliable and systematic analysis of the patterns. Table 4.1 provides estimates for the impact of wealth (measured as previously) on democracy. The models use cross-sectional time-series (CSTS) data where the country-year is the unit of analysis. Ordinary least squares regression analysis is employed with panel-corrected standard errors, which Beck and Katz suggest is the most appropriate way to model this type of data.[17] The estimates are run for all four standardized 100-point scales of democracy, to test whether the results remain robust irrespective of the particular indicator selected for analysis. The standardized scales facilitate comparison across the results of each indicator, as well as simplifying the interpretation of substantive meaning of the beta coefficients. The democracy scales are each lagged by one year, which Beck recommends as a simple way to model the dynamics.[18]

The models monitor the impact of the *size of the population* and the *physical area* of each country. Ever since Dahl and Tufte, the idea that size matters for democracy has been widely assumed, and Alesina and Spolaore have provided the most detailed recent examination of this proposition.[19] Smaller nation-states, both in physical geography and in the number of citizens, are expected to be easier to govern democratically: for example, the smaller the state, the greater the potential for citizen participation in key decisions. The physical and population sizes of states can be regarded as structural conditions which are endogenous both to economic growth and to democracy. Indeed it is hard to imagine a variable which is more immutable than geography; at least in peacetime, the physical boundaries of a nation-state are rarely altered historically except through cases of annexation or merger with neighboring territories (as occurred in East and West Germany), or the dissolution of federal states and associations (such as the breakup of the Union of Soviet Socialist Republics [USSR] and the former Republic of Yugoslavia, and the independence from Indonesia gained by East Timor). In the long term, government policy can also attempt to modify the size of the population, whether through the availability

TABLE 4.1. *Wealth and Democracy, All Societies Worldwide*

	Liberal Democracy Freedom House			Constitutional Democracy Polity IV			Participatory Democracy Vanhanen			Contested Democracy Przeworski et al./ Cheibub and Gandhi		
	B	PCSE	P	B	PCSE	P	B	PCSE	P	B	PCSE	P
Log GDP/ capita (US$)	13.54	(.682)	***	11.64	(.758)	***	22.16	(.423)	***	1.13	(.088)	***
CONTROLS												
Ex-British colony (0/1)	9.83	(.709)	***	11.46	(1.44)	***	.019	(.945)	N/s	.778	(.094)	***
Middle East (0/1)	−15.41	(1.11)	***	−21.39	(1.22)	***	−22.58	(.539)	***	−1.056	(.186)	***
Regional diffusion of democracy	.644	(.029)	***	.685	(.032)	***	.007	(.004)	N/s	.047	(.002)	***
Ethnic fractionalization (0–100-pt scale)	−10.24	(.597)	***	−5.94	(1.34)	***	−18.28	(.687)	***	−.921	(.175)	***
Population size (thou)	−0.01	(.001)	***	−.001	(.001)	***	−.001	(.001)	N/s	.001	(.001)	N/s
Area size (sq mi)	.001	(.001)	***	.001	(.001)	***	.001	(.001)	N/s	.001	(.001)	***
Constant	−20.55			−12.59			−38.45			−5.89		
No. of observations	5,115			4,205			4,586			4,852		
No. of countries	187			157			180			185		
Adjusted R²	.583			.525			.523			.602		

Note: Entries for liberal democracy, constitutional democracy, and participatory democracy are unstandardized beta OLS regression coefficients (B) with panel-corrected standard errors (PCSE) and the significance of the coefficients (P) for the pooled time-series cross-national dataset obtained using Stata's xtpcse command. With PCSE the disturbances are, by default, assumed to be heteroskedastic (each nation has its own variance) and contemporaneously correlated across nations. Models for contested democracy were run using logistic regression for the binary dependent variable, with the results summarized by Nagelkerke R square. For the measures of democracy, standardized to 100-point scales and lagged by one year, see Chapter 2. For details of all the variables, see the Technical Appendix. Significant at * the 0.05 level, ** the 0.01 level, and *** the 0.001 level.

of contraception and abortion, or through implementation of welfare incentives either to restrict or to boost fertility rates. But the impact of such policies on basic demographic trends of fertility and mortality rates is expected to be relatively modest and slow. To explore the effects of size on democracy, the models entered the total population per annum and the physical size of each country (in square miles).

The study also tests the effects of the *historical pattern of colonial legacies*. An association between the past type of colonial rule and contemporary patterns of democracy has been noted by several observers; for example, Clague, Gleason, and Knack report that lasting democracies (characterized by contestation for government office) are most likely to emerge and persist among poor nation-states in ex-British colonies, even controlling for levels of economic development, ethnic diversity, and the size of the population.[20] Under British rule, they suggest, colonies such as Canada, Australia, and India gained experience with electoral, legislative, and judicial institutions, in contrast with countries under French or Spanish rule. Arguing along similar lines, Lipset and Lakin also suggest that what mattered in ex-colonial states was whether the previous occupying power was itself democratic.[21] Settlers in the British colonies, they argue, inherited a pluralist and individualist culture and legislative institutions of self-government, which would prove critical to the development of democracy, notably in the United States, Canada, India, and New Zealand. By contrast, colonists in Latin America were strongly influenced by the Spanish and Portuguese culture, with a more centrally controlled, hierarchical, and paternalistic form of rule, at a time when the Spanish monarchy had few institutionalized checks on their power. To examine the path-dependent role of colonial legacies, countries are coded for whether they were ex-British colonies or not.

The models also examine the impact of *regional patterns of democratic diffusion*; Starr and Lindborg emphasize the influence of regime transitions experienced by states within each world region, most dramatically exemplified by the rapid downfall of dictators and the spread of multiparty elections in Central Europe following the fall of the Berlin Wall and the collapse of the Soviet grip over states.[22] Another example would be the November 2003 people-power rose revolution that deposed veteran president Eduard Shevardnadze in Georgia, which seems to have inspired the orange revolution which followed the next year in Ukraine. It is suggested that countries learn from each other, particularly where there is a shared culture and language, and this is particularly important for regional hegemonic powers which influence their neighbors, such as the role of the United States in Latin America. Another example concerns the growth of democracy in postapartheid South Africa, which may have helped to shape politics among neighboring states in the southern cone. Conversely, despite some recent moves toward liberalization, the predominance of a variety of autocratic regimes throughout the Arab world also suggests a regional effect.[23] To examine their impact, regional factors are measured in two ways. For diffusion effects, the mean strength of democracy (measured by each of the four indicators used in this study) is entered into the models. In addition, since the Middle East seems to be the region most isolated from democratic developments elsewhere, this region is entered as a dummy variable.

Last, the degree of *ethnic heterogeneity* is also entered into the models, on the grounds that deeply divided societies are widely assumed to experience greater problems of democratic consolidation. As discussed in Chapter 2, one of the most complex issues facing empirical research on consociationalism concerns the most appropriate concept and measurement of ethnic fractionalization, and the available data to estimate ethnic identities is often limited and unreliable.[24] The models compare systematic cross-national evidence worldwide by classifying nation-states according to the degree of ethnic fractionalization, based on a global dataset created by Alesina and his colleagues.[25] It needs to be emphasized that this index estimates the objective distribution of different linguistic and religious groups in the population, but it does not seek to measure the subjective meaning or the political importance of these forms of identity. Thus plural societies may have multiparty competition which closely reflects divisions into multiple languages and religions, or they may have a few large parties where these social identities are less salient political cleavages. In the long term, the objective distribution of ethno-linguistic and ethno-religious groups in the population can be strongly shaped by government policies, and thus reinforced or weakened by political actors, for example, by language policy used to determine the school curricula or by the degree of religious freedom and by official subsidies for established religions. As a constructionist perspective emphasizes, the social meaning and political relevance of these ethnic identities can also be reinforced by rhetorical appeals and party platforms which focus on these forms of identity. Nevertheless in the short term the distribution of the linguistic and religious populations can be regarded as endogenous constraints on political developments. The relationships of ethnicity, economic development, and democracy also commonly remain undertheorized. Economists have demonstrated that ethnic fractionalization has a direct relationship to economic growth; Easterly and Levine found that more ethnically divided societies in sub-Saharan Africa were also characterized by greater poverty, low schooling, political instability, underdeveloped financial systems, distorted foreign exchange markets, high government deficits, and insufficient infrastructure.[26] It is commonly assumed that ethnic fractionalization has a direct impact upon democracy (for example, by producing greater intercommunal violence and instability). What remains unclear is whether ethnicity also has an indirect impact (by lowering economic growth and therefore undermining the social conditions thought conducive to democracy).

The results of the analysis presented in Table 4.1 confirm that wealth (log GDP per capita) was significantly and positively associated with each measure of democracy, as many others have found. The unstandardized beta coefficient estimating the impact of wealth on democracy proved significant across each of the OLS models. Moreover each of the structural controls (except physical size) also proved significant and with signs pointing in the expected direction; hence democracy was usually more probable in countries which shared an ex-British colonial legacy, in regions which had seen the spread of democracy, in states outside the Middle East, in ethnically homogeneous societies, and in countries with smaller populations. Contrary to our initial assumption, however, geographically larger countries proved slightly more democratic than physically smaller states. These coefficients proved consistent across each indicator of democracy, lending greater confidence to the results, which remain robust independently of their specific measurement. The models explained between half and two-thirds of the variance in democratization across the comparison, suggesting a relatively good fit, although, as observed earlier, many outlier cases can also be found among both rich autocracies and poor democracies.

Human Capital and Democracy

Despite confirming the previous literature, the meaning and interpretation of the commonly observed relationship between wealth and democracy continue to generate heated debate.[27] We still understand remarkably little about the underlying causal mechanisms which are at work. Is it widespread literacy among the population which is critical, and thus the spread of education and the availability of mass communications, as Lipset and Rustow originally emphasized? Or does the relationship depend upon the social structure and inequalities among classes, as others suggest? Rueschemeyer, Stephens, and Stephens argue that industrialization reduced the power of the landed gentry in comparison with the middle classes and the organized working class.[28] More egalitarian societies, with a growing middle class, are also thought to provide the stability most conducive to successful and enduring political liberalization.[29] The organizational capacity of the middle classes and urban working class may function as a buffer between citizens and the state. Or alternatively is it the effects of industrialization processes more generally, as world trade in manufactured goods generates greater international contact and openness with the global economy, and thus pressures on states to conform to international standards of human rights and political liberties?

The limited time-series data measuring cross-national patterns of economic inequality, social status, and occupational class with any degree of reliability prevents us from examining the impact of these plausible candidates on the growth of democracy. Nevertheless we can look at the evidence testing the original Lipset hypothesis, which placed considerable emphasis on the role of human capital in the democratization process, a pattern also suggested by Borro.[30] In particular we can see whether democracy is associated with growing levels of literacy and schooling (measured by the number of secondary school enrollments per capita). As a result of problems of multicollinearity and problems of missing data, it is not possible to test the combined effects of wealth, education, and literacy on democracy, but each of these can be entered into separate models. As shown in Table 4.2, the results of the analysis suggest that

TABLE 4.2. *Wealth, Literacy, Education, and Liberal Democracy, All Societies Worldwide*

	Liberal Democracy Freedom House			Liberal Democracy Freedom House			Liberal Democracy Freedom House		
	B	PCSE	P	B	PCSE	P	B	PCSE	P
Log GDP/capita	13.54	(.682)	***						
% Literacy				.114	(.011)	***			
% Secondary education							.150	(.015)	***
CONTROLS									
Ex-British colony	9.83	(.709)	***	8.73	(.064)	***	8.42	(.726)	***
Middle East	−15.41	(1.11)	***	−1.93	(.716)	***	−8.16	(.750)	***
Regional diffusion of democracy	0.644	(.029)	***	0.77	(.026)	***	0.77	(.026)	***
Ethnic fractionalization	−10.24	(.597)	***	−4.24	(1.00)	***	−9.86	(.833)	***
Population size	−0.01	(.001)	***	−0.01	(.001)	***	−.001	(.001)	***
Area size	.001	(.001)	***	.001	(.001)	***	.001	(.001)	***
Constant	−20.55			.797			.625		
No. of observations	5115			3158			4328		
No. of countries	187			120			169		
Adjusted R²	.583			.415			.561		

Note: Entries for liberal democracy are unstandardized beta OLS regression coefficients (with their standard errors in parentheses) for the pooled time-series cross-national analysis obtained using Stata's xtpcse command with panel-corrected standard errors. For the measures of democracy, standardized to 100 points and lagged by one year, see Chapter 2. For details of all the variables, see the Technical Appendix. Significant at * the 0.05 level, ** the 0.01 level, and *** the 0.001 level.

each of these factors proves a significant predictor of levels of democratization, with the overall fit of the model strengthening slightly through the role of education. This suggests that societies which invest in the human capital of their populations are more likely to sustain democratic regimes, as literacy and education help to generate the access to political information and the cognitive skills needed to process this information. The results therefore serve to confirm the findings reported in much of the previous literature, irrespective of the indicator of democracy which is selected for analysis. The findings also strongly suggest that any subsequent models estimating the impact of political institutions on democratic consolidation will only be properly specified if they incorporate this range of structural conditions, understood as prior controls.

THE CASES OF SOUTH KOREA AND SINGAPORE

Yet although wealth is strongly related to democracy, as we have seen there remain many important outliers to this relationship. What explains these countries? Here we can compare nation-states in Asia, an area with remarkable contrasts today among varying types of regimes and levels of democratization, including the Communist states of China and Vietnam; repressive military juntas such as in Burma; traditional monarchies such as Bhutan which are transitioning to more liberal constitutional monarchies; a range of unstable states which are struggling with elections but with a recent history of deep-rooted conflict including Bangladesh, Nepal, and Pakistan; newer democracies such as the Philippines and Indonesia; and long-standing and stable democracies such as Japan and Australia (see Figure 4.2). The cases of South Korea and Singapore help to illustrate the nature of this relationship between wealth and democracy as well as the limitations of economic explanations to account for important outliers. These divergent cases both experienced rapid economic development until today they are among some of the most affluent in the world; according to the 2005 UNDP Human Development Index (measuring income, education/literacy, and longevity), Singapore ranks 25th and South Korea ranks 28th out of 177 nation-states (see Table 4.3). Yet one remains a one-party autocracy today, while the other has shifted since 1987 from a military dictatorship to consolidate a multiparty democracy. Why the contrasts?

South Korea

If any country best exemplifies the Lipset hypothesis, South Korea should be it. The Republic of Korea was established under the presidency of Syngman Rhee after World War II in the southern half of the Korean peninsula while a Communist regime under Kim Il Sung was installed in the north. The Korean War (1950–1953) resulted in an armistice which split the peninsula with a demilitarized zone along the 38th parallel. Once a country of rice farmers and peasants,

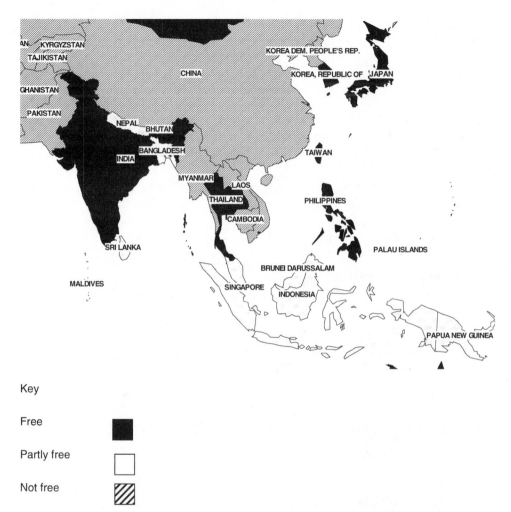

Key

Free ■

Partly free □

Not free ▨

FIGURE 4.2. Asia by Type of Regime, Freedom House, 2004. *Source:* Freedom House. *Freedom in the World*. www.freedomhouse.org (various years).

from the early-1960s South Korea experienced rapid industrialization, emphasizing the manufacture of consumer electronics and automobiles, becoming the 10th largest economy in the world today. The country has few natural mineral resources and the engine of growth is therefore highly dependent upon trade and exports. Citizens have enjoyed growing affluence; the per capita GDP quadrupled from about $4,000 in 1975 to around $18,000 in 2005 (see Figure 4.3), driven by a remarkable average annual economic growth rate of 6.1% during this period.[31] Economic growth was accompanied by rising living standards and educational levels, urbanization, and human development, as well as the widespread diffusion of new information and communication technologies.

TABLE 4.3. *Key Indicators in South Korea and Singapore*

	South Korea	Singapore
SOCIAL AND ECONOMIC INDICATORS		
Area	98,777 sq km	699 sq km
Pop., 2003	47.5 million	4.2 million
GDP, (US$) 2003	$606.3 billion	$91.3 billion
GDP per capita (PPP US$), 2003	$17,971	$24,481
Life expectancy at birth, 2003	76.9 years	78.6 years
Human Development Index, 2003	0.901	0.907
Adult literacy (% of pop. 15+), 2002	97.9	92.5
GINI coefficient economic inequality, 2004 (UNDP)	31.6	42.5
Ethnic fractionalization, 2002 (Alesina)	.002	.385
POLITICAL INDICATORS		
Year of independence	1945 (from Japan)	1965 (from Malaysian Federation)
Liberal democracy Freedom House Index, 1973 7-point scale (where 1 = high, 7 = low)	5(PR), 6(CL)	4(PR), 5(CL)
Freedom House classification, 1973	Not free	Partly free
Liberal democracy Freedom House Index, 2005	2(PR), 2(CL)	5(PR), 5(CL)
Freedom House classification, 2005	Free	Partly free
Control of corruption (Kaufmann) rank (0–100), 2004	62	99
Government effectiveness (Kaufmann) rank (0–100), 2004	80	99
Political stability (Kaufmann) rank (0–100), 2004	60	97
Rule of law (Kaufmann) rank (0–100), 2004	69	96
Voice and accountability (Kaufmann) rank (0–100), 2004	69	43
Regulatory quality (Kaufmann) rank (0–100), 2004	72	99

Note: See the Technical Appendix for details of these indices and sources of data.

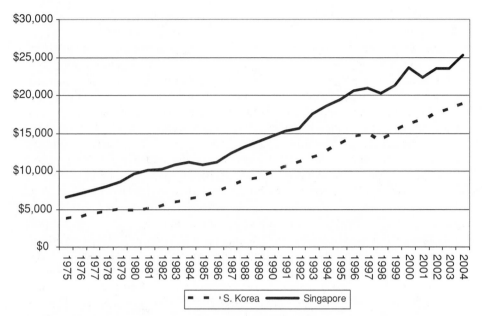

FIGURE 4.3. Economic Growth in South Korea and Singapore, 1975–2005. *Note:* GDP per capita, PPP (constant 2000 international $). *Source:* World Bank Development Indicators. www.worldbank.org

A relatively homogeneous society, with the exception of a very small minority of ethnic Chinese, the country shares a common language, and religious affiliations are spread among many faiths, including Buddhism, Christianity, Confucianism, and shamanism.

Within this context, the Lipset hypothesis predicts that the transformation of the Korean economy and society, including the expansion of the urban workers and service-sector professional middle class, would gradually generate the underlying conditions most suitable for democratic consolidation. After the end of the war, South Korea was ruled by an unstable autocracy, under a succession of military-backed dictators; President Syngman Rhee resigned in 1960 following a student-led uprising, replaced by Chang Myon, who fell after a year through a military coup led by Major General Park Chung-hee, before Park was in turn assassinated in 1979. Lieutenant General Chun Doo Hwan declared martial law and seized power until 1987, when pro-democracy activists and waves of student demonstrators forced concessions from the government, including restoration of direct presidential elections.[32] The 1987 contest elected a former general, Roh Tae-woo, to the presidency and he was succeeded in a peaceful transition in 1992 by Kim Young-sam, representing the first civilian elected president in 32 years. The 1997 elections saw a further step toward democracy, as the opposition leader, Kim Dae-jung, succeeded to power, followed by the election of a human rights advocate, President Roh

Moo-hyan, in 2002. President Roh was a prominent figure in the 1987 pro-democracy movement and had been briefly jailed for his activities.

The Sixth Republic Korean constitution, last modified in October 1987, established a strong directly elected presidency (using a simple plurality system), limited to a single five-year term. The executive is counterbalanced by a National Assembly, which plays a more minor role in political decisions. Members are elected using a combined-dependent electoral system, where 243 representatives are elected in single-member constituencies while the remaining 46 are elected from nationwide proportional representation party lists, using a simple Hare quota. The party list seats are allocated using a complicated formula which reinforces the seat allocation for larger parties, making the system less proportional than the combined-dependent system used in Germany. The 2004 parliamentary elections in Korea resulted in the inclusion of five parties, with the Uri Party and the Grand National Party fairly evenly balanced as the two main players, and the president's party ranked well behind in fourth place. The main parties are organized around the predominant regional cleavage, rather than differing by ideology or policy, although elections have shifted from being purely personality-oriented toward reflecting an evaluation of the performance of the incumbent government. On average, the series of assembly elections held under the sixth constitution have produced an ENEP of 4.0 and an ENPP of 3.0.[33] National Assembly elections no longer guarantee a legislative majority for the president's party, providing a healthy counterbalance. The Supreme Court and a Constitutional Court are established as independent bodies, checking the power of the executive and legislature. There are multiple media news outlets, including more than 100 daily newspapers with local or national coverage, and there is free criticism of the government. In its 2005 Press Freedom Index, Reporters without Borders ranks South Korea 34th out of 167 nation-states, similar to Australia, France, and Japan.[34] The country has had problems of corruption, generating some well-known government scandals, but still in 2005 Transparency International's Corruption Perception Index placed South Korea 40th (tied with Hungary and Italy) out of 158 nation-states.[35] Therefore the South Korean case serves to exemplify the relationship between growing levels of wealth and the subsequent consolidation of democracy; today the country is governed by a multiparty democracy rated 'free' by Freedom House, with political liberties and civil rights which are comparable to those in Greece, Bulgaria, and South Africa.

Singapore

But what about Singapore? As one of the East Asian 'Four Tigers', along with South Korea, the economy has forged ahead to make the nation one of the most prosperous in the world. The economy has been built upon high-tech electronics and the service sector, particularly finance, banking, investment, and trade. In 2005, Singapore produced a per capita GDP of around $25,000 (in PPP), similar to Italy and even more affluent than South Korea. The compact island nation contains just over 4 million people (compared with 48 million South Koreans), three-quarters of whom are ethnic Chinese, while the remainder are mainly Malay and Tamil Indian. The country is multilingual, divided among Malay, Chinese, Tamil, and English speakers. In terms of wealth and size, therefore, the underlying conditions for democratic consolidation are promising.

Yet the island-state remains a one-party predominant autocracy, which Freedom House rates as only 'partly free'.[36] Indeed some observers suggest that the country has become more repressive of human rights even as it has become more prosperous, turning the Lipset hypothesis upside-down.[37] Moreover from the patterns observed earlier, given the underlying conditions, Singapore should be ripe for democracy: it is a compact island state without any threats to its borders, an ex-British colony, with low to moderate ethnic fractionalization. During the nineteenth century, the island grew in population and prosperity as a major port controlled first by the British East India Company and then, after 1867, directly from London as a Crown colony as part of the Straits Settlement. After the end of World War II, demands for self-rule grew as part of the decolonization wave affecting the British Empire. In 1959, Singapore was granted full self-governance by the British authorities. In the parliamentary elections held in 1959, the People's Action Party (PAP), founded and led by Lee Kuan Yew, swept into power by winning 47% of the vote and three-quarters of all seats. Despite a regular series of multiparty contests challenging their hegemonic status, PAP has ruled continuously ever since, winning 11 successive general elections over almost half a century. The PAP has controlled parliament without effective challenge to their power, winning, on average, two-thirds of the vote but a remarkable 95% of all parliamentary seats in the series of parliamentary general elections held from 1959 to 2001 (see Figure 4.4). This has effectively squeezed out any opposition members of parliament (MPs) beyond an occasional token representative from one of the parties of the left. The share of the vote won by PAP eroded slightly from 1984 to 1997 but strengthened again in 2001. A majority of PAP candidates were returned unopposed.

One reason for the ruling party's hegemony lies in the majoritarian electoral system, which translates their share of the vote into an overwhelming majority in parliament. The unicameral parliament uses a combined-independent electoral system.[38] In the current parliament, nine members were elected from simple plurality single-member constituencies (first-past-the-post). In total, 75 other MPs were elected in a bloc vote system (termed locally 'group representation constituencies') from 14 multimember districts, where parties field a list of three to six candidates. In these, the party with a simple plurality of votes in the district wins all the seats. The bloc vote system is designed to ensure the representation of members from the Malay, Indian, and other minority communities, as each party list must include at least one candidate from these communities, encouraging parties to nominate ethnically diverse lists. Another nine members of parliament can be nominated by the president from among the opposition parties, without standing for election. Another factor contributing

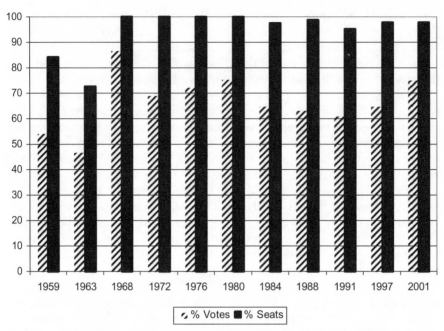

FIGURE 4.4. The Proportion of Votes and Seats Won by the Ruling People's Action Party (PAP) in Singapore General Elections, 1959–2001. *Source:* Calculated from www.singapore-elections.com

to the ruling party's predominance is alleged gerrymandering with the redrawing of electoral districts just a few months before the general election. In particular, constituencies where the PAP did relatively badly in one contest have sometimes been systematically removed from the electoral map by the next election.[39]

The 1965 constitution established a Westminster-style parliamentary democracy where the president, elected by parliament, used to be a largely ceremonial head of state. The 1991 constitutional revision introduced a more powerful president where the office is directly elected through simple plurality vote. A contested election was held in 1993, but in 1999 and in 2005 the position was filled by President Sellapan Ramanathan, as all other nominated candidates were declared ineligible by the Presidential Election Committee. A candidate can be ruled out of the contest if the committee judges that he or she is not 'a person of integrity, good character and reputation', among other stringent criteria. A nominee also must not be a member of the government or a current member of a political party. The president appoints the prime minister, the head of government, government ministers from among the members of parliament, and key members of the civil service, as well as exercising veto budgetary powers and other responsibilities. After leading the PAP in seven victorious elections since 1959, Lee Kuan Yew stepped down as prime minister in 1990, remaining 'Minister Mentor' in an advisory position but handing over to his

PAP successor, Goh Chok Tong. After a series of PAP prime ministers, in 2004 the elder son of Lee Kuan Yew, Lee Hsien Loong, took office as part of a planned handover of power.

Another way in which PAP maintains control is through its influence over the judicial system, including suing opposition members for libel, interring opposition politicians without trial under the Internal Security Act, and requiring police permits to hold any kind of public talk, exhibition, or demonstration. The government also exercises strong control of the press and news media; for example, the leading newspaper of Singapore, the *Straits Times*, is often perceived as a propaganda newspaper because it rarely criticizes government policy, and it covers little about the opposition. The owners of the paper, Singapore Press Holdings, have close links to the ruling party and the corporation has a virtual monopoly of the newspaper industry. Government censorship of journalism is common, using the threat or imposition of heavy fines or distribution bans imposed by the Media Development Authority, with these techniques also used against articles seen to be critical of the government published in the international press, including the *Economist* and *International Times Herald Tribune*. Internet access is regulated in Singapore, and private ownership of satellite dishes is not allowed. Because of this record, the Reporters without Borders assessment of Press Freedom Worldwide in 2005 ranked Singapore 140th out of 167 nation-states.

In short, compared with the situation in Togo discussed earlier, Singapore has not suffered the violent repression of opposition movements. Human rights agencies do not report cases of ballot stuffing, polling irregularities, tinkering with the electoral roll, or voter intimidation conducted in fraudulent elections by security forces. The administration of elections is widely regarded by election observers as free, fair, and well organized, within the rules.[40] Singapore is governed by the rule of law, unlike Kérékou's reign of power in Togo. Indeed the government of Singapore can be admired as a model of technocratic efficiency, delivering effective public services such as housing and transport without the widespread corruption and abuse of public office which are characteristic of many autocracies. As Table 4.3 shows, compared with South Korea, Singapore is ranked far more positively on Kaufmann measures of government effectiveness, political stability, regulatory quality, control of corruption, and rule of law. In a country with minimal natural resources, Singapore has enjoyed considerable prosperity and security under PAP rule, with a free market liberal economy. Nevertheless, although a comfortable and affluent society, Singapore remains autocratic by virtue of the hegemonic grip of the predominant ruling party, both in parliament and in government; the lack of effective checks and balances from opposition parties; and the severe restrictions on the news media. From the economic perspective, Singapore remains a puzzling outlier which fails to conform to the Lipset hypothesis. The general pattern observed worldwide suggests that certain socioeconomic and structural conditions usually prove favorable toward democracy, but they do not determine either the transition from autocracy or the steady consolidation of democracy. The contrasts observed in Singapore and South Korea strongly suggest the need to look more closely in subsequent chapters at the constitutional arrangements which may deter or sustain democracy.

CONCLUSIONS

The claim that wealth sustains democracy has important implications for public policy and for attempts to promote both poverty alleviation and democracy by the international development community. Yet two alternative interpretations dominate the policy debate and it remains unclear which one is correct.

The 'development first, democracy later' approach draws the lesson that direct attempts at democratic constitution-building in poorer nation-states may be premature and misguided, or at least a more risky investment, than similar attempts in wealthier nation-states falling above the specified threshold. In this view, investments in election-building, strengthening the independent media, or fostering human rights face considerable odds of failure in poor countries such as Afghanistan, Iraq, Cambodia, and Indonesia. In particular, initiatives attempting to build democratic constitutions in poor countries may prove irrelevant (at best), or even harmful (at worst). A more prudent strategy for the international community would be to encourage human development and economic growth in these nation-states, thus generating the social conditions conducive to sustaining democratic constitutions in the longer term. The 'development first' thesis predicts slow progress in democratization in the poorest parts of the world such as in sub-Saharan Africa, where half the population continues to live in extreme poverty, measured by the World Bank's $1 a day benchmark. There has been no sustained improvement in this situation since 1990; indeed poverty has worsened in many Africa states during this period as a result of an inadequate infrastructure, deep deficits in health and education, and severe income inequalities.[41]

By contrast, Halperin, Siegle, and Weinstein argue that societies often remain poor under authoritarian regimes, and that low-income democracies out-perform low-income autocracies in social welfare. The 'economic development first' perspective, they suggest, runs the risk of perpetuating a cycle of economic stagnation as well as political oppression.[42] Instead, Halperin, Siegle, and Weinstein argue, democracies bring internal checks and balances, making government more responsive to citizens' needs, so that development aid is more efficiently distributed and poverty is alleviated more effectively. "Citizens of democracies live longer, healthier, and more productive lives, on average, than those in autocracies. . . . At every income level considered, democracies on the whole have consistently generated superior levels of social welfare."[43] In a related study, Kosack also found that development aid improves the quality of life in democracies, although it proves ineffective or even harmful in autocracies.[44] It follows that poorer autocracies such as Togo may be victims of a vicious circle, where aid fails to generate effective development, and without human development, societies remain under the grip of autocratic regimes. A clearer understanding of the drivers at work in the link between wealth and democracy would provide more informed decisions about the best investments in political development by the international community and by domestic reformers.

An extensive literature has confirmed the relationship between wealth and democratic consolidation in a variety of contexts and circumstances. The results of the analysis presented in this chapter lend further confirmation to the Lipset proposition that democracies usually flourish in more affluent economies. Democracies are also more likely to be found in countries with a British colonial heritage, in regions where there are many other democracies and outside of the Middle East, in more homogeneous societies, and in less populous nation-states. Nevertheless the relationship between the underlying characteristics and the type of regime remains probabilistic, explaining, at most, between one-half and two-thirds of the variance in democratization found during the third wave period. The case of South Korea plausibly fits the Lipset theory but, as Singapore shows, many important outliers remain. The key question which remains is whether, even with this battery of controls, political institutions also play an important role in sustaining democracy. On this foundation, we can proceed to explore the factors which consociational theory emphasizes as important for democratic consolidation, the heart of this book, starting with one of the most fundamental, the choice of an electoral system.

PART II

THE IMPACT OF POWER-SHARING INSTITUTIONS

5

Electoral Systems

Electoral rules represent perhaps the most powerful of the instruments which undergird power-sharing arrangements, with potentially far-reaching consequences for party competition, the inclusiveness of legislatures, and the composition of governments, all of which can influence processes of democratic consolidation.[1] Formal electoral rules are understood in this study, somewhat more broadly than is common in the literature, as the official policies, legal regulations, and administrative procedures governing all steps in the sequential process of contesting elections, casting ballots, and winning elected office. Among these, most attention has conventionally focused upon the last step in the development, including the quota formula, the ballot structure, and the district magnitude, which determine how votes are cast and then converted into elected office.

The theory of consociationalism argues that power-sharing arrangements have important consequences for 'kinder, gentler' governance. Rules which recognize and seek to accommodate parties and representatives drawn from distinct ethnic groups are thought most likely to consolidate fragile democracies by facilitating accommodation and building trust among diverse communities living in deeply divided societies. The electoral mechanisms most closely associated with power-sharing include proportional representation systems, which lower the barriers facing smaller parties, and positive action strategies, such as reserved seats for ethnic communities and minority-majority constituencies. Power-sharing electoral institutions are thought especially important for accommodating diverse groups, reducing community tensions, and promoting acceptance of peace-settlements in fragmented societies emerging from a recent history of bloody civil war and regime instability.[2] If true, these claims hold critical lessons for the most effective constitutional design which can be adopted in postwar settlements.

To consider these issues, the section Consociational Theory and Its Critics in this chapter summarizes consociational arguments favoring power-sharing electoral arrangements and the doubts expressed by critics. If consociational claims are supported, the logic suggests that countries using power-sharing (either PR electoral systems or positive action strategies) should have achieved stronger democracies than equivalent states which have not employed these policies, all other factors being equal. To examine the evidence, the second section defines and classifies the major types of electoral system used in this study and then analyzes their effects on democratic consolidation, controlling for the prior social and economic conditions which the previous chapter established as important for democracy, including levels of economic development and the degree of ethnic fractionalization within each society. Case studies help to illustrate the underlying dynamic processes at work, enriching the large-N comparison. The third section describes patterns of democracy both before and after major changes to electoral systems, in the selected cases of New Zealand and Britain, to see how far reforms increased party competition, especially representation for minority communities, and thereby strengthened democracy.

CONSOCIATIONAL THEORY AND ITS CRITICS

Why might power-sharing electoral rules prove more effective for consolidating democracy, particularly in deeply divided societies? To clarify the logic underlying consociational theory, the main steps in the chain of reasoning are outlined schematically in Figure 5.1.

Multiethnic Societies Contain Distinct Ethnic Communities

Consociationalism starts from the premise that social psychological feelings of attachment to group identities – based on shared religion, language, culture, or community – are often strong, entrenched, and powerful forces dividing multiethnic societies. If not seen as fixed, innate, and immutable, then these types of cultural identities are at a minimum regarded in political sociology as derived from the earliest processes of socialization within the family, school, and community, deeply rooted in society, and thus exogenous to the political system. In the long term ethnic identities may be transformed, for example, if second-generation sons and daughters of émigré groups gradually become assimilated into the mainstream culture through language, educational opportunities, social networks, or workplace participation, but these psychological attachments are seen as enduring characteristics. In this regard, ethnicity, like gender, cues our sense of ourselves and others. Consociationalism treats ethnic identities as largely singular rather than cross-cutting categories, as reflecting group interests as well as psychological orientations, and as capable of overriding other social and political cleavages, such as those arising from socioeconomic status, gender, or ideology.[3] In this view, divisions between Protestant unionists and Catholic nationalists are taken for granted as the unshakable building blocks that have to be recognized and accommodated in Northern Ireland politics, while national identities and language divide Belgian and Canadian societies, and race demarcates American society. Even though there may be many important divisions within each group, for example, between poor

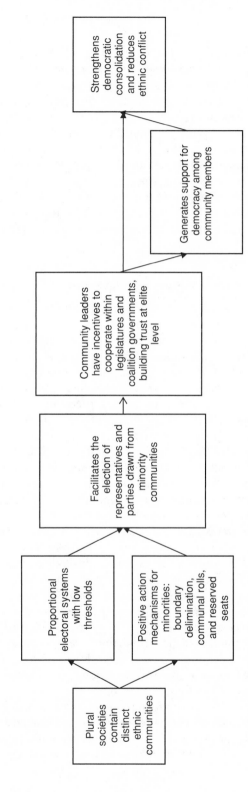

FIGURE 5.1. The Core Sequential Steps in Consociational Theory

and middle-class African Americans, or the class differences among religious communities in Belfast, this social-psychological prism regards these communities as each sharing largely homogeneous preferences and fixed boundaries, where politics represents a zero-sum game. In Iraq, in the same way, many observers consider differences among Kurds, Shi'a, and Sunnis, entrenched further by insecurities and intercommunity violence, as the intractable cleavages and deep-rooted building blocks which constitutional designers need to accommodate to achieve any realistic and lasting peace-settlement within the borders of a common nation-state. Understood through this perspective, the issue becomes how best to guarantee the incorporation of individual representatives and parties drawn from distinct communities within democratic political institutions, to protect community interests and provide safeguards for mutual security.

PR Electoral Systems Facilitate Minority Representation

If societies are deeply divided, what institutional mechanisms would ensure that representative bodies reflect the composition of the societies from which they are elected? Consociationalism regards proportional representation (PR) electoral systems as the simplest, least contentious, and most flexible way to facilitate the election of parties representing distinct minority communities. PR elections with large multimember districts lower the formal vote hurdles facing parties seeking elected office. These rules should therefore facilitate the election of smaller parties, including those representing distinct ethnic minority groups which are scattered geographically, roughly in proportion to their share of support in the electorate. By itself, PR electoral systems kick in at the final stage of translating votes into seats, so they do not automatically generate a level playing field for party competition in all prior stages in the sequential process of recruitment, campaigning, and gaining elected office. Minor parties may still commonly experience particular problems of gaining ballot access; for example, some countries impose legal bans on parties which the courts regard as extremist, such as laws restricting the expression of racial hatred by the radical right.[4] Others restrict competition through partisan redistricting processes limiting ballot access to minor parties, or strict party and candidate registration requirements.[5] Minor parties may also be disadvantaged by the official rules and statutory regulations governing direct public funding, indirect state subsidies, and access to campaign broadcasting.[6] Nevertheless, compared with majoritarian electoral systems, proportional representation systems provide lower hurdles for smaller parties and hence for those representing specific regional, linguistic, or national minority communities. Moreover unlike affirmative action policies, PR electoral systems do not need to specify and thereby freeze the size of any such minority representation, a process of legal or constitutional amendment which may well prove contentious; instead any groups and communities with a grievance may freely organize to mobilize voting support in proportion to their size.[7] Demographic shifts, such as the growing Catholic population in Northern Ireland, and hence the gathering electoral strength of Sinn Fein and other republican parties, are also incorporated flexibly into the political process over successive elections.[8]

Positive Action Strategies Also Help Minority Representation

Consociationalism regards PR as the primary, but not the only, electoral mechanism which can be designed to bring minority groups into elected office, as positive action strategies can also be used to achieve this goal.[9] This includes the creation of minority-majority districts (used in the United States to elect African Americans to the House of Representatives), the employment of communal rolls (such as those for Maoris in New Zealand), and the use of reserved seats (established in India for Scheduled Castes and Tribes).[10] Worldwide such mechanisms are employed in more than two dozen countries.[11] Positive action mechanisms commonly recognize and institutionalize the claims of certain specific historical communities, such as the position of the Maoris as the original Polynesian settlers in New Zealand, the Hungarian community who first settled in Romania in the ninth century, and indigenous Indian populations in Venezuela. At the same time, as a result of the contentious nature of affirmative action, these policies often fail to be equally inclusive for representatives and parties drawn from newer émigré communities, such as North African Muslims living in France, the Kurdish diasporas in Turkey, or Turkish 'guest workers' resident in Germany.

Legislative Office Encourages Elite Cooperation

Once elected to representative assemblies through either mechanism, consociational theory suggests, leaders of minority groups have strong incentives for cooperation, bargaining, and compromise, through the give and take of legislative politics at elite level. Party leaders can leverage their position to negotiate and gain ministerial office in coalition governments. Those working together in governing alliances develop experience of regular face-to-face negotiations and political haggling, a process expected to strengthen intercommunity cooperation and social tolerance gradually. In opposition, minority leaders can represent and safeguard the interests of their constituents, especially where specific minority vetoes are recognized constitutionally, for example, over issues involving language policy, freedom of religious expression, or cultural rights. If negotiated peace-settlements give all significant players a stake within parliament, it is anticipated that this should strengthen the incentives for the leaders of the rebellion to accept constitutional pacts, to maintain a cease-fire, and to promote conciliation among their followers. The ability of minorities to veto proposals which would threaten community interests is seen as particularly important to their security, especially in postwar pacts. At the same time, safeguards need to be built into the implementation of peace-settlements, including continued engagement by external forces or the international community, as otherwise, once in government, the majority group may simply decide to over-turn any formal constitutional agreement to protect minority rights.

Inclusiveness Strengthens Community Support for Democracy

This process, consociational theory suggests, will also have an impact upon the general public by strengthening democratic attitudes, encouraging participation, and increasing confidence in the legitimacy of the democratic channels of bargaining and compromise. Leaders have an incentive to encourage community acceptance of any peace-settlement, as this helps to preserve their power and status in elected office. The inclusion of community spokespersons in visible positions of power is expected to function as a safety valve for ethnic tensions, reducing intercommunal conflict, encouraging peaceful transitions, and strengthening the process of democratic consolidation in divided societies. Under more inclusive electoral arrangements, it is theorized that each distinct religious, linguistic, or nationalistic community will feel that their voice counts and that the rules of the game are fair and legitimate, as their leaders can articulate their concerns and protect their interests within the legislature and within government.[12] Consociational theory concludes that in the long term this process should thereby serve to stabilize deeply conflict-ridden societies and manage, or even reduce, broader ethnic tensions. The inclusion of minority groups within parliament cannot be equated automatically with their access to substantive power, especially in largely symbolic legislative bodies unable to check decisions made by the executive, and small parties may be impotent to shape the legislative agenda and government policy. Nevertheless the permanent exclusion of the leaders of any significant minority community from representative assemblies is thought to encourage alienation and violence. This situation is especially dangerous in divided societies emerging from protracted deep-rooted conflict, where parties are organized around issues of communal identity, rather than around programmatic or ideological lines, and where politics is viewed by each community as a win or lose game.

Critics of Consociational Theory. Critics have responded by raising a series of challenges to these arguments. The most important questions concern the fluidity of ethno-political identities, the strength of the electoral incentives for ethnic cooperation among elites, and the potential advantages of majoritarian electoral systems for fragile democracies.

The Political Relevance of Social Identities

As discussed earlier, consociational theory takes the existence of ethnic identities based on religion, race, or nationality as fixed and enduring psychological characteristics, acquired through socialization processes rooted in the family, school, and local community, which rarely, if ever, alter in the short term as a result of political processes. As such, community boundaries are seen as relatively stable, with each reflecting entrenched interests, and the challenge for democracy is how to include leaders from diverse minority communities within representative legislatures. This represents an essentialist or primordial view of ethnicity. Challenges arise from the alternative constructivist perspective, which suggests that people often have multiple identities, all of which are socially constructed and the salience of which is more fluid over time.[13] Hence, for instance, Hispanics in the United States may be defined as a political community by their country of origin, such as Mexican Americans, Cuban Americans, or Colombian Americans, or by other cross-cutting cleavages such as their ideological location as Democrats or Republicans, by region, class and social status, race, or gender. What matters in this regard, constructivists suggest, is not the existence of latent social identities per se, but rather the way that the shared interests arising from these identities are channeled and organized by community leadership elites into grievances and demands requiring a collective response in the political system. Modern Iraq, for example, was created after the defeat of the German-allied Ottoman Empire in World War I, when the victorious British and French carved up the territory of their defeated rival. The artificial boundaries of the new nation-state included Kurds in the north, with a distinct history and language, and the Shiite and Sunni Muslims with divergent religious viewpoints, regional areas, and cultural traditions, although Shi'a and Sunnis lived harmoniously in Iraq until the rise of the secular Baath Party and Saddam Hussein's brutal treatment of the Shiite and Kurdish communities. The fall of Saddam Hussein, and subsequent continued instability under the American-British intervention, exacerbated latent ethnic tensions. In the first elections, political leaders and factions built party support by appealing to each community. In the constructivist view, the strength of nationalist feelings toward Iraq as a single polity, and the importance of distinct ethnic communities within its borders, were reinforced and inflamed by political developments.

The constructivist approach draws on one of the longest traditions in political sociology, arising from the seminal work of Lipset and Rokkan, who suggested that contemporary European party systems reflected their historical roots within each country, with party organizations developing with the expansion of the franchise to mobilize the electorate around the major social cleavages of class, religion, and center-peripheral regions.[14] For Lipset and Rokkan, social identities became organized into partisan loyalties, with party competition subsequently institutionalizing and freezing around these core cleavages. A similar process may be occurring in new democracies, where, in the absence of other organizing principles, party systems develop around the core social cleavages, mobilizing blocs of voters. What matters for constructivists is less the multiple social identities existing in society than how some of these, but not others, are mobilized into party systems and thus legislative politics.

Incentives for Community Cooperation or Rivalry

Moreover critics charge that it is dangerous to empower leaders whose popular support is based exclusively within, rather than across, the boundaries of each community. This process provides an electoral incentive for populist leaders to appeal for popular support by reinforcing ethnic tensions and mistrust of other groups, and it serves to institutionalize and thereby freeze existing ethnic identities and community boundaries.[15] The political salience of communal identities may be unintentionally magnified by PR electoral rules (which lower the nationwide vote threshold, facilitating the election of small parties), and by positive action strategies (which explicitly recognize specific linguistic, religious, or nationalistic communal groups as the basis for allocating seats). The dangers of such arrangements are exemplified, critics suggest, by elections in Bosnia-Herzegovina after the Dayton peace-settlement, which reduced the incentive for cross-community cooperation and nonsectarian electoral appeals.[16] Rwanda also illustrates a country where international efforts promoted ethnic power-sharing between Hutu and Tutsi, but where the traditional ruling elites felt threatened by democratization. As a result, Snyder suggests, international efforts may have unintentionally backfired by heightening ethnic tensions, reinforcing the incentive for extremist politicians to make sectarian appeals reinforcing ethnic hatred within each community, generating disastrous bloodshed.[17] Communal leaders who win elected office gain a more visible platform, greater legitimacy, and the spotlight of the news media, all of which can be used to exploit, and thereby heighten, social tensions, ethnic hatred, and the politics of fear. Indeed, as illustrated by the Northern Ireland peace process, moderate parties which sought to cooperate across community lines gradually lost power to more radical politicians who regarded any compromise as a 'sellout'.[18] PR systems facilitate the election of smaller parties, not only from ethnic minorities; they also empower those drawn from the radical right, such as the French Front National, the Belgian Vlaams Blok (Flemish Bloc), and the Austrian Freiheitliche Partei Österreichs (FPÖ, Freedom Party), who exploit xenophobic fears about new immigrants, stoking racist tensions.[19] Critics charge that power-sharing formulas (PR systems with low thresholds of exclusion, and positive action strategies) fail to provide community leaders with an effective electoral incentive for cross-group cooperation. These policies may therefore serve to rigidify the boundaries dividing ethnic communities, reinforcing and heightening political instability in deeply divided postwar societies.[20]

By contrast, others propose that community cooperation and reconciliation may be strengthened most effectively by the adoption of majoritarian electoral systems. Both Horowitz and Reilly advocate adoption of the alternative vote (AV, also known as the preferential vote or 'instant runoff', used for the Australian House of Representatives).[21] The system of AV requires winning parties and candidates to gain an absolute majority of the vote ($50\% + 1$), rather than a simple plurality. This hurdle is thought to have two important consequences.[22] First, the need to gain support from a majority of the electorate encourages individual politicians to cooperate strategically with others within their party organizations. Community leaders are interested in collaborating within electoral coalitions, to build larger organizations capable of winning seats. Even more importantly, higher thresholds also create strategic incentives for vote-pooling, as politicians and parties need to emphasize broad-based moderate electoral appeals to win. Those seeking to maximize their popular support among the median voters will emphasize nonsectarian bridging issues, avoiding narrow polarizing and controversial policies which appeal only to distinct linguistic, racial, nationalistic, or religious communities.[23] This is particularly true if the electoral districts are drawn to reflect multiethnic populations, rather than drawing boundaries between ethnic communities. Majoritarian electoral systems may thereby encourage politicians to adopt cross-identity appeals, where they target diverse sectors of the electorate.[24]

Trade-Off Values in Fragile Democracies and Failed States

The final challenge to consociational theory emphasizes that the choice of electoral rules requires a trade-off among conflicting values, where the inclusiveness of all communities within the legislature is only one consideration.[25] Majoritarian systems which concentrate power in the hands of the winning party during their term of office may have other qualities that prove especially important for underpinning sustainable peace-settlements and generating stable governments in divided societies emerging from civil wars. Majoritarian and plurality electoral systems systematically exaggerate the share of seats allocated to the winning party and reduce the share of seats allocated to smaller parties. The mechanical effect of these rules is to secure a decisive outcome for the first-ranked party, so that they can form a single-party cabinet government resting on a secure overall parliamentary majority, even in a closely balanced election. This arrangement may help to maximize the transparency and accountability of government policymaking, as well as serving to produce stable and durable governments empowered to serve their full term in office. Majoritarian elections are better at generating a decisive outcome, producing governments assured of a legislative majority, without a prolonged period of uncertainty arising from postelection negotiation and haggling with coalition partners. This may be particularly important in failed states, which need to reestablish internal security destroyed by prolonged civil war and ethnic conflict. Effective government may be the overriding concern in societies emerging from deep-rooted internal conflict and failed states, such as Liberia, Somalia, Iraq, or Eritrea, where there are widespread doubts about the government's capacity to maintain internal security, to manage the economy, and to deliver basic public services. Societies emerging from a period of prolonged conflict which has destroyed intercommunity trust, and with many poorly institutionalized new parties and legislative factions elected to office, are likely to experience considerable problems in the postelection period of bargaining and compromise needed to create a workable governing coalition.

For all these reasons, while inclusive power-sharing arrangements (proportional electoral systems with low thresholds and/or positive action strategies) have often been adopted in many negotiated peace-settlements, it is by no means clear from the scholarly literature that these will necessarily prove the most effective mechanism for promoting sustainable peace, interethnic reconciliation, and democratic consolidation in the long term.

COMPARING ELECTORAL SYSTEMS

What evidence could help to resolve this debate? Case studies of the apparent success of electoral engineering (South Africa?) and apparent failure (Bosnia-Herzegovina?) can be quoted by both sides, but such examples have not proved sufficiently convincing to resolve the contemporary debate.[26] As we observed earlier, the proportional electoral system adopted by Benin in the early-1990s may have been the foundation of the broader process of power-sharing and democratic consolidation, in sharp contrast to the majoritarian rules which reinforced the military-backed autocracy in Togo, but it is difficult to know how far we can generalize from these examples. In the same way, we can compare the postwar Iraqi constitution, which followed consociational advice by adopting proportional party list elections for the National Assembly, with that of Afghanistan, which chose majoritarian elections for the Wolesi Jirga (adopting a system of single nontransferable vote). Yet case studies remain limited, as these societies differ in many other fundamental ways, so it remains difficult to isolate institutional effects arising from the electoral systems from many other factors, such as cultural traditions, levels of development, and the influence of the international community.

To examine some of the issues underlying these claims and counterclaims more systematically, broader comparisons are required. We can start by classifying power-sharing electoral arrangements, identifying both the type of electoral system and the positive action strategies for minority representation, used in all nation-states worldwide. The analysis of the effects of these arrangements builds upon the multivariate models developed in the previous chapter. Institutional effects are examined controlling for prior social and economic conditions, including levels of economic development and the degree of ethnic fractionalization within each society. The dependent variables include the indicators of democratic consolidation established earlier, as well as indicators of party systems, ethnic conflict, and political stability.

Classifying Electoral Systems

In plural societies, Lijphart theorizes that proportional representation electoral systems are most effective for democratic consolidation, while the Horowitz-Reilly vote-pooling theory predicts that majoritarian electoral systems are most likely to serve this function. To test the evidence supporting these alternative hypotheses, the major and minor types of electoral system currently used for the lower house of parliament can be classified and then compared across all independent nation-states worldwide, excluding dependent territories. The core typology used for the contemporary comparison is summarized in Figure 5.2

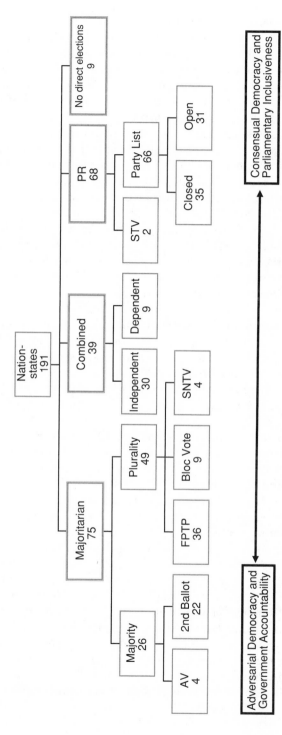

FIGURE 5.2. Classification of Contemporary Electoral Systems, Worldwide, 2004. *Note:* FPTP, first-past-the-post; 2nd Ballot, second ballot; AV, alternative vote; SNTV, single nontransferable vote; STV, single transferable vote. *Source:* Systems are classified on the basis of Appendix A in Andrew Reynolds and Ben Reilly. Eds. 2005. *The International IDEA Handbook of Electoral System Design.* 2nd ed. Stockholm: International Institute for Democracy and Electoral Assistance. For more details see http://www.aceproject.org/ and Pippa Norris. 2004. *Electoral Engineering.* New York: Cambridge University Press.

and the classification is derived from the 2nd edition of the *International IDEA Handbook of Electoral System Design* covering contemporary electoral systems used in 2004.[27] In total, out of 191 contemporary independent nation-states around the globe, 9 are excluded from the classification of electoral systems as they currently lack a directly elected national parliament. This includes the Persian Gulf royal families (in Saudi Arabia, Qatar, and the United Arab Emirates), the monarchies governing Brunei Darussalam and Bhutan, the personal dictatorship of Colonel Gaddafi in Libya, and Communist China.[28] Two additional countries are excluded as they experienced state collapse (Eritrea and Somalia) with electoral systems which remain in transition. Electoral systems for the remaining countries were categorized into three major families – majoritarian, proportional, and combined – each including a number of subcategories.

Proportional representation (PR) electoral systems are designed to translate the percentage of votes relatively proportionally into the percentage of seats won, lowering the threshold facing smaller parties. Proportional representation systems are defined in this study to include party list, as well as the single transferable vote electoral system, which is less common.[29] The main institutional variations within PR systems concern the use of open or closed lists of candidates, the quota formula for translating votes into seats, the level of the legal vote threshold, and the size of the average district magnitude. By contrast, *majoritarian-plurality* systems require a higher effective vote threshold, and they are essentially power-concentrating (by systematically squeezing the number of parliamentary parties). Majoritarian rules require the winning candidate or party to gain 50% + 1 of the vote (including the alternative vote [AV] and the second ballot [runoff or two-round] systems). Plurality rules require that the winning candidate or party in first place gain more votes than any other, but not necessarily a majority of ballots cast (including first-past-the-post single member plurality system, the party bloc vote, and the single nontransferable vote [SNTV] system).[30] Plurality rules generate a 'manufactured' majority: that is, they have a systematic exaggerative bias which usually translates a plurality of votes for the party in first place into a majority of seats. Finally, *'combined'* electoral systems (otherwise known as 'mixed', 'dual', 'hybrid', or 'side-by-side' systems) use two ballot structures within simultaneous contests for the same elected office.[31] This study follows Massicotte and Blais by classifying 'combined' systems according to their mechanics, not their outcome.[32] Combined systems have become increasingly popular during the last decade, although a great variety of alternative designs are employed. This category can be further subdivided into 'combined-independent' systems, where the distribution of seats is independent for each type of ballot, and 'combined-dependent' systems (such as Germany and New Zealand), where the distribution of seats is proportional to the share of the vote cast in the party list. As a result combined-independent systems are closer to the 'majoritarian' than the 'proportional' end of the spectrum, while 'combined-dependent' are closer to the 'proportional' end of the spectrum.

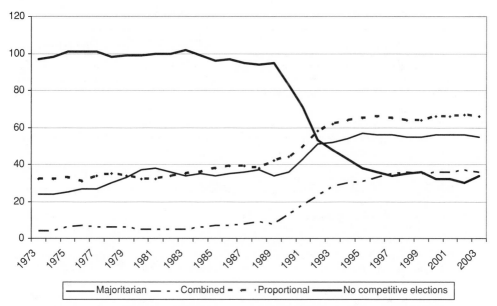

FIGURE 5.3. Trends in Types of Electoral Systems Used Worldwide, 1973–2003. *Source:*
Coded from Arthur S. Banks. 2005. *Cross-National Time-Series Data Archive;* Andrew
Reynolds and Ben Reilly. Eds. *The International IDEA Handbook of Electoral Sys-
tem Design.* 2nd ed. Stockholm: International Institute for Democracy and Electoral
Assistance.

A comparison of trends in the use of the major types of electoral systems used
worldwide since the early-1970s in Figure 5.3 illustrates the sharp fall during
the decade of the 1990s in the number of countries without any competitive
elections. The use of multiparty elections for the legislative and executive office
became far more widespread during this era; for example, International IDEA
estimates that just over 40 presidential elections were held in each decade during the 1950s, 1960s, and 1970s, rising to 67 in the 1980s, before shooting up
to 222 during the 1990s.[33] Trends in the number of parliamentary elections
show a similar rise, doubling from 196 contests held during the 1970s to 381
during the 1990s. Nevertheless many of these elections have been used in recent
years as a façade to legitimate the rule of regimes which have been conceptualized, alternatively, as 'electoral autocracies' (Diamond), 'illiberal democracies' (Fareed), or 'competitive authoritarian regimes' (Levitsky), exemplified by
Belarus, Egypt, Malaysia, Uzbekistan, or Zimbabwe.[34] As discussed in Chapter 3, electoral autocracies are often difficult to classify with any precision
as they are characterized by the formal trappings of liberal democracy, but
free and fair multiparty competition and civil liberties are sharply limited by
the ruling elites. Common techniques to limit genuine electoral competition,
often reported by observers, include major restrictions on access to the ballot

TABLE 5.1. *Characteristics of Contemporary Electoral Systems, 2000*

		PR	Combined	Majoritarian	N
(i)	Largest governing party, % of seats	44.4	53.7	68.1	158
(ii)	Rae party fractionalization index	65.2	54.6	34.6	189
(iii)	Mean number of all parliamentary parties	9.3	8.7	5.0	175
(iv)	Mean number of relevant parliamentary parties	4.7	4.4	3.2	175
(v)	Herfindahl index for all parliamentary parties	0.33	0.39	0.57	153
(vi)	Effective number of parliamentary parties	3.69	3.77	2.33	103
(vi)	Index of proportionality	90.4	83.2	83.1	110
(vii)	Effective electoral threshold	11.3	24.5	35.4	148

Notes: (i) The number of seats held by the largest governing party in the lower house of each country's national assembly (Banks 2000).
(ii) The Rae party fractionalization index (Banks 2000).
(iii) The mean number of parliamentary parties with at least one seat in the lower house of the national parliament (calculated from *Elections around the World*).
(iv) The mean number of relevant parliamentary parties (those with more than 3% of seats in the lower house of the national parliament) (calculated from *Elections around the World*).
(v) The Herfindahl index for all parliamentary parties, ranging from 0 to 1, representing the probability that two randomly selected members of the lower house of parliament belong to different parties (The Database of Political Institutions Keefer/World Bank 2005).
(vi) The Rose index of proportionality (a standardized version of the Loosemore-Hanby Index) (Rose 2001).
(vii) The effective electoral threshold, using the formula $(75/m + 1)$, where m refers to the district magnitude or the number of members returned in the electoral district (calculated from Rose 2001).

for opposition parties and intimidation of challengers; the widespread use of intimidation, coercion, or bribery by security forces at the polling station; and strong pro-government bias and limits on independent journalism in campaign coverage in the media airwaves.

Turning to trends in the type of electoral system which have been used, Figure 5.3 shows that proportional representation systems have usually been more popular than majoritarian systems, with the category of 'combined' or 'mixed' electoral systems the smallest category but rising in popularity in the 1990s. This is partly the result of the adoption of this system in many of the newer democracies which emerged following the fall of the Berlin Wall, as well as the way that this system has been adopted by some established democracies which reformed their systems, such as New Zealand.[35]

Table 5.1 summarizes a series of indicators illustrating the characteristic impact of the major types of electoral systems on party systems and levels of proportionality. The results generally conform to expectations arising from the previous literature about the mechanical workings of electoral systems. Hence, as anticipated, the exaggerative bias common in majoritarian systems usually results in a decisive electoral outcome; on average, under these rules the largest party generally wins two-thirds of all parliamentary seats. This empowers single-party cabinet governments to implement their legislative program during their term of office assured of the support of a comfortable parliamentary majority, without the need for coalition partners. By contrast, PR systems are more likely to generate coalition governments; the largest party usually wins less than a majority (44%) of seats. The indicators also confirm that PR rules systematically lower the effective electoral threshold, thereby facilitating the election of many smaller parties. This pattern is consistent irrespective of the specific indicator of party competition considered; for example, the Rae party fractionalization index is twice as strong in PR systems compared with majoritarian elections.

On the basis of this classification, the question which arises is whether there is systematic support for the core consociational claims that PR is the most effective electoral system for democratic consolidation, and that this is particularly evident in divided societies. To start to scrutinize the evidence, we can examine whether the four indicators of democracy used throughout this study differ by the major types of contemporary electoral systems used worldwide, without introducing any prior controls.

Figure 5.4 compares the scores on Freedom House's indicator of liberal democracy, Polity IV's constitutional democracy, Vanhanen's participatory democracy, or Cheibub and Gandhi's contested democracy. Irrespective of the indicator used, the results confirm that countries using list PR electoral systems consistently rate as significantly the most democratic, as consociational theory claims. The combined types of electoral system are located in an intermediate position. By contrast, majoritarian electoral systems proved consistently less democratic; for example, according to the Polity scale, nation-states using PR systems were on average twice as democratic as those using majoritarian rules. When tested by analysis of variance (ANOVA), these differences by types of electoral system all proved moderately strongly associated and statistically significant (with the ETA coefficient of association at .37 to .53 all at the $p = .001$ level).

But does this pattern also vary systematically by the type of ethnic cleavages within each society, with PR proving most important in plural societies, the second and stronger claim in consociational theory? For a preliminary look at the patterns, Figure 5.5 compares societies which were classified as either heterogeneous or homogeneous, based on dichotomizing Alesina's ethnic fractionalization index. This is a simple classification of plural societies, gauging whether populations are ethnically similar or different, but it cannot take account of whether such cleavages are politically salient. The comparison, without any prior controls, confirms that among homogeneous societies, nation-states using PR electoral systems were consistently more democratic than countries with majoritarian elections, and the difference in levels of democracy between PR and majoritarian electoral systems was greatest in heterogeneous societies, as Lijphart theorizes. Consociational theory emphasizes that majoritarian systems can work well within homogeneous societies, but that PR elections are particularly important for consolidating democracy in divided societies, and the comparison conducted so far provides preliminary support for this claim.

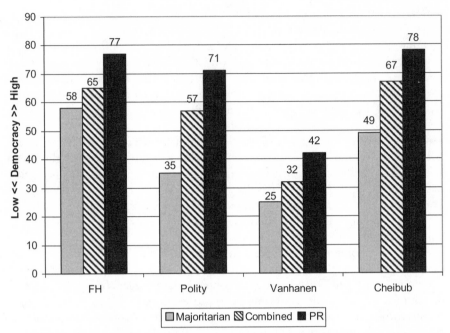

FIGURE 5.4. Levels of Democracy by Type of Electoral System, 2000. *Note:* The standardized 100-point scales of democracy are described in Table 3.1. The four scales measure *liberal democracy* (Freedom House 2000), *constitutional democracy* (Polity IV 2000), *participatory democracy* (Vanhanen 2000), and *contested democracy* (Cheibub and Gandhi 2000). When tested by ANOVA, the differences between mean scores are significant (at the $p = .001$ level). Contemporary electoral systems are classified in 191 nation-states worldwide on the basis of the Technical Appendix in Andrew Reynolds, Ben Reilly, and Andrew Ellis. 2005. *Electoral System Design: The New International IDEA Handbook*. Stockholm: International Institute for Democracy and Electoral Assistance. The type of electoral system was classified into three categories: *majoritarian/plurality* (single member plurality, second ballot, bloc vote, alternative vote, and single nontransferable vote), *proportional representation* (party list and STV), and *combined* (using more than one type of ballot in simultaneous elections for the same body).

Positive Action Mechanisms for Ethnic Minorities

As an alternative proposition, Lijphart theorizes that democratic consolidation in divided societies will also be strengthened by electoral rules which incorporate positive action policies designed to ensure the election of representatives or parties drawn from minority communities. We can compare the effects of three such mechanisms which have been employed in different countries.

District boundary delimination: In some countries, electoral boundaries are drawn to recognize certain communities of interest, creating specific single member districts where minority electorates are concentrated. In the United

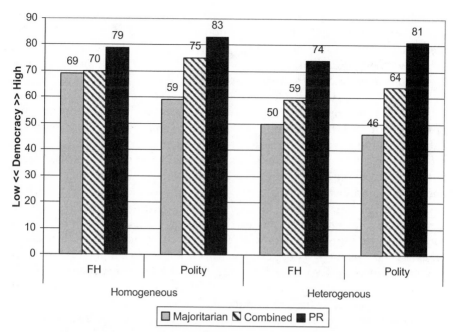

FIGURE 5.5. Contemporary Levels of Democracy by Type of Electoral System in Heterogeneous and Homogeneous Societies, 2000. *Note:* For the classification of electoral systems, see Figure 5.3. The types of heterogeneous or homogeneous society are classified by the dichotomized Alesina index of ethnic fractionalization.

States, for example, since the Voting Rights Act of 1965 and its amendment in 1982, racial redistricting processes have been based on identifying concentrations of black, Hispanic, Asian, and Native American minorities within the electorate. There are disputes about their effects but many argue that these have proved critical for the election of African-American and Latino congressional candidates to the US House of Representatives.[36] In Hungary, the boundary authority takes into account ethnic, religious, historical, or other local communities when creating districts, while Panama and Ukraine also require consideration of minority populations. Boundaries are often drawn and revised periodically to maintain population equality among districts, but some countries have overrepresented specific territories by requiring smaller electoral quotas within certain regions; until recently, for example, the population of Scotland was overrepresented by Westminster MPs in comparison with that of England. Majoritarian electoral systems are also not an insurmountable barrier for the success of smaller nationalist parties if their popular support is heavily concentrated within specific districts.[37] The Scottish National Party (SNP), for example, performed relatively well in gaining seats within their own regions; in the 2005 general election, for example, the SNP gained 17.7% of the vote in Scotland and won six seats (10%) in the region. By contrast, other minor parties more dispersed across Britain, such as the Greens, the UK Independence Party (UKIP), and the British National Party (BNP), gained no seats.[38] Electoral geography and the drawing of district boundaries are critical in this regard, with majoritarian systems most disadvantageous for smaller parties or scattered communities with dispersed support.

Reserved seats: Another alternative form of positive action is the use of reserved seats designed to compensate for historical disadvantage of communities. These are found, for example, for indigenous minorities in New Zealand, Pakistan, and Fiji, where these seats are filled by appointees of the recognized group or elected by voters from a communal electoral roll.[39] Reserved seats have been based on recognition of race/ethnicity, language, national identity, and religion and have been used for minorities on island territories detached from the nation-state landmass. There is nothing particularly novel about these arrangements; reserved seats were used in many colonially administered territories, and after the Second World War separate communal rolls with reserved seats became integral parts of power-sharing solutions to end internal conflicts in Lebanon in 1943, Cyprus in 1960, and Zimbabwe in 1980. A recent worldwide review found that at least 32 countries used reserved seats, communal rolls, race conscious districting, or special electoral arrangements designed for communal or minority representation in parliament.[40] During the last decade, these strategies were reflected in the compartmentalized ethnic arrangements of peace pacts in Bosnia, Croatia, and Kosova. In Croatia, for example, which uses list PR for most seats, specific districts are reserved for members of Hungarian, Czech and Slovak, Ruthenian and Ukrainian, and German and Austrian minorities. As we have already seen, in Singapore the Group Representative Constituencies provide a voice for Indian, Malay, and Eurasian minority candidates. Mauritius allocates eight seats for Hindu, Muslim, Chinese, and Creole recognized communities. India reserves a certain number of seats in each state for Scheduled Castes and Tribes, where only candidates drawn from these communities can stand for election. One of the best-known examples of such policies is Lebanon's parliament, which has 128 seats divided among distinct groups. Members are divided evenly among Christian and Muslim communities, each allocated 64 seats, and within those two major categories are 11 different factions, each with reserved seats. The top three sects on the Christian side are the Maronite Catholics (with 34 reserved seats), the Greek Orthodox, and the Greek Catholics. On the Muslim side, the Shi'as and Sunnis each have 27 reserved seats, while the Druze have 8. Most countries using reserved seats have majoritarian electoral systems, including within FPTP systems such as Pakistan, India, Samoa, Iran, and Kiribati. But countries with PR and combined electoral systems also include this mechanism, particularly the cases of postconflict power-sharing agreements, namely, Rwanda, Kosovo, Cyprus, Bosnia and Herzegovina, and Lebanon.

What is the effect of these mechanisms for minority representation on democratic consolidation? We can start by comparing levels of democracy, using the four indicators already employed in this study, in the countries which do and do not use at least one of these positive action mechanisms. Figure 5.6 illustrates

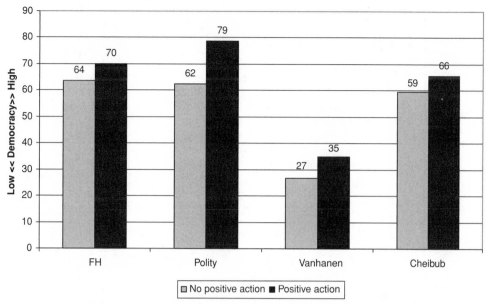

FIGURE 5.6. Contemporary Levels of Democracy by the Use of Positive Action Strategies for Ethnic Minority Representation. *Note*: The standardized 100-point scales of democracy are described in Table 3.1. The four scales measure *liberal democracy* (Freedom House 2000), *constitutional democracy* (Polity IV 2000), *participatory democracy* (Vanhanen 2000), and *contested democracy* (Cheibub and Gandhi 2000). When tested by ANOVA, the differences between mean scores are significant (at the $p = .001$ level). The use of positive action strategies in 29 out of 191 nation-states, including through reserved seats and boundary delimitation, is described in the text.

the patterns, confirming that the 29 countries employing positive action policies for minority representation are consistently more democratic across each of these indicators. ANOVA shows that the pattern is statistically significant, with the most substantial contrast found using the Polity index.

Multivariate Analysis

The preliminary comparisons so far appear to support the consociational argument favoring more proportional electoral systems or positive action strategies for minorities. But are the contrasts we have observed the product of the institutional arrangements, or can they be attributed to other features in the nation-states under comparison? Multivariate analysis is needed to see whether these patterns persist even after employing the battery of prior controls which we established in the previous chapter to be closely related to levels of democracy. One of these concerns the past colonial legacies which continue to shape the contemporary distribution of electoral systems; hence three-quarters of the former British colonies use a majoritarian electoral system today for national

TABLE 5.2. *Electoral Systems and Democracy, All Societies Worldwide*

	Liberal Democracy Freedom House			Constitutional Democracy Polity IV			Participatory Democracy Vanhanen		
	B	PCSE	P	B	PCSE	P	B	PCSE	P
INSTITUTIONAL RULES									
Majoritarian	−2.33	(.454)	***	−7.64	(.949)	***	−3.18	(.533)	***
Proportional representation	.904	(.619)	N/s	3.85	(.561)	***	1.95	(.344)	***
Positive action strategies	4.13	(.466)	***	11.41	(.777)	***	5.76	(.284)	***
CONTROLS									
Log GDP/capita	13.90	(.832)	***	11.91	(1.01)	***	14.05	(.663)	***
Ex-British colony	12.35	(.962)	***	12.36	(1.36)	***	2.05	(.803)	**
Middle East	−10.99	(1.16)	***	−16.79	(1.40)	***	−5.87	(.809)	***
Regional diffusion	.632	(.036)	***	.883	(.049)	***	.481	(.029)	***
Ethnic fractionalization	−8.45	(.878)	***	−1.98	(1.56)	N/s	−10.05	(.694)	***
Population size	.001	(.001)	N/s	.000	(.001)	***	.001	(.001)	***
Area size	.001	(.001)	***	.001	(.001)	***	.001	(.001)	***
Constant	−21.96			−38.45			−46.6		
No. of observations	4768			3946			4128		
No. of countries	174			145			167		
Adjusted R²	.487			.533			.624		

Note: Entries for liberal democracy, constitutional democracy, and participatory democracy 100-point scales are unstandardized OLS regression coefficients (with their panel-corrected standard errors) and the significance (P) of the coefficients for the pooled time-series cross-national analysis obtained using Stata's xtpcse command. For the measures of democracy, see Chapter 2. For the classification of the type of electoral system, see Figure 5.1. The default (comparison) is mixed electoral systems. For details of all the variables, see the Technical Appendix. Significant at * the 0.10 level, ** the 0.05 level, and *** the 0.01 level.

elections to the lower house of the legislature, as do two-thirds of the ex-French colonies. By contrast, proportional electoral systems are employed by three-quarters of the former Portuguese colonies, two-thirds of the ex-Spanish colonies, and all the former Dutch colonies.[41] The post-Communist states freed from rule by the Soviet Union divide almost evenly among the three major electoral families, although slightly more countries (37%) have adopted proportional systems. While Eastern Europe leans toward majoritarian arrangements, Central Europe adopted more proportional systems. To examine the impact of electoral systems on democracy, we need to expand the models already developed in Chapter 4, controlling for past colonial histories, as well as degrees of ethnic fractionalization, levels of economic development, regional diffusion, the Middle East region, and the physical and population size of the country. In these models, combined (mixed) electoral systems are the default (comparison) category.

Table 5.2 presents the results of the OLS regression models, based on analysis of the pooled time-series cross-sectional data. The coefficients confirm that, compared across all societies worldwide, countries using majoritarian electoral systems have worse democratic performance on each of the indicators, even after controlling for the range of economic and cultural factors associated with democracy. By contrast, PR electoral systems are positively associated with democracy, although the coefficient for the Freedom House index was not statistically significant. Moreover the use of positive action strategies was also positively related to levels of democracy across all the indicators. Overall the multivariate analysis confirms the comparisons observed earlier, supporting the consociational argument that countries using PR electoral systems and positive action strategies are the most successful democratically. Consociational theory predicts that these forms of power-sharing institutions are valuable in general, but nowhere more so than in divided societies. Accordingly Table 5.3 repeats the analysis but limiting the comparison to plural societies, defined by dichotomizing the Alesina measure of ethnic fractionalization. The results show that the positive impact of PR electoral systems on democracy is far stronger in these nation-states; for example, the use of PR produces a 5–10 percentage point increase in democracy on the 100-point scales. Countries using positive action strategies for ethnic minority representation were also significantly more democratic.

CASE STUDIES OF ELECTORAL REFORM

The comparisons drawn so far seem to provide considerable support for many of the consociational claims. Yet we have not been able to test all the sequential steps in the consociational argument outlined in Figure 5.1. The relationship between electoral systems and democracy could still be due to many other factors; for example, PR may facilitate multiparty competition and higher electoral turnout, without necessarily leading toward intercommunal trust among party leaders or greater satisfaction with the democratic process among community members. Paired case studies of electoral reform in Britain and New Zealand

TABLE 5.3. *Electoral Systems and Democracy, Plural Societies Only*

	Liberal Democracy Freedom House			Constitutional Democracy Polity IV			Participatory Democracy Vanhanen		
	B	PCSE	P	B	PCSE	P	B	PCSE	P
INSTITUTIONAL RULES									
Majoritarian	−4.27	(.625)	***	−3.30	(1.16)	***	.317	(.474)	N/s
Proportional representation	4.81	(.966)	***	10.68	(.915)	***	4.65	(.565)	***
Positive action strategies	.424	(.676)	N/s	13.96	(1.52)	***	3.86	(.714)	***
CONTROLS									
Log GDP/capita	10.21	(.519)	***	7.26	(1.21)	***	8.08	(.695)	***
Ex-British colony	8.35	(.744)	***	8.20	(1.10)	***	1.00	(.497)	*
Middle East	−8.39	(.974)	***	−20.72	(3.13)	***	−7.18	(.934)	***
Regional diffusion	.739	(.027)	***	1.04	(.055)	***	.548	(.025)	***
Ethnic fractionalization	14.97	(3.18)	***	26.51	(4.27)	***	15.1	(1.00)	***
Population size	−.001	(.000)	***	−.001	(.001)	***	−.001	(.001)	***
Area size	.001	(.001)	***	.001	(.001)	***	.001	(.001)	N/s
Constant	−30.9			−54.9			−50.9		
No. of observations	2116			1851			1831		
No. of countries	76			66			72		
Adjusted R²	.545			.477			.579		

Note: Entries for liberal democracy, constitutional democracy, and participatory democracy 100-point scales are unstandardized OLS regression coefficients (with their panel-corrected standard errors) and the significance (P) of the coefficients for the pooled time-series cross-national analysis obtained using Stata's xtpcse command. Only plural societies are selected (based on dichotomizing Alesina's ethnic fractionalization index). For the measures of democracy, see Chapter 2. For the classification of the type of electoral system, see Figure 5.1. The default (comparison) is mixed electoral systems. For details of all the variables, see the Technical Appendix. Significant at * the 0.10 level, ** the 0.05 level, and *** the 0.01 level.

provide a better understanding of the underlying dynamic processes at work, in particular how far changing the rules alters patterns of party competition and the representation of ethnic minority groups.

During the postwar era, both Britain and New Zealand used to exemplify the classic Westminster model, characterized by single-member plurality electoral systems and unitary states. First-past-the-post produced a two-party adversarial system in parliament, single-party cabinet governments, and strong central governments in both countries. Because of New Zealand's colonial origins, these nation-states also shared many strong cultural bonds, especially during the heyday of the British Commonwealth prior to UK entry into the European Union. Both are long-standing stable democracies, each containing important minority communities, and each society becoming increasingly diverse in recent decades. The majority of New Zealand's population is descended from British émigrés, with significant minorities of indigenous Maoris, of Polynesian descent, and more recently other European, Pacific Islander, and East Asian immigrants. By 2050, it is estimated that the white population will become a minority in New Zealand. In the United Kingdom, the primary arguments about the political representation of national identities have focused upon the peace-settlement in Northern Ireland and upon devolution in Scotland and Wales. More recent émigré communities are represented in the Muslim population in Britain, including diverse Bangladeshi and Pakistani communities, as well as Sikhs and Hindus originally from India, the black population of Afro-Caribbean descent, and other East Asian groups.

These countries have taken different paths to electoral reform, and the inclusion of specific minorities. New Zealand adopted a mixed member proportional (MMP) system (combined-dependent) for the national parliament in 1993, while continuing to use Maori communal rolls for the indigenous population. By contrast, electoral reform has been widely debated but not yet implemented for the British House of Commons and for English local elections, although the Labour government has introduced a range of alternative electoral systems used for selecting British members of the European Parliament (regional PR closed party list using the d'Hondt rule), the new Scottish Parliament and Welsh assembly (using additional member system [AMS]), and the London Assembly and London mayor (supplementary vote systems). Under devolution, Scotland was granted a parliament with considerable law-making powers, while the Welsh assembly has administrative responsibilities for a range of public services.[42] Here we can focus upon analyzing changes following the adoption of AMS for Scotland and Wales, as the most comparable combined-dependent electoral system to the MMP arrangement chosen in New Zealand.

The Regional Bodies in the United Kingdom

What have been the effects of electoral reform on party systems and minority representation in each country? Figure 5.7 illustrates party fortunes in elections

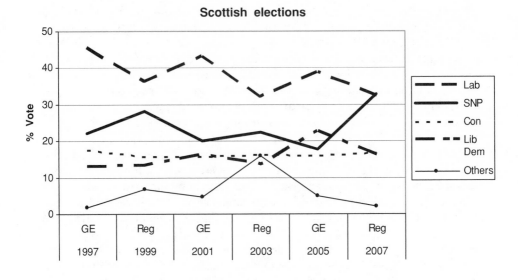

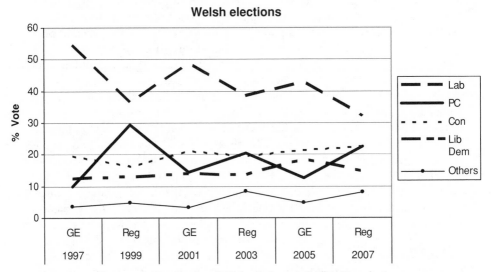

FIGURE 5.7. Elections in Scotland and Wales Before and After Devolution, 1997–2007

held before and after devolution, which was first implemented in 1999. The process of decentralization can be regarded by social scientists as a natural pre-post experiment which modified the rules in successive contests, while holding constant the broader social and economic context in each region. The electoral system used for Westminster contests also remained largely unchanged; the House of Commons continues to employ traditional single-member districts and plurality elections (first-past-the-post), although for the 2005 election, following boundary revisions, the total number of Scottish MPs was cut from 72 to 59, bringing Scottish districts into line with the size of the average electorates in England and Wales. The first elections for the Scottish Parliament and for the Welsh Assembly were held in 1999 under the additional member (combined-dependent) system and the process was repeated again in 2003 and in 2007. Scottish voters were given two ballot papers: one used the familiar system of first-past-the-post to elect each of the 72 constituency members. The second used party lists in eight regional multimember districts to elect 56 additional representatives. The latter were allocated so that the overall distribution of seats was proportional to the share of votes cast for each party in each region. The d'Hondt formula is used for allocating the top-up seats. Under the d'Hondt system, parties which perform well in constituency votes but fail to translate that success into elected constituency members will be rewarded via the additional member system. Conversely, parties which do well by securing constituencies win fewer top-up seats. Similar processes were followed for allocating the 60-seat Welsh Assembly.

As shown by the proportion of votes cast for each party, illustrated in Figure 5.7, the Labour Party has predominated in the series of elections in both regions. Indeed fear of continuous Labour hegemony was perhaps the main reason why a cross-party coalition favored the additional member system for the new bodies. But the systematic pattern evident in successive contests since devolution shows that Labour performs most strongly in general elections, with their support eroding in the regional contests. For example, compared with the 1997 general election, the first regional elections for the new Scottish Parliament in 1999 saw a striking 9-point fall in the Labour Party's share of the vote. This contest saw significant advances for the Scottish National Party (SNP) and for the smaller parties, notably the Scottish Green Party and the Scottish Socialist Party. Labour's share of the Scottish vote recovered in the 2001 general election, only to fall back again in the 2003 and 2007 regional contests. Moreover surveys monitoring nationalist sentiment from 1997 to 2004 report that this also fluctuated over time in these regions.[43] The Scottish National Party did not threaten Labour's grip on Holyrood Palace in 2003. In 2007, however, scandals within the leadership led to a dramatic loss of votes for the minor Scottish Socialist Party. The SNP benefited from this and from disillusionment with the Blair government, winning a third of the Scottish vote. As a result, the SNP formed a minority administration in the Scottish Assembly, led by Alex Salmond as first minister. This victory represents a historic breakthrough in power for the Scottish Nationalists, although SNP have only a wafer-thin one-seat lead over Labour. It was the first time that Labour failed to finish first in any Scottish election since 1955.

The fluctuating patterns of party support found in general and regional contests north of the border are also evident, but to a lesser extent, in Wales. Since devolution, waves of votes have been gained by smaller parties under the AMS combined electoral system used for the Welsh Assembly, only to fall back again in Westminster contests. Hence Plaid Cymru (PC) support peaked sharply during the 1999 regional elections before sliding back in the 2005 general election. Patterns of peaks and troughs in PC support are evident in successive regional and general elections since then. Labour remains the largest party in the Welsh Assembly, although attempts have been made to assemble a 'rainbow' coalition to challenge its hegemony. Women also proved very successful in getting elected to the regional bodies, in 2006 representing 39.5% of the Scottish Parliament and achieving parity (50%) in the Welsh Assembly, compared with just 19.7% of the House of Commons.[44]

To summarize, the electoral systems introduced with devolution in Britain generated an initial surge for the nationalist parties in 1999. The smaller parties and independents have also benefited: the Scottish Parliament currently contains seven members from the Greens, six members from the Socialist Party, two independents, and two other party representatives, most elected from the more proportional regional lists. Party fragmentation has increased in the regions. The results in the 2007 Scottish elections confirmed the hopes of the nationalist parties, who anticipated that the creation of the new bodies under devolution, and their greater visibility in these assemblies, would provide a platform which would eventually strengthen their popular support, providing a launch pad to power.

New Zealand

New Zealand adopted a different route to electoral reform when they abandoned using traditional single-member districts and plurality elections (first-past-the-post) and adopted a combined-dependent system (mixed member proportional [MMP]) in 1993.[45] The New Zealand parliament contains 120 MPs. Each elector has two votes: one for the party lists, returning 51 members, and the other for one of the 62 general or the 7 Maori seats.[46] Parties are represented in parliament if they get at least 5% vote in the lists, and above this threshold the overall distribution of parliamentary seats is proportional to the share of votes cast in the lists. Special measures are specified for the Maori population, who are recognized as an indigenous population originating in Polynesia with special cultural rights. There have been special Maori electorate seats since 1867, when Maori men were first given the vote. The number of Maori seats was fixed at four until the Electoral Act 1993 stipulated that the numbers could rise or fall, depending on whether Maori choose to go on the general or the Maori electoral roll. Increasing numbers have chosen the Maori roll; as a result, the number of special Maori electorate seats rose to seven in the 2005 parliament. Of the 19 Maori MPs in that parliament, the remaining 12 Maori MPs represented the general electorates or were list MPs.[47] In 2005, the first Maori party was created, currently with four elected representatives in parliament. New Zealand has become increasingly diverse ethnically, and, at 6.4% of the population, Asians are the third largest ethnic group. MMP has given them a political voice, currently with one Labour and one National list Asian MPs.

What have been the consequences of electoral reform in New Zealand? Prior to this change, New Zealand had an entrenched two-party 'Westminster' system during most of the twentieth century. Government office rotated between the conservative National Party and the center-left Labour Party, excluding minor party contenders from legislative and government office. Dealigning trends weakened party identification during the 1980s, and electoral volatility rose, but with little effect on parliamentary politics as a result of the use of the first-past-the-post single-member electoral system.[48] The new MMP system was used for general elections in 1996, 1999, 2002, and 2005. The results confirmed the expectations that more proportional elections would lead to multiparty competition and coalition governments, as well as more inclusive parliaments for women and minority MPs (see Figure 5.7). Under first-past-the-post, prior to reform, there were usually two or three parties in parliament. After reform, from 1996 to 2005, there were six or seven. The effective number of parliamentary parties rose from around 2.2 prior to reform in 1993 to 3.8 under the MMP system in 1996. Single-party governments were replaced by majority or minority coalitions. The proportion of women elected to office rose substantially, as did the proportion of Maori, Pacific Islander, and Asian MPs. In short, the MMP system in New Zealand fulfilled the first three steps illustrated in Figure 5.1 which are suggested by consociational theory.

There are questions, however, about subsequent steps in the chain of reasoning. Far from facilitating intercommunity understanding, as consociational accounts claim, the inclusion of more minor parties in parliament may have produced greater polarization around issues of ethnicity, following the rise of the New Zealand First. This party, founded by Winston Peters in 1993, adopted an anti-immigrant populist platform which challenged legal rights enjoyed by the Maori aboriginal population under the Treaty of Waitangi. The party won 8.3% of the vote and two seats in the 1993 general election, but their support rose sharply to 13.4% of the vote and 17 seats in 1996 after reform, and they entered government in coalition with the National Party. Their support subsequently slumped, but it rebounded again in the 2002 election, where New Zealand First was the third most popular party, with 10% of the parliamentary vote and 13 MPs.[49] New Zealand First can be seen as moderate on social policies but as part of the radical right family through its strong emphasis on economic and cultural nationalism. The party currently remains protectionist in its economic policy, calling for New Zealand ownership of key assets and infrastructure, arguing against economic globalization, and favoring limits on the extent of foreign ownership in the country. It presents a strong defense of cultural nationalism. For example, Winston Peter argued: "The public has legitimate concerns over the influx of immigrants – the dramatic changes in the ethnic mix – culture – and the other aspects of national identity – and the mindless, unthinking way change is inflicted on our society. In their contempt for the past, Labour and National have swept away many of the old landmarks – often selling them off to overseas investors – and have dismantled much that was valued and cherished by New Zealanders.... There are many apparent threats to our way of life from open door immigration policies, through to a growing obsession with the fundamentalism which has sprung up around the Treaty of Waitangi and to the disturbing increase in lawlessness in our society." The impact of electoral reform in New Zealand therefore seems to have increased the representation of ethnic minorities, but also to have politicized and polarized issues of ethnicity, leading both to the creation of the Maori party and to the popular backlash led by New Zealand First. New Zealand is an established democracy with a tolerant culture, so this process is unlikely to lead toward serious ethnic conflict; nevertheless in more fragile democracies and more deeply divided societies the politicization of latent ethnic identities carries certain well-known dangers. Moreover the last step in the logical chain of consociational theory also remains in question, as it is unclear whether electoral reform, and the inclusion of more ethnic minorities in parliament, has actually generated greater satisfaction with democracy among ethnic minority communities.[50]

CONCLUSIONS

The theory of consociationalism has been widely influential in shaping debates about the most appropriate electoral arrangements to adopt in divided societies and negotiated peace-settlements. Yet the claims have always proved controversial and systematic evidence has been lacking to test the evidence for some of the core contentions. This chapter has combined large-N cross-national time-series analysis with selected paired case studies about the consequences of changing the electoral rules in the cases of Britain and New Zealand.

The results confirm that PR electoral systems are more democratic than majoritarian systems, a pattern replicated irrespective of the choice of indicator used, and a pattern that was particularly marked in divided societies. In exploring how this process works, the case studies suggest that either PR with low thresholds or positive action strategies (or both) can be used to facilitate the election of representatives and groups drawn from minority communities. The adoption of AMS in Scotland and Wales has boosted the electoral success of nationalist parties in regional contests, although so far their support has not carried over into Westminster general elections. This process has also led toward greater party fragmentation in Scotland. In New Zealand, the MMP system has strengthened the inclusion of Maoris, Asians, and Pacific Islanders, although it has also facilitated the success of the New Zealand First party on a platform of cultural protection, and thus stirred up greater controversy about issues of Maori rights and multiculturalism. Whether this process has had a broader impact upon political attitudes and values, particular support for democracy among minority communities remains an open question and it may take successive elections over many years before any cultural impact becomes apparent. Electoral systems, moreover, are only one dimension of consociationalism. It may be that other institutions are more important for democratic consolidation, so we need to go on in the next chapter to consider the choice of types of presidential versus parliamentary executives.

6

Presidential and Parliamentary Executives

The decision to adopt either a presidential or a parliamentary executive is a critical aspect of constitutional design.[1] Considerable debate has surrounded which type is better for democratization. Reflecting upon developments in Latin America during the 1960s and 1970s, Juan Linz presented one of the most influential views, arguing that presidentialism presents substantial risks of political instability and even regime collapse.[2] The reasons, Linz suggests, are that in electoral democracies with presidential regimes, both parliaments and presidents have rival sources of popular legitimacy and authority, making it difficult to resolve disputes. Presidents hold office for a fixed term, reducing flexibility. Presidential elections are winner take all, raising the stakes and generating weak incentives for the losers to accept the legitimacy of the outcome. And the fusion of the offices of head of state and head of the government may reduce restraints on political leaders arising from checks and balances. Scholars have commonly concurred with Linz's argument.[3] Compared with parliamentary systems, for example, Riggs regards presidentialism as less capable of generating the representativeness and legitimacy required for the survival of democratic governance.[4] Stepan and Skach compared patterns of democratic consolidation until the early-1990s and concluded that parliamentary executives were indeed more effective in this regard than presidentialism. They argue that parliamentary democracies are more likely to allow the largest party to implement their program, even in multiparty systems. Unpopular or scandal-ridden prime ministers can be replaced by other senior party leaders without destabilizing the whole regime. Dual executives (where the head of government is separate from the head of state) are also less susceptible to military coups. And parliamentary democracy encourages long-term party-government careers, as backbenchers progress to ministerial office, strengthening party loyalties and the legislative experience of political leaders.[5]

Still no scholarly consensus exists about the claimed superiority of parliamentary executives for sustaining democracy. In response to Linz's diagnosis of potential maladies, Schugart and Carey argue that presidential executives display great diversity in their roles and formal powers, with different types, rather than all falling into a single category, and they challenge the notion that all contemporary presidential regimes are inherently more prone to break-down.[6] In an influential article, Mainwaring emphasized that only certain types of presidential regimes (notably those combined with multiparty systems) are particularly vulnerable to democratic instability, through generating executive-legislative deadlock, ideological polarization, and difficulties of inter-party coalition building.[7] Cheibub and Limongi conclude that if parliamentary regimes have a better record of survival than presidential regimes, this is not due to some of the causes most commonly offered to explain this phenomenon, such as the propensity of presidentialism for deadlock; indeed they speculate that regime instability may be associated with levels of centralization in the policymaking process, which is only contingently related to the structure of the executive.[8]

Much of the evidence concerning the debate about executive institutions has been derived from the experience of presidentialism in Latin America, a region strongly influenced by the US Constitution. The standard practice used in many previous studies has been to contrast the modern history of presidential regimes in Latin America with the record of parliamentary systems in Western Europe and Scandinavia. This limited analytical framework made it difficult to generate comparisons which ruled out other potentially confounding factors characteristic of each region which we have seen are also strongly associated with the success of democracy, notably lower levels of economic development and industrialization in Latin America.[9] The expansion of democracy during the third wave has facilitated a broader comparative focus; after the fall of the Berlin Wall, many post-Communist states such as Albania, Hungary, and Slovenia adopted popularly elected presidents in 'mixed' republics, which also have a prime minister leading the government.[10] A comparison of presidential powers in Central and Eastern Europe by Beliaev indicates that regimes with stronger presidential executives proved less effective at democratic consolidation during the 1990s, suggesting that the Latin American experience is not unique.[11] In Africa and Asia-Pacific, as well, many states have now adopted presidential or mixed executives. Blais, Massicotte, and Dobrynska compared 170 countries with a working parliament, and they found that, by the late-1990s, almost half had a directly elected president.[12] A comprehensive worldwide comparison also requires the analysis of other types of executives beyond elected presidents and parliamentary governments, taking account of nonelective presidencies, as well as more than a dozen contemporary states governed by ruling monarchies and a few regimes in the grip of military dictatorships without even the fig leaf of a nominal civilian president.

Therefore this chapter seeks to reexamine the evidence to see whether the type of executive influences (i) levels of democracy and democratic consolidation during the third wave over the last 30 years and (ii) broader indicators of regime instability, exemplified by the occurrence of political violence, coups d'etat, and leadership assassinations. The unit of analysis is the type of regime

TABLE 6.1. *Classification Criteria for Types of Executives*

	Military States	Ruling Monarchies	Presidential Republics	Mixed Republics	Parliamentary Monarchies
Unified or dual executive	There is a unified executive: the head of state is also head of the government.	There is a unified executive: the head of state and the head of government are fused in a single monarchical office.	There is a unified executive: the head of state and the head of government are fused in a single presidential office.	There is a dual executive: the president and the prime minister are separate posts; either office may be predominant.	There is a dual executive: the monarch is a ceremonial head of state and the prime minister leads the government.
Accession process	Usually a coup d'etat. The ruler who seizes power is a senior officer or group of officers from the military or a figurehead leader strongly backed by the armed forces.	The monarch is a hereditary ruler for life, following conventional rules of succession. The monarch appoints the head of government and the monarch may also appoint ministers and legislators.	The presidency is a nonhereditary fixed-term office. Presidents enter office through nonelective routes, indirect election, or direct election.	The posts of the president and prime minister are filled by various forms of indirect election, direct election, and appointment.	The leader of the party with an absolute parliamentary majority forms the government. Where no party has an absolute majority, conventionally the leader of the largest parliamentary party seeks to form a governing coalition.

Tenure in office	For as long as the military exert control.	The monarch cannot be removed from office except through retirement and succession, or through extraconstitutional means (a coup d'etat).	The president serves for a fixed term of office, unless removed by an exceptional process of impeachment or through extraconstitutional means (a coup d'etat).	There are varied forms of tenure; some prime ministers can be replaced by the president; others are directly elected.	The monarch cannot be removed from office except through retirement and succession. The government (including the prime minister and members of cabinet) can fall by defeat at a general election or by a nonconfidence motion passed by a majority of the legislature.
Power within the executive	There may be a military council of senior officers, or a separate civilian group of advisers.	Cabinet structures are highly hierarchical; the cabinet (and parliament) act in an advisory capacity to serve the monarch.	Cabinet structures are usually hierarchical with the president at the apex, members are appointed to serve the leader, cabinet responsibility is individualized, and major decisions may be taken by the president alone.	Cabinet structures may be hierarchical (following the model described for presidential republics) or collegial (following the model described for parliamentary monarchies).	Cabinet organization is usually collegial and composed of senior policymakers. The prime minister is conventionally regarded as 'first among equals'. Decisions are regarded as collective and binding upon all members.
Contemporary examples	Myanmar, Libya, Mauritania	Brunei, Morocco, Saudi Arabia, Swaziland, Oman, Tonga	Argentina, Costa Rica, Indonesia, Belarus, the Philippines, USA	France, India, Israel, Latvia, Hungary, Russia, Slovakia	Australia, Belgium, Denmark, Japan, Lesotho, Malaysia, Britain

in each nation-year worldwide from 1972 to 2003, and the study uses a longer time span than many previous studies, a broader range of countries and types of regimes drawn from different regions around the globe, and, to test the reliability of the results, the alternative measures of democracy already discussed earlier in the book. The standard controls used in previous chapters are also incorporated into the multivariate analysis, to see whether the relationship between the type of executive and the resilience of democracy is conditioned by factors such as patterns of socioeconomic development, the colonial history, levels of ethnic fractionalization, and the type of electoral and party systems. Finally, the conclusion considers the implications for constitutional reformers and what can be done to overcome the 'perils of presidentialism' for democratic stability.

CLASSIFYING TYPES OF EXECUTIVES

The first issue confronting any empirical study is how best to classify different types of executives. This study develops a typology according to three features: (i) the constitutional adoption of a unitary or dual executive, (ii) the constitutional process of accession for the head of state and the head of government, and (iii) the constitutional rules governing tenure in office. All these criteria are logically related to the degree of power-sharing within the regime. Five distinct categories of executives based on these factors are identified, as summarized in Table 6.1, including military dictatorships, ruling monarchies, parliamentary monarchies, presidential republics (subcategorized into nonelective, indirectly elected and directly elected types), and mixed republics. To operationalize the conceptual framework, the states falling into each of these categories are classified and identified worldwide each year from 1972 to 2003 using cross-national time-series data from Banks (2000), combining the classifications of the formal head of state and the formal head of government (derived from the constitution), along with the constitutional rules for their selection and tenure in office. Figure 6.1 illustrates the distribution of types of executives in contemporary states (classified in 2003) while Figure 6.2 shows trends over time in each category. This classification is relatively comprehensive, but worldwide, out of 191 nations, seven contemporary states failed to fit neatly into these conceptual boxes, such as Switzerland (with a rotating presidency in the federal council), Afghanistan (ruled by a theocracy in the Taliban), and San Marino (with two co-princes), as discussed later.[13]

Ruling Monarchies

One of the oldest forms of government, contemporary monarchies are associated with many titles, most commonly translated as king or queen, but there are also emirs (Kuwait, Qatar), sultans (Oman), paramount rulers (Malaysia), sovereign princes (Monaco), heavenly emperors (Japan), and co-princes (Andorra).[14] As a type of regime, *ruling* monarchies are defined by

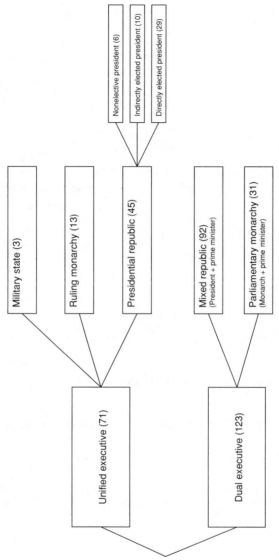

FIGURE 6.1. Types of Executives (with the Number of Contemporary States Falling into Each Category)

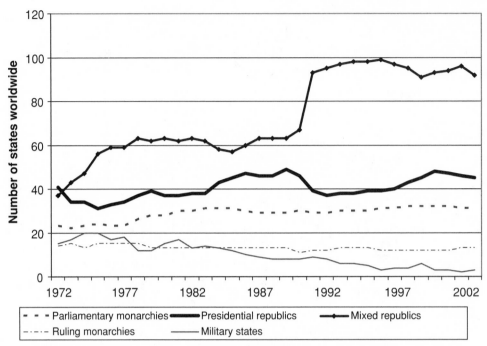

FIGURE 6.2. Trends in Types of Executives Worldwide, 1972–2003. *Note:* Coded from Arthur S. Banks. 2000. *Cross-Polity Time-Series Database.* Binghamton: State University of New York-Binghamton. www.databanks.sitehosting.net

three main rules. First, there is a unitary executive with power centralized in the monarch. All other executive, legislative, and judicial bodies are subordinate to the sovereign, and the constitution is also subject to royal decree or amendment. The monarch exercises substantive power as the head of state. The king or queen may also be the formal head of government or may appoint a premier as head of government, cabinet members, and sometimes members of the legislature as well. Second, in terms of accession, contemporary ruling monarchies are determined through a hereditary process of dynastic inheritance through the bloodline. Most European states follow the principle of primogeniture, although the specific rules determining the process of hereditary accession to the throne vary.[15] Some presidents are also succeeded in office by their sons; for example, in North Korea, Kim Il-sung (the Great Leader) was replaced after his death by his son, Kim Jong-il. In Syria, on his death in 2000, President Hafez al-Assad was succeeded by his son, Bashar al-Assad, who was confirmed in an unopposed referendum. Some dictators have also attempted to found a royal dynasty; for example, during the mid-1970s, Jean-Bédel Bokassa also proclaimed himself emperor, complete with coronation, in the Central African Republic. But new monarchies are only regarded as established if the process of succession continues over more than two generations. Third, in terms of tenure, the monarchy is a lifetime position; monarchs cannot be removed from office except through voluntary retirement and the traditional process of royal succession or through extraconstitutional means, such as a revolutionary overthrow of the royal family or coup d'etat.

Therefore the three characteristics of this type of regime (a unitary executive, dynastic accession, and a lifetime position) concentrate absolute power most effectively in the hands of the ruling monarch, the royal family, and their entourage of courtiers and advisers. Ruling monarchs lack effective checks on their power, and they remain unaccountable to other institutions of state. It might be thought that this type of regime would have passed away over time, but, in 2002 Banks classifies 13 nation-states as ruling monarchies (defined as nations with a monarch as both head of state and as head of government). Half are in the Gulf with the remainder scattered across many continents.[16] Contemporary ruling or absolute monarchies include the king of Bahrain, the sultan of Oman, the emir of Qatar, the king of Swaziland, the king or queen of Tonga, the sovereign prince of Monaco, and the sultanate of Brunei Darussalam. The total number of states governed by ruling monarchies is almost untouched by the third wave of democratization during the last three decades, although some states such as Bahrain, Morocco, and Nepal have experimented with more liberal reforms in recent years.

Ruling monarchies are perhaps best exemplified as a contemporary type of regime by Saudi Arabia. The Al Saud family, which came to power in the eighteenth century, has governed this country through successive kings. The current head of state and the head of government is King Abdullah Bin-Abd-al-Aziz Al Saud, who formally succeeded the late King Fahd, his half brother, in August 2005. The cabinet (Council of Ministers), especially the core ministries, includes many members of the royal family, such as Prince Sultan Bin-Abd-al-Aziz Al Saud (the first deputy prime minister), Prince Saud al-Faysal Bin-Abd-al-Aziz Al Saud (the foreign minister), and Prince Nayif Bin-Abd-al-Aziz Al Saud (the minister of the interior). The cabinet is appointed by the king. The consultative council or Majlis al-Shura has 120 members and a chairman appointed by the king for a four-year term. The royal family exerts strict controls over opposition forces, including stringent censorship of the news media, banning criticism of the House of Al Saud. Saudi Arabia has introduced very cautious moves toward democratic reform, with municipal elections held in 2005, but women were unable to participate as voters or candidates, political parties were banned, the opposition is organized from outside the country, and activists who publicly seek reform risk being jailed. In short, ruling monarchies are relatively rare worldwide, with most historical cases gradually evolving into parliamentary monarchies, where substantive power is transferred to the legislature led by the prime minister, or to presidential republics, where the trappings of royalty are overthrown. But in the remaining ruling monarchies, power remains highly concentrated and unaccountable.

Parliamentary Monarchies

In Western Europe and Scandinavia, most ruling monarchies lost power through incremental processes of reform which gradually strengthened the role and independence of the cabinet (led by the prime minister) and legislature. Ruling monarchies transitioned into parliamentary monarchies, exemplified by developments in Great Britain, Belgium, and Sweden. Elsewhere in Europe, where monarchies failed to adapt to pressures for reform, revolutionary processes led to the violent overthrow of royal families and the establishment of republics, notably in France and Russia. Parliamentary monarchies are defined by three criteria.

First, parliamentary monarchies have dual executives, with a clear separation of the roles of head of state and head of government. The monarch remains as a largely symbolic head of state, with some nominal ceremonial roles when representing the nation at official diplomatic events. For constitutional monarchies, all royal acts are subject to the parliament.[17] The separation of offices in dual executives is thought to promote political stability; for example, the monarch preserves continuity in a prime ministerial leadership succession or when the government is defeated by an election.[18] Moreover, this division makes the state less vulnerable to decapitation by a military coup d'etat or popular revolution.

In terms of selection and tenure, prime ministers are indirectly elected and government office always remains dependent upon maintaining support in parliament. General elections provide voters with a choice of parties, including the leadership team headed by the party leader as well as the party platform. Usually by convention the leader of the party winning an absolute majority of parliamentary seats over all other parties appoints the cabinet and heads the administration. In the case of a minority administration, the leader of the largest party in parliament engages in a period of negotiations with other party leaders, creating a coalition cabinet with an absolute majority in parliament. Substantive executive power resides with the government, consisting of the prime minister and the leadership team of cabinet ministers. The party linkage between the executive and legislature, and the government's majority in parliament, means that the cabinet is usually capable of driving through most of its legislative agenda and rarely suffers an outright defeat. The ability of the cabinet to implement its manifesto is particularly strong if the governing party has a substantial parliamentary majority and controls all cabinet portfolios. Parliamentary government reinforces the incentives for cooperation, and reduces the dangers of potential conflict or even stalemate, between the executive and legislature.

The prime minister and cabinet hold power during their term of office so long as they continue to receive the trust and support of the majority of backbenchers within the legislature. The system encourages collaboration between the legislature and executive, maintains interelectoral flexibility, and functions as an automatic safety valve in the case of an unpopular prime minister or government; if the administration loses a vote of confidence or censure in parliament, then by convention they have to resign. In this situation, the government can call fresh elections, or they can stand down to be replaced by another party or party coalition under new leadership, without the sort of constitutional crisis generated by impeachment proceedings used to remove unpopular presidents. Governments rarely face a no confidence vote, however, because legislators in the governing party or parties are reluctant to trigger the threat of a dissolution of parliament followed by an early parliamentary election, thereby risking their own positions. The threat of dissolution reinforces party discipline. Indeed leaders can sometimes use a no confidence vote attached to legislative proposals as a way to bring backbench dissidents to heel.[19] Strong party discipline also binds legislators to the government's program. The fate of party backbenchers is tied collectively to that of their leadership. Backbenchers are still prone to rebel against the party leadership on key legislative measures – they do not simply acquiesce to the whips – but this activity does not necessarily defeat government proposals, still less bring down the government.[20] The prime minister can also be replaced by a leadership contest within his or her own party, without any actions by parliament or calling a popular election; for example, this occurred with the end of Mrs. Thatcher's long dominance within the British Conservative Party and her successor as prime minister in 1990 by John Major.[21] Beyond the vote of confidence, backbenchers have many other channels of oversight to scrutinize the government's actions and proposals. The chain of accountability extends one further step, because members of parliament are accountable to the public through general elections held at regular intervals.

In terms of intra-executive powers, the prime minister generally leads a more collegial cabinet, rather than a hierarchical structure.[22] In parliamentary monarchies, cabinets are composed of a collective leadership team including seasoned senior ministers, many of whom have long experience of collaborating together within the parliamentary party as opposition shadow ministers, as well as working in different government departments when in power. There are collective decision making and the doctrine of collective responsibility; in public, ministers are expected to present a united front supporting decisions made by the majority of cabinet members. The prime minister appoints members of cabinet, reinforcing the incentive for backbenchers to remain loyal to the leadership, in the hope of career advancement to government office. Political parties act as the glue binding together the executive and legislature, as well as linking cabinet members collectively within the executive.

In summary, in parliamentary monarchies, governments are subject to multiple forms of accountability. In electoral democracies, governments are subject to occasional popular elections every few years. In between these contests, the prime minister's continued grip on power is always contingent upon maintaining the support of cabinet colleagues and carrying a majority of parliamentary backbenchers. If the government loses a vote of confidence in parliament, they fall. This creates incentives for the leadership to consult backbenchers, via party whips, and to pay attention to any potential revolts. Prime ministers are most powerful in parliamentary monarchies where they head single-party governments which enjoy a solid majority over the opposition parties. In this context, prime ministers have many opportunities to implement much of their legislative agenda and party platform or manifesto, because of the fusion of the cabinet executive and legislature within one party. Where parliamentary monarchies have coalition governments, prime ministers face greater limits on their autonomy. They share executive power with cabinet ministers from other parties, requiring a process of bargaining and negotiation over key policy decisions within the government. Leaders also remain continually dependent upon the support of a multiparty coalition in parliament to pass the government's legislative proposals. Governments face the continual threat of a no confidence vote in parliament, and they remain accountable to the electorate for their record and performance at regular intervals. In parliamentary monarchies, prime ministers also share power with the symbolic head of state. As such, prime ministers who head coalition governments also exercise considerable power but face multiple checks on their autonomy, an arrangement which comes closest to the power-sharing regime advocated by consociational theorists.

Parliamentary monarchies can be identified by the Banks dataset on the basis of the classification of the formal head of state (monarchy) and the formal head of government (prime ministerial) in constitutional conventions. The definition suggests that 23 nation-states were parliamentary monarchies in 1973, rising in number during the 1970s, with 31 such regimes in 2003. One-third of all parliamentary monarchies are located in Western Europe and Scandinavia, but many are also found in Asia-Pacific (10) and in the Caribbean (9). The influence of the British Commonwealth is evident in the distribution of parliamentary monarchies, with countries such as Canada, Australia, and Jamaica retaining the Crown as the symbolic head of state, as well as adopting the Westminster model of a bicameral parliament.

Presidential Republics

Presidential republics also have a unitary executive, where the head of state and head of government are fused into a single office.[23] The president is thus also the symbolic leader of the nation, as well as heading the day-to-day business of running administrative departments. By contrast with ruling monarchies, however, presidencies do not have dynastic accession in attaining office by the bloodline over more than two generations, and, although a few have declared themselves presidents for life, they usually hold power for a constitutionally fixed term of office.

Presidencies are a nonhereditary office, attained through three routes to power. In *nonelective presidencies*, presidents are empowered by being appointed or self-appointed to office. There is a fine line between a military junta which governs explicitly and civilian presidencies which are appointed and backed by the armed forces, sometimes as a façade for maintaining power in the hands of the military, as we have observed earlier in the case of President Faure Gnassingbe in Togo. Judgments are required for the accurate classification of regimes in countries such as Pakistan and Libya, where the military play an important role but where there are also civilian elements in government. In some states, presidents may also hold office after being appointed by a single hegemonic party, where the leadership emerged from an internal power struggle among elites or from a process of one-party internal elections. *Indirectly elected presidencies* are exemplified by the US Constitution, which specifies an Electoral College. The college is composed of a number of delegated electors drawn from each state, depending upon its population size. Each delegate is committed to voting for a specified candidate determined by the popular vote in each state, but there have been exceptional cases of 'disloyal' delegates. In several close American elections (notably in 1876, 1888, and 2000), while one candidate received the most popular votes, another candidate managed to win more electoral votes in the Electoral College and so won the presidency. Finally, *directly elected presidencies* are filled through popular elections. These may be free and fair contests with multiparty competition, but they may also be a manipulated plebiscite or referendum, characterized by restrictions on the ability of opposition forces to register and campaign, ballot rigging, or voter intimidation, where only one candidate may be listed on the ballot.[24] In most cases, contests use plurality or majoritarian electoral systems, with a few more complex or mixed procedures.[25] Blais, Massicotte, and Dobrzynska found that out of 91 countries with a directly elected president, 61 used the majority rule, most often the majority-runoff or second ballot procedure.[26]

With a few exceptional cases (Switzerland and Bosnia-Herzegovina), the one-person presidency cannot be shared, making the office a winner-take-all position.[27] This characteristic is thought to provide the losing parties and candidates with weak incentives to accept the legitimacy of the outcome. This feature may be especially destabilizing in the absence of political trust and confidence in the fairness of electoral processes, such as in states emerging from conflict or in newer electoral democracies with a history of manipulated or fraudulent electoral practices. Potential problems associated with this system are illustrated by the constitutional crisis triggered by the July 2006 presidential elections in Mexico, determining the successor to Vincente Fox. Filipe Calderón (National Action Party [PAN]) was declared the winner, although he had only a wafer-thin edge, estimated at less that 244,000 votes or 0.58 percentage point separating the main candidates. The declaration led to legal challenges by rival Manuel López Obrador (Party of the Democratic Revolution [PRD]), repeated demands that the Federal Electoral Institute (IFE) carry out a total recount, and massive protests in Zocalo Square, Mexico City. The tight result raised troubling doubts about the legitimacy of the outcome, producing months of political uncertainty and heated unrest, and called into question the stability of Mexico's 2001 transition to a competitive multiparty system. By contrast, depending upon the final distribution of seats, a similarly close result under a proportional representation electoral system in a parliamentary system would have given the government a narrow parliamentary majority but it would also have rewarded the opposition with many members of parliament and a powerful position in holding the government to account. More deep-rooted problems of executive power are illustrated by cases where presidents have been willing to trample upon the rights of the opposition and abuse power to perpetuate their rule, exemplified by President Alberto Fujimori's government in Peru and President Alexander Lukashenko's grip on power in Belarus.

In contrast to that of prime ministers, presidential tenure is not dependent upon the legislature. Indeed presidents are rarely constitutionally removed from power during their term in office except through the exceptional circumstances of impeachment, or through unconstitutional processes, such as cases where the military intervenes in a violent coup d'etat. Presidents who are directly elected for a fixed term remain accountable at intervals to the electorate, but not to the legislature in their day-to-day actions. As a result of mutual independence, there is weaker incentive for cooperation and collaboration between presidents and legislatures. If there is a headlong clash between the executive and legislature, policy stalemate and gridlock, or another form of political impasse between these bodies, it becomes difficult to overcome this condition by replacing the president through legitimate constitutional channels. During the term of office, the removal of a president normally requires an extraordinary process of impeachment by the legislature and the courts, entailing a major constitutional crisis and a period of serious political instability and uncertainty. Such initiatives have often followed revelations of major leadership scandals and financial corruption. Cases of impeachment used to be relatively rare, but in Latin America they occurred in Brazil in 1992, Venezuela and Guatemala in 1993, Ecuador in 1997, and Paraguay in 1999.[28] Elsewhere, President Bingu wa Mutharika was threatened with impeachment proceedings in Malawi in 2005, there have been a number of attempts in the Philippines against President Gloria Arroya, Lithuanian President Rolandas Paksas was removed from office in 2004 following this procedure, and President Roh Moo-hyun was impeached the same year in South Korea. Other presidencies have been removed by a mass popular uprising and extraconstitutional means, such as the downfall of President Estrada by people power in the Philippines in 2001, following a failed attempt at impeachment, entailing considerable destabilization and turmoil. In Ecuador, as well, massive protests by indigenous groups, coupled with actions by the military, led to the removal of President Mahaud in 2000. The unitary structure of the executive is believed to make presidencies more vulnerable than dual executives to decapitation via a coup d'etat.

Last, in terms of intra-executive power, in presidential systems the cabinet is also usually hierarchical, where members are appointed to serve the personal leader at the apex of the administration, rather than collegial.[29] Hierarchical structures generate weak notions of collective cabinet responsibility, the doctrine that decisions are taken by majority vote and all members are then bound by these decisions. Instead loyalties are to the person of the president. The leader consults the cabinet, but major decisions may be taken by the president alone, or in conjunction with a few core advisers, even if he or she overrules the wishes of the majority of cabinet members.[30]

All these characteristic features usually concentrate considerable power in the hands of a single chief executive who is relatively autonomous in relation to both the legislature and the judiciary, and who thus has less incentive to cooperate and compromise with these institutions. The defining feature of presidential republics is that unitary executives combine the positions of nonhereditary head of government (running the country) and head of state (the symbolic national leader). This combination of roles in one office removes an important source of checks and balances across institutions which are evident in dual executives. In terms of the formal head of the government (as specified in the constitution) the Banks dataset estimates that there were 41 presidential republics in 1972, and this number remains fairly stable over time, with 45 states falling into this category in 2003. Today presidential republics predominate throughout Latin America, as is well known, but this form of regime is also fairly common in sub-Saharan Africa and in Asia and the Pacific. It should be noted that if the Banks dataset is classified by the *effective* head of government (rather than the formal head of government), then the estimated number of presidential regimes expands substantially. But this requires a subjective judgment of the coders about the real location of power in the regime, whether with the premier or president. For example, President Putin exerts considerable power within the Russian Federation, including appointing the premier. Should this system be classified as a mixed republic with a dual executive or as an effective presidential system? This study chooses to focus on the formal office as defined in the constitution or legal system, as the most reliable and consistent source of classifications.

Mixed Republics

As Figure 6.2 illustrates, recent years have seen a growing number of formal constitutions which share powers between a president and prime minister, with a sharp jump in the number of these regimes in the early-1990s. Mixed republics are exemplified by the constitution adopted by the French Fifth Republic. Maurice Duverger introduced the notion of 'semipresidential' or 'mixed' executives and subsequent scholars have debated how best to define and label this category.[31] This is the most complicated category to classify, depending upon the precise distinctions which are drawn by different scholars. In this study, regimes are categorized as 'mixed republics' when they contain a dual executive containing both a nonhereditary president as head of state and a prime minister as the formal or constitutional head of government. No judgment is made about the location of power within the executive, which can vary substantially. Whether the president or prime minister is dominant in these systems, and hence who is the effective head of government, depends substantially upon the selection processes and specific constitutional arrangements, for example, the distribution of the powers of veto, nomination, decree, budgetary, and legislative initiative, as well as whether the premier is indirectly elected (and thus with a democratic mandate) or appointed to office (and thus dependent upon the president). In mixed republics, in reality presidents can be predominant over the legislature and the prime minister, such as in Russia under President Putin, but presidents may also hold office as purely symbolic national figureheads, as, for example, in Ireland, India, and Germany. In mixed republics, prime ministers also differ in their roles and powers; some run the government fairly independently with a largely symbolic presidency. Other premiers are appointed by the president and they remain weak figureheads.

The best-known example of mixed republics is probably the Constitution of the French Fifth Republic, which established a prime minister who is chosen by the president but who nevertheless needs to gain support in the National Assembly. When the president is drawn from one party, but the opposition parties are in control of the legislature, then the president often has to select an opposition prime minister, a process known as cohabitation. Traditionally only a few countries could be categorized as mixed republics; Duverger, for example, recognized France, Finland, Austria, Ireland, Iceland, Weimar Germany, and Portugal within Western Europe. In recent years, however, many more nations outside this region have included both presidents and prime ministers within the constitution, including many post-Communist states. The Banks dataset estimates that there were 37 mixed executives in 1972 (defined as states with a presidential head of state and a prime minister as the *formal* head of government). By 2003, this category had almost tripled to 92. Rejecting both the classical form of parliamentarianism and presidentialism, one of the most striking developments in new constitutions has been the popularity of this form of regime, for example, throughout Central Europe.

Military States

The last type of unitary executive concerns military states, where power resides with the armed forces. Where a junta rules, there is a small group of senior officers who exert control; in other cases, a single senior commander takes over the reins of head of state. Military regimes are also characterized by the use of martial law. Since the early-1990s, this type of regime has declined. After the end of the cold war, military regimes throughout Latin America were replaced with electoral democracies. In the Middle East, states such as Syria and Egypt that were once clearly military dictatorships have switched to other forms of autocracy. Nevertheless some clear cases remain among contemporary states which are run by military dictatorships, notably Myanmar after the military invalidated the results of the 1990 assembly elections. Other contemporary examples include Libya under Colonel Gaddafi, Guinea-Bissau after a coup led to the empowerment of President Joao Bernardo Vieira in 2003, and Mauritania after a military coup in August 2005. Pakistan fell into this category after a coup in October 1999 led by General Pervez Musharraf, who assumed the title of chief executive as head of state and then, in June 2001, of president.

Nevertheless this country's classification remains complicated, as the regime has seen growing elements of civilian rule in a mixed republic, with parliamentary elections, and in April 2002 Musharraf held a flawed referendum to extend his rule for another five years. Accordingly, to be consistent, Pakistan is probably best described today as a presidential republic (with military backing) rather than a pure military state. In Thailand the military ruled on and off from 1947 to 1992, when they were replaced in democratic elections by a parliamentary monarchy. In September 2006, however, with the endorsement of the king, the army commander in chief, General Sonthi Boonyaratglin, seized power in a bloodless coup while Thaksin Shinawatra, the prime minister, was overseas. In Fiji, persistent racial tensions have led to considerable instability, including a military coup in 2006, the fourth time this has occurred in the last 20 years. According to the Banks dataset, the number of military states rose from 15 in 1972 to 20 in 1975 (under what Huntington termed the second reverse wave of democratization), then fell steadily over the years to 5 states in 2006.

TYPES OF EXECUTIVES VERSUS SCALED MEASURES OF EXECUTIVE POWER

Before proceeding to analyze the data, we need to consider whether the typology is adequate for the purpose. In recent years some revisionist scholars have questioned the older tradition of classifying types of executives, on the grounds that this process fails to capture important cross-national variations in the distribution of power among chief executive, cabinets, ministers, bureaucrats, and legislatures.[32] Echoing the debate we have already reviewed about alternative measures of democracy, both typologies of executives and continuous scaled indices of the powers of the chief executive have been used for comparison. Such a scale could potentially help to resolve difficult issues of classification, such as contrasts evident between the effective power of presidents in Russia and in Ireland, both with formal dual executives in mixed republics but, in practice, with very different roles. A number of power indices have been developed; for example, to explain institutional choices in post-Communist presidencies, Frye created a scale of executive powers and classified regimes on the basis of a checklist of 27 functions, such as the formal constitutional powers of the president to propose legislation, appoint judges, and call elections.[33] Shugart and Carey compared presidencies by using a simpler list of 10 powers, weighted with a scoring system, for example, whether presidents have a full or partial veto over legislative bills, whether they have budgetary powers, and whether they can appoint cabinet ministers with or without the need for legislative confirmation processes.[34] Building on this approach, Metcalf sought to develop and refine the Shugart and Carey scoring system.[35]

Yet it remains problematic to classify regimes in terms of the formal legal and constitutional powers, which may differ substantially from informal practices. Attempts to evaluate the underlying distribution of power are inherently subjective. Executive powers can also vary substantially over time, according to the specific officeholders. In established democracies such as Britain, for example, with certain established conventions but without a written constitution, both relatively weak and strong prime ministers are evident historically; some leaders have exerted an iron grip over decisions made by their cabinet, with other opting for a more collegiate role.[36] It is often difficult to distinguish the personal style adopted by individual leaders, and the way they use the constraints and opportunities of office, from the constitutional roles allocated to the institution. Other sources shaping leadership power include the status, skills, popularity, and expertise of particular prime ministers and presidents. The role of the particular leader is particularly important during periods of democratic transition, such as those occurring during the early-1990s in Central and Eastern Europe, when the distribution of authority between the executive and legislature remains fluid and ambiguous, and there is a contested struggle over the appropriate roles for each body.[37] Classifying the changing powers of the executive branch over time in one country is a formidable task, let alone attempting such an exercise on a consistent basis over time and across countries.

Continuous scales of executive power also remain sensitive to the specific indicators used for identifying the functions of the chief executive, and the subjective and somewhat arbitrary weighting which is given to these measures. Is it more important, for example, if a president has the constitutional power to dissolve the legislative assembly, to appoint ministers, or to veto proposed bills? There are no agreed guidelines or yardsticks to evaluate these functions. It is also unclear whether a similar approach could be applied to assess and compare prime ministerial powers across a wide range of parliamentary systems, an area which is strikingly underresearched.[38] Moreover the overall powers of the executive and legislature are also dependent upon many broader constitutional arrangements, such as whether the regime is unitary or federal, whether the courts and judiciary are powerful or circumscribed, and whether the bureaucracy is part of a hierarchical structure within departments headed by a minister, or whether it functions relatively autonomously. Tsebelis has proposed an alternative comparative framework, which counts the number of institutional and partisan veto players in the process of policy change.[39] This approach is valuable, for example, in emphasizing that presidential systems can have multiple institutional veto players, whereas prime ministers in single-party parliaments and unitary states can have a single institutional veto player. But the veto players approach is less useful for analyzing the specific impact of types of executives on democracy, since many other institutional factors, such as party systems, are brought into the analysis. Therefore although scaled indicators of the powers of the executive appear better suited for capturing subtle constitutional differences among states, in practice, given the current state of research, the lack of precision involved in generating the existing indices reduces their consistency and reliability.

By contrast, simpler and more parsimonious typologies of major types of executives, focusing on a few core constitutional features, attract greater consensus in the research literature.[40] As with any attempt at developing clear and comprehensive institutional typologies, difficult boundary issues remain in certain cases which refuse to fit neatly into conceptual boxes. This is especially true for attempts to classify mixed republics, where it is unclear whether the president or prime minister is effectively the more powerful office.[41] Nevertheless, despite this qualification, comparative typologies of executive institutions generate more consistent comparisons than continuous scales of executive power. The classifications developed here aim to be comprehensive, covering all or nearly all contemporary states worldwide. There remain some cases which are not classified, for example, failed states where it is difficult to identify the form of central authority, such as Afghanistan prior to adoption of the new constitution, Iraq immediately after the downfall of Saddam Hussein, and states which were experiencing radical regime change in any particular year, such as the Central African Republic in 2003. The classification rules generate categories which are independent of the measures of democracy, in order to prevent conflating the independent and dependent variables. Hence this study classifies all types of presidential executives, including those rising through nonelective routes, not merely those leaders who hold office through direct elections. The typology which is employed is also relatively parsimonious, as it is founded on a few simple and observable rules, a process which facilitates replication, encourages transparency, and generates greater consensus about the results of the classification. The typology also does not stray too far from the normal distinctions and commonsense categories found in everyday language.

TYPES OF EXECUTIVES AND DEMOCRACY

Are democracies less stable under presidential executives, as Linz claims? In the light of the ongoing debate, we can reexamine the evidence for this issue by comparing the record of democracy, using the indicators employed in earlier chapters, against the different types of executive arrangements which have been delineated. To operationalize the typology, the classification of the head of state and the chief executive office is derived from the cross-national time-series dataset provided by Arthur S. Banks.[42] This dataset measures the type of executive used worldwide in 191 nations on an annual basis, so that again nation-year is the unit of analysis. The dataset provides about 5,000 cases (regime-year) which can be classified. The multivariate models which are used for analysis incorporate the battery of controls which we have already established as relevant for explaining processes of democratization in previous chapters. The models control patterns of socioeconomic development, the colonial history of each country, levels of ethnic fractionalization, and the type of electoral and party systems. The models used for analysis focus upon three alternative dependent variables, namely, whether the type of executive influences (i) contemporary levels of democracy and patterns of democratic consolidation during the third wave over the last 30 years, and (ii) broader indicators of regime instability, exemplified by the occurrence of political violence, coups d'etat, and leadership assassinations. In each case, after applying controls,

TABLE 6.2. *Mean Democracy Scores by Type of Executive*

		FH Liberal Democracy	Vanhanen Participatory Democracy	Polity IV Constitutional Democracy	Cheibub Contested Democracy
Parliamentary monarchy	Mean	88.3	43.0	92.4	86.0
	N	911	774	570	852
PM indirectly elected		89.2	43.7	93.0	87.7
PM nonelected		37.1	3.0	40.6	0.0
Mixed executive	Mean	53.0	21.5	49.2	39.9
	N	2344	2023	2027	2243
Directly elected		49.4	16.9	42.4	32.6
Indirectly elected		64.5	32.3	67.7	58.7
Nonelected		27.2	1.7	18.6	2.7
Presidential republic	Mean	58.5	15.9	54.2	45.4
	N	1306	1115	1115	1246
Directly elected		64.0	21.2	63.8	57.7
Indirectly elected		64.3	12.0	51.4	40.4
Nonelected		24.9	0.2	14.2	1.0
Monarchy	Mean	40.9	0.5	8.2	0.9
	N	404	326	322	349
Military state	Mean	30.2	1.0	17.4	0.6
	N	321	308	282	313
TOTAL	Mean	57.2	20.2	49.8	42.2
	N	5885	4798	4553	5366
Coefficient of association (eta)		0.506	0.547	0.506	0.481
Sig. (P)		0.000	0.000	0.000	0.000

Note: See text for details. All democracy scales are standardized to 100 points, for comparison.
Source: Coded from Arthur S. Banks. 2000. *Cross-Polity Time-Series Database.* Binghamton: State University of New York-Binghamton. www.databanks.sitehosting.net

military states and ruling monarchies would be expected to prove the least democratic of all regimes. Military states are also expected to be the most vulnerable to political instability; many came to power through a coup d'etat, often in states with a history of regime instability and violent conflict, and they may also be overthrown in this way. If the Linz thesis is correct, then all forms of presidential republics (nonelective, indirectly elected, and directly elected) would be expected to prove less democratic and less stable than all parliamentary monarchies. Mixed republics would be expected to fall somewhere between the position of presidential republics and parliamentary monarchies.

Does systematic evidence demonstrate these propositions, in particular the supposed virtues of parliamentary executives for sustaining the process of democratization and preventing democratic breakdown, as Linz suggests? Table 6.2 first compares the mean score of different regimes on the four indicators of democracy (Freedom House, Polity IV, Vanhanen, and Cheibub

TABLE 6.3. *Classification of Types of Executives by Region, 2003*

	Parliamentary Monarchy	Presidential Republic	Mixed Republic	Monarchy	Military State	Other	Total
Sub-Saharan Africa	1	17	27	1	1	2	49
Asia-Pacific	10	8	14	4	1	0	37
Central and Eastern Europe	0	0	26	0	0	1	27
Middle East	0	1	8	7	1	2	19
North America	1	2	0	0	0	0	3
Central and South America	9	16	7	0	0	0	32
Scandinavia	3	0	2	0	0	0	5
Western Europe	7	1	8	1	0	2	19
TOTAL	31	45	92	13	3	7	191

Note: The number of states falling into each category in 2003.

Source: Coded from Arthur S. Banks. 2000. *Cross-Polity Time-Series Database.* Binghamton: State University of New York-Binghamton. www.databanks.sitehosting.net

and Ghandi), examining the significance of the difference in the mean scores (using ANOVA), without applying any prior controls.

The initial results appear to confirm the Linz thesis; irrespective of the indicator of democracy chosen for analysis, all cases of parliamentary monarchies achieve higher mean scores than all types of presidential republics. Moreover the difference in scores by type of regime is statistically significant and also substantially large; on the 100-point scales, presidential regimes have democracy scores which are between one-third and one-half of those recorded for parliamentary monarchies. Also confirming expectations, monarchies and military states achieve the lowest scores according to these indicators. Mixed republics, however, are more difficult to interpret, but overall they score closer to presidential republics than to parliamentary monarchies. Moreover the difference between presidential republics and parliamentary monarchies is not simply the product of whether the executive is nonelected, indirectly elected, or directly elected. As the mean scores show, the directly and indirectly elected presidential republics continued to display consistently far lower scores on all the democracy indices than the indirectly elected premiers in parliamentary monarchies. All these estimates, however, remain preliminary since there are no controls for the prior conditions in each state, for example, levels of economic development. As already observed, the types of executives cluster by region (see Table 6.3); for example, more than half of all the contemporary ruling monarchies are in Middle Eastern states. Presidential republics are rare in Western Europe, although fairly common in sub-Saharan Africa and Latin America, while mixed republics

TABLE 6.4. *Types of Executives and Democracy, All Societies Worldwide*

	Liberal Democracy Freedom House			Constitutional Democracy Polity IV			Participatory Democracy Vanhanen		
	B	PCSE	P	B	PCSE	P	B	PCSE	P
INSTITUTIONAL RULES									
Presidential republics	−5.79	.873	***	−9.80	1.38	***	−5.46	.731	***
Mixed republics	−10.77	.803	***	−14.25	1.26	***	−3.40	.655	***
Ruling monarchies	−15.13	1.43	***	−44.50	2.31	***	−21.09	1.18	***
Military states	−24.19	1.37	***	−34.12	2.06	***	−13.65	1.07	***
CONTROLS									
Log GDP/capita	12.91	.589	***	10.1	.886	***	11.88	.482	***
Ex-British colony	9.35	.616	***	10.7	.968	***	2.56	.503	***
Middle East	−7.57	1.19	***	−2.69	1.79		−3.81	.914	***
Regional diffusion	.556	.020	***	.582	.020	***	.662	.019	***
Ethnic fractionalization	−7.91	1.14	***	−1.86	1.80		−5.60	.946	***
Population size	.000	.000	***	.000	.000	***	.000	.000	***
Area size	.001	.000	***	.002	.000	***	.000	.000	***
PR electoral system for lower house	2.71	.596	***	6.32	.886	***	3.00	.488	***
Constant	−6.70			5.17					
No. of observations	4766			3939			4127		
Adjusted R²	.620			.585			.688		

Note: The default (comparison) is parliamentary monarchies. Entries for liberal democracy, constitutional democracy, and participatory democracy 100-point scales are unstandardized OLS regression coefficients (with their panel-corrected standard errors) and the significance (P) of the coefficients for the pooled time-series cross-national analysis obtained using Stata's xtpcse command. For the measures of democracy, see Chapter 2. For the classification of the type of executives, see Figure 6.1. For details of all the variables, see the Technical Appendix. Significant at * the 0.10 level, ** the 0.05 level, and *** the 0.01 level.

are found in most countries in Central and Eastern Europe. Many countries with parliamentary monarchies are within the British Commonwealth. This geographic distribution reinforces the need for multivariate analysis to rule out other confounding factors, such as levels of development or colonial traditions, which affect both the adoption of a particular type of constitutional executive and levels of democratic consolidation.

Table 6.4 presents the results of the multivariate analysis. The models for the 100-point standardized scales of liberal democracy, constitutional democracy, and participatory democracy use ordinary least squares regression (with their panel-corrected standard errors), where the unit of analysis is the regime-year, as in previous chapters. After applying the standard range of controls employed earlier, the results confirm that, as Linz argued, compared with parliamentary republics (as the default category), presidential republics are indeed significantly associated with lower levels of democracy. This pattern is confirmed irrespective of the indicator of democracy which is selected for analysis. Yet at the same time, mixed republics have an even worse record (according to the Freedom House and Polity measures), while, as might be expected, ruling monarchies and military states fare among the worst. The other control

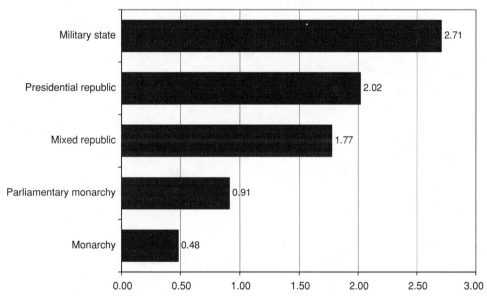

FIGURE 6.3. Mean Scores on the Political Crisis Scale by Types of Executives. *Note:* The political crisis scale is constructed from events recorded in the Banks dataset including the number of coups d'etat, major constitutional changes, political assassinations, general strikes, cases of guerrilla warfare, government crises, purges of opposition, riots, revolutions, and antigovernment demonstrations. The measure is constructed for every regime-year as a simple additive scale without any weighting. *Source:* Coded from Arthur S. Banks. 2000. *Cross-Polity Time-Series Database*. Binghamton: State University of New York-Binghamton. www.databanks.sitehosting.net

indicators behave as expected from the analysis in previous chapters. The overall models are fairly successful by explaining between 58% and 68% of the
variance in patterns of democracy worldwide.

In addition, we can look more directly at indicators of political crisis, to see
whether presidentialism is also associated with less stability, and even regime
breakdown, as Linz suggests. A political crisis scale was constructed from events
recorded in the Banks dataset, derived from records in the *New York Times*,
including for each nation-year, the number of coups d'etat, major constitutional
changes, political assassinations, general strikes, cases of guerrilla warfare,
government crisis, purges of opposition, riots, revolutions, and antigovernment
demonstrations. The scale was created by adding together all these events,
without any weighting of their relative importance for threatening the survival
of the regime. The comparison of the mean score on the crisis scale in Table 6.5
and Figure 6.3, without any controls, shows that as Linz predicted, presidential
republics are more often associated with political crisis than parliamentary

TABLE 6.5. *Types of Executives and the Indicators of Political
Crisis, All Societies Worldwide*

	Political Crisis Scale		
	Freedom House		
	B	PCSE	P
INSTITUTIONAL RULES			
Presidential republics	.656	.174	***
Mixed republics	.246	.160	N/s
Ruling monarchies	−616	.286	*
Military states	1.67	.272	***
CONTROLS			
Log GDP/capita	−.289	.098	***
Ex-British colony	−.321	.124	***
Middle East	.731	.215	***
Ethnic fractionalization	−.793	.222	***
Population size	.000	.000	***
Area size	.000	.000	***
PR electoral system for lower house	.606	.119	***
Constant	2.04		
No. of observations	4719		
Adjusted R^2	.114		

Note: The default (comparison) is parliamentary monarchies. Entries are
unstandardized OLS regression coefficients (with their panel-corrected standard errors) and the significance (P) of the coefficients for the pooled time-series
cross-national analysis obtained using Stata's xtpcse command. For the classification of the type of executives, see Figure 6.1. For details of all the variables,
including the political crisis scale, see the Technical Appendix. Significant at *
the 0.10 level, ** the 0.05 level, and *** the 0.01 level.

monarchies; the difference is substantively large since presidential republics record almost twice as many crisis events as parliamentary monarchies. At the same time, the worst record is displayed by military states, as might be expected given the extreme nature of this type of regime and the way in which it usually comes to power through a coup d'etat. And the small number of ruling monarchies in the dataset emerge as the most stable and immune to political crisis, possibly because they maintain the strongest autocratic grip by banning political parties, organized opposition forces, and dissident movements from challenging their rule. The regression analysis in Table 6.4 confirms the significance of these results, even with the standard controls.

CONCLUSIONS

There has long been concern that presidential democracies are less stable and more prone to regime breakdown, but the evidence has been challenged by scholars who argue that there are many different types of presidential regimes, rather than just one category. Moreover comparisons of the empirical evidence have often been limited to historical patterns in Latin America and Western Europe, rather than considering executives elsewhere. This chapter has proposed a new typology of executives, based on a few simple criteria derived from the formal constitutional structure of a unified or dual executive, and the forms of selection and tenure for executives. In terms of this typology, the conclusions from this analysis are that parliamentary monarchies have a better record at democratic consolidation, as many have argued, compared with presidential republics. This is also true if the comparison is limited to elected presidential republics compared with parliamentary monarchies. Mixed republics – the type of executive which has proved most popular for new constitutions during the last decade – show a somewhat inconsistent record, but this category performs worse on democracy than parliamentary republics, at least according to the indicators provided by Freedom House and Polity IV. And presidential republics also have a poorer record than parliamentary monarchies according to direct indicators of crisis events, such as experience of coups d'etat, political assassinations, and riots.

The broader lesson, reinforcing the conclusions from earlier chapters, is that constitutional design plays an important role in driving democracy. Even after cultural, social, and economic factors are taken into account, the choice of executive institutions is systematically related to the success (or failure) of democracy. These findings support the argument that power-sharing arrangements, which are characteristic of parliamentary monarchies, are at the heart of this process. In these types of executives, there are multiple checks and balances on political leaders. The dual executive divides the ceremonial monarch as the symbolic head of state from the prime minister, functioning as the effective head of government. The government faces the electorate at regular intervals, and between these contests, the cabinet remains collectively accountable in their daily actions to the scrutiny of the legislature, and, if they lose the confidence and trust of their backbenchers, they pay the ultimate penalty and lose office. The flexibility in the prime minister's tenure, so that the leadership can be replaced without a major constitutional crisis if he or she loses support, provides an additional safety valve. And the incentives for cooperation and consultation between the executive and legislature are also likely to promote accommodation and compromise, fostering stability. Horizontal power-sharing is particularly evident where the government rests on a multiparty coalition. The results of the analysis of types of executives are consistent with those we have already observed with electoral systems. The question which remains to be considered in the next chapter is whether vertical power-sharing also serves the same function, and therefore whether federal arrangements and decentralization of decision making also strengthen democracy, as consociational theory suggests.

7

Federalism and Decentralization

Parliamentary republics and proportional electoral systems generate horizontal checks and balances in the core institutions of state. By contrast, federalism and decentralization lead toward *vertical* power-sharing among multiple layers of government. Contemporary debates about decentralized governance have arisen in many plural democracies, notably among the Francophone majority living in Quebec, the Basques in Spain, and the Scots in the United Kingdom. These arguments have been particularly influential in fragile multinational states afflicted with deep-rooted civil wars where decentralization has been advocated as a potential constitutional solution aiming to reduce conflict, build peace, and protect the interests of marginalized communities. In Sri Lanka, for example, federalism has been proposed in a peace-agreement designed to settle the long-running tensions between the majority Buddhist Sinhalese community and the mainly Hindu Tamils in the northeast. In Sudan the 2005 peace-settlement proposed a high degree of federal autonomy for the south and a constitutionally guaranteed regional division of oil revenues, in the attempt to bind together a country afflicted for two decades by a bloody civil war between the mainly Muslim north and the animist and Christian south.[1] Federal arrangements have also been advocated, more controversially, in Iraq as a mechanism seeking to stem violence among Shi'a and Sunni Muslims, as well as to provide some degree of autonomy for the Kurds in the north.[2]

This chapter focuses on one of the most influential claims made by consociational theory, namely, that the adoption of decentralized forms of governance – notably federal constitutions – facilitates social stability and democratic consolidation in multinational states. As illustrated in Figure 7.1, several distinct and diverse institutional mechanisms can be used for decentralization, understood as the devolution of power and responsibilities from the national to the subnational level. Federal constitutions which strengthen state's rights and regional autonomy represent some of the most important strategies, as these safeguard some guaranteed areas of self-government for geographically concentrated minorities. Other common approaches include

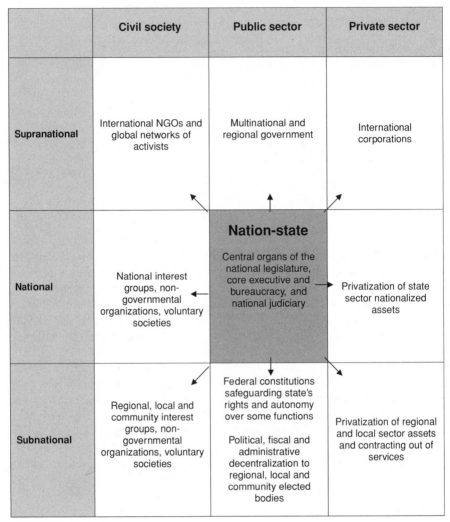

	Civil society	**Public sector**	**Private sector**
Supranational	International NGOs and global networks of activists	Multinational and regional government	International corporations
National	National interest groups, non-governmental organizations, voluntary societies	**Nation-state** Central organs of the national legislature, core executive and bureaucracy, and national judiciary	Privatization of state sector nationalized assets
Subnational	Regional, local and community interest groups, non-governmental organizations, voluntary societies	Federal constitutions safeguarding state's rights and autonomy over some functions Political, fiscal and administrative decentralization to regional, local and community elected bodies	Privatization of regional and local sector assets and contracting out of services

FIGURE 7.1. Model of Vertical Power-Sharing Arrangements

devolution of powers to elected and nonelected regional and local government bodies; shrinking the state through the privatization of public assets, private-public partnerships, and the contracting out of services to the nonprofit and private sectors; delegation of central departmental responsibilities and decision making to local managers in field offices; and using traditional village councils or urban communities for consultation and planning processes.

Encouraged by international agencies, many industrialized and developing societies have been experimenting with these strategies.[3] For example, the

World Bank reports that in 1980, subnational governments around the world collected on average 15% of revenues and spent 20% of expenditures. By the late-1990s, those figures had risen to 19% and 25%, respectively, and had even doubled in some regions and countries.[4] A comparison of trends in West European government during the last three decades noted a widespread shift from direct control and intervention by central government to more indirect control exercised primarily through regulation.[5] Organization for Economic Co-Operation and Development (OECD) data suggests that fiscal decentralization has expanded among most industrialized nations during the last three decades, notably with growing regional autonomy controlling taxation revenue and public expenditure in Spain and Belgium, but also in other nations such as France, Italy, and Denmark.[6] Proponents argue that decentralization has many potential advantages for making decisions closer to the community; for allowing policy flexibility, innovation, and experimentation; and for ensuring government responsiveness to local needs.[7] Nevertheless no consensus surrounds the impact of these reforms, and the assumed benefits of this strategy have come under vigorous challenge. Skeptics charge that many of the theoretical claims advanced in favor of decentralized governance have not been sustained by careful empirical analysis.[8] Indeed some have detected evidence of a backlash against this movement occurring in Western Europe, with some recentralization happening in the Netherlands and Sweden. Most seriously, far from maintaining stability and unity in multination states, critics argue that federalism and decentralization strategies risk the serious dangers of rigidifying community differences, encouraging partition or even succession and thus the ultimate breakup of fragile nation-states.

To evaluate these issues, the first part of this chapter outlines the theoretical arguments surrounding the debate about decentralization, including considering the claims and counterclaims of the consequences for democratic participation and representation, for the effectiveness of government policymaking, and for the representation of minorities in multinational states, as suggested by proponents and critics. To sort out support for these arguments, the next section develops a two-dimensional matrix classifying forms of vertical power-sharing and discusses suitable measures and evidence. Much of the previous literature has drawn upon historical case studies of particular federal systems, focused especially on the US Constitution. Yet it often remains difficult to generalize from the American experience to other types of societies and contexts; for instance, Stepan points out that strong states' rights embodied in the US Constitution represent only one type of federalism.[9] To develop a global comparison, a classification of ideal types of vertical power-sharing is developed conceptually, based on two dimensions: the degree of fiscal, administrative, and political decentralization in the public sector and the type of constitutional rules governing the relationship between the national and subnational tiers. Formal constitutional structures in all nations around the world are classified as 'unitary states', 'federal states', or an intermediate category of 'hybrid unions'. Each of these categories can be further subdivided according to the degree of decentralized governance, where fiscal, administrative, and political powers and functions are transferred to provincial and local levels. As with previous chapters, regression models with cross-national time-series data help to analyze the performance of federal states on the four standard indicators of democracy which have already been employed, after applying the prior battery of controls.

The interpretation of the results is further enriched and illuminated by examining detailed paired case studies comparing processes of historical development in India and Bangladesh. These cases were selected for comparison as Southeast Asian bordering states sharing a common history and culture for centuries, although one was predominately Hindu while the other was predominately Muslim. Both are plural societies, with an agrarian workforce characterized by low levels of literacy and endemic poverty, although with different decentralized structures of governance and political histories. Contrasts in the vertical power-sharing arrangements used in India and Bangladesh can help to illustrate the origins of institutions, their evolution, and their consequences for processes of democratic stability and the containment and management of ethnic violence. The conclusion summarizes the results and considers their policy implications, particularly the lessons for fragile multinational states emerging from a history of conflict and civil war.

THE DEBATE ABOUT DECENTRALIZED GOVERNANCE

From Montesquieu to Madison, classical theorists suggest that decentralized governance has many advantages, especially (i) for democratic participation, representation, and accountability; (ii) for public policy and governmental effectiveness; and (iii) for the representation and accommodation of territorially based ethnic, cultural, and linguistic differences.[10]

In particular, it is argued that the transfer of central decision making to democratically elected local and regional bodies gives citizens multiple points of access, thereby enhancing opportunities for public participation, increasing the accountability and responsiveness of elected officials to local citizens, and hence providing incentives for more responsive democratic government. The capacity of this process to expand public engagement in community decision making is illustrated by processes of participatory budget making and deliberative policy councils, as exemplified by developments in Sao Paulo, Brazil.[11] Fiscal decentralization is believed to reduce corruption by strengthening the transparency of decision making and the accountability of elected officials to local communities.[12]

Advocates believe that the proliferation of decision-making units at local and regional levels also strengthens public policymaking, through potentially encouraging creative new solutions to tough problems. This process is thought to encourage learning from social innovations and flexible experimentation, thereby reinventing governance to deal with complex challenges, for example, in urban development and welfare policies.[13] Rather than 'one size fits all', devolved government bodies may also tailor public services and regulations more efficiently and flexibly to meet the needs of each particular community.[14] Privatization policies, where state industries are transferred to the free market, have been widely advocated as part of a broader package of liberalization designed to shrink the state and thereby lead toward programs which boost economic growth and sustainable human development.[15] In short, decentralization efforts are widely identified with the promotion of managerial efficiency and the enhancement of public services, as well as with more open, transparent, and accountable forms of representative democracy and the qualities of good governance. For all these reasons, if these claims are valid, a strong linkage should be found between levels of government decentralization and patterns of democracy.

The advantages of decentralization should be particularly evident in deeply divided plural societies. Different institutional forms of decentralization, notably federal constitutions, have long been recommended as the preferred mode of democratic governance designed to maintain stability within multinational states. Lijphart theorizes that if political boundaries for subnational governments reflect social boundaries, diverse plural societies can become homogeneous within their regions, thereby reducing communal violence, promoting political stability, and facilitating the accommodation of diverse interests within the boundaries of a single state.[16] Plural societies are characterized by the existence of multiple groups, whether demarcated by class, linguistic, religious, racial, tribal, or caste-based identities. Federalism and decentralization are thought to be particularly important strategies for plural societies where groups live in geographically concentrated communities and where the administrative boundaries for political units reflect the distribution of these groups. These arrangements allow spatially concentrated groups a considerable degree of self-determination to manage their own affairs and to protect their own cultural, social, and economic interests within their own communities, for example, to control religious teachings in school curriculums, to determine levels of local taxation and expenditure for poorer marginalized areas, to administer internal security forces and justice systems, and to establish language policy regulating public broadcasting and official documents.

Federal constitutions represent only one form of decentralization, and similar claims can be advanced for other related institutions. In plural societies, where ethnic groups are geographically dispersed, Lijphart theorizes that administrative and political decentralization also helps to promote accommodation, for example, allowing minorities to elect local representatives who could manage policies toward culturally sensitive issues such as education. Local forms of decision making can be regarded as particularly important for the management of tensions among specific ethnic communities living within particular areas, by facilitating the inclusion of leaders drawn from ethnic minorities through municipal and state elections. In England, for example, municipal councils facilitate the election of representatives drawn from the Bangladeshi, Pakistani, Indian, and Afro-Caribbean communities in the inner-city areas of Birmingham, Bradford, Leeds, and London, where minority populations are concentrated. Through decentralization, ethnic communities can protect their rights and defend their interests in specific local areas, even within unitary states.

Lijphart is far from alone in emphasizing the importance of decentralization for stability, peace building, and democratic consolidation in fragile multinational states. For example, when comparing data from the Minorities at Risk project, Bermeo concludes that armed rebellions are three times more common among groups living in unitary than in federal states, while these groups also experience lower levels of discrimination and grievances.[17] Stepan is also a strong proponent of this form of government, suggesting that plural societies such as the Russian Federation, Indonesia, and Burma/Myanmar will never become consolidated democracies without workable federal systems. All stable contemporary multinational democracies are federal, including Switzerland, Canada, Belgium, Spain, and India. At the same time he warns that federal arrangements pose serious risks for the emergence of ethnic nationalist parties in transitional states emerging from autocracy where regional elections are held prior to nationwide contests.[18] Elsewhere, Gurr has also advocated power-sharing arrangements and group autonomy as a solution to deep-rooted ethnic conflict and civil wars.[19] Hechter also suggests that plural states such as India and Nigeria would probably not have survived without some form of decentralized governance.[20]

And Potential Criticisms

Skeptics, however, challenge the assumptions and cast doubt on the evidence supporting these predictions about the benefits of decentralized governance. In terms of administrative efficiency, critics charge that compared with a unitary state, decentralization may encourage overly complex, duplicative, and wasteful forms of government; structures which are slow to respond to major challenges because of the existence of multiple veto points; and uneven development and inequality across constituency units.[21] By generating another layer of government bureaucracy, some studies suggest, decentralization may generate increased costs, poorer service efficiency, worse coordination, greater inequality among administrative areas, and macroeconomic instability.[22] By contrast, centralized government is thought to enhance integration, decisiveness, uniformity, economies of scale, and cost efficiency.[23] The claims concerning participation and representation have also been challenged; in particular decentralization may encourage the fragmentation of party systems through the growth of regional parties. Multilevel governance may also reduce clear channels of electoral accountability, as a result of overlapping functions and roles across national, regional, and local governments. By contrast centralized governments have a clearer definition of responsibilities for 'where the buck stops' in decision-making processes. Corruption may also expand in decentralized governance as a result of the spread of clientalistic relationships and 'elite capture' which links local politicians, public officials, and business leaders.

In particular, the benefit of decentralization for accommodating political stability in multinational states has come under strong challenge. Critics highlight certain federations which illustrate the most serious risks associated with these arrangements, including the cases of persistent violence and continued conflict in the Russian Federation (in Chechnya), in the Basque region of Spain, in India (in Kashmir), Nigeria, and Sudan (in Darfur). Federations which disintegrated, whether peacefully or violently, include the West Indies (1962), Pakistan (1971), Czechoslovakia (1993), the Soviet Union (1991), most of the constituent units in the Federal Republic of Yugoslavia (1991), and the expulsion of Singapore from Malaysia (1965). Federalism has had a checkered record in much of Africa, the Middle East, and Asia.[24] Critics argue that the creation of federal structures may encourage a dynamic unraveling and breakup of the nation-state, in which accession to demands for increased autonomy fuels the flames which lead eventually to instability, partition, and even outright succession.[25]

A number of reasons have been suggested for the apparent failure of federal arrangements in cases such as Pakistan, Czechoslovakia, and the Federal Republic of Yugoslavia. Watts argues that extreme disparities in the population, size, or wealth of constituent federal units contribute to stress, along with the special problems facing bicommunal two-unit federations (such as Bangladesh's succession from Pakistan in 1971) and the peaceful 'velvet revolution' divorcing Slovakia and the Czech Republic. Moreover many cases of failed federations occurred where democratic institutions were weak or lacking, so that these cannot be regarded as genuine tests of the consociational claim. Watts argues that there have not yet been any cases of 'genuinely' democratic federations which have failed.[26] Hale suggests that where federal borders are drawn along ethnic lines, this system encourages local politicians to 'play the ethnic card' when seeking popularity. This process, he argues, heightens and reinforces ethnic identities in the electorate, generating stronger intra-ethnic rivalries and destabilizing fledgling democracies, rather than rewarding politicians who seek to resolve or accommodate group differences.[27] Cross-cutting cleavages, by contrast, moderate the sharpness of internal divisions, exemplified by Switzerland. Federal states which possess a single core region which enjoys dramatic superiority in population, such as in Nigeria and Russia, are regarded as particularly vulnerable to collapse.[28] Nordlinger also excludes federalism from his recommended conflict-regulating practices in divided societies, fearing that it may result in the breakup of the state.[29] Some researchers attribute the dramatic collapse of the Soviet Union, Yugoslavia, and Czechoslovakia, at least in part, to federal arrangements, on the grounds that new post-Communist democracies with federal structures are more vulnerable to secessionist pressures.[30] Mozaffar and Scarritt have argued that in Africa, because of the dispersion and intermingling of diverse multiethnic communities, territorial autonomy does not work well as a way of managing ethnic conflict.[31] In this perspective, institutional arrangements which facilitate territorial autonomy in states or provinces may reinforce ethnic differences and provide resources for leaders who play the 'nationalist' card, for example, by providing access to media coverage and a public platform in the legislature, thereby promoting incentives for ethnic intolerance, and even in extreme cases nationalist succession, partition, or state failure.[32] Yet Brancati argues that much of the debate has been based on faulty premises, since it is the existence of regional parties competing in only one part of a country which is responsible for the negative effects of decentralization, not federalism per se.[33]

CLASSIFYING TYPES OF VERTICAL POWER-SHARING

How can we evaluate the evidence concerning this debate, focusing particularly on understanding the consequences of decentralization for consolidating democracy in multination states? One difficulty is that many distinct types of reforms, structures, and agencies can all be regarded legitimately as part of the decentralization process, making the core concepts excessively vague and imprecise. As a result, not surprisingly, it becomes difficult to evaluate the effects of this process. As discussed earlier, decentralization takes multiple institutional forms, as the general principle refers to the process of dispersing political, administrative, and/or fiscal powers from the central state to subnational agencies or authorities. What matters is the negative transfer of functions and responsibilities *away* from the central organs in the nation-state, but the principle is silent about the flow of powers in a positive direction. Privatization to corporations, devolution to elected local authorities, and fiscal federalism to the regions are all policies broadly designed to shrink the role and responsibilities of the central government, but nevertheless the impacts of these changes on democratic values can be expected to differ and some important trade-offs among values may occur, for example, in terms of government accountability, public participation, and service efficiency.

To clarify the conceptual assumptions, this study focuses upon the central pillar of transfers of power from the central government to subnational tiers within the public sector, thereby excluding an analysis of the impact of broader dimensions of decentralization, such as privatization and engagement of the nonprofit sector. Figure 7.2 illustrates the two-dimensional matrix of vertical power-sharing arrangements used in this study. The vertical dimension refers to the degree of decentralization within the public sector, which in turn falls into three categories – administrative, fiscal, and political.[34] The horizontal dimension represents the classification of the constitutional arrangements determining relations between the national and subnational units of government.

Classifying Types of Decentralization

Administrative decentralization transfers bureaucratic decision-making authority and managerial responsibilities for the delivery and regulation of public services and for raising revenues from the central government to subnational tiers. This is the most basic form of decentralization, for example, where ministerial

		Type of constitution		
		Unitary states (144)	**Hybrid unions** (22)	**Federal states** (25)
Degree of administrative, fiscal and political decentralization	**Centralized**	E.g., Kenya Zimbabwe	E.g., Indonesia Azerbaijan	E.g., Malaysia Belgium
	Decentralized	E.g., Norway Denmark	E.g., Italy	E.g., Canada Switzerland

FIGURE 7.2. Matrix of Vertical Power-Sharing Arrangements. *Note:* See the text for definitions of each type of constitution and the measures of decentralization which are used. The numbers in parentheses represent the distribution of each type out of 191 contemporary states worldwide in 2000.

departments based in the national capital transfer administrative functions to provincial administrative bureaus and local field offices responsible for implementing central directives, regulating local areas, and running public health services, community planning, and schools. More radical options involve delegating responsibilities from the public sector to nonprofit bodies, such as public enterprises or corporations, housing authorities, transportation authorities, school districts, regional development corporations, or special project implementation units, as well as 'contracting out' services to the private sector.

Fiscal decentralization transfers some forms of resource allocation, usually by giving subnational units authority over local taxes and spending. The prime emphasis has been to locate decisions about resources (revenues and expenditures) closest to the equivalent level of government. An extensive literature in political economy has examined the causes and consequences of fiscal decentralization, and this process has been widely advocated as it is theorized to generate conditions most conducive to economic stability, allocative efficiency, and distributive equity, thus maximizing social welfare.[35] The share of subnational government expenditure in consolidated general government expenditure is widely used as a proxy measure of the degree of fiscal decentralization in the public sector, for example, by the World Bank. Nevertheless this measure may systematically exaggerate the political distribution of localized decision making; in Austria and Germany, for example, subnational governments collect local taxes but they have relatively little autonomy or discretion in determining taxation policy.[36] By contrast, Canadian and Swedish local governments have considerable control over their own tax revenues.

Last, from the perspective of the democratization process the most radical type of vertical power-sharing involves *political decentralization* which transfers authority and responsibility from the central government to public bodies at subnational level, such as village assemblies, city mayors and state governors, and elected municipal councils. The prime motivation of political decentralization has been to strengthen opportunities for local control over public services and to expand opportunities for electoral accountability, political representation, and civil society engagement. The aim has been to give citizens, or their representatives, more voice in the formulation and implementation of local policies. The most common practices involve expanding elections for representative office from the national to the local, municipal, or state levels. Some of the most innovative strategies designed to broaden public deliberation have been through innovative mechanisms, such as participatory budgeting and community planning, where citizens have a direct say in local decision making.[37]

Classifying Types of Constitution

Building upon this foundation, a few simple rules can be used to classify the formal constitutional arrangements governing the relationship between the national and subnational units of government into three major types, including unitary states, federal states, and hybrid unions. In simple binary classifications, federalism is sometimes assumed to be equated automatically with decentralized decision making while unitary states are regarded as most centralized.[38] In reality, the situation is more complex, however, as important variations can be observed.[39] Federal states differ, for instance, in whether state/provincial or central government has primary decision-making authority over public sector services and functions such as safety and public order, economic and social planning, control of natural resources, educational policy, public health care, and taxation. Federal constitutions also differ in whether a strong upper house represents and defends states' rights in a bicameral national legislature. Unitary states also vary in the devolution of administrative, fiscal, and political decision making at regional and local levels. Accordingly, given this understanding, all the basic types of unitary and federal constitutions can be further subdivided into centralized and decentralized variants. We can then consider suitable measures and sources of evidence to operationalize the conceptual framework and compare the distribution of vertical power-sharing arrangements in countries worldwide.

Federal Constitutions

Given a long tradition of philosophical debate there are, of course, multiple ways to understand the related concepts of 'federalism', 'federations', and 'confederations'.[40] *Federal constitutions* are understood in the conceptual framework used in this study as those which distinguish between the national and subnational tiers of government, where each tier has certain specified areas of autonomy.[41] This understanding draws upon Riker's well-known definition, where a federal state is defined by two rules: (i) it must have (at least) two levels of government, and (ii) each level must have at least one area of action in which it is autonomous. The latter requirement must be formally guaranteed, most commonly in a written constitution where disputes between tiers are usually resolved by an independent court.[42] As well as subnational tiers of government, including state or provincial legislatures and executives, most (although not all) federations have bicameral legislatures where the second chamber includes representatives drawn from territorial provinces or states.[43] There may also be mutual veto points, for example, where supramajorities are required in the legislature to alter the balance of power among tiers. The subnational constituent units in a federal system are usually territorially defined geographic regions, such as Nigerian states, German Länder, or Canadian provinces. But the subnational units may also be nonterritorial bodies, for example, the tripartite cultural councils in Belgium.

Decentralized federal constitutions are characterized by fairly autonomous provinces and a weak central authority in the powers granted to the executive and national parliament. The Brazilian and American versions both exemplify cases with strong regional states and a relatively weak central government. In the American model, when coming together states voluntarily pooled their sovereignty and designed a constitution to protect their rights against encroachments by the central government, and hence to limited majority rule.[44] In the US Senate, all states are equally weighted, with two members per state, whether California or Nebraska, irrespective of the size of their electorate. The powers of the US Senate are also roughly counterbalanced by the House of Representatives. The US model of federalism therefore limits the powers of the executive and the popular branch of the legislature. The Brazilian constitution also illustrates this model with a political system combining a fragmented multiparty system with personalistic and undisciplined parties, the separation of executive-legislative powers, and vigorous state federalism.[45] As a result of divided government and the weaknesses of parties, Brazilian democracy has frequently experienced legislative-executive stalemate and policymaking logjams, generating what has been termed 'deadlocked democracy', or a crisis of governability.[46]

By contrast, *centralized federal constitutions* grant only limited autonomy to states and allocate the predominant power and authority to the central government, whether the president and executive branch or the prime minister representing the largest party in the lower house of parliament. These cases are closer to the unitary model. In Austria, Belgium, and India, for example, the number of state representatives sitting in the upper chamber is weighted by the size of the electorate within each state, and the lower house retains greater powers than the upper. Moreover in cases of asymmetrical federalism, such as in India and Canada, some rights are limited to specific linguistic or cultural minorities, such as those granted to Francophones in Quebec or to Muslim family courts in India, rather than being universal. The Indian and Belgian constitutions retained greater powers for the central state, with some concessions made to states' rights in order to contain pressures for succession. In Malaysia, power is shared among a few main regions, with restricted political or fiscal decision making among lower tiers of government.[47] The Malaysian constitution grants the central government strong formal powers over an extensive list of functions, including over civil and criminal law, state and federal elections, finance, trade and commerce, taxation, education, health and social security, with federal law taking precedence over state laws. The Senate includes two members from each state, but the remaining two-thirds of all senators are appointed on the basis of their loyalty to the ruling party, and hence this body has served to rubber-stamp the government's policies rather than protecting states' rights. As all major taxing powers reside with the central government, state and local authorities rely for their revenues upon transfers. An even clearer example concerns federalism during the period of Communist control in the Soviet Union, where power was highly centralized within the Politburo, and there were strong asymmetries of federal power due to the predominance of Russia, despite the formal constitutional provisions for federal territories.[48] During the early-1990s, powerful ethnically based republics challenged the central authorities in the Russian Federation on key reforms, and a weak federal government appeared unable to counter their claims to sovereignty.[49] The interpretation of recent developments remains a matter of dispute, with some observers seeing Russia persisting as a weak federation, while others suggest that regional prerogatives have been substantially curtailed since the election of 2000, with Moscow reasserting central control.[50]

Unitary Constitutions

Unitary constitutions are defined as those states with national and subnational tiers, where the national government is defined as sovereign over all its territorial units. The national government retains the authority and legitimacy to control the activities of subnational units even though some roles and administrative functions can still be devolved to lower tiers of government, such as to regional, local, or village assemblies; governors and mayors; or departmental agencies at local levels. In the case of any conflict, however, the national government remains constitutionally sovereign so that executive decisions and laws passed by the national legislature cannot be overruled by lower units.

Important variations are also evident within this category. *Decentralized unitary constitutions* are defined as those unitary regimes with considerable devolution of administrative, fiscal, and political powers among subnational levels, such as to county, provincial, local, urban, and municipal governments. This category includes unitary states where locally elected legislatures and executive bodies plan, finance, and manage issues such as levels of local property taxes, the administration of schools, or related issues of community development.[51] In Norway, for example, the national parliament in Oslo (Stortinget) remains sovereign, although local government is run through 19 counties (*fylke*) and 432 municipalities (*kommune*). The latter are responsible for a wide range of functions, such as primary and lower secondary education, social services, municipal roads, water and sewerage and zoning regulation, raising revenues through local taxation, fees, and local business management as well as from allocations from the central authorities. A prefecture system (with bureaucrats drawn from central government ministries but working at subnational levels) supervises, regulates, and standardizes administrative and legal processes across different regions and areas. Counties and municipalities are responsible for spending about one-third of all government expenditure in Norway, a higher share than is spent at subnational level in some federal states, such as Malaysia. This type of regime is also exemplified by the United Kingdom. The Westminster system exemplifies a strong unitary state, with the major party in government controlling parliament. Yet the United Kingdom now has a multitier system which has become increasingly complex, with elections at supranational level (for the European parliament) and at the subnational levels of regions (Scottish Parliament, Welsh Assembly, and the Greater London Authority and mayor), as well as for local councils in counties, unitary authorities, metropolitan districts, London boroughs, districts, wards, and local parishes. In recent decades broader processes of decentralization have also reduced the size of the state sector, notably privatization of industry and utilities and contracting out of services such as social services, the prison service, and health care. The power-sharing agreement in Northern Ireland (NI), endorsed in April 1998, has also contributed toward decentralization within the United Kingdom through the NI Assembly, the multiparty Executive, and the consultative Civic Forum.

By contrast, *centralized unitary constitutions* exercise most functions from the national legislature and executive, with administrative decisions implemented at provincial and local levels, although with minimal political or fiscal decentralization. Less democratic regimes are often characterized by a 'command-and-control' structure with limited local autonomy or decision making outside the ruling party, the core leadership elites, and the executive bureaucracy. In Singapore, for example, the country is administered as a unified city-state, with local government bodies abolished and absorbed in 1959 by departments of the central government. These arrangements are part of the reason why the predominant party, the People's Action Party (PAP), has exerted power for almost six decades, as discussed in Chapter 4.[52] The centralized state makes it impossible for opposition parties to develop a grassroots base of local leaders who could then challenge the governing party more effectively in parliamentary elections. Another example of a centralized unitary state is Syria, where there are 13 provinces and the City of Damascus for administrative purposes. Each province is headed by a centrally appointed governor who acts in conjunction with a partially elected Provincial Council. Real power is centralized in the hands of the president and People's Assembly, however, controlled by the Baath Party in a coalition as the National Progressive Front. Provincial governments are therefore used as agencies extending popular control by the state outside Damascus, rather than as decentralized bodies exercising genuine autonomy.

Hybrid Unions

Classifications and typologies of vertical power-sharing arrangements have therefore commonly drawn a clean conceptual line in the sand between federations and unitary constitutions. Nevertheless another variant can be distinguished in the form of *hybrid unions* with constitutions which lie somewhere between these polar extremes.[53] Hybrid unions are defined as states where the common organs of the national government remain sovereign but where some independent powers are constitutionally recognized for certain constituent territorial units. This form of vertical power-sharing is exemplified by the United Kingdom, constituting Wales, Scotland, England, and Northern Ireland, as well as five self-governing islands (including Jersey, Guernsey, and the Isle of Man). Devolution in the United Kingdom has strengthened the political influence of the Celtic regions, through the creation in 1999 of the Scottish Parliament and Welsh Assembly. Nevertheless these bodies have limited powers and autonomy; for example, the Scottish Parliament can adjust taxes but only within certain limits, while the Westminster parliament retains sovereignty and thus the formal right to legislate on devolved matters. The new devolved bodies gained powers unavailable to the English regions, a process designed to dampen the pressures for Scottish independence and thus prevent the breakup of the United Kingdom.[54] Other hybrid arrangements can also be identified worldwide, such as *associated statehood* (found in Andorra, France-Monaco, India-Bhutan), a few special cases of *federacies* where unitary states develop a federal relationship with particular dependent territories (such as Denmark's relationship with Greenland and Finland's with the Aaland Islands), and *confederations* (such as the Benelux Union, a social union among citizens in Belgium, the Netherlands, and Luxembourg).[55] Hybrid unions are therefore in themselves a fairly diverse category but in their performance can be expected to fall roughly between the full unitary and federal ideal types. This category can also be subdivided further into relatively centralized and decentralized versions.

CLASSIFYING AND MEASURING VERTICAL FORMS OF POWER-SHARING

Given this understanding, how can we best operationalize and apply the matrix? Some studies opt for the clarity and parsimony of binary categories dividing federal versus unitary states, based on a few key logical rules for classification. Others prefer gradations of the degree of decentralization using continuous scales which try to capture more subtle variations of roles and responsibilities which occur within and across each category.[56] Rather than arbitrarily opting for one or the other, it seems preferable to combine both approaches, thereby generating greater confidence if the results of the analysis remain robust and reliable independently of the specific measurement employed.

For the major types of federal, hybrid, and unitary constitutions, based on these definitions, the formal arrangements of the national and subnational tiers of government were categorized for 191 countries worldwide on the basis of information provided by standard reference handbooks, with information cross-checked against four independent sources (Elazar, Watts, Griffiths, and Banks).[57] These categories were then compared against the degree of decentralized power-sharing in each state, based on measures developed by Schneider, which are derived from Government Finance Statistics gathered by the International Monetary Fund (IMF)/World Bank.[58] This scale gauges the transfer of authority and responsibility for public functions from the national government to subnational tiers in the public sector, distinguishing three main types: political, administrative, and fiscal decentralization. Political decentralization is measured by the existence of municipal and state elections, as monitored by Schneider. Fiscal decentralization is measured by the level of subnational expenditures and revenues as a proportion of total government expenditure, with data estimates provided by the IMF/World Bank. Administrative decentralization is gauged here according to levels of taxation as a percentage of subnational grants and revenues, again using IMF/World Bank data. The data on decentralization was collected for 68 nations in 1996. The Schneider measures for each scale are factor scores based on confirmatory factor analysis which are standardized to range from 0 to 1.0.

DOES DECENTRALIZED GOVERNANCE STRENGTHEN DEMOCRACY?

Drawing upon this conceptual framework, we can first compare the world-wide distribution of the different constitutional types and examine how this relates to the degree of decentralization. The comparison of 191 contemporary nation-states worldwide showed that only 25 (13%) could be identified as having federal constitutions, according to this definition. Despite this, some of the geographically largest and the most populous societies are federations – including the United States, Canada, Germany, Nigeria, Brazil, India, and Russia – hence about 41% of the world's population currently lives under this system of government. Federal constitutions are found in many global regions (see Table 7.1 and Figure 7.2), particularly in North America and Western Europe, although none are in Scandinavia and only one is found in the Middle East (the United Arab Emirates). In the comparison, another 22 constitutions could be classified in the intermediate category as hybrid unions, with this form of government particularly common in the Western European and Asia-Pacific regions. Finally, three-quarters of all contemporary states (144 out of 191 nations) were classified as having unitary constitutions, where the central government was sovereign although with subnational tiers.

To see how far the constitutional typology reflected the indicators of vertical decentralization, in Table 7.2 the mean scores for each category were estimated for the measures of fiscal, administrative, and political decentralization developed by Schneider, available for 68 states. As expected, fiscal

TABLE 7.1. *Type of Constitution by Region*

	Unitary Constitutions	Hybrid Unions	Federal Constitutions	Total
Sub-Saharan Africa	41	4	4	49
South America	26	2	4	32
Asia-Pacific	23	9	5	37
Central and Eastern Europe	22	2	3	27
Middle East	18	0	1	19
Western Europe	9	5	5	19
Scandinavia	5	0	0	5
North America	0	0	3	3
TOTAL	144	22	25	191

Note: The type of constitution was classified using the definitions defined in the text according to data derived from Griffiths (2005), Watts (1999), and Banks (2004). The mean level of fiscal, administrative, and political decentralization was estimated in 68 nations based on the measure developed by Schneider (2003). The coefficient of association (eta) and its significance were calculated in terms of the difference between means using ANOVA.

Sources: Ann L. Griffiths. 2005. Ed. *Handbook of Federal Countries, 2005.* Montreal: Forum of Federations/McGill University Press; Ronald L. Watts. 1999. *Comparing Federal Systems.* 2nd ed. Kingston, Canada: McGill-Queen's University Press; Aaron Schneider. 2003. 'Decentralization: Conceptualization and measurement.' *Studies in Comparative International Development* 38 (3): 32–56.

TABLE 7.2. *Typology of Constitutions and the Mean Decentralization of Power, 68 States*

Type of Federalism	Fiscal Decentralization	Administrative Decentralization	Political Decentralization
Unitary constitutions (44)	.337	.575	.507
Hybrid unions (8)	.414	.431	.436
Federal constitutions (15)	.639	.537	.748
Coefficient of association	.555	.200	.391
Significance (P)	.000	N/s	.005
TOTAL	.414	.549	.553

Note: The type of constitution was classified using the definitions defined in the text according to data derived from Griffiths (2005), Watts (1999), and Banks (2004). The mean level of fiscal, administrative, and political decentralization was estimated in 68 nations on the basis of the measure developed by Schneider (2003). The coefficient of association (eta) and its significance were calculated in terms of the difference between means using ANOVA.

Sources: Ann L. Griffiths. 2005. Ed. *Handbook of Federal Countries, 2005.* Montreal: Forum of Federations/McGill University Press; Ronald L. Watts. 1999. *Comparing Federal Systems.* 2nd ed. Kingston, Canada: McGill-Queen's University Press; Aaron Schneider. 2003. 'Decentralization: Conceptualization and measurement.' *Studies in Comparative International Development* 38 (3): 32–56.

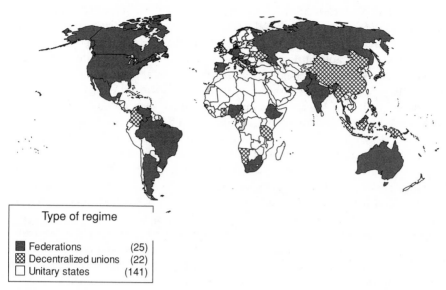

FIGURE 7.3. Map of Constitutional Types. *Note:* The type of constitution was classified using the definitions defined in the text according to data derived from Griffiths (2005), Watts (1999), and Banks (2004).

and political decentralization was significantly higher in countries with federal rather than unitary constitutions; for example, the fiscal decentralization measure proved twice as strong in federal as in unitary states. Nevertheless the overall mean showed considerable variations among countries governed by federal constitutions. The distribution of nations across the fiscal and political decentralization scales is illustrated in the scatter-plot shown in Figure 7.3. Countries such as Canada and Switzerland exemplify the most decentralized forms of federalism on both these dimensions, and indeed most of the states with federal constitutions can be found in the top-right quadrant, representing those with the highest levels of fiscal and political decentralization. At the same time there are some clear outliers, notably Malaysia and Belgium, both with federal constitutions but which fail to conform to this pattern. Moreover there are a number of unitary states which still have a considerable degree of political and fiscal decentralization, including Sweden, Norway, and Denmark. These Scandinavian states have unitary states yet are also highly decentralized, as discussed earlier. The plot also displays a widely distributed scatter, suggesting only a poor fit between levels of political and fiscal decentralization; some countries such as the Philippines and Panama elect local representatives but nevertheless the central government continues to exert considerable fiscal control through tightly regulating levels of local government expenditure. Elsewhere, such as in some of the post-Communist states, subnational units absorb a relatively high proportion of total government expenditure but have little political decentralization of power. Therefore the assumption that federal constitutions are automatically always the most decentralized states can be questioned; most states with federal constitutions do fit this expectation, but there are some notable outliers, while some other states with unitary constitutions can also be highly decentralized in terms of fiscal and political measures. Watts also found that as a proportion of total government expenditures (after transfers), the federal government share varied from 96% in Malaysia and 69% in Austria down to 40% in Canada and 37% in Switzerland.[59]

The key issue to be analyzed is whether systematic variations are evident in the democratic performance of federal states, hybrid unions, and unitary states, even after controlling for the standard battery of factors established in previous chapters as being closely linked to patterns of democracy. In analyzing the impact of these arrangements on democracy we face similar analytical challenges to those addressed earlier, particularly questions concerning institutional endogeneity. As with other institutional explanations, plausible arguments about the impact of multilevel forms of governance also need to consider carefully whether the causes and consequences are mixed up. Did processes of democratization in plural societies lead toward the adoption of federal constitutions? Or did the adoption of such constitutional arrangements in plural societies lead toward more stable consolidated democracies? Studies also need to consider other possible underlying historical forces or social characteristics which could have led toward both the adoption of federal constitutions and levels of democracy, such as the colonial legacy inherited by newly independent states, patterns of ethnic fractionalization, and the dynamics of economic development. As with the study of electoral systems, in principle evidence for the impact of institutional change should often be easiest to discern in classic 'before' and 'after' natural experiments when states have experienced a major constitutional reform, such as the processes of devolution which occurred in Belgium (1970), in Spain (1978), in Nigeria (1999), and in the United Kingdom (1999). In practice, however, when states adopt sweeping constitutional revisions it often becomes difficult to isolate the distinct effects of federalism from other simultaneous institutional reforms, for example, following the introduction of the new constitution in postapartheid South Africa. The impact is often also difficult to discern in countries where patterns of fiscal or political decentralization evolve incrementally through a series of small steps, for example, where there are multiple revisions to the exact roles and boundaries of local government bodies. Recent decades have seen few cases of countries which have switched directly from unitary or hybrid to federal constitutions.

One alternative strategy is to compare the mean levels of democracy associated with federal, hybrid unions, and unitary constitutions, using the cross-sectional time-series data, without any prior controls. The results in Figure 7.4 show substantial and significant contrasts between unitary and federal constitutions across all four standard indicators of democracy; in the Polity IV 100-point index of democracy, for example, federal constitutions scored 69 percentage points on average, 25 points higher than unitary constitutions. Hybrid

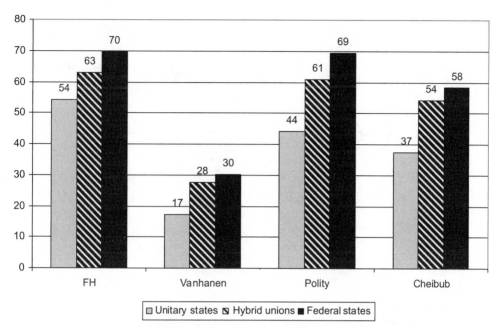

FIGURE 7.4. Levels of Democracy by Type of Constitution. *Note:* The type of constitution was classified using the definitions in the text according to data derived from Griffiths (2005), Watts (1999), and Banks (2004). The standardized 100-point scales of democracy are described in Table 3.1. The four scales measure *liberal democracy* (Freedom House 2000), *constitutional democracy* (Polity IV 2000), *participatory democracy* (Vanhanen 2000), and *contested democracy* (Cheibub and Gandhi 2000). When tested by ANOVA, the differences between mean scores are all significant (at the $p = .001$ level).

unions were located between these scores. Moreover the 30-year trends in the Freedom House scale, illustrated in Figure 7.5, show that federal constitutions have consistently displayed a better record of democracy than unitary states, with hybrid unions falling in between these polar extremes, as expected. The differences between types which are apparent are not just the result of one or two years but instead appear to be a robust and consistent pattern which persists despite the major changes in levels of democracy occurring during the third wave era. The period since the end of the cold war sees a slight closing of the contrasts between constitutional types but not a reversal of these persistent patterns.

Nevertheless many other factors may be generating these differences, above and beyond the type of regimes, for example, if federal constitutions are more common among nations which have affluent industrialized economies or in more homogeneous societies. To control for other potentially confounding factors, the cross-sectional time-series models used OLS linear regression with PCSEs to measure the impact of federalism on levels of democratization in each

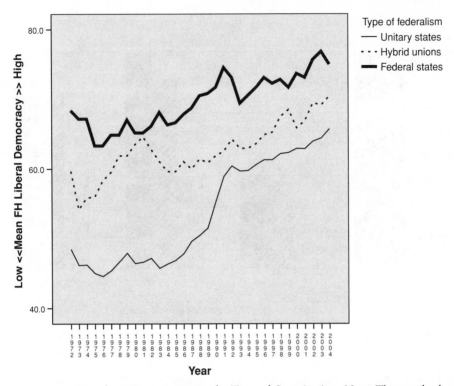

FIGURE 7.5. Trends in Democratization by Type of Constitution. *Note:* The standard-ized 100-point scale of democracy is described in Table 3.1. The scale measures *liberal democracy* (Freedom House 2000). For the classification of types of constitution, see text.

nation-year, while controlling for other variables associated with democracy. The results of the analysis presented in Table 7.3 show that the type of vertical power-sharing was significantly associated with the four indicators of democ-racy, even after applying the series of controls for socioeconomic development, colonial origins, regional patterns of democratic diffusion, ethnic fractionaliza-tion, area size, and the other institutional arrangements which we have already identified as related to levels of democracy (proportional representation elec-toral systems for the lower house and parliamentary monarchies for the type of executive). Even with this battery of controls, federalism proved to be positively linked to democracy, across each of the four models using different measures, as consociational theory argued. The models explained a substantial amount of variance in levels of democracy (between 45% and 66%). Unfortunately it is not possible to monitor the impact of decentralization on democracy by replicating similar time-series models by using the Schneider scales of fiscal, administrative, and political decentralization since these are only available for

TABLE 7.3. Federalism and Democracy, All Societies Worldwide

	Liberal Democracy Freedom House			Constitutional Democracy Polity IV			Participatory Democracy Vanhanen			Contested Democracy Przeworski et al./ Cheibub and Gandhi		
	B	PCSE	P	B	PCSE	P	B	PCSE	P	B	PCSE	P
INSTITUTIONS												
PR electoral system	4.30	(.949)	***	10.54	(.530)	***	4.72	(.401)	***	13.74	(.921)	***
Parliamentary monarchy	11.68	(.569)	***	18.74	(1.17)	***	7.87	(.848)	***	21.54	(1.83)	***
Federal constitution	.70	(.222)	***	1.60	(.204)	***	.939	(.127)	***	1.27	(.269)	***
CONTROLS												
Log GDP/capita (US$)	11.46	(.979)	***	7.75	(.737)	***	10.1	(.551)	***	21.0	(1.13)	***
Ex-British colony (0/1)	9.27	(.627)	***	9.66	(1.14)	***	1.65	(.596)	***	7.24	(.719)	***
Middle East (0/1)	−13.33	(1.88)	***	−16.94	(1.53)	***	−11.00	(.632)	***	−28.3	(2.44)	***
Regional diffusion of democracy	.59	(.052)	***	.621	(.039)	***	.688	(.034)	***	.307	(.045)	***
Ethnic fractionalization (0–100-pt scale)	−9.78	(.634)	***	−2.40	(1.48)	N/s	−6.12	(.776)	***	−16.7	(2.11)	***
Population size (thou)	−.000	(.001)	***	−.001	(.001)	N/s	−.001	(.001)	***	.000	(.001)	***
Area size (sq mi)	.001	(.001)	***	.001	(.001)	***	.001	(.001)	***	.001	(.001)	***
Constant	−14.76			−7.45			−30.51			−39.9		
No. of observations	5125			4221			4446			.4902		
No. of countries	187			156			180			185		
Adjusted R²	.513			.560			.666			.448		

Note: Entries for liberal democracy, constitutional democracy, and participatory democracy are unstandardized beta OLS regression coefficients (B) with panel-corrected standard errors (PCSE) and the significance of the coefficients (P) for the pooled time-series cross-national dataset obtained using Stata's xtpcse command. With PCSE the disturbances are, by default, assumed to be heteroskedastic (each nation-state has its own variance) and contemporaneously correlated across states. Models for contested democracy were run using logistic regression for the binary dependent variable, with the results summarized by Nagelkerke R square. For the measures of democracy, standardized to 100-point scales and lagged by one year, see Chapter 2. For details of all the variables, see the Technical Appendix. Significant at * the 0.05 level, ** the 0.01 level, and *** the 0.001 level.

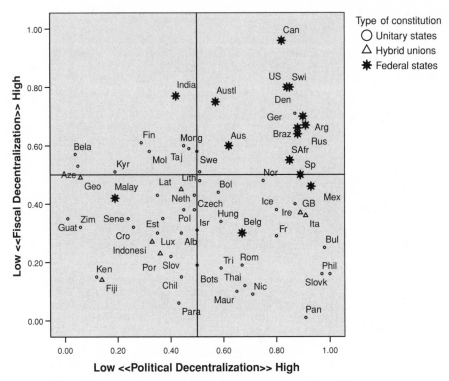

FIGURE 7.6. Types of Constitution and the Degree of Fiscal and Political Decentralization. *Note:* The type of constitution was classified using the definitions in the text according to data derived from Griffiths (2005), Watts (1999), and Banks (2004). The mean level of fiscal and political decentralization was estimated for 68 nations in the mid-1990s, based on the measures developed by Schneider (2003).

the mid-1990s in 68 nations. Moreover there are problems in using this data for a broader cross-national comparison, since detailed levels of subnational government expenditure were often not reported in many autocratic states. As Figure 7.6 illustrates, most of the federal systems tend to have relatively high levels of fiscal and political decentralization, exemplified by Canada, but a few such as Malaysia and Belgium do not follow this pattern. Moreover some unitary states such as Norway are also fairly highly decentralized through local governance. Figure 7.7 looks at the simple correlation between liberal democracy and the degree of fiscal decentralization, in those countries where data is available, and it shows a relatively poor fit, with notable outliers such as Russia, Belarus, and Turkey. Accordingly further research is required to see whether the conclusions drawn here about the impact of different types of federal constitution on democracy also hold for broader patterns of administrative, fiscal, and political decentralization.

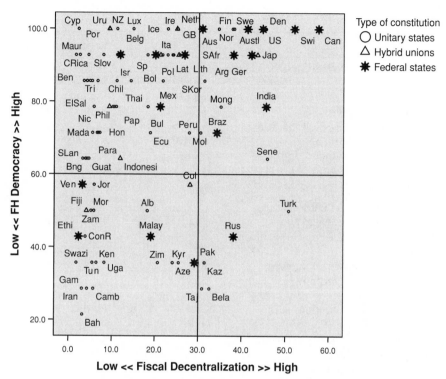

FIGURE 7.7. Freedom House Liberal Democracy and the Degree of Fiscal Decentralization. *Note:* The standardized 100-point scale of democracy is described in Table 3.1. The scale measures *liberal democracy* (Freedom House 2000). The type of constitution was classified using the definitions in the text according to data derived from Griffiths (2005), Watts (1999), and Banks (2004). The mean level of fiscal decentralization was estimated for 98 nations on the basis of the mean level of subnational expenditure reported for the period 1972–2000.

CASE STUDIES OF CONSTITUTIONAL CHANGE: INDIA AND BANGLADESH

To understand the impact of federal and decentralized arrangements in greater depth, we can turn to the paired case-study comparisons contrasting historical developments which occurred in India and Bangladesh. These bordering states were selected as they shared a common history and colonial government for many centuries, as well as displaying many similar social and economic characteristics (see Table 7.4). With a population of over 1.1 billion spread over 3.3 million square kilometers, Indian society is divided among multiple ethnic identities, languages, religions, and cultures. Hindi is the national language and primary tongue of a third of the people, but there are more than a dozen other official languages. About 80% of the population is Hindu but India

TABLE 7.4. *Key Indicators in India and Bangladesh*

	India	Bangladesh
SOCIAL AND ECONOMIC INDICATORS		
Area	3,287,590 sq km	144,000 sq km
Pop., 2007	1.13 bn	150.4m
Pop. below poverty line (%)	25%	45%
GDP per capita (PPP US$), 2006	$3,700	$2,200
Life expectancy at birth, 2003	68 years	63 years
Human Development Index, 2003	.501	.600
Adult literacy (% of pop. 15+), 2003	59%	43%
Ethnic fractionalization (Alesina), 2002	.418	.045
POLITICAL INDICATORS		
Year of independence (from)	1947 (Britain)	1971 (W. Pakistan)
Liberal democracy Freedom House Index, 1973	2.5	3
Freedom House classification, 1973	Free	Partly free
Liberal democracy Freedom House Index, 2007	2.5	4
Freedom House classification, 2007	Free	Partly free
Control of corruption (Kaufmann), 2005	47	8
Government effectiveness (Kaufmann), 2005	52	21
Political stability (Kaufmann), 2005	22	7
Rule of law (Kaufmann), 2005	56	20
Voice and accountability (Kaufmann), 2005	56	31
Regulatory quality (Kaufmann), 2005	41	15

Note: See the Technical Appendix for details of these indices and full sources of data. The Kaufmann indices rank each country on 0–100-point scales where high = better governance ratings.
Source: Daniel Kaufmann, A. Kraay, and M. Mastruzzi. 2006. *Governance Matters V: Governance Indicators for 1996–2005.* Washington, DC: World Bank. www.worldbank.org

also contains sizable minorities of Muslims (13%), Christians (2%), and Sikhs (2%). According to World Bank estimates, one-quarter of the Indian population live below the poverty level ($1 a day), with 59% literacy. Despite the immense challenges of governing such a vast, poor, and diverse society, Indian democracy has persisted and deepened since independence was achieved in 1947. This endurance is a remarkable achievement, given the odds, despite the fact that Indian democracy has been flawed by intermittent ethnic violence in many states, persistent conflict in Kashmir, a major suspension of civil liberties under Mrs. Ghandi's emergency rule for 19 months in 1975–1977, rising economic inequalities, and sporadic crisis from political assassinations.[60]

The neighboring state of Bangladesh, by contrast, is far smaller in area and population, as well as more ethnically homogeneous as a predominantly Muslim state. The population is 98% Bengali and 83% Muslim, with a sizable Hindu minority (16%), and the main languages are Bangla and English. These structural characteristics should make it easier to govern than India, but it in fact has had a checkered history of democracy and continued instability, conflict, and confrontation. Bangladesh came into being in 1971 following a civil war with West Pakistan, and the years since independence have been marred by political turmoil and violence, symbolized by two presidential assassinations, 13 heads of government, three military coups, and 19 failed coup attempts. After independence, the next 15 years were governed under military rule. In 1991 civilian rule was restored, with elections which were regarded as meeting international standards, but subsequent elections have been troubled and marred by violence. Throughout 2006, there were signs that the forthcoming electoral process would face difficulties, due to high levels of political violence and major cities facing paralyzing street actions. The opposition Awami League declared a boycott of the elections which had been planned for 2007 and called for their supporters to take direct action. The country appeared to be descending into chaos, with riots, strikes, transport blockades, and business instability adding to an already strong sense of tension. In January 2007, a state of emergency was declared and the military-backed caretaker government banned all political activities, while the security forces have arrested many political leaders. Deep tensions and antagonisms persist between the leaders of the major parties, the Bangladesh Nationalist Party and the Awami League, and their minor party alliances, with attacks on opposition rallies and public meetings, and hundreds of people have been killed by political violence in recent years. Rather than a process of bargaining and compromise, during periods in power each major party seeks to monopolize politics in a zero-sum game, as if the other did not have a right to exist. Leadership has been dynastic and bitterly personal, based on patronage placement for supporters in bureaucratic positions, rather than development of institutionalized and programmatic party organizations.[61] The caretaker government has sought to stamp out corruption, by arresting and detailing many political leaders since the state of emergency was first declared.[62] Some estimates suggest that more than 50,000 people have been arrested since the announcement of the state of emergency in January 2007, many of whom have not been charged. The Emergency Power Ordinance gave the caretaker government sweeping powers to ban all political activities, suspend fundamental civil rights, and detain and arrest high-ranking party leaders on charges of corruption and crime. According to the Fund for Peace's global comparison in 2006, based on indicators of instability such as suspension of the rule of law, intercommunal violence, and delegitimization of the state, Bangladesh was ranked as the 19th most vulnerable out of 148 nations worldwide to becoming a 'failed state'.[63]

What explains these contrasts? The countries have similar first-past-the-post (single-member district) electoral systems for parliament, but the federal-unitary constitutional arrangements, the degree of decentralization, and the contemporary structures of local governance present striking contrasts between the states.

India has had a two-tier federal constitution since independence, with decision making divided among 28 states. The form of power-sharing has been
regarded as asymmetrical federalism, with Kashmir being given special provisions, although this view has been challenged.[64] The states vary greatly in
population size – the ratio between the population of the largest and smallest
states is 307 to 1 – and there are also significant inequalities among states in levels of economic growth and economic development.[65] Under the constitution,
India's form of federalism has been described as relatively centralized, with
state powers circumscribed in several important regards and the central government having overriding powers.[66] Nevertheless the constitutional arrangements have had certain important consequences. Most importantly, for such
a divided society, since the breakdown of Congress Party dominance in 1967,
federalism has facilitated the proliferation of a range of state-based political
parties, aggregating varied regional interests based on region, language, caste,
class, or views on secularism. This, in turn, has had an impact on the complex mosaic of parliamentary national elections. Reflecting Duverger's law, the
single-member simple plurality electoral system (first-past-the-post) in use for
the lower house of parliament, where voting support is spread relatively evenly
geographically, can usually be expected to generate a two-party system. After
the general elections of 1999, however, more than 20 parties provided a stable
national coalition government, transforming the political process. A national
multiparty coalition again formed the government following the elections of
2004. Federalism therefore facilitates multiparty competition and the politics
of coalition building, as smaller parties can gain credibility and expand electoral support within each state.[67] India's federal structure has also facilitated a
remarkable capacity for innovation, for example, in terms of diverse strategies
of economic policy or in language policy. The federal structure is also reflected
in the bicameral national parliament (Sansad), which includes the Council of
States, with not more than 250 members with most chosen by elected members
of state and territorial assemblies plus a dozen selected by the president. The
federal state has allowed flexibility in the containment and management of
ethnic conflict, for example, through the creation of the separate federal state
of Nagaland in 1963, Tripura in 1972, Mizoram in 1986, and an autonomous
Bodo council created in 2003 following negotiations with a rebel group. Inter-
mittent fighting and sporadic conflict continue with Assamese, Tripuras, and
Acehnese communities, along with ongoing violence with Kashmiri Muslims,
but nevertheless the federal structure of the state has allowed some important
intercommunal conflicts to be settled.[68]

Since 1993, the Indian state has been radically decentralized into a three-
tier structure.[69] Reformers sought to challenge the existing structure of power
exerted primarily through landownership, patriarchy, and the caste system.
Political decentralization through local government aimed to eliminate rural
poverty and to expand human development. Today India's government is
divided into 28 states, seven union territories, and a complex system of local
government in 600,000 villages and towns. The 73rd and 74th Constitutional

Amendments of 1993 introduced radically new institutions through several significant innovations, including reservations of seats for marginal groups, women, Dalits, and Adivasis; creation of decentralized planning mechanisms; establishment of state election commissions to oversee local elections and state finance commissions to prepare a blueprint for sharing of state revenues; and institutionalization of the direct-participation village assembly (*gram sabha*).[70] Urban areas are governed by municipal corporations, municipal councils, town area committees, and notified area committees. Rural areas have a three-tier structure consisting of 474 district legislative bodies (*zilla parishads*), at the top; 5,906 block councils (*panchayats samitis*); and 227,698 village councils (*gram panchayats*) at the base. Together these institutions have added approximately 3 million elected local offices to the 5,000 state representatives and the 500 or more members of parliament. Among the new local officeholders, one-third or about 1 million are women. Nearly 700,000 are drawn from the Scheduled Castes and Scheduled Tribal communities (the Dalits and Adivasis). The expansion in representatives has considerably increased the density of the political system, drawing literally millions into elected office for the first time. Moreover the inclusion of women as council leaders through reserved seats is not just of symbolic importance, but has been found to influence public policy. In particular, a study which examined village councils reported that women leaders invested more in public goods which were more closely related to women's concerns, such as drinking water, while by contrast male leaders invested more heavily in education.[71] The village assemblies were institutionalized in the new structure, with direct forms of decision making among all members of the village. The assembly was designed to function as a watchdog over the workings of the village council.[72]

By contrast, the Bangladeshi state has always centralized power. The national parliament (Jatiya Sangsad) is a unicameral body where 300 members are popularly elected from single-territorial constituencies. Many parties are registered to stand for parliamentary elections, but the single-member plurality electoral system concentrates seats in just four parties: the Awami League, the Bangladesh Nationalist Party, the Jatiya Party, and the Jamaat-i-Islami Bangladesh. The two major parties remain in confrontational mode under dynastic leaders, gaining power from patron-clientalistic relationships which protect and reward their supporters. Intolerance, corruption, and malfeasance are rife. Distinctive regional parties have been unable to break the hold of the major players without a state legislature to develop an electoral base. Moreover local government also remains seriously underdeveloped. During the 1980s, the military government introduced some wide-ranging structural reforms in local government, partly in the attempt to create a rural power base and to increase their legitimacy. Contrary to expectations, however, the country has not moved further toward decentralization since the early-1990s, when democracy was restored, and indeed in some cases there have been significant attempts at recentralization.[73] In short, the multiparty diversity characteristic of contemporary India could never have developed in this country, in part because of the vertical centralization of power within the Bangladeshi state, coupled with the majoritarian electoral system for parliament. With more significant forms of vertical power-sharing, the Bangladesh party system could have developed more checks and balances, breaking the feudal hold of dynastic leadership which has encouraged kleptocracy and the destabilization of the state.

CONCLUSIONS

To summarize, processes of decentralization take diverse forms. Federalism is one important mechanism, but fiscal, administrative, and political decentralization can also transfer power to bodies in the public sector (local government elected officials and executive bodies), as well as those in civil society (nongovernmental organizations and community, philanthropic, and voluntary associations) and in the private sector (such as through privatization and contracting out of services). A wide variety of elected and nonelected authorities operate in different nations at the level of departments, prefectures, counties, municipalities, boroughs, districts, or villages, including governors and mayors, as well as administrative agencies and units representing a sub-branch of national ministries and departments. Complex structures determine how far decision-making powers, control of taxation and spending, and administrative responsibilities are dispersed among governing units at local, state, provincial, and central levels, such as roles and responsibilities over public health care, social services, and education.

Decentralization is often thought to strengthen democratic participation, representation, and accountability, as well as improving government efficiency and effectiveness. Federal forms of power-sharing are commonly regarded as especially suitable for accommodating cultural diversity in fragile multinational states. Nevertheless critics argue that decentralized arrangements may fail to strengthen democracy and federalism may dilute a sense of unity and commitment to the nation-state, thereby undermining fragile multicultural states such as Iraq and Sudan.

The typology of vertical power-sharing constitutional arrangements used in this study defined *unitary* constitutions as those where the national government retains sovereignty over all subnational tiers. In this system, the presidential executive branch, or the prime minister heading the largest party in the lower house of the national parliament, has both de jure and de facto authority to override all other regulations, directives, and decisions emanating from subnational units. Constitutions were classified as *federal* if governments had national and subnational units, in a compound polity where each tier possesses some autonomous powers and functions. *Hybrid unions*, the intermediate category, represent those constitutions where some independent powers are granted for certain subnational units or dependent territories, but where sovereignty remains ultimately with the central government. The results of the time-series cross-national analysis served to confirm the consociational claims that compared with unitary states, federal arrangements were associated with stronger performance of democracy, even after controlling for many other factors commonly linked with democratization. Finally, the illustrative cases strongly suggest that the federal and decentralized vertical forms of power-sharing are one major reason why democracy has flourished in India, despite the odds in a vast, poor, and deeply divided society, while it has foundered in neighboring Bangladesh. More radical constitutional reforms through decentralized governance could be one way to break the stranglehold of the major parties in Bangladesh and therefore to lay the basis for more genuine and sustained multiparty competition.

8

The Fourth Estate

What is the role of the free press in strengthening democracy, good governance, and human development?[1] Liberal theorists have long argued that the existence of an unfettered and independent press within each nation is essential in the process of democratization, by contributing to the right of freedom of expression, thought, and conscience; strengthening the responsiveness and accountability of governments to all citizens; and providing a pluralist platform and channel of political expression for a multiplicity of groups and interests.[2] The guarantee of freedom of expression and information is recognized as a basic human right in the Universal Declaration of Human Rights adopted by the UN in 1948, the European Convention on Human Rights, the American Convention on Human Rights, and the African Charter on Human and Peoples' Rights. In particular, Article 19 of the 1948 Universal Declaration of Human Rights states: "Everyone has the right to freedom of opinion and expression; this right includes freedom to hold opinions without interference and to seek, receive and impart information and ideas through any media and regardless of frontiers." The positive relationship between the growth of the free press and the process of democratization is thought to be reciprocal. The core claim is that in the first stage the initial transition from autocracy opens up the state control of the media to private ownership, diffuses access, and reduces official censorship and government control of information. The public thereby receives greater exposure to a wider variety of cultural products and ideas through access to multiple radio and TV channels, as well as the diffusion of new technologies such as the Internet and mobile telephones. Once media liberalization has commenced, in the second stage democratic consolidation is strengthened where journalists in independent newspapers and radio and television stations facilitate greater transparency and accountability in governance, by serving in their watchdog role to deter corruption and malfeasance, as well as providing a civic forum for multiple voices in public debate, and highlighting problems to inform the policy agenda.[3]

Through this process, numerous observers have emphasized, a free press is valuable for democracy, for good governance, and for human development. This perspective is exemplified by Amartya Sen's famous argument that in independent and democratic countries, the free press encourages government responsiveness to public concerns, by highlighting cases of famine and natural disasters: "in the terrible history of famines in the world, no substantial famine has ever occurred in any independent and democratic country with a relatively free press."[4] The independent media, Sen suggests, enhances the voice of poor people and generates more informed choices about economic needs and priorities.[5] James D. Wolfensen echoed these sentiments when he was the president of the World Bank: "A free press is not a luxury. A free press is at the absolute core of equitable development, because if you cannot enfranchise poor people, if they do not have a right to expression, if there is no searchlight on corruption and inequitable practices, you cannot build the public consensus needed to bring about change."[6] Systematic evidence supporting these claims has been reported by Besley and Burgess, who found that Indian state governments proved more responsive to external shocks, such as falls in crop production and crop flood damage, by expanding local public relief in places where newspaper circulation was higher and electoral accountability greater.[7] Similarly, greater transparency and more open information are thought to be particularly important for stamping out malfeasance and misappropriations by public officials; for example, economic studies have reported that places with widespread newspaper circulation and the existence of freedom of information laws have less corruption.[8] Many case studies also emphasize the vital role of the mass media in transitions from autocracy, for instance, in Georgia's 'rose' revolution.[9] Likewise in Serbia, Georgia, and Ukraine, McFaul argues that the presence of the independent media was one of the key components of successful transitions from post-Communist states, for instance, their role in highlighting news about rigged votes and publicizing popular protests and dissent expressed against the authorities, encouraging opposition movements onto the streets.[10]

More liberal media landscapes are therefore widely regarded among popular commentators, donor agencies, and the international community as strengthening democratization processes. But what systematic comparative evidence supports these claims? Much existing research has focused on assessing the impact of media structures and access, such as the diffusion of independent newspapers or the existence of private television channels or radio stations, rather than comparing press freedom per se.[11] Cross-national work on democratic institutions has usually emphasized the classic constitutional arrangements analyzed in earlier chapters, including the impact of electoral and party systems, federal or unitary states, and parliamentary or presidential executives, while neglecting to analyze comparable evidence about the institutional role and function of the news media as an integral part of power-sharing arrangements.[12] Yet many constitutions contain general provisions respecting rights to freedom of speech and the press, and more detailed freedom of information and data protection laws implementing these rights have been passed in more than six dozen nations worldwide, often a fairly recent development, as part of the anticorruption drive to promote transparency and open government.[13] Many other statutory provisions can limit or promote media independence, including requirements for registration or licenses for journalists or newspapers, broadcasting regulations and the degree of public and commercial ownership of radio and television stations, as well as laws governing broadcasting contents, concentration of ownership, official secrecy, intellectual property, libel, and taxation.[14] Levels of access to radio, television, newspapers, and the Internet also vary substantially around the globe, affecting patterns of information reach and availability.[15]

To explore the role of the independent media in the democratization process, the first section outlines the analytical framework and summarizes the previous research on this topic. The second outlines the comparative evidence where Freedom House provides the principal measure of Press Freedom, with annual data available from 1992 to 2007. This indicator is strongly correlated with the independently developed Press Freedom Index created by Reporters without Borders, increasing confidence in the reliability of the Freedom House measure. The next sections describe the distribution and trends in press freedom. The analytical models using time-series cross-national regression present the results after controlling for many factors commonly associated with processes of democratization, as observed earlier, including levels of economic development, colonial origins, population size, and regional effects, as well as other institutional arrangements. Two paired cases drawn from Eurasia are then compared, in Ukraine and Uzbekistan, to illustrate the underlying processes at work and the role of the media in regime change. The study confirms that even with prior controls, freedom of the press contributes toward democratic governance, with important consequences as another check and balance on government.

THE ROLES OF THE NEWS MEDIA AS WATCHDOG, CIVIC FORUM, AND AGENDA SETTER

In the late-1950s and early-1960s, early modernization theories assumed fairly simple and unproblematic relationships among the spread of access to modern forms of mass communications, economic development, and the process of democratization. Accounts offered by Lerner, Lipset, Pye, Cutright, and others suggested that the diffusion of mass communications represented one sequential step in the development process. In this view, urbanization and the spread of literacy led to growing access to modern technologies such as telephones, newspapers, radios, and television, all of which laid the basis for an informed citizenry able to participate effectively in political affairs.[16] Hence, on the basis of a strong connection between the spread of communications and political development, Daniel Lerner theorized: "The capacity to read, at first acquired by relatively few people, equips them to perform the varied tasks required in the modernizing society. Not until the third stage, when the elaborate technology of industrial development is fairly well advanced, does a society begin to produce newspapers, radio networks, and motion pictures on a massive scale. This, in turn, accelerates the spread of literacy. Out of this interaction develop those institutions of participation (e.g. voting) which we find in all advanced modern societies."[17]

By the late-1960s and early-1970s, however, the assumption that the modernization process involved a series of sequential steps gradually fell out of fashion. Skepticism grew, faced with the complexities of human development evident in different parts of the world, and the major setbacks for democracy with the 'second reverse wave' experienced in Latin America, sub-Saharan Africa, and Asia.[18] There was growing recognition that widening public *access* to newspapers, radio, and television was insufficient by itself to promote democracy and development, as these media could be used to maintain autocracies, to reinforce crony capitalism, and to consolidate the power of media oligopolies, as much as to provide a democratic channel for the disadvantaged.[19] Access remains important, but this study theorizes that the news media is most effective in strengthening the process of democratization, good governance, and human development where journalists function as a *watchdog* over the abuse of power (promoting accountability and transparency), as a *civic forum* for political debate (facilitating informed electoral choices), and as an *agenda setter* for policymakers (strengthening government responsiveness to social problems).[20]

The Role of Journalists as Watchdogs of the Powerful

In their 'watchdog' role, the channels of the news media can function to promote government transparency, accountability, and public scrutiny of decision makers in power, by highlighting policy failures, maladministration by public officials, corruption in the judiciary, and scandals in the corporate sector.[21] Since Edmund Burke, the 'fourth estate' has traditionally been regarded as one of the classic checks and balances in the division of powers.[22] Investigative journalism can open the government's record to external scrutiny and critical evaluation and hold authorities accountable for their actions to the public as well as scrutinizing the record of public sector institutions, nonprofit organizations, or private companies. Comparative econometric studies, and historical case studies of developments within particular countries such as Taiwan, have explored evidence for the impact of the news media upon corruption. Brunetti and Weder, among others, found that there was less corruption in nations with a free press. The reason, they argue, is that journalists' roles as watchdogs promote the transparency of government decision-making processes and thereby expose and hinder misuse of public office, malfeasance, and financial scandals.[23] In competitive multiparty democracies, voters can use information provided by the media to hold parties and leaders to account by 'kicking the rascals out'.

By contrast, control of the news media is used to reinforce the power of autocratic regimes and to deter criticism of the government by independent journalists, through official government censorship, state ownership of the main radio and television channels, legal restrictions on freedom of expression and publication (such as stringent libel laws and restrictive official secrets acts), limited competition through oligopolies in commercial ownership, and use of outright violence and intimidation against journalists and broadcasters.[24] In Malaysia, for example, human rights observers report that the state has manipulated the media to stifle internal dissent and forced journalists employed by the international press to modify or suppress news stories unflattering to the regime.[25] Elsewhere governments in Myanmar, Sri Lanka, and Saudi Arabia, among others, commonly place serious restrictions on press freedom to criticize government rulers through official regulations, legal restrictions, and state censorship.[26] It remains more difficult for governments to censor online communications, but nevertheless in nations such as China and Cuba, state-controlled monopolies provide the only Internet service and thereby filter both access and content.[27] Media freedom organizations demonstrate that each year dozens of media professionals are killed or injured in the course of their work. In Colombia, Sierra Leone, Liberia, Zimbabwe, and Egypt, for example, many journalists, broadcasters, and editors have experienced intimidation or harassment, while journalists in many parts of the world face the daily threat of personal danger from wars or imprisonment by the security services.[28]

The Role of the News Media as Civic Forum

Equally vital, in their civic forum role, the free press can strengthen the public sphere, by mediating between citizens and the state, facilitating debate about the major issues of the day, and informing the public about party leadership, political issues, and government actions.[29] If the channels of communication reflect the social and cultural pluralism within each society, in a fair and impartial balance, then multiple interests and voices are heard in public deliberation. On the other hand, if the airwaves and press overwhelmingly favor the government, this state of affairs can drown out credible opponents. The role of the media is particularly important during election campaigns, as balanced and open access to the airwaves by opposition parties, candidates, and groups is critical for competitive and fair multiparty contests. During campaigns, the media provides citizens with information to compare and evaluate the retrospective record, prospective policies, and leadership characteristics of parties and candidates, providing the essential conditions for informed voting choices.[30] The role of the news media as a civic forum remains deeply flawed where major newspapers and television stations heavily favor the governing party, in the total balance or else the tone of coverage, rather than being open to a plurality of political viewpoints and parties during campaigns. This principle has been recognized in jurisprudence from countries as varied as Ghana, Sri Lanka, Belize, India, Trinidad and Tobago, and Zambia.[31] There are many cases where electoral observers have reported that bias on television and radio toward the party or leader in government has failed to provide a level playing field for all contenders, exemplified by election campaigns in Russia, Belarus, and Mozambique.[32] As observed earlier, in Benin and Mali the process of liberalization and privatization has undermined the older state-controlled media, which once consolidated the grip of autocrats, facilitating competitive multiparty electoral democracies.[33]

By contrast, where the media fails to act as an effective civic forum, this can hinder democratic consolidation, as observed earlier in Togo. State ownership and control of the primary broadcasting channels are important issues, but threats to media pluralism are also raised by overconcentration of private ownership of the media, whether in the hands of broadcasting oligopolies within each nation or of major multinational corporations with multimedia empires.[34] It is feared that the process of media mergers may have concentrated excessive control in the hands of a few multinational corporations, which remain unaccountable to the public, reducing the diversity of news media outlets.[35] Contemporary observers caution that the quality of democracy remains limited where state ownership of television has been replaced by private oligopolies and crony capitalism, for example, in nations such as Russia, Brazil, and Peru, which have failed to create fully independent and pluralistic media systems. Broadcasting cartels, coupled with the failure of regulatory reform, legal policies which restrict critical reporting, and uneven journalistic standards, can all limit the role of the media in its civic forum or watchdog role.[36]

Speaking Truth to Power

Last, the news media also functions as an agenda setter, providing information about urgent social problems and thereby channeling citizens' concerns to decision makers in government. Particularly in cases of natural disaster, public officials often suffer from a breakdown in the usual channels of communication. Poor internal communications among official agencies can hinder the delivery of effective emergency relief, so that timely and accurate information about the scope and nature of any disaster is vital as the first component of any effective official response. Similar observations can be made concerning reporting about social issues such as the extent of any food shortages, the spread of diseases such as HIV/AIDS, or problems of crime and violence. In these situations, independent journalists can act as a vital conduit for decision makers, helping to make governments more responsive to the needs of the people. For example, Besley and Burgess examined the Indian case and established that regions with higher levels of newspaper circulation proved more active during an emergency in responding to food shortages.[37] The reason, they suggest, is that political leaders learn about local problems more accurately and in a timely fashion when journalists function as an intermediary by reporting living conditions at the grass roots, and the role of news headlines as an agenda setter can also pressure officials to respond to local problems and report cases of corruption and misuse of public money.

INDICATORS OF PRESS FREEDOM

For all of these reasons, where the press is effective in these roles, greater media freedom and journalistic independence can be expected to promote and sustain democracy, as well as to improve broader indicators of good governance, such as limiting corruption. To explore some of the evidence, the annual Freedom House Index of Press Freedom was used as the standard cross-national indicator.[38] Press freedom is measured by this index according to how much the diversity of news content is influenced by the structure of the news industry, legal and administrative decisions, the degree of political influence or control, the economic influences exerted by the government or private entrepreneurs, and actual incidents violating press autonomy, including censorship, harassment, and physical threats to journalists. The *legal environment* category examines the laws and regulations that could influence media content, as well as the government's inclination to use these laws and legal institutions to restrict the media's ability to operate. The organization assesses the positive impact of legal and constitutional guarantees for freedom of expression; the potentially negative aspects of security legislation, the penal code, and other criminal statutes; penalties for libel and defamation; the existence of and ability to use freedom of information legislation; the independence of the judiciary and of official media regulatory bodies; registration requirements for both media outlets and journalists; and the ability of journalists' groups to operate freely. Under the *political environment* category, Freedom House evaluates the degree of political control over the content of news media. Issues examined here include the editorial independence of both state-owned and privately owned media, access to information and sources, official censorship and self-censorship, the vibrancy of the media, the ability of both foreign and local reporters to cover the news freely and without harassment, and the intimidation of journalists by the state or other actors, including arbitrary detention and imprisonment, violent assaults, and other threats. The last category examines the *economic environment* for the media. This includes the structure of media ownership, transparency and concentration of ownership, the costs of establishing media as well as of production and distribution, the selective withholding of advertising or subsidies by the state or other actors, the impact of corruption and bribery on content, and the extent to which the economic situation in a country impacts the development of the media. The assessment of press freedom distinguishes between the broadcast and print media, and the resulting ratings are expressed as a 100-point scale for each country under comparison. Evaluations of press freedom in 191 contemporary nations were available in the Freedom House annual index from 1992 to 2007.

As with any such indicators, however, it is important to check whether the results of this measure proved reliable or biased. To do this, the Freedom House index was compared against the Worldwide Press Freedom Index, which is independently produced by Reporters without Borders. The Worldwide Press Freedom Index is constructed to reflect the degree of freedom journalists and news organizations enjoy in each country, and the efforts made by the state to respect and ensure respect for this freedom. The organization compiled a questionnaire with 52 criteria for assessing the state of press freedom in each country. It includes every kind of violation directly affecting journalists (such as murders, imprisonment, physical attacks, and threats) and news media (censorship, confiscation of issues, searches, and harassment). It registers the degree of impunity enjoyed by those responsible for such violations. It also takes account of the legal situation affecting the news media (such as penalties for press offenses, the existence of a state monopoly in certain areas, and the existence of a regulatory body), the behavior of the authorities toward the state-owned news media and the foreign press, and the main obstacles to the free flow of information on the Internet. The Worldwide Press Freedom Index reflects not only abuses attributable to the state, but also those by armed militias, clandestine organizations, or pressure groups that can pose a real threat to press freedom.

The results of the comparison of these two indices in the 160 nations where there are data, illustrated in Figure 8.1, show a strong correlation across both these measures (R = .755, sig .001), with just a few outliers such as Sao Tome and Principe where the organizations disagree in their rankings. The indices differ in their construction, data sources, and conceptualization. Despite this, these organizations largely report similar judgments, a correspondence which increases confidence in the reliability of the measures. The Freedom House measure was selected for the analysis since it provides the longer time-series, with data available since 1994, compared with the start of the Reporters without Borders index in 2002. Nevertheless replication of the basic models in this study suggests that the results remain robust irrespective of the particular measure used for analysis, which is hardly surprising given their intercorrelation. Many countries scoring most highly on press freedom by both these indicators are highly developed nations, such as New Zealand, the Netherlands, and Sweden, as expected given the strong linkage established earlier between affluence and democracy. But other countries with high press freedom are classified by the UNDP as having only moderate or even low development, as Mali and Benin, Jamaica, Nicaragua, and El Salvador, as well as Burkina Faso and Senegal. The countries ranked as having the minimal freedom of the press by both organizations include Cuba, Eritrea, China, and Turkmenistan. Alternative indicators which are available for comparison include whether countries recognize rights to freedom of expression in their written constitutions, or whether they have passed a freedom of information act.[39] These measures were not used in this study, however, because what matters is the implementation of such rights or legislation; after all, the Kyrgyz republic, Russia, and Colombia have such freedom of information laws on their books, while Uzbekistan's constitution has a nominal guarantee protecting freedom of speech and the press, but this does not mean that journalists are safe in these countries or that such regulations have proved effective in promoting freedom of the press.

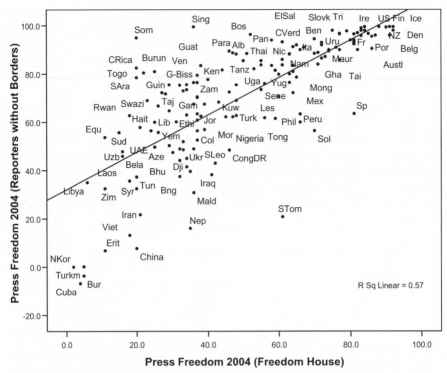

FIGURE 8.1. Press Freedom in 161 Nations Worldwide, 2004. *Note:* Freedom House Global Press Freedom Index, 100 points (100 = high). Reporters without Borders Press Freedom Index, 100 points (100 = high). See the Technical Appendix for the construction of each index. *Sources:* Freedom House. *Freedom in the World.* www.freedomhouse.org (various years); Reporters without Borders.

THE DISTRIBUTION OF THE FREE PRESS

What do these indices show about the contemporary distribution of press freedom? The pattern shows considerable variations around the world. As illustrated in Figure 8.2, as expected, the most liberal media were usually found in industrialized nations, including the most affluent economies and longest-standing democracies. Latin America and Southeast Asia proved the regions which also scored relatively high in freedom of the press, and the Arab states the least free. Despite the growing audience for the more independent and aggressive style of journalism found in Al Jazeera, and moves to liberalize the press in other nations in the region, this region lagged behind others to a marked extent. Nevertheless important contrasts can be found within regions; for example, some relatively affluent nations have serious restrictions on an independent press, notably Saudi Arabia, Singapore, and Malaysia. In Singapore, as observed earlier, the People's Action Party (PAP), founded and

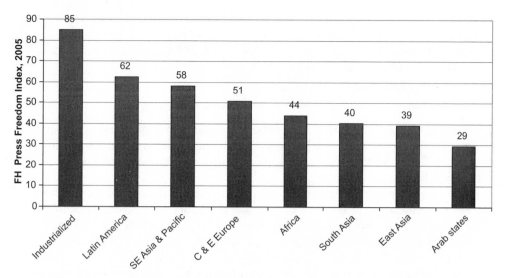

FIGURE 8.2. Press Freedom by Global Region, 2005. *Note:* Freedom House Press Freedom Index, 100 pts. *Source:* Freedom House. *Freedom in the World.* www. freedomhouse.org (various years).

originally led by Lee Kuan Yew, has maintained its unbroken rule in government since 1959, despite a regular series of multiparty contests challenging their hegemonic status. One reason contributing to the ruling party's predominance is their strong control of the press and news media; for example, the leading newspaper of Singapore, the *Straits Times*, is often perceived as a propaganda newspaper because it rarely criticizes government policy and covers little about the opposition. The owners of the paper, Singapore Press Holdings, have close links to the ruling party and the corporation has a virtual monopoly of the newspaper industry. Government censorship of journalism is common, using the threat or imposition of heavy fines or distribution bans imposed by the Media Development Authority, with these techniques also used against articles seen to be critical of the government published in the international press, including the *Economist* and *International Times Herald Tribune*. Internet access is regulated in Singapore, and private ownership of satellite dishes is not allowed. As a result of this record, the Reporters without Borders assessment of Press Freedom Worldwide in 2005 ranked Singapore 140th out of 167 nations.

By contrast, some poorer developing nations, such as Bolivia, Mali, Benin, and South Africa, also scored well on journalistic freedom. As discussed earlier, Benin is widely regarded as a successful African democracy with constitutional checks and balances, multiple parties, a high degree of judicial independence, and a lively partisan press, which is often critical of the government. Benin ranks 161st lowest out of 177 states in the 2003 UNDP Human Development Index, with a per capita GDP (in purchasing power parity) of $1,115. One-third of the population lives with income below the poverty level and two-thirds of the adult population is illiterate. Despite this, the country is categorized as 66th out of 195 nations in the 2007 Freedom House Global Press Freedom Index, comparable to Italy, Israel, and Chile in its record.

THE IMPACT OF THE FREE PRESS ON DEMOCRACY

The key question is whether press freedom is related to democracy, even using multivariate regression models controlling for many other institutions and control variables which previous chapters established are commonly associated with political development.

As in previous chapters, in the multivariate models the dependent variables are two indicators of levels of democracy: the Polity IV project's measure of constitutional democracy and Vanhanen's indicator of participatory democracy. Freedom House's index of liberal democracy was not employed in this chapter as the measure contains freedom of the press as one of its core components. By contrast, the other two indicators do not suffer from this problem as neither contains data on freedom of the press. As discussed in Chapter 3, Polity IV excludes civil liberties in its measure of constitutional democracy, focusing instead on constructing a measure based on the competitiveness and openness of executive recruitment, constraints on the chief executive, and the competitiveness of political participation. Vanhanen's participatory democracy also excludes any classification of freedom of the press as it is based on the degree of electoral competition and the level of electoral participation. The most prudent strategy, as adopted by earlier chapters, is to compare the results of analytical models using alternative indicators, to see whether the findings remain robust and consistent irrespective of the specific measures of democracy which are employed for analysis. If so, as Collier and Adcock suggest, this procedure generates greater confidence in the reliability of the results and we can conclude that the main generalizations hold irrespective of the particular measures which are used.[40]

As noted in Chapter 4, the relationship between *wealth* and democracy is a long-standing observation which has withstood repeated tests in the social sciences, and accordingly the models were initially tested controlling for levels of economic development (measured by logged per capita GDP in purchasing power parity [PPP]), but this variable was dropped from the final model, after checking for tolerance, as a result of problems of collinearity with the strength of the free press. The models control for the effects of the *historical pattern of colonial legacies*. An association between the past type of colonial rule and contemporary patterns of democracy has been noted by several observers; for example, Clague, Gleason, and Knack report that lasting democracies (characterized by contestation for government office) are most likely to emerge and persist among poor nations in ex-British colonies, even controlling for levels of economic development, ethnic diversity, and the size of the population.[41] The *Middle East* is also entered into the analysis, since many observers have pointed out that this region has been least affected by the trends in democratization since the start of the third wave, and indeed to be the least democratic region worldwide. The degree of *ethnic heterogeneity* is also entered, on the grounds that deeply divided societies are widely assumed to experience greater problems of democratic consolidation. Nations were classified according to the degree of ethnic fractionalization, based on a global dataset created by Alesina and his colleagues.[42] The models also control for the impact of the *size of the population* and the *geographic size* of each country. Ever since Dahl and Tufte, the idea that size matters for democracy has been widely assumed, and Alesina and Spolaore have provided the most detailed recent examination of this proposition.[43] Smaller nations are expected to be easier to govern democratically; for example, the smaller the population, the greater the potential for citizen participation in key decisions. Finally, the institutions already observed as linked to patterns of democracy are added, namely, proportional representation electoral systems, parliamentary monarchies as a type of executive, and federal constitutions. The number of cases used for analysis dropped substantially, compared with previous chapters, given the shorter period available for the data on freedom of the press.

The results of the multivariate analysis in Table 8.1 confirm that the free press is significantly associated with levels of democracy, even after employing the battery of controls. The impact of the free press appears to be robust irrespective of the particular indicator of democracy which is selected, despite major differences in the conceptualization and measurement processes used by Polity IV and by Vanhanen. Indeed the impact of media liberalization was one of the most consistent predictors of democracy out of any of the factors under comparison. The institutions of the type of electoral system (proportional representation) and the type of executive (parliamentary monarchies) also remained significantly associated with levels of democracy, although the measure of federalism dropped out of the analysis in one model. The results of the overall models explained in total between 55% and 62% of the variance in the Polity IV and Vanhanen measures of democracy. The contemporary pattern was inspected visually in Figure 8.3, using the Polity IV measure of democracy, to examine the goodness of fit and to identify any obvious outliers. As the scatter-plot shows, a few countries fall quite far below the line, such as Russia, Guatamala, and Bangladesh, suggesting that limits on independent journalism in these nations may be more severe than might be expected from other indicators of democracy, such as holding free and fair elections for the major government offices. And there are other countries well above the line where the free press is particularly strong, given their overall level of democratization.

CASE STUDIES: UKRAINE AND UZBEKISTAN

To understand the underlying processes at work in this relationship, cases examining the role of the independent media in regime transitions and in multiethnic societies were selected from post-Soviet Eurasia. Significant and

TABLE 8.1. *The Free Press and Democracy, All Societies Worldwide*

	Constitutional Democracy			Participatory Democracy		
	Polity IV			Vanhanen		
	B	PCSE	P	B	PCSE	P
INSTITUTIONS						
PR Electoral system	10.88	(.091)	***	6.46	(1.00)	***
Parliamentary monarchy	10.67	(3.13)	***	2.36	(1.13)	*
Federal constitution	1.24	(.926)	N/s	2.79	(.468)	***
Freedom of the press	.501	(.091)	***	.251	(.055)	***
CONTROLS						
Ex-British colony (o/1)	2.22	(2.46)	N/s	−1.56	(.697)	*
Middle East (o/1)	−16.16	(1.58)	***	−.965	(1.12)	N/s
Regional diffusion of democracy	.295	(.058)	***	.654	(.037)	***
Ethnic fractionalization (0–100-pt scale)	−5.67	(4.25)	N/s	−10.30	(2.27)	***
Population size (thou)	−.001	(.001)	N/s	−.001	(.001)	**
Area size (sq mi)	.001	(.001)	N/s	.001	(.001)	*
Constant	19.7			−7.89		
No. of observations	1,495			1,256		
No. of countries	154			181		
Adjusted R^2	.616			.554		

Note: Entries for constitutional democracy and participatory democracy are unstandardized beta OLS regression coefficients (B) with panel-corrected standard errors (PCSE) and the significance of the coefficients (P) for the pooled time-series cross-national dataset obtained using Stata's xtpcse command. With PCSE the disturbances are, by default, assumed to be heteroskedastic (each nation has its own variance) and contemporaneously correlated across nations. Models for contested democracy were run using logistic regression for the binary dependent variable, with the results summarized by Nagelkerke R square. For the measures of democracy, standardized to 100-point scales and lagged by one year, see Chapter 2. For details of all the variables, see the Technical Appendix. Significant at * the 0.05 level, ** the 0.01 level, and *** the 0.001 level.

sustained progress toward democracy has transformed the political landscape in Central and Eastern Europe since the fall of the Berlin Wall in the late-1980s and early-1990s, including the extension of the 27-member European Union to the borders of the Black Sea. This was followed in a second stage by the 'color revolutions' in the mid-1990s signifying a radical transition in the political leadership in Georgia (the 2003 rose revolution), Ukraine (the 2004 orange revolution), and Kyrgyzstan (the 2005 tulip revolution).[44] Each time massive street protests followed disputed elections and led to the resignation or overthrow of unpopular authoritarian leaders. As Hale points out, these dramatic events all occurred when countries were entering a period of succession, with the previous leader either too old, too unpopular, or too afraid of legal term limits to continue.[45] Although triggering processes of regime change, it remains unclear at this stage whether the dramatic events in Ukraine will lead toward the transition and consolidation of a stable democratic state. Instead of a smoothly sequential process, some observers interpret the process of regime

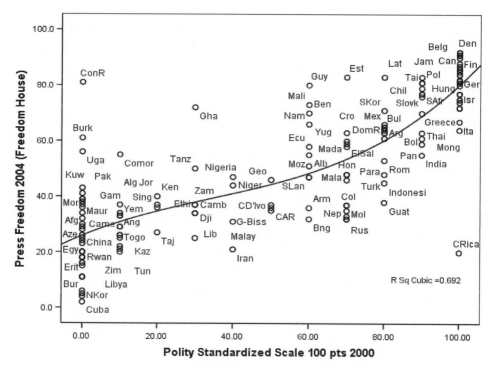

FIGURE 8.3. Press Freedom by Level of Democratization. *Notes:* Freedom House Press Freedom Index 2004, 100-pt scale. Polity IV autocracy-democracy scale, standardized to 0–100 points. *Sources:* Freedom House. *Freedom in the World.* www.freedomhouse.org (various years); Polity IV.

change as cyclical, with incremental steps ebbing and flowing, and with omissions and deviations, rather than a steady march toward democracy.[46] At the same time, other Eurasian states such as Belarus, Uzbekistan, and Turkmenistan, which also gained independence following the collapse of the Soviet Union in 1991, have failed to make any consistent transition from authoritarian rule. These states have not witnessed a peaceful handover of power from the governing leader to opposition parties following elections, or any substantial gains in human rights. Presidents in these nations continue to exert rigid control, through a series of manipulated elections. Their power is bolstered through restricting the independent media, intimidating government critics and crushing dissent, persecuting journalists, and limiting reporting about unrest or public discontent.

The striking contrasts which are apparent between Uzbekistan and Ukraine today illustrate the role of the mass media in the process of regime transitions. Those countries were selected for comparison as they shared common political histories for more than a century under the dominance of the Russian Empire and then the Soviet Union, attaining roughly similar levels of

TABLE 8.2. *Key Indicators in Ukraine and Uzbekistan*

	Ukraine	Uzbekistan
SOCIAL AND ECONOMIC INDICATORS		
Area	603,700 sq km	447,400 sq km
Pop., 2007	46.3m	27.8m
Pop. below poverty line (%)	29%	33%
GDP per capita (PPP US$), 2006	$7,600	$2,000
Life expectancy at birth, 2003	68 years	65 years
Human Development Index, 2003	.780	.710
Adult literacy (% of pop. 15+), 2003	99.7%	99.3%
Ethnic fractionalization (Alesina), 2002	.473	.412
POLITICAL INDICATORS		
Year of independence (from)	1991 (Soviet Union)	1991 (Soviet Union)
Liberal democracy (Freedom House), (USSR), 1973	6	6
Freedom House classification (of USSR), 1973	(Not free)	(Not free)
Liberal democracy (Freedom House) Index, 2007	2.5	7
Freedom House classification, 2007	Free	Not free
Press freedom rank (Freedom House), 2006	113th/194	187th/194
Press freedom (Reporters without Borders), 2006	105th/168	158th/168
Control of corruption (Kaufmann), 2005	35	13
Government effectiveness (Kaufmann), 2005	40	10
Political stability (Kaufmann), 2005	32	3
Rule of law (Kaufmann), 2005	35	7
Voice and accountability (Kaufmann), 2005	40	4
Regulatory quality (Kaufmann), 2005	47	4

Note: See the Technical Appendix for details of these indices and full sources of data. The Kaufmann indices rank each country on 0–100-point scales where high = better governance ratings. Press freedom is ranked out of 194 nations by Freedom House and 168 nations by Reporters without Borders; in both higher scores = better ranked.

Source: Daniel Kaufmann, A. Kraay, and M. Mastruzzi. 2006. *Governance Matters V: Governance Indicators for 1996–2005.* Washington, DC: World Bank. www.worldbank.org

human development, poverty, education, and literacy today, although Ukraine is considerably more affluent in per capita GDP (see Table 8.2). Both are presidential republics, with few significant checks on the powers of the presidency in Uzbekistan, although parliament provides more effective checks and balances in the Ukrainian constitution, particularly after recent amendment. Both states are multiethnic societies; a significant proportion of those living in Ukraine are Russians or Russian-speaking (24%), and the country also contains sizable Romanian, Polish, and Hungarian linguistic minorities. This is comparable to Uzbekistan, located in Central Asia, where about three-quarters of the population speaks Uzbek and there are Russian, Tajik, and other linguistic groups. By religion, Ukraine is divided among Orthodox churches, although with high levels of secularization, while Uzbekistan is predominantly Muslim with

Orthodox minorities. Uzbekistan is the most populous Central Asian country and has the largest armed forces.

Uzbekistan

In 1991 Uzbekistan emerged as a sovereign country after more than a century of Russian rule – first as part of the Russian Empire and then as a component of the Soviet Union. The country continues to be governed by a Soviet-style autocrat, President Islam Karimov, who has dominated the leadership since 1989, when he rose to be Communist Party leader in the Soviet era. The following year he became Uzbek president and he has continued to rule ever since. A referendum held in 1995 extended his term until 2000, when he won the presidential elections with a reported 91.9% of the vote. A further referendum in 2002 extended the presidential term from five to seven years and there are no constitutional term limits on the presidency. President Karimov has sweeping powers as he appoints the prime minister and cabinet. The 100-seat upper house in the bicameral parliament contains 84 members indirectly elected by regional governing councils and the remainder appointed by the president. The lower house contains 120 members popularly elected by a majoritarian electoral system. The few OSCE international observers who monitored parliamentary elections at the end of 2004 condemned them as having failed to meet international standards, noting that although there were competing parties, all the candidates supported President Karimov.[47] There are also a dozen provinces functioning as administrative divisions, and the president selects and replaces provincial governors.

In this context, the state maintains tight control of the media, through owning or running most major national newspapers. Despite a formal constitutional ban on censorship, the media rights body Reporters without Borders said in 2005 that the use of violence against journalists and disinformation by the authorities were commonplace. According to the Committee to Protect Journalists, in 2006 Uzbekistan was in the top 10 countries for censorship of the media, ahead of Syria, Belarus, China, and Russia.[48] Uzbekistan saw an unsuccessful imitation of the color revolutions, with violence on both sides, at and around Andijan, on 13 May 2005. In this case, the events were triggered by the trial of 23 local businessmen, who were subsequently imprisoned. Several hundred demonstrators stormed the jail to release the businessmen and other prisoners. The military swiftly intervened to stamp out antigovernment protest by firing into the crowd of demonstrators.[49] Dispute continues to surround the number of fatalities, ranging from 173 in official figures given by the authorities to an estimated 750 by human rights groups. In the aftermath of the deadly unrest, activists were arrested, journalists were expelled from the area, Russian Web sites were blocked, and foreign TV news broadcasts by Russian broadcasters, CNN, BBC, and others were restricted, replaced by music videos on cable TV. Amnesty International reports that restrictions on press reporting worsened in the year following these events, along with the imprisonment, ill treatment, and torture of human rights activists.[50] Indeed two years later an Uzbek journalist was imprisoned for seven years for seeking to investigate events at Andijan. Prepublication state censorship of the press was officially abolished in 2002, but nevertheless OSCE observers report that many techniques used to stifle investigation of controversial subjects remain widespread, including tough regulations of the press, prosecution through strict libel or defamation laws, limits on newspaper licenses, intimidation or harassment of reporters, visa restrictions on entry for foreign journalists, restrictions on bloggers and Web sites, and self-censorship by journalists.[51]

The government in Uzbekistan controls much of the printing and distribution infrastructure, although private TV and radio stations operate alongside state-run broadcasters. There are no private publishing houses or printing presses, and the establishment of a new newspaper is subject to political approval. Foreign channels are carried via cable TV, which is widely available. The Committee to Protect Journalists notes that many Uzbeks rely on foreign sources – including Russian TV and other broadcasters – as a counterpoint to the stifled domestic news media.[52] The law limits criticism of the president, and public insults are a crime punishable by up to five years in prison. The law also specifically prohibits articles that incite religious confrontation and ethnic discord or advocate subverting or overthrowing the constitutional order. In short, the post-Communist authoritarianism exercised by Karimov has not yet been successfully challenged by other elites, opposition parties, or reform movements in part because of the severe repressions of critical coverage. In a ranking of press freedom worldwide, Uzbekistan was rated in 2007 as 189th out of 195 nations by Freedom House, and it was ranked 158th out of 164 countries by the Reporters without Borders World Press Freedom Index. Indeed, far from any improvement, the last decade has seen a glacial erosion in freedom of the press in Uzbekistan, according to the Freedom House index.

Ukraine

Ukraine also gained independence as a presidential republic after the collapse of the Soviet Union in 1991. After independence, former Communist Party official Leonid Kravchuk gained almost two-thirds of the popular vote in the 1991 presidential elections. His support was slashed in the 1994 elections, however, following a period of economic decline and runaway inflation. The contest was won by the former prime minister, Leonid Kuchma. The new constitution adopted in June 1996 specified popular elections for the president for a five-year term (limited to two successive terms) using a second ballot majoritarian system. Under this system, President Kuchma was reelected for a second term in 1999, with 56% of the vote.

The unicameral 450-member parliament (Supreme Council) is directly elected using a system which has been amended on a number of occasions.[53]

Since Ukrainian independence, parliamentary contests were held in 1994 and 1998 using a combined-independent (mixed parallel) system, where Ukrainian voters could each cast two ballots. Half the deputies (225) were elected by a second ballot majoritarian system in single-member districts, and the remainder were elected from nationwide closed PR party lists, with a 4% national vote threshold. The two electoral systems operated separately, so that many smaller parties were elected from the single-member districts. The 1998 elections were contested by 30 parties and party blocs, although only 10 of these groups could be said to have a clear programmatic profile and organizational base. The Ukrainian result in 1998 produced a party system that was both extremely fragmented and unstable: 8 parties were elected via party lists and 17 won seats via the single-member districts, along with 116 Independents. The election produced one of the highest effective numbers of parliamentary parties (5.98) in the region, and it also generated a fairly disproportional votes/seats ratio that benefited the larger parties. Ethnicity was reflected in the appeal of particular parties, including the Russophile Social Liberal Union, the Party of Regional Revival, and the Soyuz (Union) Party, and in the way that ethnic Russians were twice as likely to support the Communist Party as ethnic Ukrainians.[54] In turn, the largest parties in parliament select the prime minister, providing a greater check and balance than the system in Uzbekistan.

In the presidential elections held in October 2004, election observers reported government intimidation of the opposition and of independent media, abuse of state administrative resources, and skewed press coverage. The two major candidates were Prime Minister Viktor Yanukovych and opposition leader (and former prime minister) Viktor Yushchenko. Outgoing president Leonid Kuchma backed as his successor Viktor Yanukovych, a candidate also supported by Russia. Each candidate garnered between 39% and 40% of the vote and proceeded to a winner-take-all second round ballot. On 24 November 2004, the Central Electoral Commission (CEC) declared Prime Minister Yanukovych the winner with 49.46% compared to 46.61% for Yushchenko. Observers widely reported that the results were rigged, however, generating the mass protest of this outcome for 10 days. The November 21 runoff election was marred by credible reports of widespread and significant violations, including illegal expulsion of opposition representatives from election commissions, multiple voting by busloads of people, abuse of absentee ballots, reports of coercion of votes in schools and prisons, and an abnormally high number of (easily manipulated) mobile ballot box votes.[55] Hundreds of thousands of people took to the streets of Kyiv and other cities to protest electoral fraud and express support for Yushchenko and conducted peaceful demonstrations during what came to be known as the "orange revolution." In the turmoil that followed, journalists at the state-run TV rejected the network's usual pro-government line. For the first time in years, opposition views were aired in a balanced way. On 1 December, the Rada passed a vote of no confidence in the government. On 3 December, Ukraine's Supreme Court invalidated the CEC's announced results and mandated a repeat of the second-round vote to take place on December 26. The new ballot led to the victory of President Viktor Yushchenko by 51.99% of the votes, compared with 44.20% for Yanukovych. Just two years later, however, following parliamentary elections in 2006, divisions in the pro-presidential Our Ukraine bloc let Vikton Yanukovych make a comeback as prime minister, heading a coalition of the Party of Regions, Our Ukraine, and the Socialist Party.

The history of Ukraine since independence has therefore been characterized by an unstable transition, marked by continued strong clashes for power between the executive and legislative branches, and a lack of consensus about the constitutional rules of the game concerning the powers of the presidency, as well as many modifications to the electoral system used for parliament. A series of multiparty competitive elections have been held since independence, with far more effective legislative and judicial checks and balances on the powers of the executive than exist in Uzbekistan. Nevertheless numerous observers have raised doubts about Ukraine's ability to consolidate democratic institutions.[56] In this context, one important institutional check on the power of the executive, and a watchdog over corruption and cronyism, lies in the role of the news media. Independent reporting has contributed on certain occasions to decisive events in Ukrainian politics, notably during the 'orange revolution'. Ukraine is characterized by a vibrant and politically diverse newspaper industry, which is largely free of censorship and government interference, although observers note the continued harassment of journalists for reporting on stories critical of government officials. The decade under President Kuchma's rule saw the closure of a number of opposition papers and a marked deterioration in human rights. Moreover, several journalists investigating high-profile crimes died in mysterious circumstances. The most prominent case was the journalist Georgiy Gongadze, who disappeared in September 2000; his body was found two months later.

Today all the main newspapers are privately owned, some by oligarchs and individuals with close ties to the government, and offer a wide range of opinions as well as factual reporting. For example, *Zerkalo Nedeli* is Ukraine's most influential analytical weekly, published in Ukrainian and Russian. Widely read by the Ukrainian elite, the paper is nonpartisan. It was highly critical of both major parties in Ukraine. It employs high journalistic standards and offers political analysis, exclusive interviews, and opinion. There are hundreds of state and private television and radio stations, and Radio Free Europe has resumed broadcasting after being shut down in 2004. In contrast to Uzbekistan, in the same ratings of press freedom worldwide, Ukraine was rated in 2007 as 112th out of 195 nations by Freedom House, and it was ranked 105th out of 164 countries by the Reporters without Borders Press Freedom Index. The last few years have also seen resurgence in press freedom according to the Freedom House index (see Figure 8.4). The future of democracy in Ukraine remains uncertain but the constitutional reforms brought in under Yushchenko seem likely to strengthen the consensual arrangements, by increasing the proportionality of the electoral system, boosting the power of parliament, and limiting the

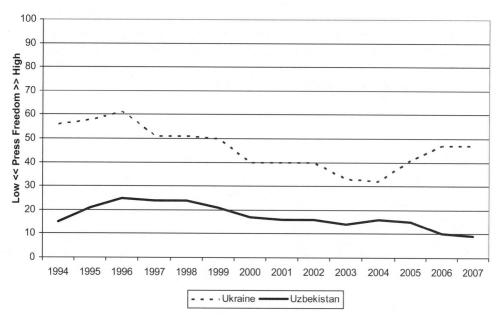

FIGURE 8.4. Press Freedom in Ukraine and Uzbekistan, 1994–2007. *Note:* Freedom House Press Freedom Index, 1994–2007, 100-pt scale (reversed, higher = greater freedom).

role of the president. If this lays the foundation for a genuine power-sharing constitutional settlement which is accepted by all parties, then in the long term this should help to promote consolidation, given the evidence presented throughout this study.

CONCLUSIONS

Overall the cross-national analysis lends considerable support to the claims of liberal theorists about the critical role of the free press, as one of the major components buttressing democratic transitions and consolidation. The independent media functions as another check and balance on government, although it remains unclear which of the roles of the free press – as watchdog, as civic forum, or as agenda setter – is most important in this relationship. Plausibly, for example, the effectiveness of the press as watchdogs should have the greatest impact upon stamping out corruption and promoting transparency and freedom of information, while their function in calling attention to social problems should influence government responsiveness to policy problems.

The illustrative case studies from post-Soviet Eurasia reinforce many of the claims about the role of independent journalism which are pervasive in liberal theory, including the core argument that independent journalism matters, both intrinsically and instrumentally. Policies which eradicate limits on the freedom of information and communication, whether due to state censorship, intimidation and harassment of journalists, or private media oligopolies, therefore have important consequences for those seeking to strengthen transitions from autocracy, although how far freedom expression and communication can contribute to the consolidation of democratic development in the particular cases compared here remains an open question at this stage.

PART III

CONCLUSIONS

9

What Works?

Lessons for Public Policy

In conclusion, what are the implications of this study for comparative research in the social sciences seeking to understand processes of democratization, as well as for practical reformers, NGOs, and agencies in the international community actively engaged in peace building and promoting democracy? This chapter summarizes the main findings developed throughout the book, and it considers further issues which skeptics could raise in response to the argument. One potential methodological criticism concerns the dangers of self-selection bias in the cases used for illustration and whether this invalidates the evidence. In addition, are power-sharing constitutions a practical and viable reform which should be advocated by domestic reformers and the international development community, as an effective strategy with a realistic chance of success? There are many reasons for caution about this claim. In particular, it should be emphasized that many alternative political reforms should also be implemented, beyond those discussed within this study; opportunities for major constitutional reform often remain extremely restricted; the odds of success in generating durable ends to civil wars are daunting; and the conditions of deep-rooted poverty and fragile states make democratic development through power-sharing agreements extremely challenging. Reflecting upon these issues provides insights into the fundamental role, and also limits, of institutional reforms.

THE IMPACT OF POWER-SHARING ARRANGEMENTS

Power-sharing arrangements are understood here to include four features as the basic building blocks, used singly or in combination. Proportional electoral systems with low vote thresholds and reserved seats facilitate the inclusion of minority parties in the legislature, opening the door to representation in multiparty coalitional cabinet government. Federal and decentralized arrangements allow minor parties to build a local power base and a degree of regional autonomy in the communities where their support is most concentrated. In parliamentary monarchies, prime ministers face many checks and balances on their decision-making authority within the cabinet and the legislature, including the ultimate sanction of removal from office. And an independent pluralistic news media in civil society, free of state control, scrutinizes the conduct of the powerful; expands transparency, accountability, and open government; and provides the foundation for informed choice by the electorate.

As outlined in the opening chapter, advocates make strong claims that power-sharing regimes encourage moderate and cooperative behavior among contending groups in divided societies.[1] Through inclusive processes in representative bodies, consociational democracies are thought to manage and contain ethnic tensions, armed uprisings, and intercommunal violence, helping to build peace and stabilize fragile democracies in plural societies. Rebel factions are encouraged to lay down their arms and to contest power as political parties, gradually becoming integrated into the conventional process of bargaining and compromise. These assumptions have shaped constitutional agreements in many recent peace-settlements, as exemplified by the Dayton Agreement governing Bosnia-Herzegovina and the Good Friday agreement in Northern Ireland. They remain at the heart of constitutional talks and peace-building initiatives in many countries, such as Nepal, Sudan, and Sri Lanka, which are currently searching for a solution for deep-rooted armed conflict.[2] Despite the popularity of these ideas, theories about power-sharing constitutions always attracted many critics challenging the core claims, the precise classification of cases, and the consequences of these arrangements.[3] Skeptics have emphasized the breakdown of these arrangements, such as in Lebanon and Cyprus. Controversy surrounding consociational theory has continued for almost 40 years. Despite a wealth of case studies cited by both proponents and critics, many issues remain unresolved. Over successive elections, proponents argue that power-sharing regimes generally serve to reduce conflict in deeply divided societies by providing rivals with a stake in the government, thereby facilitating a durable constitutional settlement, political stability, and the underlying conditions under which democracy flourishes. In response, critics suggest, the incentives under power-sharing regimes can unintentionally serve to freeze group boundaries and heighten latent ethnic identities, thus failing to ensure the long-term conditions leading toward stability and democratic consolidation.[4] This long-standing controversy generates important questions for scholarly researchers seeking to understand the underlying drivers of the democratization process. It raises even more pressing issues for domestic reformers and the international community trying to implement effective peace-settlements, rebuild failed states, and promote democratic governance.

The opening chapter outlined the theoretical reasons why power-sharing arrangements have been thought to generate incentives leading toward more stable processes of democratic consolidation, especially in plural societies divided into distinct communities. The study has presented the results of the systematic cross-national time-series analysis for patterns of regimes worldwide since the early-1970s, along with the selected paired case-study narratives, which point in a consistent direction. The cumulative results reinforce and confirm the advantages of power-sharing institutions which have often been assumed, irrespective of which particular indicators are selected to measure democracy, even with the controls used in the series of multivariate models. Societies which are deeply divided, whether by identities based on religion, language, region/nationality, ethnicity, or race, which are emerging from deep-rooted conflict should consider adopting power-sharing arrangements in democratic constitutional settlements.

Before examining the role of institutions, models have to control for broader conditions associated with democratic consolidation. Previous chapters confirmed the relationship between wealth and democratic consolidation in a variety of contexts and circumstances. The results of the analysis presented in this study lend further confirmation to the classic Lipset proposition that democracies usually flourish in wealthy economies. Democracies are also more likely to be found in countries with a British colonial heritage, in regions where there are many other democracies and outside the Middle East, in more homogeneous societies, and in nations with smaller populations. Nevertheless the relationship between the underlying characteristics and the type of regime remains probabilistic, and it was found to explain, at most, between one-half and two-thirds of the variance in democratization found during the third wave period. The case of South Korea plausibly fits the Lipset theory, but, as Singapore shows, many important outliers remain.

Electoral rules are some of the most basic institutional features of a regime and these determine much else about how democracy works, including patterns of party competitions, levels of electoral participation, and the representation of women and cultural minorities. The results of the analysis presented in this study confirmed that PR electoral systems are more democratic than majoritarian systems, especially in divided societies. The case studies of electoral reform in the United Kingdom and New Zealand suggested that either PR with low thresholds or positive action strategies (or both) can be used to facilitate the election of representatives and groups drawn from minority communities. The adoption of the additional member system in Scotland and Wales boosted the electoral success of nationalist parties in regional contests, with the Scottish National Party taking the reins of the regional government in a minority administration in 2007, although so far their increased support has not translated into greater representation in Westminster general elections. This process has also led to greater party fragmentation in Scotland. In New Zealand, the mixed member proportional electoral system strengthened the inclusion of Maoris, Asians, and Pacific Islanders, although it has also facilitated the success of the New Zealand First party on a platform of cultural protection, and thus stirred up greater controversy about issues of Maori rights and multiculturalism.

Another critical aspect of constitutional choice concerns the type of executive. The idea that presidential democracies are less stable and more prone to regime breakdown has a long pedigree, but the comparative evidence has been challenged by those who argue that there are many different types of

presidential regimes, rather than just one category. Comparisons of the empirical evidence have usually been limited to historical patterns in Latin America
and Western Europe, rather than considering types of executives found elsewhere. This study developed a new typology of executives, based on a few
simple criteria, including the formal constitutional structure of a unified or
dual executive and the forms of selection and tenure for executives. The conclusions from the analysis using this typology are that parliamentary monarchies have a demonstrably better record at democratic consolidation, as many
have commonly argued, compared with presidential republics. This is also true
if the comparison is limited to elected presidential republics compared with
parliamentary monarchies. Mixed republics – the type of executive which has
proved most popular for many new constitutions during the last decade –
display a somewhat inconsistent record. Nevertheless this type of executive
has a poorer record of democracy than parliamentary republics, according to
the indicators provided by Freedom House and Polity IV. And presidential
republics also have a poorer record than parliamentary monarchies according
to direct indicators of crisis events, such as experience of coups d'etat, political
assassinations, and riots. The reasons are that parliamentary systems are led by
a prime minister who can be replaced without a major constitutional crisis if
he or she loses backbench support, a mechanism which provides an additional
safety valve. The incentives for cooperation and consultation between the executive and legislature are likely to promote accommodation and compromise in
parliamentary systems, fostering stability. The dual executive found in parliamentary monarchies divides the ceremonial head of state from the prime
minister, who functions as the effective head of government. This ensures state
continuity even when governments collapse in crisis.

Parliamentary republics and proportional electoral systems generate horizontal checks and balances in the core institutions of state. By contrast, federalism and decentralization lead toward *vertical* power-sharing among multiple
layers of government. Processes of decentralization take diverse forms. Federalism is one important mechanism, but fiscal, administrative, and political
decentralization can also transfer power to bodies in the public sector (local
government elected officials and executive bodies), as well as those in civil
society (nongovernmental organizations and community, philanthropic, and
voluntary associations), and in the private sector (such as through privatization and contracting out of services). The typology of vertical power-sharing
constitutional arrangements used in this study defined *unitary* constitutions as
those where the national government retains sovereignty over all subnational
tiers. In this system, the presidential executive branch, or the prime minister
heading the largest party in the lower house of the national parliament, has
both de jure and de facto authority to override all other regulations, directives,
and decisions emanating from subnational units. Constitutions were classified as *federal* if governments had national and subnational units, in a compound polity where each tier possesses certain autonomous functions. *Hybrid
unions*, the intermediate category, represent those constitutions where some

independent powers are granted for certain subnational units or dependent territories, but where sovereignty remains ultimately with the central government. The results of the time-series cross-national analysis using this typology confirmed the claims that compared with unitary states, federal arrangements were associated with a stronger performance of democracy, even after controlling for many other factors commonly linked with democratization. Moreover the illustrative cases drawn from Southeast Asia explain the underlying reasons why federal and decentralized vertical forms of power-sharing have helped democracy persist in India, despite the odds in a vast, poor, and deeply divided society, while it has foundered in neighboring Bangladesh.

The free press is one of the major institutions buttressing democratic transitions and consolidation. The cross-national time-series data demonstrates that the independent media functions as another check and balance on the government executive, even after controlling for other democratic institutions. This relationship operates primarily through the roles of the media as watchdog, civic forum, and agenda setter. The case studies of Ukraine and Uzbekistan in post-Soviet Eurasia reinforce many of the claims about the role of independent journalism, showing how this mattered in facilitating the orange revolution in the former, while suppressing dissent in the latter. Policies which eradicate limits on the freedom of information and communication, whether due to state censorship, intimidation and harassment of journalists, or private media oligopolies, therefore have important consequences by deterring transitions from autocracy.

SELF-SELECTION BIAS IN THE CHOICE OF CASES?

The evidence used to support these arguments combines qualitative and quantitative analysis. One legitimate question which arises concerns the choice of cases for comparison in this book. Small-N qualitative case studies have often been used to illustrate the pros and cons of power-sharing regimes. This approach is invaluable as a way to explore the complex processes of regime change, using historical narrative to describe detailed developments and specific practices within each nation.[5] Cases help to develop grounded theories, to derive testable propositions, and to explore the underlying causal mechanisms driving processes of regime change. This approach is particularly illuminating in considering outliers which are atypical, such as the one-party rule persisting in wealthy Singapore in contrast to the persistence of Indian democracy despite widespread poverty, and the reasons why these nations deviate from the generally observed pattern.

This method is unable to resolve the debate between proponents and critics of power-sharing, however, since the potential danger of selection bias means that different cases can be cited on both sides of the argument. The paired examples used in this book were chosen to illustrate the underlying processes established in the broader cross-national time-series data, but, arguably, other particular cases could always be used to challenge the argument. For every apparent success of power-sharing arrangements, there are other notable failures.[6] Many historical examples can be cited, exemplified by Lebanon, where the 1943 National Pact divided power among the major religious communities, a system which collapsed in 1975 when civil war erupted. Other cases include Cyprus prior to 1963, when civil war led to partition between the Greek and Turkish communities. Another potential failure concerns the intricate consociational arrangements for power-sharing along ethnic lines developed in the new constitution for Bosnia and Herzegovina set up by the Dayton Agreement, which have been blamed for reinforcing ethnic divisions.[7] Czechoslovakia also experimented with these arrangements briefly from 1989 to 1993, before the 'velvet revolution' produced peaceful succession into two separate states. Elsewhere, many peace-building negotiations and treaties have offered a degree of self-autonomy for rebel groups and armed factions through regional government and decentralization, with different degrees of success.[8]

Elsewhere, even within the same region, power-sharing has been judged to have very different degrees of success, such as in the West African cases of Rwanda, the Democratic Republic of Congo, and Burundi.[9] Given the mixed bag of positive and negative experiences in different nations, clearly the power-sharing arrangements compared in this study cannot be claimed to be *sufficient* for containing communal violence and preventing outbreaks of open hostility, as multiple other factors may outweigh the institutional arrangements. Not surprisingly, given the complexity of the challenge, there is no single solution which can automatically be applied to guarantee peace-building operations will succeed. Constitutional design is more of an art than a science. Nor can it be claimed that power-sharing arrangements are *necessary* for containing potential sources of communal conflict; the outright suppression of ethnic identities and minority rights is another strategy employed by strong states, as illustrated by the containment of ethnic divisions in the Federal Republic of Yugoslavia prior to dissolution and the outbreak of the Balkan wars, the bloodiest conflicts in Europe since the end of World War II.[10] The paired cases selected for comparison in successive chapters are striking illustrations of countries which are similar in many (although not all) important regards and yet which took divergent pathways in their political development, arriving at contrasting end points today.

Nevertheless because of the methodological limitations of potential selection bias, case studies alone are unable to resolve the debate over power-sharing. Greater weight should be given to the more systematic evidence presented in this research, derived from the cross-national time-series data, covering all countries worldwide since the early-1970s. As Brady and Collier argue, it is the combination of econometric techniques and qualitative case studies which becomes more powerful than either method used in isolation.[11] What this evidence demonstrates is that power-sharing arrangements increase the probability of democratic governance's succeeding, even after controlling for factors such as economic development, ethnic heterogeneity, and colonial background, all of which are also significantly associated with patterns of democratization.

ARE POWER-SHARING CONSTITUTIONAL REFORMS A REALISTIC STRATEGY FOR REFORMERS?

The last issue which needs to be addressed concerns the claim that power-sharing, even if effective in reducing or managing conflict, is not necessarily the most practical and realistic strategy to achieve a peace-settlement and consolidate democracy in divided societies. There are four reasons, in particular, offered to support this claim. The first emphasizes that there are many other types of initiatives which help to strengthen democratic governance, beyond the institutional reforms discussed here. The second stresses the rigidity of constitutional arrangements. The third concerns the fundamental difficulties of achieving any success in peace building and resolving conflict. The last is derived from the sequential arguments that the economic conditions and/or the basic functions of the state have to be established first before power-sharing arrangements can be implemented with any realistic chance of success. These are important considerations, but these claims rest, ultimately, on flawed assumptions.

WHAT OF OTHER STRATEGIES FOR STRENGTHENING DEMOCRATIC GOVERNANCE?

One potential issue which arises concerns the narrow institutional focus of the book. The study should certainly not be read as suggesting that these are the *only* constitutional reforms which are important for power-sharing agreements, still less that this is the only strategy possible for building sustainable democratic governance and resolving conflict. Of course many other political institutions associated with democracy and good governance, which are not discussed in this limited study, may also contribute toward dispersing decision making in power-sharing regimes. Most notably, this includes the vital role of the independent judiciary and constitutional courts, functioning as a classic check on the executive, protecting human rights, and establishing the rule of law as an essential function of the state. The bureaucratic structure of the public sector provides the chain of accountability for the delivery of public goods and services which stretches from public servants to elected leaders and thus to the electorate. Pluralistic competition among multiple voluntary groups, community associations, and new social movements is widely seen as critical for the vitality of civil society, as well as promoting bargaining and compromise among rival interests and providing opportunities for civic engagement and voluntary community work. Positive action mechanisms such as legal quotas help ensure the inclusion of women and cultural minorities in public office, widening social diversity within legislatures and executives. Limits on the political powers and role of the security forces maintain the military, police, and secret service under civilian control. The parliamentary voting rules and provisions for minority vetoes provide checks and balances within coalition multiparty governments. Reforms which promote transparency, such as rights to access to information laws, encourage open government, increase the ability of citizens and journalists to scrutinize the policymaking process, and reduce opportunities for corruption and malfeasance in public office. Liberalization through market mechanisms is another way of dispersing economic power and divesting patronage from state control, through a variety of privatization, private-public partnerships, deregulation, and contracting out policies. Central bank independence can be regarded as playing a similar role, through limiting state control of macroeconomic policy.

Reflecting recognition of these considerations, an emerging set of international norms and standards supporting democratic governance has been promoted by many global and regional bodies. The last decade has experienced growing initiatives and a range of activities by national reformers, bilateral donors, regional multinational bodies, nonprofit foundations, and democracy movements in many countries designed to strengthen and consolidate democratic institutions and processes.[12] The international emphasis on strengthening democratic governance is reflected in the activities of regional multilateral bodies, including the Organization of American States, the European Union, the Organization for Security and Cooperation in Europe, the North Atlantic Treaty Organization, the Commonwealth of Nations, the African Union, the Association of Southeast Asian Nations, and the Arab League.[13] Major bilateral donors in the development community, such as USAID, Dfid in the United Kingdom, and CIDA in Canada, have devoted growing resources to promoting democracy.[14] Under the Bush administration, the notion of democracy promotion to root out extremism and violence has taken center stage in American foreign policy, but although the priority given to this idea has been higher than usual, this rhetoric reflects a long tradition within the United States.[15] In the nonprofit sector, the democracy promotion process is exemplified by programs run by the International Foundation for Electoral Systems (IFES), the Soros Foundation and Open Society Institute, the Forum of Federations, Transparency International, and International IDEA.[16] Transnational activist networks and NGOs have also been very active, including those concerned with monitoring human rights, such as Amnesty International, the Committee to Protect Journalists, and Human Rights Watch, among others.[17]

Within the international community, the United Nations plays a lead role in this activity.[18] The United Nations Development Programme spends approximately $1.4 billion per year in this area, making it the largest organization providing technical assistance on democratic governance worldwide. The UN Department of Economic and Social Affairs (UNDESA) works on issues of ethics and public administration, decentralization, and e-government. In the areas of human rights, the UN Office of the High Commissioner for Human Rights (UNOHCHR) has the normative mandate and specific responsibility to monitor human rights violations. The Department of Political Affairs (DPA), specifically the Electoral Administration Division, has played an important role in elections, while the UN Department of Peace Keeping Operations (DPKO) has focused on state-building and transitional governance issues, along with the UNDP Bureau for Crisis Prevention and Recovery. The UN Capital

Development Fund (UNCDF) has emphasized decentralization, local governance, and microfinance initiatives to achieve the Millennium Development Goals. The UN Office on Drugs and Crime (UNODC) has the normative mandate on corruption and helps build national capacities for the implementation and monitoring of the UN Convention against Corruption. On the issue of women's participation in the political process, the UN Development Fund for Women (UNIFEM) is a key agency. UNESCO has led on activities promoting freedom of expression and protecting cultural diversity. The World Bank has emphasized the importance of strengthening 'good governance' to achieve sustainable development, emphasizing the principles of transparency, accountability, and efficiency in the public sector and the role of private-public partnerships in development. The World Bank has also pioneered work on indicators of good governance. Work by these organizations within the United Nations therefore seeks to promote democratic governance and development assistance, both at global and at country level, through multiple strategies and approaches.

Much of the emphasis of the international democracy promotion efforts has focused upon building civil society, including sustained efforts to strengthen voluntary associations and community organizations and interest groups, building social capital and networks which connect citizens and the state. Voter and civic education programs have played an important part in these activities. USAID, for example, one of the largest international democracy assistance agencies, spent over $2.4 million on civil societies initiatives from 1990 to 2003, about 40% of its total budget on democracy assistance.[19] Another major set of activities and programs have been devoted to promoting effective electoral systems and processes, including developing the capacity of electoral management bodies to administer elections, training professional staff, and sending international observers to monitor and report on standards.[20] Many foundations have also emphasized providing assistance for party-building initiatives and programs, through strengthening party organizations and internal party democracy. The attack on corruption through strengthening transparency and integrity in government, as well as traditional work on public administration reform, has been given added impetus by development agencies concerned that basic public services will fail to be delivered, and aid will not meet its objectives, if there is widespread inefficiency, venality, and malfeasance in the public sector. As discussed in Chapter 7, one of the major trends in activities involves decentralizing government through strengthening local authorities and engaging local communities in development. Human rights monitoring is critical to calling the attention of the world to abuses of civil liberties, by international agencies and local NGOs, along with establishing human rights commissions, legal reforms, truth commissions, and war crime tribunals. Law enforcement, the courts, and judicial agencies have also been strengthened, along with civilian control over the military.

All these initiatives, and many others, are part of the difficult long-term process of facilitating democracy and building capacity, especially in fragile and postconflict states. The impact of each of these institutions on patterns of democratization remains to be classified and analyzed systematically in further research, beyond the limits of this study, to explore their role and relative importance in this process. The book does not claim to provide a comprehensive and thorough examination of *all* the diverse mechanisms of power-sharing. There is no simple set of institutional reforms which can reduce conflict and build peace without many other conditions. What is claimed here is that the four types of power-sharing arrangements within each state which are analyzed at the heart of this book are some of the most important building blocks in any constitutional arrangements designed to build sustainable democracy, whether promoted by domestic reformers or influenced by the international development community. There are serious measurement problems in classifying and developing suitable comparative indicators for all these institutional arrangements with any degree of reliability, especially for longitudinal time-series analysis. New work with a database classifying and comparing constitutional provisions is emerging which will eventually help to overcome some of these hurdles.[21] It seems likely that other forms of power-sharing will probably have a similar impact on patterns of democratization to that of those we have studied here, using the same basic theoretical logic, although this remains to be confirmed in further research.

HOW OFTEN ARE CONSTITUTIONS AMENDED?

Another related argument rests on the way that the institutional arrangements which define the role of the head of state and government, the federal division of powers, and the basic type of electoral system, embodied in written constitutions or special laws, are relatively fixed and immutable. As such, even if reform is highly desirable, it is not a practical step which could be considered by practitioners. As a result, it could be concluded that alternative strategies such as providing technical support designed to strengthen grassroots NGOs in civil society, to provide civic education, or to facilitate community participation may prove more effective reforms which could be implemented by governments and supported by the international community to strengthen democratic governance in the short to medium term.

As noted, the institutional features which are the focus of this study are only one way that democracy can be strengthened, and many other initiatives need to be implemented, especially in electoral democracies and countries which are in the process of deepening the quality of democratic governance. It is true that major constitutional reforms which generate regime change are relatively rare, especially in established democracies. Formal written constitutions are often resilient pacts which are designed to be difficult to alter by formal amendment, especially where these documents are regarded as legitimate and an important symbol of the nation-state. At the same time, more minor reforms, for example, adjusting detailed features of electoral systems and processes, such as the average district magnitude, the ballot structure, or the vote threshold, have been found to be far more common than is usually assumed, even within established democracies.[22] The powers of the states and the federal government are often revised, including through the creation of new states to resolve communal conflict (such as in India), while further reforms for devolution and the decentralization of government are widespread in many nations. Although fundamental constitutions are often enduring, a recent comprehensive review has compared all national constitutions worldwide since 1789 and estimated that the average life span is only 16 years.[23] Wholesale constitutional revision is particularly common among newer democracies in Latin America. More minor constitutional amendments are often far more frequent, depending upon the requirements established for revision and the role of constitutional courts in this process. The establishment of a new constitution, specifying the core normative principles and the rules determining the structure of the state, represents an integral part of the peace-building process for newly independent nations, for 'failed' states where the previous central authority has collapsed, and for societies emerging from civil conflict. As a result, understanding the options which are available for designing and implementing new constitutions is vital; once the rules of the game are negotiated and agreed, they will determine much else in the regime.

THE ODDS OF SUCCESS?

Another critique emphasizes that most postconflict agreements often have poor chances of success: for example, Collier estimated that 40% of civil wars recur within a decade and thus, on average, a country that has terminated civil war can expect the outbreak of a new round of fighting within six years.[24] Research on civil wars suggests that cease-fires imposed by external powers on a country after intense ethnic conflict seem least likely to survive and to provide durable peace-settlements, particularly once the outside powers withdraw and cease to enforce the arrangement.[25] Furthermore, in civil wars where third parties intervene by economic, diplomatic, or military means, conflicts persist, except when the intervention clearly supports the stronger party, in which case it generally shortens conflict. Compared to a peace agreement or a cease-fire, civil wars that end with an outright victory are three times less likely to recur, possibly because one party is sufficiently subdued or deterred from fighting again.[26]

Given these patterns, it is true that institutional theories of power-sharing which focus upon societies such as Belgium, Switzerland, or the Netherlands (or even Lebanon, South Africa, and Malaysia) may underestimate certain practical realities about achieving durable agreements in contemporary societies, such as the DRC, Liberia, or Sierra Leone, which are emerging from decades of violent rebellion, prolonged militant hostilities, and armed uprisings. The initial period of state building and controlling conflict is one fraught with considerable uncertainties and risks, where a few spoilers may use violent tactics to block full implementation of any constitutional settlement. If there is one outright victor at the end of a prolonged civil war, this situation may strengthen the chances of a durable peace, although, equally, it may make achieving initial agreement to any negotiated power-sharing arrangement more difficult. Moving toward reconstruction and reconciliation is an even more challenging stage of conflict resolution.[27] Against this argument, it should be emphasized that both PR electoral systems and decentralized decision making through territorial autonomy have been confirmed as important peace-building strategies, leading toward a lasting conflict reduction after civil war.[28] Again, no single strategy of reform can guarantee peace building; there will be multiple cases of failure. Given the odds, the claim is not that power-sharing will guarantee the end of prolonged conflict or prevent its future recurrence. But the odds of power-sharing will improve under power-sharing constitutions such as federalism and decentralization, proportional electoral systems, and parliamentary monarchy executives. The vast research on the many complex conditions leading to the end of conflict has often examined the classic issue of whether democracy leads toward peace. International relations scholars should place far greater emphasis on understanding the particular type of institutions which are agreed and implemented in any postconflict constitutional settlement, issues which are surprisingly neglected in the peace-building literature.

DEVELOPMENT FIRST?

Finally, the 'sequencing' argument asserts that in practice the adoption of any power-sharing arrangements has to wait until the conditions are ripe, in particular until economic development or rebuilding of the core functions of the state is achieved, where this is regarded as an essential foundation for achieving a sustainable democratic government. The continuing strong and robust relationship between wealth and democracy was confirmed in Chapter 4, irrespective of the controls and the particular indicator of democracy which are selected in alternative models. Rich nations are not inevitably more democratic, as we observed earlier with the case of Singapore. Nevertheless in poorer nations it remains hard to generate the conditions of sustained economic prosperity which facilitate and buttress lasting institutional reforms.

The sequencing argument is also seen as a barrier to power-sharing agreements, where it is argued that first the state needs to be capable of maintaining security and basic services, prior to the stage of agreeing upon any power-sharing constitutional arrangement and then holding any democratic elections. The case of Iraq illustrates the complexities of this claim. Multiple reasons can be offered to help explain political failure in Iraq and this case draws attention to the limits of constitutional engineering alone. The design of the Iraqi constitution adopted in October 2005 contained many elements of power-sharing. This included the use of a closed list proportional representation electoral system for the 275-member House of Representatives, as well as positive action mechanisms used most successfully to achieve the election of women candidates. A multiparty coalition government was established with a mixed type of executive, where powers were divided between the prime minister, Nuri al-Maliki, and an indirectly elected three-person presidential council, headed by Jalal Talabani. After the January 2005 elections, there were some initial hopes that the Shi'a and Sunni parties within the National Assembly and members of the coalition government would start to engage in an effective political process of bargaining and coalition building. Instead the National Assembly and the coalition government headed by Prime Minister Nuri al-Maliki appeared to be immobilized from making any effective gestures to bridge the chasm which deepened between the Shi'a and Sunni communities. Widespread sectarian strife and carnage on the streets of Iraq accelerated after the election, despite the formal power-sharing arrangements.

The special circumstance of contemporary Iraq remains to be played out, along with the historical debate about the precise causes of the failure.[29] The role of the power-sharing arrangements in the constitutional settlement, however, is open to alternative perspectives. One perspective emphasizes that it was premature to sign a power-sharing constitutional settlement in October 2005, along with holding popular elections a few months later, as these events occurred prior to establishing effective state institutions capable of maintaining security and delivering basic public services. In the sequencing view, the heart of the governability crisis in the Iraqi state arose from the complete collapse of both the administrative and coercive capacities, including its ministries, their civil servants, police force, and army, in part due to the radical policy of de-Baathification which deconstructed the machinery of state.[30] Delaying the elections and the implementation of the power-sharing arrangements until after basic public institutions had been rebuilt, in this perspective, might have prevented the legislative stalemate and lack of state capacity to deal with the conflict and violence which ensued.

Yet alternatively, it is also arguable that a more radical power-sharing agreement in Iraq could have worked better by building trust in the legitimacy of the new constitution and reducing popular resentment among the Sunni community, as well as greater autonomy for the Kurds in the north. This logic has led to a proposal to share the division of oil and gas revenues among rival communities and regions, to end laws preventing former Baathist Party members from taking government jobs, and to consider further steps in the contentious issue of federalism.[31] Historians will have to decide which interpretation provides the more accurate assessment once events have unfolded more fully. What can be concluded with greater confidence at this stage is that the power-sharing constitutional arrangements which governed the country after October 2005 have not proved capable of overcoming the deep divisions within the administration to produce a viable and legitimate state, capable of acting with unity to restore basic public services, let alone led to any rebuilding of security and cessation of the broader conflict in society.

At the same time, despite these observations, it would be too pessimistic to conclude that reforms for more democratic governance should be delayed until the 'right' conditions are achieved. One reason is that this course would unduly

delay opportunities for democratic reform when they arise in many developing countries in Africa and Asia which are afflicted with deep and enduring poverty. The 2006 Millennium Development Goals Report suggests some
significant signs of global progress in human development: rates of extreme
poverty fell globally since 1990, from 29% to 19% of the world's population,
largely as a result of economic growth in Asia.[32] Universal primary education is in sight, with great strides registered in Southern Asia. Some countries
have made rapid and sustained improvements in the lives of their citizens. But
positive gains remain uneven worldwide and the situation in some places has
stagnated or even worsened. Estimates suggest that on the basis of projections
from current trends, the world will fall short of achieving many of the key
Millennium targets. More people now experience chronic hunger than in the
early-1990s. Deaths and new infections from HIV are growing. Rapid defor-
estation continues. Half the population in developing countries still lacks basic
sanitation. Surging economic growth has markedly improved the average GDP
in China and India, but inequalities within each society have simultaneously
worsened. Sub-Saharan Africa trails far behind on multiple developmental
indicators, where many countries remain mired in deep-rooted poverty, and
social deprivation and poverty have worsened during the last two decades, not
improved.[33] At the same time, democracies can persist and flourish in poorer
nations, as illustrated by the cases of Benin, Mali, and South Africa. It is a
false and outdated assumption that democratic institutions can only be developed successfully once a basic level of economic and social development is
realized. Moreover the constitutional arrangements are often decided as part
of any cease-fire and negotiated or imposed peace-settlement, so that if the
core functions of the state are rebuilt without an initial agreement to power-
sharing among rival communities, it seems unlikely that this will happen once
incumbents are entrenched in power or that the government which arises from
this process will be based on any sense of popular legitimacy. While focusing
upon understanding the outcome and impact of institutions, the book has not
discussed how power-sharing arrangements are negotiated and agreed, a topic
well deserving its own future study.

Therefore it should be recognized that power-sharing arrangements are the
best chance of success for sustaining democracy, while recognizing that this
claim should be interpreted cautiously, with many qualifiers. Many alternative
political reforms should also be implemented, beyond those discussed here;
opportunities for regime change often remain extremely limited; the odds of
success in peace building and peace maintenance in fragile postconflict states
are daunting; and the conditions of enduring poverty and rebuilding of the
state make democratic development through power-sharing extremely challenging. Against the odds, the indicators of trends in democratization in this
book demonstrate that there has been considerable progress around the globe
from the early-1970s, with the start of the 'third wave' of democratization, to
the end of the twentieth century. Still today many developing nations remain
in the gray zone stranded between democracy and autocracy.[34] The world may

be experiencing a recent backlash against democracy promotion; some major nations which had experienced periods of electoral democracy have regressed in recent years, whether afflicted by violence at the ballot box and outbreaks of rioting (Nigeria), problems of rampant corruption (Bangladesh, Kenya), greater restrictions on human rights and civil liberties (Russia), limits on freedom of the press and an expansion of executive powers (Venezuela), or the suspension of democratic constitutional processes through outright military coups (Thailand, Pakistan, Fiji). In 2007, Freedom House reported that the proportion of 'free' countries has failed to increase during the last decade, while authoritarian rule has become further entrenched in some of the world's poorest countries, including in Zimbabwe, Burma, and Uzbekistan.[35] In this context, given the complexity of the challenge, no single initiative or program can succeed alone. Among the alternative strategies which can be used to assist and strengthen the democratization process, however, the evidence presented here indicates that reforms which promote and implement power-sharing constitutional arrangements should be more widely recognized as one of the most promising avenues to contribute toward lasting peace-settlements and sustainable democracy.

Technical Appendix

Description of the Variables and Data Sources

Name	Description and Source	Obs.
Ethno-linguistic fractionalization	The share of languages spoken as 'mother tongues' in each country, generally derived from national census data, as reported in the *Encyclopaedia Britannica 2001*. The fractionalization index is computed as one minus the Herfindahl index of ethno-linguistic group share, reflecting the probability that two randomly selected individuals from a population belonged to different groups. *Alesina, Devleeschauwer, Easterly, Kurlat, and Wacziarg 2003.*	181
Religious fractionalization	The share of the population adhering to different religions in each country, as reported in the *Encyclopaedia Britannica 2001* and related sources. The fractionalization index is computed as one minus the Herfindahl index of ethnoreligious group share, reflecting the probability that two randomly selected individuals from a population belonged to different groups. *Alesina, Devleeschauwer, Easterly, Kurlat, and Wacziarg 2003.*	190
Freedom House liberal democracy index	The Gastil index, the 7-point scale used by Freedom House, measuring political rights and civil liberties annually since 1972. *Freedom in the World. www.Freedomhouse.com*	191

(continued)

(continued)

Name	Description and Source	Obs.
Change in Freedom House index	The mean change in the Gastil index, the 7-point scale used by Freedom House, measuring political rights and civil liberties every year. *Freedom in the World. www.Freedomhouse.com*	167
Polity IV constitutional democracy index	The Polity IV Project classifies democracy and autocracy in each nation-year as a composite score of different characteristics relating to authority structures. The dataset constructs a 10-point democracy scale by coding the competitiveness of political participation (1–3), the competitiveness of executive recruitment (1–2), the openness of executive recruitment (1), and the constraints on the chief executive (1–4). Autocracy is measured by negative versions of the same indices. The two scales are combined into a single democracy-autocracy score varying from −10 to +10. The democracy-autocracy index for 2000 was recoded to a 20-point positive scale from low (autocracy) to high (democracy). *Marshall and Jaggers 2002.*	
Vanhanen participatory democracy index	Vanhanen developed a scaled measure of democracy in each country according to two criteria, the degree of *electoral competition* (measured by the share of the vote won by the largest party in the national legislature) and the degree of *electoral participation* (the proportion of the total population who voted in national legislative elections), which are combined to yield a 100-pt index of participatory democracy. *Vanhanen 2000.*	
Cheibub and Gandhi contested democracy classification	This classification of regimes from 1950 to 1990 was originally developed by Przeworski, Alvarez, Cheibub, and Limongi, and the time-series was subsequently extended to 2000 by Cheibub and Gandhi. This approach defines regimes as autocratic if the chief executive is not elected, the legislature is not elected, there is only one party, or there has been no alternation in power. All other regimes are classified as democratic. In democratic states, therefore, those who govern are selected through contested elections. *Cheibub and Gandhi 2004.*	

Name	Description and Source	Obs.
Political stability	Indicators which measure perceptions of the likelihood that the government in power will be destabilized or overthrown by unconstitutional or violent means, including terrorism. *Kaufmann, Kray, and Zoido-Lobaton 2002.*	177
Voice and accountability	Indicators measuring the extent to which citizens are able to participate in the selection of governments. This includes the political process, civil liberties, political rights, and media independence. *Kaufmann, Kray, and Zoido-Lobaton 2002.*	190
Government effectiveness	Indicators of the ability of the government to formulate and implement sound policies. This includes perceptions of the quality of public services, the competence and independence of civil servants, and the ability of the government to implement and deliver public goods. *Kaufmann, Kray, and Zoido-Lobaton 2002.*	186
Human Development Index (HDI)	The Human Development Index (HDI) is based on longevity, as measured by life expectancy at birth; educational achievement; and standard of living, as measured by per capita GDP (PPP $US). *UNDP 2004.*	170
Population size	Estimates are for total population per state (thousands). *World Bank World Development Indicators.*	187
BritCol	The past colonial history of countries was classified into those which shared a British colonial background (1) and all others (0). CIA *The World Factbook.* www.cia.gov	191
Middle East	This classified the regional location of nations into those Arab states in the Middle East and North Africa (1) and all others (0).	191
Electoral systems	This classified the type of electoral systems used for the lower house of the national parliament. *Majoritarian formulas* include first-past-the-post, second ballot, the bloc vote, the single nontransferable vote, and the	191

(*continued*)

(continued)

Name	Description and Source	Obs.
	alternative vote. *Proportional formulas* are defined to include party list as well as the single transferable vote systems. *Combined* (or 'mixed') formulas use both majoritarian and proportional ballots for election to the same body.	
	International IDEA. 2005.	
Federations	Federations are defined as compound polities where the directly elected constituent units possess independent powers in the exercise of their legislative, fiscal, and administrative responsibilities.	191
	Watts 1999.	
	Banks, Muller, and Overstreet. *Political Handbook of the World 2000–2002.*	
Decentralized unions	Constituent units of government work through the common organs of government although constitutionally protected subunits of government have some functional autonomy.	191
	Watts 1999.	
	Banks, Muller, and Overstreet. *Political Handbook of the World 2000–2002.*	
Unitary states	All states which are not either federations or decentralized unions.	191
Press freedom	The Freedom House survey of press freedom has been conducted every year since 1980. Countries are given a total score from 0 (best) to 100 (worst) on the basis of a set of 23 methodology questions divided into three subcategories. Assigning numerical points allows for comparative analysis among the countries surveyed and facilitates an examination of trends over time. The degree to which each country permits the free flow of news and information determines the classification of its media as 'free,' 'partly free,' or 'not free.' Countries scoring 0 to 30 are regarded as having 'free' media; 31 to 60, 'partly free' media; and 61 to 100, 'not free' media.	

Name	Description and Source	Obs.
	The examination of the level of press freedom in each country currently comprises 23 methodology questions divided into three broad categories: the legal environment, the political environment, and the economic environment. *Freedom House Index of Press Freedom 1994–2007.*	
Press freedom	The Reporters without Borders *Worldwide Annual Press Freedom Index* measures the state of press freedom in the world. It reflects the degree of freedom journalists and news organizations enjoy in each country, and the efforts made by the state to respect and ensure respect for this freedom. The organization compiled a questionnaire with 52 criteria for assessing the state of press freedom in each country. It includes every kind of violation directly affecting journalists (such as murders, imprisonment, physical attacks, and threats) and news media (censorship, confiscation of issues, searches, and harassment). It registers the degree of impunity enjoyed by those responsible for such violations. It also takes account of the legal situation affecting the news media (such as penalties for press offenses, the existence of a state monopoly in certain areas, and the existence of a regulatory body), the behavior of the authorities toward the state-owned news media and the foreign press, and the main obstacles to the free flow of information on the Internet. The index reflects not only abuses attributable to the state, but also those by armed militias, clandestine organizations, or pressure groups that can pose a real threat to press freedom. The questionnaire was sent to partner organizations of Reporters without Borders (14 freedom of expression groups in five continents) and its 130 correspondents around the world, as well as to journalists, researchers, jurists, and human rights activists. A scale devised by the organization was then used to give a country-score to each questionnaire. The 100-pt index is reversed for analysis, so that a higher score represents greater press freedom.	

Notes

Chapter 1: What Drives Democracy?

1. For more details about these cases, see Mathurin C. Houngnikpo. 2001. *Determinants of Democratization in Africa: A Comparative Study of Benin and Togo.* Lanham, MD: University Press of America; Boubacar Diaye, Abdoulaye Saine, and Mathurin Houngnikpo. 2005. *Not Yet Democracy: West Africa's Slow Farewell to Authoritarianism.* Durham, NC: Carolina Academic Press.

2. As discussed later in this chapter, during his lifetime Arend Lijphart published a long series of articles and books devoted to developing the ideas of consociationalism and consensus democracy. The seminal works are Arend Lijphart. 1969. 'Consociational democracy.' *World Politics* 21: 207–225; Arend Lijphart. 1975. *The Politics of Accommodation: Pluralism and Democracy in the Netherlands.* Berkeley: University of California Press; Arend Lijphart. 1999. *Patterns of Democracy: Government Forms and Performance in 36 Countries.* New Haven, CT: Yale University Press; Arend Lijphart. 2008. *Thinking about Democracy: Power Sharing and Majority Rule in Theory and Practice.* New York: Routledge.

3. For a half-dozen comparative case studies, see Ulrich Schneckener. 2002. 'Making power-sharing work: Lessons from successes and failures in ethnic conflict regulation.' *Journal of Peace Research* 39 (2): 203–228; Ulrich Schneckener and Stefan Wolff. Eds. 2004. *Managing and Settling Ethnic Conflicts: Perspectives on Successes and Failures in Europe, Africa and Asia.* London: C. Hurst. On Kosovo, see Andrew Taylor. 2001. 'Electoral systems and the promotion of 'consociationalism' in a multi-ethnic society: The Kosovo Assembly elections of November 2001.' *Electoral Studies* 24 (3): 435–463.

4. For a review of the extensive literature, see Rudy B. Andweg. 2000. 'Consociational democracy.' *Annual Review of Politics* 3: 509–536. For the development of alternative versions of this concept, see Gerhard Lehmbruch. 1967. *Proporzdemokratie. Politisches System und politische Kultur in der Schweiz und Osterreich.* Tubingen: Mohr; Jurg Steiner. 1974. *Amicable Agreement versus Majority Rule: Conflict Resolution in Switzerland.* Chapel Hill: University of North Carolina Press; Hans Daalder. 1974. 'The consociational democracy theme.' *World Politics* 26: 604–621; Kenneth McRae. Ed. 1974. *Consociational Democracy: Conflict Accommodation in Segmented Societies.* Toronto: McClelland and Stewart; Klaus

Armingeon. 2002. 'The effects of negotiation democracy: A comparative analysis.' *European Journal of Political Research* 41: 81; Arend Lijphart. 2002. 'Negotiation democracy versus consensus democracy: Parallel conclusions and recommendations.' *European Journal of Political Research* 41 (1): 107–113; Wolf Linder and Andre Baechtiger. 2005. 'What drives democratization in Asia and Africa?' *European Journal of Political Research* 44: 861–880. For an early and influential critique, see Brian Barry. 1975. 'Review article: Political accommodation and consociational democracy.' *British Journal of Political Science* 5 (4): 194.

5. The primary works are Donald L. Horowitz. 1985. *Ethnic Groups in Conflict*. Berkeley: University of California Press; Donald L. Horowitz. 1991. *A Democratic South Africa? Constitutional Engineering in a Divided Society*. Berkeley: University of California Press; Donald L. Horowitz. 2002. *The Deadly Ethnic Riot*. Berkeley: University of California Press.

6. S. G. Simonsen. 2005. 'Addressing ethnic divisions in post-conflict institution-building: Lessons from recent cases.' *Security Dialogue* 36 (3): 297–318.

7. For a discussion of the advantages of adopting a mixed research design, see Henry Brady and David Collier. 2004. *Rethinking Social Inquiry: Diverse Tools, Shared Standards*. New York: Rowman & Littlefield.

8. Amnesty International. 1999. *Togo: Rule of Terror*. http://web.amnesty.org/library/Index/engAFR570011999

9. Amnesty International. 2003. 'Opposition silenced in Togo elections.' http://web.amnesty.org/wire/July2003/Togo; West African Civil Society Forum (WASCOF). 2005. Report of the West African Civil Society Forum Observation Mission on the Togo Presidential elections held on 24th April 2005. http://www.cdd.org.uk/pdf/wascof_togo.pdf

10. Thomas Carothers. 2002. 'The end of the transition paradigm.' *Journal of Democracy* 13: 5–21; Fareed Zakaria. 1997. 'The rise of illiberal democracy.' *Foreign Affairs* 76 (6): 22–41; Larry Diamond. 2002. 'Thinking about hybrid regimes.' *Journal of Democracy* 13 (2): 21–35; Steven Levitsky and Lucan A. Way. 2002. 'The rise of competitive authoritarianism.' *Journal of Democracy* 13 (2): 51–65; Stephen Levitsky. 2003. 'Autocracy by democratic rules: The dynamics of competitive authoritarianism in the post–cold war era.' Paper presented at the Conference, 'Mapping the Great Zone: Clientelism and the Boundary between Democratic and Democratizing.' Columbia University, April 4–5, 2003; Andreas Schedler. Ed. 2006. *Electoral Authoritarianism: The Dynamics of Unfree Competition*. Boulder, CO: Lynne Reinner.

11. See Samuel Decalo. 1997. 'Benin: First of the new democracies.' In John F. Clarke and David E. Gardiner (Eds.), *Political Reform in Francophone Africa*, pp. 41–61. Boulder, CO: Westview Press.

12. Juan Linz and Alfred Stepan. 1978. *The Breakdown of Democratic Regimes*. Baltimore: The Johns Hopkins University Press; Juan Linz and Alfred Stepan. 1996. *Problems of Democratic Transition and Consolidation*. Baltimore: The Johns Hopkins University Press.

13. Seymour Martin Lipset. 1959. 'Some social requisites of democracy: Economic development and political legitimacy.' *American Political Science Review* 53: 69–105.

14. See, for example, M. L. Ross. 2001. 'Does oil hinder democracy?' *World Politics* 53: 325–361; N. Jensen and L. Wantchekon. 2004. 'Resource wealth and political regimes in Africa.' *Comparative Political Studies* 37: 816–841; Carles Boix. 2003.

Democracy and Redistribution. Cambridge: Cambridge University Press; M. L. Ross. 2004. 'How do natural resources influence civil war? Evidence from thirteen cases.' *International Organization* 58 (1): 35–67.

15. Paul Collier and Nicholas Sambanis. Eds. 2005. *Understanding Civil War.* Washington, DC: World Bank; M. Humphreys. 2005. 'Natural resources, conflict, and conflict resolution – uncovering the mechanisms.' *Journal of Conflict Resolution* 49 (4): 508–537; Richard Snyder. 2006. 'Does lootable wealth breed disorder? A political economy of extraction framework.' *Comparative Political Studies* 39 (8): 943–968.

16. E. R. Larsen. 2005. 'Are rich countries immune to the resource curse? Evidence from Norway's management of its oil riches.' *Resources Policy* 30 (2): 75–86.

17. J. A. Robinson, R. Torvik, R. Verdier, and T. Verdier. 2006. 'Political foundations of the resource curse.' *Journal of Development Economics* 79 (2): 447–468; H. Mehlum, K. Moene, and R. Torvik. 2006. 'Institutions and the resource curse.' *Economic Journal* 116 (508): 1–20.

18. Stuart J. Kaufman. 2001. *Modern Hatreds: The Symbolic Politics of Ethnic War.* Ithaca, NY: Cornell University Press; Paul Collier and Nicholas Sambanis. Eds. 2005. *Understanding Civil War.* Washington, DC: World Bank; Michael W. Doyle and Nicholas Sambanis. 2006. *Making War and Building Peace.* Princeton, NJ: Princeton University Press.

19. For an argument challenging the conventional wisdom that more ethnically or religiously diverse countries are more likely to experience significant civil violence, however, see James D. Fearon and David D. Laitin. 2003. 'Ethnicity, insurgency, and civil war.' *American Political Science Review* 97 (1): 75–90.

20. Jack Snyder. 2000. *From Voting to Violence: Democratization and Nationalist Conflict.* New York: W. W. Norton; Edward D. Mansfield and Jack Snyder. 2007. *Electing to Fight: Why Emerging Democracies Go to War.* Cambridge, MA: MIT Press.

21. See, for example, Roland Paris. 2005. *At War's End: Building Peace after Civil Conflict.* Cambridge: Cambridge University Press; Paul Collier and Nicholas Sambanis. Eds. 2005. *Understanding Civil War.* Washington, DC: World Bank; Michael W. Doyle and Nicholas Sambanis. 2006. *Making War and Building Peace.* Princeton, NJ: Princeton University Press; Chaim Kaufmann. 1996. 'Possible and impossible solutions to ethnic civil wars.' *International Security* 20 (4): 136–175.

22. Lucy Creevey, Paul Ngomo, and Richard Vergroff. 2005. 'Party politics and different paths to democratic transitions – a comparison of Benin and Senegal.' *Party Politics* 11 (4): 471–493.

23. For a discussion, see James R. Scarritt and Shaheen Mozaffar. 1999. 'The specification of ethnic cleavages and ethnopolitical groups for the analysis of democratic competition in contemporary Africa.' *Nationalism and Ethnic Politics* 5: 82–117; Shaheen Mozaffar, James R. Scarritt, and Glen Galaich. 2003. 'Electoral institutions, ethnopolitical cleavages, and party systems in Africa's emerging democracies.' *American Political Science Review* 97: 379–390.

24. Daniel Posner. 2004. 'The political salience of cultural difference: Why Chewas and Tumbukas are allies in Zambia and adversaries in Malawi.' *American Political Science Review* 98: 4: 529–545; Daniel Posner. 2005. *Institutions and Ethnic Politics in Africa.* Cambridge: Cambridge University Press.

25. Daniel Posner. 2004. 'Measuring ethnic fractionalization in Africa.' *American Journal of Political Science* 48 (4): 849–863.

26. Daron Acemoglu and James A. Robinson. 2006. *Economic Origins of Dictatorship and Democracy*. Cambridge: Cambridge University Press.

27. Daron Acemoglu and James A. Robinson. 2006. *Economic Origins of Dictatorship and Democracy*. Cambridge: Cambridge University Press, p. 27

28. See, for example, Raffaele Romanelli. 1998. *How Did They Become Voters? The History of Franchise in Modern European Representation*. Germany: Springer.

29. David Allan Hamer. 1977. *The Politics of Electoral Pressure: A Study of the History of Victorian Reform Agitations*. Hassocks: Harvester Press; John K. Walton. 1987. *The Second Reform Act*. London: Methuen.

30. Ted Piccone and Richard Youngs. Eds. 2006. *Strategies for Democratic Change: Assessing the Global Response*. Washington, DC: Democracy Coalition Project.

31. Edward Neuman and Roland Rich. Eds. 2004. *The UN Role in Promoting Democracy: Between Ideals and Reality*. New York: UN University Press; Richard D. Caplan. 2005. *International Governance of War-Torn Territories: Rule and Reconstruction*. Oxford/New York: Oxford University Press; Thomas G. Weiss, David P. Forsythe, and Roger A. Coate. 2004. *United Nations and Changing World Politics*. Boulder, CO: Westview Press; Craig N. Murphy. 2006. *The United Nations Development Programme: A Better Way?* Cambridge: Cambridge University Press.

32. For a review of some of these initiatives, see Thomas Carothers. 1999. *Aiding Democracy Abroad*. Washington, DC: Carnegie Endowment for International Peace; Jean Grugel. 1999. *Democracy without Borders: Transnationalisation and Conditionality in New Democracies*. London: Routledge; Peter Burnell. Ed. 2000. *Democracy Assistance: International Co-Operation for Democratization*. London: Frank Cass; Jon C. Pevehouse. 2002. 'With a little help from my friends? Regional organizations and the consolidation of democracy.' *American Journal of Political Science* 46 (3): 611–626; Jon C. Pevehouse. 2002. 'Democracy from the outside-in? International organizations and democratization.' *International Organization* 56 (3): 515; Jon C. Pevehouse. 2004. *Democracy from Above: Regional Organizations and Democratization*. Cambridge: Cambridge University Press; *Critical Mission: Essays on Democracy Promotion*. Washington, DC: Carnegie Endowment for International Peace; Andrew F. Cooper and Thomas Legler. 2007. *Intervention without Intervening? The OAS Defense and Promotion of Democracy in the Americas*. New York: Palgrave Macmillan.

33. Joshua Muravchik. 1992. *Exporting Democracy*. Washington, DC: AEI Press; Michael Cox, G. John Ikenberry, and Takashi Inoguchi. Eds. 2000. *American Democracy Promotion: Impulses, Strategies, and Impacts*. New York: Oxford University Press.

34. National Endowment for Democracy. 6 November 2003. 'President Bush Discusses Freedom in Iraq and Middle East: Remarks by the President at the 20th Anniversary of the National Endowment for Democracy.' United States Chamber of Commerce, Washington, DC. http://www.ned.org/events/anniversary/20thAniv-Bush.html

35. The White House. 20 January 2005. 'President sworn in to second term.' www.whitehouse.gov/news/releases/2005. See Jonathan Monten. 2005. 'The roots of the Bush doctrine: Power, nationalism and democracy promotion in U.S. Strategy.' *International Security* 29 (4): 112–156.

36. Karen Elizabeth Smith. 2003. *European Union Foreign Policy in a Changing World*. Oxford: Polity Press.

37. James Manor. 2007. *Aid That Works: Successful Development in Fragile States.* Washington, DC: World Bank.

38. Nicolas Guilhot. 2005. *The Democracy Makers: Human Rights and International Order.* New York: Columbia University Press.

39. Stephen Knack. 2001. 'Aid dependence and the quality of governance.' *Southern Economic Journal* 68 (2): 310–329; Stephen Knack. 2004. 'Does foreign aid promote democracy?' *International Studies Quarterly* 48 (1): 251–266.

40. Steven E. Finkel, Anibal Perez-Linan, and Mitchell A. Seligson with Dinorah Azpuru. 2005. *Effects of U.S. Foreign Assistance on Democracy Building: Results from a Cross-National Quantitative Study.* Washington, DC: USAID.

41. See, for example, Ted Piccone and Richard Youngs. Eds. 2006. *Strategies for Democratic Change: Assessing the Global Response.* Washington, DC: Democracy Coalition Project.

42. Richard Youngs. 2002. *The European Union and the Promotion of Democracy.* Oxford: Oxford University Press; Thomas Carothers. 2004. *Critical Mission: Essays on Democracy Promotion.* Washington, DC: Carnegie Endowment for International Peace.

43. David L. Cingranelli and Thomas E. Pasquarello. 1985. 'Human rights practices and the distribution of U.S. foreign aid to Latin America.' *American Journal of Political Science* 29 (3): 539–563; James M. McCormick and Neil Mitchell. 1988. 'Is U.S. aid really linked to human rights in Latin America?' *American Journal of Political Science* 32 (1): 231–239; Graham T. Allison and R. P. Beschel. 1992. 'Can the United States promote democracy?' *Political Science Quarterly* 107 (1): 81–98.

44. Thomas Carothers. 'Promoting democracy and fighting terror.' *Foreign Affairs* 2003.

45. Harvey Starr and Christina Lindborg. 2003. 'Democratic dominoes: Diffusion approaches to the spread of democracy in the international system.' *Journal of Conflict Resolution* 35 (2): 356–381; D. Brinks and Michael Coppedge. 2006. 'Diffusion is no illusion: Neighbor emulation in the third wave of democracy.' *Comparative Political Studies* 39 (4): 463–489; Kristian Skrede Gleditsch and Michael D. Ward. 2006. 'Diffusion and the international context of democratization.' *International Organization* 60: 911–933.

46. Valerie Bunch and Sharon L. Wolchik. 2006. 'International diffusion and post-Communist electoral revolutions.' *Communist and Post-Communist Studies* 39 (3): 283–304.

47. UNDP. 2004. *Arab Human Development Report 2004.* New York: UNDP/Oxford University Press. For a critique of the conventional lens, however, see Lisa Anderson. 2006. 'Searching where the light shines: Studying democratization in the Middle East.' *Annual Review of Political Science* 9: 189–214.

48. For a review of some of these initiatives, see Thomas Carothers. 1999. *Aiding Democracy Abroad.* Washington, DC: Carnegie Endowment for International Peace; Jean Grugel. 1999. *Democracy without Borders: Transnationalisation and Conditionality in New Democracies.* London: Routledge; Peter Burnell. Ed. 2000. *Democracy Assistance: International Co-Operation for Democratization.* London: Frank Cass; Jon C. Pevehouse. 2002. 'With a little help from my friends? Regional organizations and the consolidation of democracy.' *American Journal of Political Science* 46 (3): 611–626; Jon C. Pevehouse. 2002. 'Democracy from the outside-in? International organizations and democratization.' *International Organization*

56 (3): 515; Jon C. Pevehouse. 2004. *Democracy from Above: Regional Orga-*
nizations and Democratization. Cambridge: Cambridge University Press; Thomas
Carothers. 2005. *Critical Mission: Essays on Democracy Promotion.* Washington,
DC: Carnegie Endowment for International Peace; Andrew F. Cooper and Thomas
Legler. 2007. *Intervention without Intervening? The OAS Defense and Promotion*
of Democracy in the Americas. New York: Palgrave Macmillan.

49. Rachel Murray. 2005. *Human Rights in Africa: From the OAU to the African*
    Union. Cambridge: Cambridge University Press; B. Manby. 2004. 'The African
    Union, NEPAD, and human rights: The missing agenda.' *Human Rights Quarterly*
    26 (4): 983–1027.

50. The African Union. http://www.africa-union.org/root/au/Documents/Treaties/text/
    Charter%20on%20Democracy.pdf

51. Robert A. Dahl and E. R.Tufte. 1973. *Size and Democracy.* Stanford, CA: Stanford
    University Press; Alberto Alesina and Enrico Spolaore. 2003. *The Size of Nations.*
    Cambridge, MA: MIT Press.

52. For details about the Togelese and Benin electoral systems and results see Dieter
    Nohlen, Michael Krennerich, and Bernhard Thibaut. Eds. 1999. *Elections in Africa:*
    A Data Handbook. Oxford: Oxford University Press.

53. Andrew Reynolds, Ben Reilly, and Andrew Ellis. 2005. *Electoral System Design:*
    The New International IDEA Handbook. Stockholm: International IDEA, p. 53.

54. Reporters without Borders. 2005. *Worldwide Index of Press Freedom.* http://www.
    rsf.org/rubrique.php3?id_rubrique=554

55. Russell Hardin. 1989. 'Why a constitution?' In Bernard Grofman and Donald
    Wittman (Eds.), *The Federalist Papers and the New Institutionalism.* New York:
    Agathon Press; Sammy Finer. 1995. *Comparing Constitutions.* Oxford: Oxford
    University Press; Barry Weingast. 2005. *Self-Enforcing Constitutions.* Stanford,
    CA: Stanford University Press.

56. Samuel P. Huntington. 1991. *The Third Wave.* Norman: The University of Okla-
    homa Press.

57. UNDP. 2004. *Arab Human Development Report 2004.* New York: UNDP.
    www.undp.org

58. Freedom House estimated that 76 out of 157 independent nation-states (48.4%)
    were 'free' or 'partly free' in 1973, compared with 148 out of 193 (76.6%) in 2007.
    See *Freedom in the World.* www.freedomhouse.org. For a discussion, see Arch
    Puddington and Aili Piano. 2004. 'The 2004 Freedom House Survey: Worrisome
    signs, modest shifts.' *Journal of Democracy* 16 (1): 103–108; Arch Puddington.
    2006. 'Freedom in the World 2006: Middle East progress amid global gains.'
    Journal of Democracy 17 (1); Arch Puddington. 2007. 'The pushback against
    democracy.' *Journal of Democracy* 18 (2): 125–137.

59. Francis Fukiyama. 1992. *The End of History and the Last Man.* New York: Free
    Press.

60. Arch Puddington. 2007. 'The pushback against democracy.' *Journal of Democracy*
    18 (2): 125–137.

61. Jonathan Monten. 2005. 'The roots of the Bush Doctrine: Power, nationalism, and
    democracy promotion in U.S. strategy.' *International Security* 29 (4): 112–156;
    Thomas Carothers. 'Promoting democracy and fighting terror.' *Foreign Affairs*
    2003.

62. See Larry Diamond. 2002. 'Thinking about hybrid regimes.' *Journal of Democracy*
    13 (2): 21–35; Fareed Zakaria. 2007. *The Future of Freedom: Illiberal Democracy*

at Home and Abroad, revised ed. New York: W. W. Norton; Marc M. Howard and P. G. Roessler. 2006. 'Liberalizing electoral outcomes in competitive authoritarian regimes.' *American Journal of Political Science* 50 (2): 365–381; A. C. Armony and H. E. Schamis. 2005. 'Babel in democratization studies.' *Journal of Democracy* 16 (4): 113–128.

63. For a discussion, see Barbara Geddes. 1999. 'What do we know about democratization after twenty years?' *Annual Review of Political Science* 2: 115–144.

64. See, for example, the discussion of the cases contained in Barbara F. Walter and Jack Snyder. Eds. *Civil Wars, Insecurity, and Intervention.* New York: Columbia University Press; Andrew Reynolds. Ed. 2002. *The Architecture of Democracy: Constitutional Design, Conflict Management and Democracy.* Oxford: Oxford University Press; Adrian Guelke. Ed. 2004. *Democracy and Ethnic Conflict.* New York: Palgrave.

65. For a useful discussion of the distinction between "Big C" Constitutions and the "little c" constitutional structure of a country, see Zachary Elkins, Thomas Ginsburg, and James Melton. 2007. *The Lifespan of Written Constitutions.* University of Illinois, unpublished paper.

66. Albert Venn Dicey. 1960. *Introduction to the Study of the Law of the Constitution,* 10th ed. London: MacMillan.

67. For the early development of this concept, see Gerhard Lehmbruch. 1967. *Proporzdemokratie: Politisches System und politische Kultur in der Schweiz und Osterreich.* Tubingen: Mohr; Jurg Steiner. 1974. *Amicable Agreement versus Majority Rule: Conflict Resolution in Switzerland.* Chapel Hill: University of North Carolina Press; Hans Daalder. 1974. 'The consociational democracy theme.' *World Politics* 26: 604–621; Kenneth McRae. Ed. 1974. *Consociational Democracy: Conflict Accommodation in Segmented Societies.* Toronto: McClelland and Stewart.

68. Arend Lijphart. 1969. 'Consociational democracy.' *World Politics* 21: 207–225; Arend Lijphart. 1975. *The Politics of Accommodation: Pluralism and Democracy in the Netherlands.* Berkeley: University of California Press; Arend Lijphart. 1977. *Democracy in Plural Societies: A Comparative Exploration.* New Haven, CT: Yale University Press; Arend Lijphart and Bernard Grofman. Eds. 1984. *Choosing an Electoral System: Issues and Alternatives.* New York: Praeger; Arend Lijphart. 1984. *Democracies.* New Haven, CT: Yale University Press; Arend Lijphart. 1986. 'Degrees of proportionality of proportional representation formulas.' In Bernard Grofman and Arend Lijphart (Eds.), *Electoral Laws and Their Political Consequences.* New York: Agathon Press; Arend Lijphart. 1991. 'Constitutional choices for new democracies.' *Journal of Democracy* 2: 72–84; Arend Lijphart. 1991. 'Proportional representation: Double checking the evidence.' *Journal of Democracy* 2: 42–48; Arend Lijphart. 1994. *Electoral Systems and Party Systems: A Study of Twenty-Seven Democracies, 1945–1990.* New York: Oxford University Press; Arend Lijphart. 1995. 'Electoral systems.' In Seymour Martin Lipset (Ed.), *The Encyclopedia of Democracy.* Washington, DC: Congressional Quarterly Press; Arend Lijphart. 1999. *Patterns of Democracy: Government Forms and Performance in 36 Countries.* New Haven, CT: Yale University Press; Arend Lijphart. 2004. 'Constitutional design for divided societies.' *Journal of Democracy* 15 (2): 96–109; Arend Lijphart. 2008. *Thinking about Democracy: Power Sharing and Majority Rule in Theory and Practice.* New York: Routledge.

69. Arend Lijphart. 1969. 'Consociational democracy.' *World Politics* 21: 207–225.

70. Arend Lijphart. 1968. *The Politics of Accommodation: Pluralism and Democracy in the Netherlands*. Berkeley: University of California Press; Arend Lijphart. 1977. *Democracy in Plural Societies: A Comparative Exploration*. New Haven, CT: Yale University Press.

71. Arend Lijphart. 1999. *Patterns of Democracy: Government Forms and Performance in 36 Countries*. New Haven, CT: Yale University Press.

72. Arend Lijphart. 1999. *Patterns of Democracy: Government Forms and Performance in 36 Countries*. New Haven, CT: Yale University Press, p. 33.

73. W. Arthur Lewis. 1965. *Politics in West Africa*. London: Allen & Unwin.

74. Arend Lijphart. 1999. *Patterns of Democracy: Government Forms and Performance in 36 Countries*. New Haven, CT: Yale University Press, chapters 15 and 16.

75. Matthijs Bogaards. 2000. 'The uneasy relationship between empirical and normative types in consociational theory.' *Journal of Theoretical Politics* 12 (4): 395–423. See also Arend Lijphart. 2000. 'Definitions, evidence and policy: A response to Matthijs Bogaards' Critique.' *Journal of Theoretical Politics* 12 (4): 425–431.

76. Daniel L. Byman. 2002. *Keeping the Peace: Lasting Solutions to Ethnic Conflict*. Baltimore: The Johns Hopkins University Press.

77. Timothy D. Sisk. 1998. 'Elections and conflict management in Africa: Conclusions and recommendations.' In Timothy D. Sisk and Andrew Reynolds (Eds.), *Elections and Conflict Management in Africa*. Washington, DC: US Institute of Peace Press; Daniel P. Sullivan. 2005. 'The missing pillars: A look at the failure of peace in Burundi through the lens of Arend Lijphart's theory of consociational democracy.' *Journal of Modern African Studies* 43 (1): 75–95.

78. Arend Lijphart. 2004. 'Constitutional design for divided societies.' *Journal of Democracy* 15 (2): 96–109.

79. Wolf Linder and Andre Baechtiger. 2005. 'What drives democratization in Asia and Africa?' *European Journal of Political Research* 44: 861–880.

80. See, for example, Stuart J. Kaufman. 2001. *Modern Hatreds: The Symbolic Politics of Ethnic War*. Ithaca, NY: Cornell University Press; Daniel N. Posner. 2004. 'The political salience of cultural difference: Why Chewas and Tumbukas are allies in Zambia and adversaries in Malawi.' *American Political Science Review* 98 (4): 529–546; Daniel N. Posner. 2005. *Institutions and Ethnic Politics in Africa*. Cambridge: Cambridge University Press.

81. Donald L. Horowitz. 1985. *Ethnic Groups in Conflict*. Berkeley: University of California Press; Donald L. Horowitz. 1991. *A Democratic South Africa? Constitutional Engineering in a Divided Society*. Berkeley: University of California Press; Donald L. Horowitz. 1993. 'Democracy in divided societies.' *Journal of Democracy* 4: 18–38; Donald L. Horowitz. 2002. 'Constitutional design: Proposals versus processes.' In Andrew Reynolds (Ed.), *The Architecture of Democracy: Constitutional Design, Conflict Management and Democracy*. Oxford: Oxford University Press; Donald L. Horowitz. 2003. *The Deadly Ethnic Riot*. Berkeley: University of California Press.

82. Ben Reilly and Andrew Reynolds. 1998. *Electoral Systems and Conflict in Divided Societies*. Washington, DC: National Academy Press, p. 30; Susan L. Woodward. 'Bosnia and Herzegovina.' In Barbara F. Walter and Jack Snyder (Eds.), *Civil Wars, Insecurity and Intervention*. New York: Columbia University Press, p. 96.

83. Jack Snyder. 2000. *From Voting to Violence: Democratization and Nationalist Conflict*. New York: W. W. Norton, p. 36; Edward D. Mansfield and Jack Snyder.

2007. *Electing to Fight: Why Emerging Democracies Go to War.* Cambridge, MA: MIT Press.

84. S. G. Simonsen. 2005. 'Addressing ethnic divisions in post-conflict institution-building: Lessons from recent cases.' *Security Dialogue* 36 (3): 297–318.

85. Pippa Norris. 2004. *Electoral Engineering.* New York and Cambridge: Cambridge University Press.

86. See also Ben Reilly and Andrew Reynolds. 1998. *Electoral Systems and Conflict in Divided Societies.* Washington, DC: National Academy Press; Ben Reilly. 2001. *Democracy in Divided Societies: Electoral Engineering for Conflict Management.* Cambridge: Cambridge University Press.

87. On developments in Fiji, see Brij V. Lal. 2002. 'Constitutional engineering in post-coup Fiji.' In Andrew Reynolds (Ed.), *The Architecture of Democracy: Constitutional Design, Conflict Management and Democracy.* Oxford: Oxford University Press.

88. Joel D. Barkan. 1998. 'Rethinking the applicability of proportional representation for Africa.' In Timothy D. Sisk and Andrew Reynolds (Eds.), *Elections and Conflict Management in Africa.* Washington, DC: US Institute of Peace Press.

89. Andre Kaiser, Matthias Lehnert, Bernhard Miller, and Ulrich Sieberer. 2002. 'The democratic quality of institutional regimes: A conceptual framework.' *Political Studies* 50: 313–331.

90. William I. Zartman. 1995. *Elusive Peace: Negotiating an End to Civil Wars 1995–1996.* Washington, DC: Brookings Institution; Caroline Hartzell, Matthew Hoddie, and Donald Rothchild. 2001. 'Stabilizing the peace after civil war: An investigation of some key variables.' *International Organization* 55 (1): 183–208; Donald Rothchild. 2002. 'Settlement terms and post-agreement stability.' In Stephen Stedman, Donald Rothchild, and Elizabeth Cousens (Eds.), *Ending Civil Wars.* Boulder, CO: Lynne Reinner; Paul Collier and Nicholas Sambanis. Eds. 2005. *Understanding Civil War: Evidence and Analysis.* Volume 1. Washington, DC: World Bank.

91. Paul Collier and Nicholas Sambanis. Eds. 2005. *Understanding Civil War.* Washington, DC: World Bank.

92. Robert H. Wagner. 1993. 'The causes of peace.' In Roy Licklider (Ed.), *Stopping the Killing.* New York: New York University Press; Patrick M. Regan. 2002. 'Third party interventions and the duration of intrastate conflict.' *Journal of Conflict Resolution* 46 (1): 55–73.

93. Philip Roeder and Donald Rothschild. 2005. *Sustainable Peace: Power and Democracy after Civil Wars.* Ithaca, NY: Cornell University Press; Edward D. Mansfield and Jack Snyder. 2007. *Electing to Fight: Why Emerging Democracies Go to War.* Cambridge, MA: MIT Press.

94. Denis M. Tull and Andreas Mehler. 2005. 'The hidden costs of power-sharing: Reproducing insurgent violence in Africa.' *African Affairs* 104: 375–398.

95. Olga Shvetsova. 1999. 'A survey of post-communist electoral institutions, 1900–1998.' *Electoral Studies* 18: 397–409; Joseph M. Colomer. 2004. *Handbook of Electoral System Choice.* New York: Palgrave Macmillan.

96. Aníbal Perez-Linan. 2007. *Presidential Impeachment and the New Political Instability in Latin America.* Cambridge: Cambridge University Press.

97. For a discussion, see Alfred Stepan and Cindy Skach. 1993. 'Constitutional frameworks and democratic consolidation: Parliamentarism and presidentialism.' *World Politics* 46 (1): 1–22.

98. See, for example, Mathew Soberg Schugart and John Carey. 1992. *Presidents and Assemblies: Constitutional Design and Electoral Dynamics*. Cambridge: Cambridge University Press; Juan J. Linz and Arturo Valenzuela. Eds. 1994. *The Failure of Presidential Democracy: Comparative Perspectives*. Baltimore: The Johns Hopkins University Press; Scott Mainwaring and Matthew Soberg Shugart. Eds. 1997. *Presidential Democracy in Latin America*. Cambridge: Cambridge University Press; Jose Antonio Cheibub. 2007. *Presidentialism, Parliamentarism, and Democracy*. Cambridge: Cambridge University Press.

99. M. Stephen Fish. 2006. 'Stronger legislatures, stronger democracies.' *Journal of Democracy* 17 (1): 5–20.

100. Ronald L. Watts. 1999. *Comparing Federal Systems*, 2nd ed. Kingston, Canada: McGill-Queen's University Press, p. 3.

101. Chaim Kaufmann. 1996. 'Possible and impossible solutions to ethnic civil wars.' *International Security* 20 (4): 136–175.

102. Dawn Brancati. 2006. 'Decentralization: Fueling the fire or dampening the flames of ethnic conflict and secessionism.' *International Organization* 60 (3): 651–685.

103. Daniel Treisman. 2007. *The Architecture of Government: Rethinking Political Decentralization*. Cambridge: Cambridge University Press.

104. Timothy Besley and Robin Burgess. 2002. 'The political economy of government responsiveness: Theory and evidence from India.' *Quarterly Journal of Economics* 117 (4): 1415–1451.

Chapter 2: Evidence and Methods

1. For a discussion of mixed research designs, see Henry Brady and David Collier. 2004. *Rethinking Social Inquiry: Diverse Tools, Shared Standards*. New York: Rowman & Littlefield.

2. For a discussion of the pros and cons of case study methods, see Alexander L. George and Andrew Bennett. 2004. *Case Studies and Theory Development*. Cambridge, MA: MIT Press.

3. U. Kloti. 'Consensual government in a heterogeneous polity.' *West European Politics* 24 (2): 19–25.

4. Arend Lijphart. 1977. *Democracy in Plural Societies: A Comparative Exploration*. New Haven, CT: Yale University Press.

5. Anna Morawiec Mansfield. 'Ethnic but equal: The quest for a new democratic order in Bosnia and Herzegovina.' *Columbia Law Review* 103: 2020–2051.

6. Sid Noel. Ed. 2005. *From Power Sharing to Democracy: Post-Conflict Institutions in Ethnically Divided Societies*. Montreal: McGill-Queen's University Press.

7. Freedom House. 2007. *Freedom in the World, 2006*. www.freedomhouse.org

8. Susan A. Banducci, Todd Donovan, and Jeffrey A. Karp. 2004. 'Minority representation, empowerment, and participation.' *Journal of Politics* 66 (2): 534–556.

9. L. Mees. 2001. 'Between votes and bullets: Conflicting ethnic identities in the Basque Country.' *Ethnic and Racial Studies* 24 (5): 798–827.

10. Liesbet Hooghe. 1991. *A Leap in the Dark: Nationalist Conflict and Federal Reform in Belgium*. Ithaca, NY: Cornell University Press.

11. John Curtice. Ed. 2002. *New Scotland, New Society? Are Social and Political Ties Fragmenting?* Edinburgh: Polygon.

12. Andrew Reynolds, Ben Reilly, and Andrew Ellis. 2005. *Electoral System Design: The New International IDEA Handbook*. Stockholm: International IDEA.

13. Joseph M. Colomer. 2004. *Handbook of Electoral System Choice*. New York: Palgrave Macmillan.

14. Matthew Golder. 2005. 'Democratic electoral systems around the world, 1946–2000.' *Electoral Studies* 24 (2): 103–121.

15. Kenneth Benoit. 2002. 'The endogeneity problem in electoral studies: A critical re-examination of Duverger's mechanical effect.' *Electoral Studies* 21 (1): 35–46; Kenneth Benoit. 2007. 'Electoral laws as political consequences: Explaining the origins and change of electoral institutions.' *Annual Review of Political Science* 10: 363–390.

16. Arend Lijphart. 1984. *Democracies: Patterns of Majoritarian and Consensus Government in 21 Countries*. New Haven, CT: Yale University Press; Arend Lijphart. 1999. *Patterns of Democracy: Government Forms and Performance in 36 Countries*. New Haven, CT: Yale University Press.

17. For a discussion of the potential problem of selection bias in comparative politics, see Barbara Geddes. 2003. *Paradigms and Sand Castles: Theory Building and Research Design in Comparative Politics,* chapter 3. Ann Arbor: The University of Michigan Press; David Collier, James Mahoney, and Jason Seawright. 2004. 'Claiming too much: Warnings about selection bias.' In Henry E. Brady and David Collier (Eds.), *Rethinking Social Inquiry: Diverse Tools, Shared Standards.* Lanham, MD: Rowman & Littlefield.

18. Ted Robert Gurr. 2000. *Peoples versus States: Minorities at Risk in the New Century*. Washington, DC: US Institute for Peace Press.

19. Minorities at Risk. *Data User Manual 030703*. Project Director Christian Davenport. University of Maryland. http://www.cidcm.umd.edu/inscr/mar/margene/mar-codebook_040903.pdf; Ted Robert Gurr. *People versus States: Minorities at Risk in the New Century,* chapter 1. http://www.bsos.umd.edu/cidcm/mar/trgpvs.html; Minorities at Risk database http://www.cidcm.umd.edu/inscr/mar/

20. David Broughton and Hans-Martien ten Napel. Eds. 2000. *Religion and Mass Electoral Behavior in Europe*. London: Routledge.

21. Arend Lijphart. 1999. *Patterns of Democracy: Government Forms and Performance in 36 Countries*. New Haven, CT: Yale University Press, pp. 280–282; see also a similar strategy in Rein Taagepera. 1994. 'Beating the law of minority attrition.' In Wilma Rule and Joseph Zimmerman (Eds.), *Electoral Systems in Comparative Perspective*. Westport, CT: Greenwood, p. 244.

22. Wilma Rule and Joseph Zimmerman. Eds. 1992. *United States Electoral Systems: Their Impact on Women and Minorities*. New York: Greenwood Press.

23. Pippa Norris. 1985. 'Women in European legislative elites.' *West European Politics* 8 (4): 90–101; Wilma Rule. 1994. 'Women's under-representation and electoral systems.' *PS: Political Science and Politics* 4: 689–692; Pippa Norris. 2000. 'Women's representation and electoral systems.' In Richard Rose (Ed.), *The International Encyclopedia of Elections*. Washington, DC: CQ Press.

24. Karen Bird. 2003. 'The political representation of women and ethnic minorities in established democracies: A framework for comparative research.' Working Paper for AMID, Aalborg University.

25. Chandler Davidson and Bernard Grofman. Eds. 1994. *Quiet Revolution in the South: The Impact of the Voting Rights Act 1965–1990*. Princeton, NJ: Princeton University Press; David Lublin. 1997. *The Paradox of Representation: Racial Gerrymandering and Minority Interests*. Princeton, NJ: Princeton University Press.

26. Mala Htun. 2004. 'Is gender like ethnicity? The political representation of identity groups.' *Perspectives on Politics* 2 (3).

27. Anna Jarstad. 2001. *Changing the Game: Consociational Theory and Ethnic Quotas in Cyprus and New Zealand.* Uppsala: Department of Peace and Conflict, Uppsala University; Andrew Reynolds. 2005. 'Reserved seats in national legislatures.' *Legislative Studies Quarterly* 30 (2): 301–310.

28. See, for example, Charles C. Ragin. 2000. *Fuzzy-Set Social Science.* Chicago: University of Chicago Press.

29. See Jon M. Carey. 'Parchment, equilibria, and institutions.' *Comparative Political Studies* 33 (6–7): 735–761.

30. Maurice Duverger. 1954. *Political Parties: Their Organization and Activity in the Modern State.* New York: Wiley.

31. For a discussion of the general issue, see Kenneth Benoit. 2002. 'The endogeneity problem in electoral studies: A critical re-examination of Duverger's mechanical effect.' *Electoral Studies* 21 (1): 35–46; Kenneth Benoit. 2007. 'Electoral laws as political consequences: Explaining the origins and change of electoral institutions.' *Annual Review of Political Science* 10: 363–390. For a study of stability and change, see also Bernard Grofman and Arend Lijphart. Eds. 2002. *The Evolution of Electoral and Party Systems in the Nordic Countries.* New York: Agathon Press.

32. Bridget Taylor and Katarina Thomson. Eds. 1999. *Scotland and Wales: Nations Again?* Cardiff: University of Wales Press; John Curtice. Ed. 2002. *New Scotland, New Society? Are Social and Political Ties Fragmenting?* Edinburgh: Polygon.

33. Michael Gallagher. 1998. 'The political impact of electoral system change in Japan and New Zealand, 1996.' *Party Politics* 4 (2): 203–228; Jack Vowles, Peter Aimer, Susan Banducci, and Jeffrey Karp. 1998. *Voters' Victory? New Zealand's First Election under Proportional Representation.* Auckland: Auckland University Press.

34. Joseph M. Colomer. 2004. *Handbook of Electoral System Choice.* New York: Palgrave Macmillan; Joseph M. Colomer. 2005. 'It's parties that chose electoral systems (or, Duverger's Laws upside down).' *Political Studies* 53: 1–21.

35. Carles Boix. 1999. 'Setting the rules of the game: The choice of electoral systems in advanced democracies.' *American Political Science Review* 93 (3): 609–624.

36. Pippa Norris. 2004. *Electoral Engineering.* New York and Cambridge: Cambridge University Press, chapter 4.

37. Roger Petersen. 2002. *Understanding Ethnic Violence: Fear, Hatred and Resentment in Twentieth-Century Eastern Europe.* Cambridge: Cambridge University Press.

38. *Constitution of Bosnia and Herzegovina.* Annex 4. December 1995. http://www.ohr.int/dpa/default.asp?content_id=372

39. Stuart J. Kaufman. 2001. *Modern Hatreds: The Symbolic Politics of Ethnic War.* Ithaca, NY: Cornell University Press; Dan Posner. 2004. 'The political salience of cultural difference: Why Chewas and Tumbukas are allies in Zambia and adversaries in Malawi.' *American Political Science Review* 98 (4): 529–546.

40. V. P. Gagnon Jr. 1994. 'Ethnic nationalism and international conflict: The case of Serbia.' *International Security* 19 (3): 130–166.

41. Jack L. Snyder. 2000. *From Voting to Violence: Democratization and Nationalist Conflict.* New York: W. W. Norton.

42. Benedict Anderson. 1983. *Imagined Communities: Reflections on the Origins and Spread of Nationalism.* London: Verso; Dawn Brancati. 2006. 'Decentralization:

Fueling the fire or dampening the flames of ethnic conflict and secessionism.' *International Organization* 60 (3): 651–685.

43. Daniel L. Byman. 2002. *Keeping the Peace: Lasting Solutions to Ethnic Conflicts.* Baltimore: Johns Hopkins University Press.

44. James A. Stimson. 1985. 'Regression in time and space: A statistical essay.' *American Journal of Political Science* 29: 914–947; Cheng M. Hsiao. 1986. *Analysis of Panel Data.* Cambridge: Cambridge University Press.

45. Nathaniel Beck and Jonathan Katz. 1995. 'What to do (and not to do) with time-series cross-section data.' *American Political Science Review* 89: 634–647; Nathaniel Beck and Jonathan Katz. 1996. 'Nuisance vs. substance: Specifying and estimating time-series cross-sectional models.' In J. Freeman (Ed.), *Political Analysis.* Ann Arbor: University of Michigan Press. Beck and Katz argue that feasible generalized least squares approaches that estimate the error process with an AR1 model are less accurate and efficient than OLS with panel-corrected standard errors.

46. See Sven E. Wilson and David M. Butler. 2007. 'A lot more to do: The sensitivity of time-series cross-section analyses to simple alternative specifications.' *Political Analysis* 15 (2): 101–123.

47. Cheng M. Hsiao. 1986. *Analysis of Panel Data.* Cambridge: Cambridge University Press.

48. Nathaniel Beck and Jonathan Katz. 1995. 'What to do (and not to do) with time-series cross-section data.' *American Political Science Review* 89: 634–647.

49. Arend Lijphart. 1984. *Democracies: Patterns of Majoritarian and Consensus Government in 21 Countries.* New Haven, CT: Yale University Press; Arend Lijphart. 1999. *Patterns of Democracy: Government Forms and Performance in 36 Countries.* New Haven, CT: Yale University Press.

50. See, for example, Thomas Carothers. 1999. *Aiding Democracy Abroad: The Learning Curve.* Washington, DC: The Carnegie Foundation; G. Shabbir Cheema. 2005. *Building Democratic Institutions in Developing Countries.* Bloomfield, CT: Kumarian Press; Ted Piccone and Richard Youngs. Eds. 2006. *Strategies for Democratic Change: Assessing the Global Response.* Washington, DC: The Democracy Coalition; Edward Neuman and Roland Rich. Eds. 2004. *The UN Role in Promoting Democracy: Between Ideals and Reality.* New York: UN University Press.

51. George Tsebelis. 2002. *Veto Players: How Political Institutions Work.* Princeton, NJ: Princeton University Press.

52. Wolf Linder and André Bächtiger. 2005. 'What drives democratization in Asia and Africa?' *European Journal of Political Research* 44: 861–880.

53. Alberto Alesina and Eliana La Ferrara. 2005. 'Ethnic diversity and economic performance.' *Journal of Economic Literature* 43 (3): 762–800.

54. *Atlas Narodov Mira.* 1964. Moscow: Miklukho-Maklai Ethnological Institute.

55. William Easterly and Ross Levine. 1997. 'Africa's growth tragedy: Policies and ethnic divisions.' *Quarterly Journal of Economics* 111 (4): 1203–1250.

56. Daniel Posner. 2004. 'Measuring ethnic fractionalization in Africa.' *American Journal of Political Science* 48 (4): 849–863.

57. Alberto Alesina, Arnaud Devleeschauwer, William Easterly, Sergio Kurlat, and Romain Wacziarg. 2003. 'Fractionalization.' *Journal of Economic Growth* 8: 155–194. For details see: www.stanford.edu/~wacziarg/papersum.html

58. Stuart J. Kaufman. 2001. *Modern Hatreds: The Symbolic Politics of Ethnic Wars.* Ithaca, NY: Cornell University Press; Daniel Posner. 2004. 'Measuring ethnic fractionalization in Africa.' *American Journal of Political Science* 48 (4): 849–863.

Chapter 3: Democratic Indicators and Trends

1. Kenneth A. Bollen. 1990. 'Political democracy: Conceptual and measurement traps.' *Studies in International Development* 25 (2): 7–24; Geraldo L. Munck and Jay Verkuilen. 2002. 'Conceptualizing and measuring democracy: Evaluating alternative indices.' *Comparative Political Studies* 35 (1): 5–34; Geraldo L. Munck and Jay Verkuilen. 2002. 'Generating better data: A response to discussants.' *Comparative Political Studies* 35 (1): 52–57.

2. Merilee Grindle. 2004. 'Good enough governance: Poverty reduction and reform in developing countries.' *Governance* 17 (4): 525–548; Derick W. Brinkerhoff and Arthur A. Goldsmith. 2005. 'Institutional dualism and international development: A revisionist interpretation of good governance.' *Administration and Society* 37 (2): 199–225.

3. A useful review of these, and also the other measures which are available but covering a shorter period or more limited range of nation-states, is available from Geraldo L. Munck and Jay Verkuilen. 2002. 'Conceptualizing and measuring democracy: Evaluating alternative indices.' *Comparative Political Studies* 35 (1): 5–34.

4. David Collier and Robert Adcock. 1999. 'Democracy and dichotomies: A pragmatic approach to choices about concepts.' *Annual Review of Political Science* 1: 537–565.

5. Geraldo L. Munck and Jay Verkuilen. 2002. 'Conceptualizing and measuring democracy: Evaluating alternative indices.' *Comparative Political Studies* 35 (1): 5–34.

6. Karl Popper. 1963. *Conjectures and Refutations.* Oxford: Clarendon Press.

7. Joseph A. Schumpeter. 1950. *Capitalism, Socialism and Democracy*, 3rd ed. New York: Harper & Row.

8. José Cheibub and Jennifer Gandhi. 2004. 'A six-fold measure of democracies and dictatorships.' Unpublished paper presented at the Annual Meeting of the American Political Science Association.

9. Monty G. Marshall and Keith Jaggers. 2002. *Polity IV Project: Political Regime Characteristics and Transitions, 1800–2002. Dataset Users' Manual.* College Park: University of Maryland. www.cidm.umd.edu/inscr/polity

10. Thomas Carothers. 2002. 'The end of the transition paradigm.' *Journal of Democracy* 13: 5–21; Fareed Zakaria. 1997. 'The rise of illiberal democracy.' *Foreign Affairs* 76 (6): 22–41; Larry Diamond. 2002. 'Thinking about hybrid regimes.' *Journal of Democracy* 13 (2): 21–35; Steven Levitsky and Lucan A. Way. 2002. 'The rise of competitive authoritarianism.' *Journal of Democracy* 13 (2): 51–65; Stephen Levitsky. 2003. 'Autocracy by democratic rules: The dynamics of competitive authoritarianism in the post–cold war era.' Paper presented at the Conference, 'Mapping the Great Zone: Clientelism and the Boundary between Democratic and Democratizing.' Columbia University, April 4–5.

11. Ariel C. Armony and Hector E. Schamis. 2005. 'Babel in democratization studies.' *Journal of Democracy* 16 (4): 113–128.

12. M. M. Howard and P. G. Roessler. 2006. 'Liberalizing electoral outcomes in competitive authoritarian regimes.' *American Journal of Political Science* 50 (2): 365–381.

13. Robert A. Dahl. 1956. *A Preface to Democratic Theory.* Chicago: University of Chicago Press; Robert A. Dahl. 1971. *Polyarchy.* New Haven, CT: Yale University Press; Robert A. Dahl and Charles E. Lindblom. 1953. *Politics, Economics, and*

Welfare. New York: Harper Collins; Robert A. Dahl. 1989. *Democracy and Its Critics*. New Haven, CT: Yale University Press, p. 221; Robert A. Dahl. 2005. 'What political institutions does large-scale democracy require?' *Political Science Quarterly* 120 (2): 187–197.

14. Robert Dahl. 1989. *Democracy and Its Critics*. New Haven, CT: Yale University Press, p. 221.

15. Freedom House. 2007. *Freedom in the World, 2007*. 'Methodology.' www.freedomhouse.org

16. Monty G. Marshall and Keith Jaggers. 2002. *Polity IV Project: Political Regime Characteristics and Transitions, 1800–2002. Dataset Users' Manual*. College Park: University of Maryland. www.cidm.umd.edu/inscr/polity

17. Axel Hadenius. 1992. *Democracy and Development*. Cambridge: Cambridge University Press.

18. Joe Foweraker and Roman Krznaric. 2003. 'Differentiating the democratic performance of the West.' *European Journal of Political Research* 42 (3): 313–341.

19. Joe Foweraker and Roman Krznaric. 2000. 'Measuring liberal democratic performance: An empirical and conceptual critique.' *Political Studies* 48: 759–787.

20. Larry Diamond. 1996. *Developing Democracy: Toward Consolidation*. Baltimore: The Johns Hopkins University Press; Robert J. Barro. 1999. 'Determinants of democracy.' *Journal of Political Economy* 107 (6): 158–183; Ronald Inglehart and Christopher Welzel. 2005. *Modernization, Cultural Change, and Democracy: The Human Development Sequence*. Cambridge: Cambridge University Press.

21. David Collier and Robert Adcock. 1999. 'Democracy and dichotomies: A pragmatic approach to choices about concepts.' *Annual Review of Political Science* 1: 537–565.

22. Freedom House. 2007. *Freedom in the World, 2007*. Washington, DC: Freedom House. www.freedomhouse.org

23. Geraldo L. Munck and Jay Verkuilen. 2002. 'Conceptualizing and measuring democracy: Evaluating alternative indices.' *Comparative Political Studies* 35 (1): 5–34.

24. See, for example, R. E. Burkhart. 2000. 'Economic freedom and democracy: Post-cold war tests.' *European Journal of Political Research* 37 (2): 237–253.

25. For a disaggregated approach, see Bruce Bueno De Mesquita, G. W. Downs, Alistair Smith, and F. M. Cherif. 2005. 'Thinking inside the box: A closer look at democracy and human rights.' *International Studies Quarterly* 49 (3): 439–457.

26. Ted Robert Gurr. 1974. 'Persistence and change in political systems.' *American Political Science Review* 74: 1482–1504.

27. Monty Marshall and Keith Jaggers. 2003. *Polity IV Project: Political Regime Characteristics and Transitions, 1800–2003*. http://www.cidcm.umd.edu/inscr/polity/; Monty Marshall, Ted Robert Gurr, Christian Davenport, and Keith Jaggers. 2002. 'Polity IV, 1800–1999: Comments on Munck and Verkuilen.' *Comparative Political Studies* 35 (1): 40–45.

28. Geraldo L. Munck and Jay Verkuilen. 2002. 'Conceptualizing and measuring democracy: Evaluating alternative indices.' *Comparative Political Studies* 35 (1): 5–34; Monty G. Marshall, Ted Robert Gurr, Christian Davenport, and Keith Jaggers. 2002. 'Polity IV, 1800–1999: Comments on Munck and Verkuilen.' *Comparative Political Studies* 35 (1): 40–45.

29. Tatu Vanhanen. 1990. *The Process of Democratization: A Comparative Study of 147 States: 1980–88*. New York: Crane Russak; Tatu Vanhanen. 1997. *Prospects*

for Democracy: A Study of 172 Countries. New York: Routledge; Tatu Vanhanen. 2000. 'A new dataset for measuring democracy, 1810–1998.' *Journal of Peace Research* 37 (2): 251–265.

30. Pamela Paxton, Kenneth A. Bollen, Deborah M. Lee, and Hyo Joung Kim. 2003. 'A half century of suffrage: New data and a comparative analysis.' *Studies in Comparative International Development* 38 (1): 93–122; Teri L. Caraway. 2004. 'Inclusion and democratization: Class, gender, race, and the extension of suffrage.' *Comparative Politics* 36 (4): 443.

31. International IDEA. *Voter Turnout since 1945.* Stockholm: International IDEA.

32. Mark N. Franklin. 2004. Voter Turnout and the Dynamics of Electoral Competition in Established Democracies since 1945. Cambridge: Cambridge University Press.

33. Tatu Vanhanen. 1990. *The Process of Democratization: A Comparative Study of 147 States: 1980–88.* New York: Crane Russak; Tatu Vanhanen. 1997. *Prospects for Democracy: A Study of 172 Countries.* New York: Routledge; Tatu Vanhanen. 2000. 'A new dataset for measuring democracy, 1810–1998.' *Journal of Peace Research* 37 (2): 251–265.

34. M. Laakso and Rein Taagepera. 1979. 'Effective number of parties: A measure with application to Western Europe.' *Comparative Political Studies.* 12: 3–27.

35. Mike Alvarez, José Antonio Cheibub, Fernando Limongi, and Adam Przeworski. 1996. 'Classifying political regimes.' *Studies in International Comparative Development* 31: 3–36; Adam Przeworski, Michael E. Alvarez, José Antonio Cheibub, and Fernando Limongi. 2000. *Democracy and Development: Political Institutions and Well-Being in the World, 1950–1990.* Cambridge: Cambridge University Press; José Cheibub and Jennifer Gandhi. 2005. 'A six-fold measure of democracies and dictatorships.' Paper presented at the Annual Meeting of the American Political Science Association. For a discussion of the virtues of adopting a minimalist conceptualization and measure, see Adam Przeworski. 1999. 'Minimalist conception of democracy: A defense.' In Ian Shapiro and Casiano Hacker-Cordon (Eds.), *Democracy's Value.* Cambridge: Cambridge University Press.

36. The earliest conceptualization was offered by Joseph Schumpeter. 1947. *Capitalism, Socialism, and Democracy.* New York: Harper and Bros. Similar definitions are offered by Seymour Martin Lipset: "Democracy (in a complex society) is defined as a political system which supplies regular constitutional opportunities for changing the governing officials." Seymour Martin Lipset. 1959. 'Some social requisites of democracy: Economic development and political legitimacy.' *American Political Science Review* 53: 71.

37. Robert Dahl. 1989. *Democracy and Its Critics.* New Haven, CT: Yale University Press.

38. Elmer Eric Schattschneider. 1942. *Party Government.* New York: Holt, Rinehart & Winston. Anckar and Anckar argue, however, that a half-dozen small independent island states can be classified as democratic regimes without political parties, namely, Belau (Palau), the Federated States of Micronesia, Kiribati, Marshall Islands, Nauru, and Tuvalu. Their size, an extremely archipelagic geography, and an intense cultural resistance all contribute to an absence of political parties in these democracies. See D. Anckar and C. Anckar. 2000. 'Democracies without parties.' *Comparative Political Studies* 33 (2): 225–247.

39. Adam Przeworski, Michael E. Alvarez, José Antonio Cheibub, and Fernando Limongi. 2000. *Democracy and Development: Political Institutions and Well-Being*

in the World, 1950–1990. Cambridge: Cambridge University Press; José Cheibub and Jennifer Gandhi. 2004. 'A six-fold measure of democracies and dictatorships.' Paper Presented at the Annual Meeting of the American Political Science Association.

40. André Blais, Louis Massicote, and A. Yoshinaka. 2001. 'Deciding who has the right to vote: A comparative analysis of election laws.' *Electoral Studies* 20 (1): 41–62.

41. Pamela Paxton. 2000. 'Women's suffrage in the measurement of democracy: Problems of operationalization.' *Studies in Comparative International Development* 35 (3): 92–111; Teri L. Caraway. 2004. 'Inclusion and democratization: Class, gender, race, and the extension of suffrage.' *Comparative Politics* 36 (4): 443–450; Pamela Paxton, Kenneth A. Bollen, Deborah M. Lee, and Hyo Joung Kim. 2003. 'A half century of suffrage: New data and a comparative analysis.' *Studies in Comparative International Development* 38 (1): 93–122.

42. The Committee to Protect Journalists. 'Journalists killed in the line of duty during the last ten years: 1995–2004.' http://www.cpj.org/killed/Ten_Year_Killed/Intro.html

43. David L. Cingranelli and David L. Richards. 2004. *The Cingranelli-Richards (CIRI) Human Rights Database Coder Manual*. http://ciri.binghamton.edu/

44. World Bank. 2007. *Strengthening World Bank Group Engagement on Governance and Anticorruption*. http://www.worldbank.org/html/extdr/comments/governancefeedback/

45. David L. Cingranelli and David L. Richards. 2004. *The Cingranelli-Richards (CIRI) Human Rights Database Coder Manual*. http://ciri.binghamton.edu/

46. Derick W. Brinkerhoff and Arthur A. Goldsmith. 2005. 'Institutional dualism and international development: A revisionist interpretation of good governance.' *Administration and Society* 37 (2): 199–225.

47. Merilee Grindle. 2004. 'Good enough governance: Poverty reduction and reform in developing countries.' *Governance* 17 (4): 525–548.

48. David Collier and Robert Adcock. 1999. 'Democracy and dichotomies: A pragmatic approach to choices about concepts.' *Annual Review of Political Science* 1: 537–565; Zachary Elkins. 2000. 'Gradations of democracy? Empirical tests of alternative conceptualizations.' *American Journal of Political Science* 44 (2): 293–300; Geraldo L. Munck and Jay Verkuilen. 2002. 'Conceptualizing and measuring democracy: Evaluating alternative indices.' *Comparative Political Studies* 35 (1): 5–34.

49. John Gerring. 2001. *Social Science Methodology: A Critical Framework*. Cambridge: Cambridge University Press, pp. 89–117.

50. Nancy Bermeo. 2003. *Ordinary People in Extraordinary Times: The Citizenry and the Breakdown of Democracy*. Princeton, NJ: Princeton University Press.

51. Guillermo O'Donnell. 1973. *Modernization and Bureaucratic-Authoritarianism: Studies in South American Politics*. Berkeley: University of California Press.

52. Geraldo L. Munck. 2001. 'The regime question: Theory building in democracy studies.' *World Politics* 54 (1): 119.

53. Michael Coppedge. 1999. 'Thickening thin concepts and theories: Combining large N and small in comparative politics.' *Comparative Politics* 31 (4): 465–476.

54. Donald P. Green and Ian Shapiro. 1994. *Pathologies of Rational Choice Theory*. New Haven, CT: Yale University Press.

55. Nathaniel Beck and Jonathan Katz. 1995. 'What to do (and not to do) with time-series cross-section data.' *American Political Science Review*. 89: 634–647.

Chapter 4: Wealth and Democracy

1. B. Davidson. 1992. *The Black Man's Burden: Africa and the Curse of the Nation-State*. New York: Random House.
2. Robert A. Dahl. 1998. *On Democracy*. New Haven, CT: Yale University Press.
3. John Stuart Mill. 1964. *Considerations on Representative Government* (1859). London: Dent. Lipset also attributed the original notion to Aristotle: Seymour Martin Lipset. 1959. 'Some social requisites of democracy: Economic development and political legitimacy.' *American Political Science Review* 53: 69–105.
4. Seymour Martin Lipset. 1959. 'Some social requisites of democracy: Economic development and political legitimacy.' *American Political Science Review* 53: 69–105. See also Seymour Martin Lipset. 1960. *Political Man: The Social Basis of Politics*. New York: Doubleday; Seymour Martin Lipset, Kyoung-Ryung Seong, and John Charles Torres. 1993. 'A comparative analysis of the social requisites of democracy.' *International Social Science Journal* 45 (2): 154–175; Seymour Martin Lipset and Jason M. Lakin. 2004. *The Democratic Century*. Norman: The University of Oklahoma Press.
5. Seymour Martin Lipset. 1959. 'Some social requisites of democracy: Economic development and political legitimacy.' *American Political Science Review* 53: 75.
6. Seymour Martin Lipset. 1959. 'Some social requisites of democracy: Economic development and political legitimacy.' *American Political Science Review* 53: 75. The most recent statement of this relationship by Lipset and Lakin suggests that capitalist free-market economies produce multiple commodities which are critical for democracy, by creating more heterogeneous and diverse centers of wealth and power. This process reduces the economic control of the state and provides the basis for opposition organizations, they suggest, and the economic foundation for an active civil society. See Seymour Martin Lipset and Jason M. Lakin. 2004. *The Democratic Century*. Norman: The University of Oklahoma Press, chapter 5.
7. Dankwart Rustow. 1970. 'Transitions to democracy.' *Comparative Politics* 2: 337–363.
8. J. Krieckhaus. 2004. 'The regime debate revisited: A sensitivity analysis of democracy's economic effect.' *British Journal of Political Science* 34 (4): 635–655.
9. Robert W. Jackman. 1973. 'On the relation of economic development and democratic performance.' *American Journal of Political Science* 17: 611–621; Kenneth A. Bollen. 1979. 'Political democracy and the timing of development.' *American Sociological Review* 44: 572–587; Kenneth A. Bollen. 1983. 'World system position, dependency and democracy: The cross-national evidence.' *American Sociological Review* 48: 468–479; Kenneth A. Bollen and Robert W. Jackman. 1985. 'Political democracy and the size distribution of income.' *American Sociological Review* 50: 438–458; Gregory C. Brunk, Gregory A. Caldeira, and Michael S. Lewis-Beck. 1987. 'Capitalism, socialism, and democracy: An empirical inquiry.' *European Journal of Political Research* 15: 459–470; Evelyne Huber, Dietrich Rueschmeyer, and John D. Stephens. 1993. 'The impact of economic development on democracy.' *Journal of Economic Perspectives* 7 (3): 71–85; Ross E. Burkhart and Michael S. Lewis-Beck. 1994. 'Comparative democracy: The economic development thesis.' *American Political Science Review* 88: 903–910; John F. Helliwell. 1994. 'Empirical linkages between democracy and economic growth.' *British Journal of Political Science* 24 (2): 225–248; Tatu Vanhanen. 1997. *Prospects for Democracy: A Study of 172 Countries*. New York: Routledge; Robert J. Barro. 1999. 'Determinants of

democracy.' *Journal of Political Economy* 107 (6): 158–183; Adam Przeworski, Michael E. Alvarez, José Antonio Cheibub, and Fernando Limongi. 2000. *Democracy and Development: Political Institutions and Well-Being in the World, 1950–1990*. Cambridge: Cambridge University Press; Seymour Martin Lipset, Kyoung-Ryung Seong, and John Charles Torres. 1993. 'A comparative analysis of the social requisites of democracy.' *International Social Science Journal* 45 (2): 154–175; Seymour Martin Lipset and Jason M. Lakin. 2004. *The Democratic Century*. Norman: The University of Oklahoma Press.

10. Adam Przeworski, Michael E. Alvarez, José Antonio Cheibub, and Fernando Limongi. 1996. 'What makes democracies endure?' *Journal of Democracy* 7 (1): 39–55; Adam Przeworski and F. Limongi. 1997. 'Modernization: Theories and facts.' *World Politics* 49: 155–183; Adam Przeworski, Michael E. Alvarez, José Antonio Cheibub, and Fernando Limongi. 2000. *Democracy and Development: Political Institutions and Well-Being in the World, 1950–1990*. Cambridge: Cambridge University Press.

11. See David Collier and Robert Adcock. 1999. 'Democracy and dichotomies: A pragmatic approach to choices about concepts.' *Annual Review of Political Science* 1: 537–565; Michael Coppedge. 1999. 'Thickening thin concepts and theories: Combining large N and small in comparative politics.' *Comparative Politics* 31 (4): 465–476; Adam Przeworski. 1999. 'Minimalist conception of democracy: A defense.' In Ian Shapiro and Casiano Hacker-Cordon (Eds.), *Democracy's Value*. Cambridge: Cambridge University Press; Geraldo L. Munck and Jay Verkuilen. 2002. 'Conceptualizing and measuring democracy: Evaluating alternative indices.' *Comparative Political Studies* 35 (1): 5–34; Pamela Paxton. 2000. 'Women's suffrage in the measurement of democracy: Problems of operationalization.' *Studies in Comparative International Development* 35 (3): 92–111; Teri L. Caraway. 2004. 'Inclusion and democratization: Class, gender, race, and the extension of suffrage.' *Comparative Politics* 36 (4): 443–460.

12. See Robert J. Barro. 1997. *Determinants of Economic Growth: A Cross-Country Empirical Study*. Cambridge, MA: MIT Press; Robert J. Barro. 1999. 'Determinants of democracy.' *Journal of Political Economy* 107 (6–2): 158–183.

13. Seymour Martin Lipset and Jason M. Lakin. 2004. *The Democratic Century*. Norman: The University of Oklahoma Press, chapter 11.

14. M. L. Ross 2001. 'Does oil hinder democracy?' *World Politics* 53: 325–361.

15. Torsten Perrson and Guido Tabellini. 2003. *The Economic Effects of Constitutions*. Cambridge, MA: MIT Press.

16. Guillermo O'Donnell. 1973. *Modernization and Bureaucratic-Authoritarianism: Studies in South American Politics*. Berkeley: University of California Press.

17. Nathaniel Beck and Jonathan N. Katz. 1995. 'What to do (and not to do) with time-series cross-section data.' *American Political Science Review* 89: 634–647.

18. Nathaniel Beck. 2001. 'Time-series/cross-section data: What have we learned in the past few years?' *Annual Review of Political Science* 4: 271–293.

19. Robert A. Dahl and E. R. Tufte. 1973. *Size and Democracy*. Stanford, CA: Stanford University Press; Robert A. Dahl. 1998. *On Democracy*. New Haven, CT: Yale University Press; Alberto Alesina and Enrico Spolaore. 2003. *The Size of Nations*. Cambridge, MA: MIT Press.

20. Christopher Clague, Suzanne Gleason, and Stephen Knack. 2001. 'Determinants of lasting democracy in poor countries: Culture, development and institutions.' *Annals of the American Academy of Social Sciences* 573: 16–41.

21. Seymour Martin Lipset and Jason M. Lakin. 2004. *The Democratic Century.* Norman: The University of Oklahoma Press, chapter 11. See also similar findings in Axel Hadenius. 1994. 'The duration of democracy.' In David Beetham. 1994. *Defining and Measuring Democracy.* London: Sage.

22. Harvey Starr and Christina Lindborg. 2003. 'Democratic dominoes: Diffusion approaches to the spread of democracy in the international system.' *Journal of Conflict Resolution* 35 (2): 356–381; see also Barbara Wejnart. 2005. 'Diffusion, development and democracy, 1800–1999.' *American Sociological Review* 70 (1): 53–81.

23. UNDP. 2004. *Arab Human Development Report 2004.* New York: UNDP/Oxford University Press.

24. Alberto Alesina and E. LaFerrara. 2005. 'Ethnic diversity and economic performance.' *Journal of Economic Literature* 43 (3): 762–800.

25. Alberto Alesina, Arnaud Devleeschauwer, William Easterly, Sergio Kurlat, and Romain Wacziarg. 2003. 'Fractionalization.' *Journal of Economic Growth* 8: 155–194. For details see: www.stanford.edu/~wacziarg/papersum.html

26. William Easterly and Ross Levine. 1997. 'Africa's Growth Tragedy: Policies and Ethnic Divisions.' *The Quarterly Journal of Economics* 112 (4): 1203–1250.

27. See, for example, David Lerner. 1958. *The Passing of Traditional Society.* Glencoe, IL: The Free Press; P. Cutright. 1963. 'National political development: Measurement and analysis.' *American Sociological Review* 28: 253–264; Larry Diamond. 1999. *Developing Democracy.* Baltimore: The Johns Hopkins University Press; Adam Przeworski, Michael E. Alvarez, José Antonio Cheibub, and Fernando Limongi. 2000. *Democracy and Development: Political Institutions and Well-Being in the World, 1950–1990.* Cambridge: Cambridge University Press.

28. Dietrich Rueschemeyer, Evelyne Huber Stephens, and John D. Stephens. 1992. *Capitalist Development and Democracy.* Chicago: University of Chicago Press; Evelyne Huber Stephens, Dietrich Rueschemeyer, and John D. Stephens. 1993. 'The impact of economic development on democracy.' *Journal of Economic Perspectives* 7 (3): 71–85; Ruth Berins Collier. 1999. *Paths toward Democracy: Working Class and Elites in Western Europe and South America.* Cambridge: Cambridge University Press.

29. Kenneth Bolen and Robert Jackman. 1985. 'Political democracy and the size distribution of income.' *American Sociological Review* 52 (2): 50–68; Ross E. Burkhart. 1997. 'Comparative democracy and income distribution: Shape and direction of the causal arrow.' *Journal of Politics* 59 (1): 148–164; Manus I. Midlarsky. Ed. 1997. *Inequality, Democracy and Economic Development.* Cambridge: Cambridge University Press.

30. Robert J. Barro. 1999. 'Determinants of democracy.' *Journal of Political Economy* 107 (6): 158–183.

31. Per capita gross domestic product is measured in US$ in purchasing power parity. See UNDP. 2005. *Human Development Report 2005.* New York: Oxford University Press.

32. For details, see Carl J. Saxer. 2002. *From Transition to Power Alternation: Democracy in South Korea, 1987–1997.* New York: Routledge; Sunhyuk Kim. 2000. *The Politics of Democratization in Korea: The Role of Civil Society.* Pittsburgh: University of Pittsburgh Press; Young W. Kihl. 2005. *Transforming Korean Politics: Democracy, Reform, and Culture.* Armonk, NY: M. E. Sharpe.

33. Chan Wook Park. 2002. 'Elections in Democratizing Korea.' In John Fuh-Sheng Hsieh and David Newman (Eds.), *How Asia Votes*. New York: Chatham House, Table 6.5.

34. Reporters sans Frontiers. 2005. *Annual Worldwide Press Freedom Index – 2005*. www.rfs.org

35. Transparency International. 2005. *Corruption Perceptions Index 2005*. http://www.transparency.org/policy_and_research/surveys_indices/cpi/2005

36. For more details about the historical development and contemporary nature of the political system, see Carl A. Trocki. 2006. *Singapore: Wealth, Power and the Culture of Control*. New York: Routledge; Diane K. Mauzy and R. S. Milne. 2002. *Singapore Politics under the People's Action Party*. New York: Routledge.

37. Michael Haas. Ed. 1999. *The Singapore Puzzle*. Westport, CT: Praeger.

38. For details of the electoral system, see http://www.elections.gov.sg/index.html

39. Diane K. Mauzy. 2002. 'Electoral innovation and one-party dominance in Singapore.' In John Fuh-Sheng Hsieh and David Newman (Eds.), *How Asia Votes*. New York: Chatham House.

40. Jorgen Elkit anhd Palle Svensson. 1997. 'What makes elections free and fair?' *Journal of Democracy* 8 (3): 32–46.

41. UNDP. 2005. *The Human Development Report, 2004*. New York: Oxford University Press.

42. Morton H. Halperin, Joseph T. Siegle, and Michael M. Weinstein. 2005. *The Democracy Advantage: How Democracies Promote Prosperity and Peace*. New York: Routledge.

43. Morton H. Halperin, Joseph T. Siegle, and Michael M. Weinstein. 2005. *The Democracy Advantage: How Democracies Promote Prosperity and Peace*. New York: Routledge, pp. 35–43.

44. Stephen Kosack. 2003. 'Effective aid: How democracy allows development aid to improve the quality of life.' *World Development* 31 (1): 1–22.

Chapter 5: Electoral Systems

1. See Giovanni Sartori. 1994. *Comparative Constitutional Engineering: An Inquiry into Structures, Incentives, and Outcomes*. New York: Columbia University Press; Arend Lijphart and Carlos Waisman. 1996. *Institutional Design in New Democracies*. Boulder, CO: Westview Press.

2. Arend Lijphart. 1999. *Patterns of Democracy: Government Forms and Performance in 36 Countries*. New Haven, CT: Yale University Press; Arend Lijphart. 2004. 'Constitutional design for divided societies.' *Journal of Democracy* 15 (2): 96–109.

3. Kanchan Chandra. 2001. 'Ethnic bargains, group instability, and social choice theory.' *Politics & Society* 29 (3): 337–362; Kanchan Chandra. 2005. 'Ethnic parties and democratic stability.' *Perspectives on Politics* 3 (2): 235–252.

4. Meindert Fennema. 2000. 'Legal repression of extreme-right parties and racial discrimination.' In Ruud Koopmans and Paul Statham (Eds.), *Challenging Immigration and Ethnic Relations Politics*. Oxford: Oxford University Press.

5. For a study of these factors, see Shaun Bowler, Elisabeth Carter, and David M. Farrell. 2003. 'Changing party access to elections.' In Bruce Cain, Russell Dalton, and Susan Scarrow (Eds.), *Democracy Transformed?* Oxford: Oxford University Press. For an application of these factors to the radical right, see Elisabeth Carter. 2005.

The Extreme Right in Western Europe: Success or Failure? Manchester: Manchester University Press, chapter 5; Pippa Norris. 2005. *Radical Right.* Cambridge: Cambridge University Press, chapter 4.

6. International IDEA. 2003. *Funding of Political Parties and Election Campaigns.* Stockholm: International IDEA.

7. Arend Lijphart. 1997. 'Unequal participation: Democracies' unresolved dilemma.' *American Political Science Review* 91: 1–14.

8. Brendan O'Leary and John McGarry. 2006. 'Consociational theory, Northern Ireland's conflict and its agreement: 1. What consociationalists can learn from Northern Ireland.' *Government & Opposition* 41 (1): 43–63.

9. Arend Lijphart. 1986. 'Proportionality by non-PR methods: Ethnic representation in Belgium, Cyprus, Lebanon, New Zealand, West Germany and Zimbabwe.' In Bernard Grofman and Arend Lijphart (Eds.), *Electoral Laws and Their Political Consequences.* New York: Agathon Press; Arend Lijphart. 1997. 'Unequal participation: Democracies' unresolved dilemma.' *American Political Science Review* 91: 1–14.

10. Kanchan Chandra. 2004. *Why Ethnic Parties Succeed: Patronage and Ethnic Headcounts in India.* Cambridge: Cambridge University Press; Kanchan Chandra. 2005. 'Ethnic parties and democratic stability.' *Perspectives on Politics* 3 (2): 235–252.

11. Anna Jarstad. 2001. *Changing the Game: Consociational Theory and Ethnic Quotas in Cyprus and New Zealand.* Uppsala: Department of Peace and Conflict, Uppsala University; Andrew Reynolds. 2005. 'Reserved seats in national legislatures.' *Legislative Studies Quarterly* 30 (2): 301–310; Lisa Handley. 2005. 'Comparative Redistricting Practices.' Paper Presented at the Annual Meeting of the American Political Science Association, Washington, DC; Andrew Reynolds. 2007. 'Minority MPs in national legislatures: Existing research and data gaps.' Minority Rights Group International/ UNDP.

12. For a critical comparison of the evidence supporting this proposition, see Pippa Norris. 2002. 'Ballots not bullets: Electoral systems, ethnic minorities and democratization.' In Andrew Reynolds and Scott Mainwaring (Eds.), *The Architecture of Democracy: Constitutional Design, Conflict Management and Democracy.* Oxford: Oxford University Press.

13. Kanchan Chandra. 2001. 'Ethnic bargains, group instability, and social choice theory.' *Politics & Society* 29 (3): 337–362; Kanchan Chandra. 2004. *Why Ethnic Parties Succeed: Patronage and Ethnic Headcounts in India.* Cambridge: Cambridge University Press.

14. Seymour Martin Lipset and Stein Rokkan. 1967. *Party Systems and Voter Alignments.* New York: Free Press; Peter C. Ordeshook and Olga Shvetsova. 1994. 'Ethnic heterogeneity, district magnitude and the number of parties.' *American Journal of Political Science* 38: 100–123; Octavio Amorim Neto and Gary Cox. 1997. 'Electoral institutions, cleavage structures and the number of parties.' *American Journal of Political Science* 41 (1): 149–174.

15. Donald L. Horowitz. 1985. *Ethnic Groups in Conflict.* Berkeley: University of California Press.

16. Susan L. Woodward. 'Bosnia and Herzegovina.' In Barbara F. Walter and Jack Snyder (Eds.), *Civil Wars, Insecurity and Intervention.* New York: Columbia University Press, p. 96.

17. Jack Snyder. 2000. *From Voting to Violence: Democratization and Nationalist Conflict.* New York: W. W. Norton, pp. 296–308.

18. Brendan O'Leary and John McGarry. 2004. *The Northern Ireland Conflict: Consociational Engagements*. Oxford: Oxford University Press.

19. Pippa Norris. 2005. *Radical Right*. Cambridge: Cambridge University Press.

20. Donald Rothschild. 2002. 'Settlement terms and post-agreement stability.' In Stephen Stedman, Donald Rothchild, and Elizabeth Cousens (Eds.), *Ending Civil Wars*. Boulder, CO: Lynne Reinner; Paul Collier and Nicholas Sambanis. Eds. 2005. *Understanding Civil War: Evidence and Analysis*. Volume 1. Washington, DC: World Bank.

21. Donald L. Horowitz. 1985. *Ethnic Groups in Conflict*. Berkeley: University of California Press; Ben Reilly. 2001. *Democracy in Divided Societies: Electoral Engineering for Conflict Management*. Cambridge: Cambridge University Press; Ben Reilly. 2002. 'Electoral systems for divided societies.' *Journal of Democracy* 13 (2): 156–170.

22. Gary Cox. 1997. *Making Votes Count: Strategic Coordination in the World's Electoral Systems*. Cambridge: Cambridge University Press; Gary Cox. 1999. 'Electoral rules and electoral coordination.' *Annual Review of Political Science* 2: 145–161.

23. Donald L. Horowitz. 1985. *Ethnic Groups in Conflict*. Berkeley: University of California Press; Donald L. Horowitz. 1991. *A Democratic South Africa? Constitutional Engineering in a Divided Society*. Berkeley: University of California Press; Donald L. Horowitz. 1993. 'Democracy in divided societies.' *Journal of Democracy* 4: 18–38; Donald L. Horowitz. 2002. 'Constitutional design: Proposals versus processes.' In Andrew Reynolds and Scott Mainwaring (Eds.), *The Architecture of Democracy: Constitutional Design, Conflict Management and Democracy*. Oxford: Oxford University Press; Andrew Reynolds and Ben Reilly. 1999. *Electoral Systems and Conflict in Divided Societies*. Washington, DC: National Academy Press; Ben Reilly. 2001. *Democracy in Divided Societies: Electoral Engineering for Conflict Management*. Cambridge: Cambridge University Press; J. Fraenkel and Bernie Grofman. 2004. 'A neo-Downsian model of the alternative vote as a mechanism for mitigating ethnic conflict in plural societies.' *Public Choice* 121 (3–4): 487–506; Donald L. Horowitz. 2004. 'The alternative vote and interethnic moderation: A reply to Fraenkel and Grofman.' *Public Choice* 121 (3–4): 507–516.

24. Pippa Norris. 2004. *Electoral Engineering*. Cambridge: Cambridge University Press.

25. Patrick Dunleavy and Helen Margetts. 1995. 'Understanding the dynamics of electoral reform.' *International Political Science Review* 16 (1): 9–29; Michael Gallagher. 2005. 'Conclusions.' In Michael Gallagher and Paul Mitchell (Eds.), *The Politics of Electoral Systems*. Oxford: Oxford University Press.

26. See, for example, Andrew Reynolds. Ed. 2002. *The Architecture of Democracy: Constitutional Design, Conflict Management and Democracy*. Oxford: Oxford University Press.

27. Andrew Reynolds, Ben Reilly, and Andrew Ellis. 2005. *International IDEA Handbook of Electoral System*. Stockholm: International IDEA Design. http://www.idea.int/esd/index.cfm

28. The first direct national parliamentary elections were due to be held in Qatar in 2007 and in Bhutan in 2008.

29. Shaun Bowler and Bernard Grofman. Eds. 2000. *Elections in Australia, Ireland and Malta under the Single Transferable Vote: Reflections on an Embedded Institution*. Ann Arbor: University of Michigan Press.

30. For a detailed discussion of the subtype classification, see chapter 3 in Pippa Norris. 2004. *Electoral Engineering*. Cambridge: Cambridge University Press, and Andrew Reynolds, Ben Reilly, and Andrew Ellis. 2005. *International IDEA Handbook of Electoral System*. Stockholm: International IDEA Design. http://www.idea.int/esd/index.cfm. For a brief history of the evolution of these systems, see Joseph M. Colomer. 2004. *Handbook of Electoral System Choice*. New York: Palgrave Macmillan.

31. Matthew Soberg Shugart and Martin P. Wattenberg. Eds. 2001. *Mixed-Member Electoral Systems: The Best of Both Worlds?* New York: Oxford University Press.

32. For a discussion and classification of 'mixed systems,' see Louise Massicotte and Andre Blais. 1999. 'Mixed electoral systems: A conceptual and empirical survey.' *Electoral Studies* 18 (3): 341–366.

33. International IDEA. *Voter Turnout*. 'Total number of democratic elections from 1945 to 2000.' www.idea.int/vt

34. Fareed Zakaria. 1997. 'The rise of illiberal democracy.' *Foreign Affairs* 76 (6): 22–41; Larry Diamond. 2002. 'Thinking about hybrid regimes.' *Journal of Democracy* 13 (2): 21–35; Steven Levitsky and Lucan A. Way. 2002. 'The rise of competitive authoritarianism.' *Journal of Democracy* 13 (2): 51–65; Stephen Levitsky. 2003. 'Autocracy by democratic rules: The dynamics of competitive authoritarianism in the post–cold war era.' Paper presented at the Conference, "Mapping the Great Zone: Clientelism and the Boundary between Democratic and Democratizing," Columbia University, April 4–5.

35. Matthew Soberg Shugart and Martin P. Wattenberg. Eds. 2001. *Mixed-Member Electoral Systems: The Best of Both Worlds?* New York: Oxford University Press.

36. David Lublin. 1997. *The Paradox of Representation: Racial Gerrymandering and Minority Interests*. Princeton, NJ: Princeton University Press; Chandler Davidson and Bernard Grofman. Eds. 1994. *Quiet Revolution in the South: The Impact of the Voting Rights Act 1965–1990*. Princeton, NJ: Princeton University Press.

37. J.-O. Kim and M.-G. Ohn. 1992. 'A theory of minor-party persistence: Election rule, social cleavage, and the number of political parties.' *Social Forces* 70: 575–599.

38. Pippa Norris and Christopher Wlezien. Eds. 2005. *Britain Votes 2005*. Oxford: Oxford University Press.

39. Anna Jarstad. 2001. *Changing the Game: Consociational Theory and Ethnic Quotas in Cyprus and New Zealand*. Uppsala: Department of Peace and Conflict, Uppsala University; Andrew Reynolds. 2005. 'Reserved seats in national legislatures.' *Legislative Studies Quarterly* 30 (2): 301–310; Lisa Handley. 2005. 'Comparative Redistricting Practices.' Paper Presented at the Annual Meeting of the American Political Science Association, Washington, DC; Andrew Reynolds. 2007. 'Minority MPs in national legislatures: Existing research and data gaps.' Minority Rights Group International/UNDP. http://www.minorityrights.org/?lid=674?.

40. Andrew Reynolds. 2006. *Electoral Systems and the Protection and Participation of Minorities*. Minority Rights Group Report.

41. Pippa Norris. 2004. *Electoral Engineering*. Cambridge: Cambridge University Press.

42. Patrick Dunleavy and Helen Margetts. 2004. 'The United Kingdom: Reforming the Westminster Model.' In Josep M. Colomer (Ed.), *Handbook of Electoral System*

Choice. London: Palgrave; Brigitte Taylor and Katarina Thomson. 1999. *Scotland and Wales: Nations Again?* Cardiff: University of Wales Press.

43. James Tilley, Sonia Exley, and Anthony Heath. 2004. 'Dimensions of British identity.' In Alison Park et al. (Eds.), *British Social Attitudes: The 21st Report.* London: Sage; A. Trench. Ed. 2004. *Has Devolution Made a Difference? The State of the Nations, 2004.* Exeter: Imprint Academic.

44. Equal Opportunity Commission. 2006. *Sex and Power: Who Runs Britain 2006?* http://www.eoc.org.uk/pdf/sexandpower_GB_2006.pdf. Note, however, that the number of women MPs dropped to 43 (33.3%) in May 2007, following the retirement of some incumbents.

45. See Jack H. Nagel. 2004. 'New Zealand: Reform by (nearly) immaculate design.' In Josep M. Colomer (Ed.), *Handbook of Electoral System Choice.* London: Palgrave.

46. A. Hampton. 1995. 'The limitations of the prescriptive dimensions of Lijphart's consensus model: A case study of the incorporation of Māori within New Zealand's democratic system, 1984–1995.' *Political Science* 47 (2): 215–237.

47. D. Alves. 1999. *The Maori and the Crown: An Indigenous People's Struggle for Self-Determination.* Westport, CT: Greenwood Press; F. Barker, J. Boston, S. Levine, E. McLeay, and N. S. Roberts. 2003. 'An initial assessment of the consequences of MMP in New Zealand.' In Matthew S. Shugart and Marty P. Wattenberg (Eds.), *Mixed-Member Electoral Systems: The Best of Both Worlds?* Oxford: Oxford University Press, pp. 297–322.

48. Jack Vowles. 2002. 'Parties and society in New Zealand.' In Paul Webb, David Farrell, and Ian Holliday (Eds.), *Political Parties in Advanced Industrial Democracies.* Oxford: Oxford University Press, Table 14.3.

49. Jonathan Boston, Stephen Levine, Elizabeth McLeay, and Nigel S. Roberts. 1996. *New Zealand under MMP: A New Politics?* Auckland: Auckland University Press; Jack Vowles, Peter Aimer, Susan Banducci, and Jeffrey Karp. 1998. *Voters' Victory? New Zealand's First Election under Proportional Representation.* Auckland: Auckland University Press; Raymond Miller. 1998. 'New Zealand First.' In Hans-Georg Bens and Stefan Immerfall. Eds. *The New Politics of the Right.* New York: St. Martin's Press; D. Denemark and Shaun Bowler. 2002. 'Minor parties and protest votes in Australia and New Zealand: Locating populist politics.' *Electoral Studies* 21 (1): 47–67. Another new right-wing party is ACT New Zealand, but their party program emphasizes libertarian principles governing the market and immigration policies as well, so that they do not qualify for the radical right as such.

50. Pippa Norris. 2002 'Ballots not bullets: Electoral systems, ethnic minorities and democratization.' In Andrew Reynolds and Scott Mainwaring (Eds.), *The Architecture of Democracy.* Oxford: Oxford University Press; Susan A. Banducci, Todd Donovan, and Jeffrey A. Karp. 2004. 'Minority representation, empowerment, and participation.' *Journal of Politics* 66 (2): 534–556.

Chapter 6: Presidential and Parliamentary Executives

1. Giovanni Sartori. 1996. *Comparative Constitutional Engineering: An Inquiry into Structures, Incentives and Outcomes.* London: Macmillan.

2. Juan Linz. 1990. 'The perils of presidentialism.' *Journal of Democracy* 1 (1): 51–69; Juan Linz and Arturo Valenzuela. Eds. 1994. *The Failure of Presidential Democracy: The Case of Latin America.* Baltimore: The Johns Hopkins University

Press; Juan Linz and Alfred Stepan. 1996. *Problems of Democratic Consolidation.* Baltimore: The Johns Hopkins University Press; Arendt Lijphart. Ed. 1996. *Presidential v. Parliamentary Government.* Oxford: Oxford University Press.

3. See, for example, Alfred Stepan and Cindy Skach. 1993. 'Constitutional frameworks and democratic consolidation: Parliamentarism and presidentialism.' *World Politics* 46 (1): 1–22; Adam Przeworski, Michael Alvarez, José Cheibub, and Fernando Limongi. 2000. *Democracy and Development.* Cambridge: Cambridge University Press.

4. Fred W. Riggs. 1997. 'Presidentialism versus parliamentarism: Implications for representativeness and legitimacy.' *International Political Science Review* 18 (3): 253–278.

5. For a discussion, see Alfred Stepan and Cindy Skach. 1993. 'Constitutional frameworks and democratic consolidation: Parliamentarism and presidentialism.' *World Politics* 46 (1): 1–22.

6. Mathew Soberg Schugart and John Carey. 1992. *Presidents and Assemblies: Constitutional Design and Electoral Dynamics.* Cambridge: Cambridge University Press.

7. Scott Mainwaring. 1993. 'Presidentialism, multipartism, and democracy – the difficult combination.' *Comparative Political Studies* 26 (2): 198–228; Scott Mainwaring and Matthew Soberg Shugart. 1997. *Presidentialism and Democracy in Latin America.* Cambridge: Cambridge University Press. See also Mark Jones. 1995. *Electoral Laws and the Survival of Presidential Democracies.* Notre Dame, IN: University of Notre Dame Press.

8. José Cheibub and Fernando Limongi. 2002. 'Democratic institutions and regime survival: Parliamentary and presidential democracies reconsidered.' *Annual Review of Political Science* 5: 151; José Cheibub, Adam Przeworski, and S. M. Saiegh. 2004. 'Government coalitions and legislative success under presidentialism and parliamentarism.' *British Journal of Political Science* 34: 565; José Cheibub. 2002. 'Minority governments, deadlock situations, and the survival of presidential democracies.' *Comparative Political Studies* 35: 284; José Cheibub. 2007. *Presidentialism, Parliamentarism, and Democracy.* Cambridge: Cambridge University Press.

9. See, for example, Mathew Soberg Schugart and John Carey. 1992. *Presidents and Assemblies: Constitutional Design and Electoral Dynamics.* Cambridge: Cambridge University Press; Juan J. Linz and Arturo Valenzuela. Eds. 1994. *The Failure of Presidential Democracy: Comparative Perspectives.* Baltimore: The Johns Hopkins University Press; Scott Mainwaring and Matthew Soberg Shugart. Eds. 1997. *Presidential Democracy in Latin America.* Cambridge: Cambridge University Press.

10. Timothy Frye. 1997. 'A politics of institutional choice: Post-communist presidencies.' *Comparative Political Studies* 30: 523. See also M. Stephen Fish. 2006. 'Stronger legislatures, stronger democracies.' *Journal of Democracy* 17 (1): 5–20.

11. M. V. Beliaev. 2006. 'Presidential powers and consolidation of new post-communist democracies.' *Comparative Political Studies* 39 (3): 375–398.

12. André Blais, Louis Massicotte, and Agnieszka Dobrynska. 1997. 'Direct presidential elections: A world summary.' *Electoral Studies* 16 (4): 441–455.

13. Notably some cases of co-presidencies (Switzerland and Bosnia-Herzegovina).

14. The most authoritative and sweeping historical account of forms of monarchies is provided by Samuel E. Finer. 1999. *The History of Government.* Oxford: Oxford University Press. The most comprehensive historical reference work is John Middleton. Ed. 2005. *World Monarchies and Dynasties.* New York: Sharpe Reference.

15. One exception is that technically the supreme pontiff of the Catholic Church, the pope, is monarch of Vatican City and elected by the College of Cardinals. In Malaysia, the paramount ruler is nominally elected, but in practice the position rotates among nine hereditary rulers.

16. Traditional monarchs also persist in some specific subnational territories.

17. For this reason, these systems are sometimes termed 'constitutional' monarchies.

18. Jean Blondel. 1984. 'Dual leadership in the contemporary world: A step towards executive and regime stability?' In Denis Kavanagh and Gillean Peele (Eds.), *Comparative Government and Politics*. London: Heinemann.

19. John D. Huber. 1996. 'The vote of confidence in parliamentary democracies.' *American Political Science Review* 90: 269.

20. Philip Cowley. 2004. 'Parliament: More *Bleak House* than *Great Expectations*.' *Parliamentary Affairs* 57 (2): 301–314.

21. For details, see N. G. Jesse. 1996. 'Thatcher's rise and fall: An institutional analysis of the Tory leadership selection process.' *Electoral Studies* 15 (2): 183–202.

22. T. A. Baylis. 1989. *Governing by Committee: Collegial Leadership in Advanced Societies*. Albany: State University of New York Press; Michael Laver and Kenneth Shepsle. Eds. 1994. *Cabinet Ministers and Parliamentary Government*. Cambridge: Cambridge University Press.

23. The terminology can be somewhat confusing and inconsistent in common usage, since some countries such as Poland have presidents who are head of the government but not head of state. In such cases, these officeholders are termed here 'prime ministers' to maintain consistency. As such, 'presidents' are always defined here as presidents of the nation-state who hold both the office of nonhereditary head of state and that of head of government.

24. Andreas Schedler. Ed. 2005. *Electoral Authoritarianism: The Dynamics of Unfree Competition*. Boulder, CO: Lynne Reinner.

25. André Blais, Louis Massicotte, and Agnieszka Dobrynska. 1997. 'Direct presidential elections: A world summary.' *Electoral Studies* 16 (4): 441–455. One exception is Switzerland, with a rotating head of state (presidency) chosen from among the seven ministers in the Federal Council.

26. André Blais, Louis Massicotte, and Agnieszka Dobrynska. 1997. 'Direct presidential elections: A world summary.' *Electoral Studies* 16 (4): 441–455.

27. The exceptions are co-presidencies used with rotation among the seven members of the Federal Council in Switzerland, and the powers shared among three co-presidencies in Bosnia-Herzegovina following the Dayton agreement.

28. For details, see John M. Carey. 2003. 'Presidentialism and representative institutions.' In Jorge I. Dominguez and Michael Shifter (Eds.), *Constructing Democratic Governance in Latin America*. Baltimore: The Johns Hopkins University Press.

29. Jean Blondel and N. Manning. 2002. 'Do ministers do what they say? Ministerial unreliability, collegial and hierarchical governments.' *Political Studies* 50 (3): 455–476.

30. Colin Campbell and M. J. Wyszimirski. Eds. 1991. *Executive Leadership in Anglo-American Systems*. Pittsburgh: University of Pittsburgh Press.

31. Maurice Duverger. 1980. 'A new political-system model – semi-presidential government.' *European Journal of Political Research* 8: 165; H. Bahro. 1998. 'Duverger's concept: Semi-presidential government revisited.' *European Journal of Political Research* 34: 201; Alan Siaroff. 2003. 'Comparative presidencies: The inadequacy

of the presidential, semi-presidential, and parliamentary distinction.' *European Journal of Political Research* 42 (3): 287–312.

32. Robert Elgie. 1997. 'Models of executive politics: A framework for the study of executive power relations in parliamentary and semi-presidential regimes.' *Political Studies* 155: 217–231; Lee Kendall Metcalf. 2000. 'Measuring presidential power.' *Comparative Political Studies* 33 (5): 660–685.

33. Timothy Frye. 1997. 'A politics of institutional choice: Post-communist presidencies.' *Comparative Political Studies* 30: 523.

34. Mathew Soberg Schugart and John Carey. 1992. *Presidents and Assemblies: Constitutional Design and Electoral Dynamics*. Cambridge: Cambridge University Press.

35. Lee Kendall Metcalf. 2000. 'Measuring presidential power.' *Comparative Political Studies* 33 (5): 660–685.

36. Ludger Helms. 2005. *Presidents, Prime Ministers and Chancellors: Executive Leadership in Western Democracies*. New York: Palgrave.

37. T. A. Baylis. 1996. 'President versus prime ministers: Shaping executive authority in Eastern Europe.' *World Politics* 48 (3): 297; O. Protsyk. 2006. 'Intra-executive competition between president and prime minister: Patterns of institutional conflict and cooperation under semi-presidentialism.' *Political Studies* 54 (2): 219–244; M. V. Beliaev. 2006. 'Presidential powers and consolidation of new post-communist democracies.' *Comparative Political Studies* 39 (3): 375–398.

38. Some regard parliamentary regimes as increasingly following a presidential style of leadership. See, for example, the discussion in Thomas Poguntke and Paul Webb. Eds. 2005. *The Presidentialization of Politics: A Comparative Study of Modern Democracies*. Oxford/New York: Oxford University Press/ECPR.

39. From the veto-power perspective, presidential systems (especially in divided governments, where different parties hold the presidency and control the legislature) could have more power-sharing features than some parliamentary systems (especially where a single party dominates in the lower house of the legislature and therefore holds the premiership). See G. Tsebelis. 1995. 'Decision-making in political-systems – veto players in presidentialism, parliamentarism, multicameralism and multipartyism.' *British Journal of Political Science* 25 (3): 289–325.

40. Arendt Lijphart. Ed. 1996. *Presidential v. Parliamentary Government*. Oxford: Oxford University Press.

41. Alan Siaroff. 2003. 'Comparative presidencies: The inadequacy of the presidential, semi-presidential, and parliamentary distinction.' *European Journal of Political Research* 42 (3): 287–312.

42. Arthur S. Banks. *Cross-National Time-Series Data Archive (CNTS)*. The Cross-National Time-Series Data Archive (also referred to as CNTS), assembled at the State University of New York, Binghamton, provides a comprehensive listing of international and national country data facts. The database has statistical information on a range of countries, with data entries ranging from 1815 to the present. The data was provided by Banner Software, Inc., Binghamton, NY 13905.

Chapter 7: Federalism and Decentralization

1. Rohan Edrisinha and Lee Seymour with Ann Griffiths. 2005. 'Adopting federalism: Sri Lanka and Sudan.' In Ann L. Griffiths. Ed. *Handbook of Federal Countries, 2005*. Montreal: Forum of Federations/McGill University Press.

2. Remy Prudhomme. 1995. 'The dangers of decentralization.' *World Bank Research Observer* 10 (2): 201–220.

3. James Manor. 1999. *The Political Economy of Democratic Decentralization*. Washington, DC: World Bank; Richard M. Bird and François Vaillancourt. Eds. 1999. *Fiscal Decentralization in Developing Countries*. Cambridge: Cambridge University Press; Ehtisham Ahmad. Ed. 2002. *Fiscal Decentralization*. London: Routledge; Erik Wibbels. 2005. *Federalism and the Market: Intergovernmental Conflict and Economic Reform in the Developing World*. Cambridge: Cambridge University Press; Bas Denters and Lawrence Rose. Eds. 2005. *Comparing Local Governance: Trends and Developments*. London: Palgrave/Macmillan.

4. http://www1.worldbank.org/publicsector/decentralization/webfiscal.pdf

5. See, for example, Ed C. Page and Michael Goldsmith. 1987. *Central and Local Government Relations*. London: Sage; Ed C. Page. 1991. *Localism and Centralism in Europe*. Oxford: Oxford University Press; Michael Goldsmith. 2002. 'Central control over local government: A Western European comparison.' *Local Government Studies* 28 (3): 91.

6. Dan Stegarescu. 2005. 'Public sector decentralisation: Measurement concepts and recent international trends.' *Fiscal Studies* 26 (3): 301–333.

7. Michiel S. De Vries. 2000. 'The rise and fall of decentralization: A comparative analysis of arguments and practices in European countries.' *European Journal of Political Research* 38: 193–224.

8. Daniel Treisman. 2007. *The Architecture of Government: Rethinking Political Decentralization*. Cambridge: Cambridge University Press.

9. Alfred Stepan. 1999. 'Federalism and democracy: Beyond the U.S. model.' *Journal of Democracy* 10 (4): 19–34.

10. For a critical discussion and review of these claims, see Jan Erk. 2006. 'Does federalism really matter?' *Comparative Politics* 39 (1): 103; Daniel Treisman. 2007. *The Architecture of Government: Rethinking Political Decentralization*. Cambridge: Cambridge University Press.

11. See R. A. Nickson. 1995. *Local Government in Latin America*. Boulder, CO: Lynne Reinner; B. D. Santos. 1998. 'Participatory budgeting in Porto Alegre: Toward a redistributive democracy.' *Politics & Society* 26 (4): 461–510; A. Acharya, A. G. Lavalle, and P. P. Houtzager. 2004. 'Civil society representation in the participatory budget and deliberative councils of Sao Paulo, Brazil.' *IDS Bulletin-Institute of Development Studies* 35 (2): 40.

12. R. Fisman and R. Gatti. 2002. 'Decentralization and corruption: Evidence across countries.' *Journal of Public Economics* 83 (3): 325–345.

13. David Osborne and T. Gaebler. 1993. *Reinventing Government*. New York: Addison Wesley; Hans Keman. 2000. 'Federalism and policy performance.' In Ute Wachendorfer-Schmidt (Ed.), *Federalism and Policy Performance*. London: Routledge.

14. Stuart Ranson and John Stuart. 1994. *Management for the Public Domain*. Basingstoke: Macmillan.

15. Classic arguments in favor of federalism and decentralization can be found in William H. Riker. 1964. *Federalism: Origins, Operations, Significance*. Boston: Little, Brown; W. Oates. 1972. *Fiscal Federalism*. New York: Harcourt, Brace, Jovanovich.

16. Arend Lijphart. 1999. *Patterns of Democracy*. New Haven, CT: Yale University Press, p. 196.

17. Nancy Bermeo. 2002. 'The import of institutions.' *Journal of Democracy* 13 (12): 96–110.

18. Alfred Stephan. 1999. 'Federalism and democracy: Beyond the U.S. model.' *Journal of Democracy* 10 (4): 19–34.

19. Ted Robert Gurr. 1993. *Minorities at Risk: A Global View of Ethnopolitical Conflicts*. Washington, DC: US Institute of Peace Press.

20. M. Hechter. 2000. *Containing Nationalism*. New York: Oxford University Press.

21. See the literature review in Erik Wibbels. 2005. *Federalism and the Market: Intergovernmental Conflict and Economic Reform in the Developing World*. Cambridge: Cambridge University Press.

22. Remy Prudhomme. 1995. 'The dangers of decentralization.' *World Bank Research Observer* 10 (2): 201–220.

23. Stuart Ranson and John Stuart. 1994. *Management for the Public Domain*. Basingstoke: Macmillan.

24. For regional overviews, see Daniel Elazar. 1994. *Federal Systems of the World: A Handbook of Federal, Confederal and Autonomy Arrangements*. Essex: Longman; Ann L. Griffiths. Ed. *Handbook of Federal Countries, 2005*. Montreal: Forum of Federations/McGill University Press.

25. Richard Simeaon and Daniel-Patrick Conway. 2001. 'Federalism and the management of conflict in multinational societies.' In Alain-G. Gagnon and James Tully (Eds.), *Multinational Democracies*. Cambridge: Cambridge University Press.

26. Ronald L. Watts. 2006. *Models of Federal Power-Sharing*. Washington, DC: National Democratic Institute.

27. Henry E. Hale. 2004. 'Divided we stand: Institutional sources of ethno-federal state survival and collapse.' *World Politics* 56: 165–193.

28. Henry E. Hale. 2004. 'Divided we stand: Institutional sources of ethno-federal state survival and collapse.' *World Politics* 56: 165–193.

29. Eric A. Nordlinger 1972. *Conflict Regulation in Divided Societies*. Cambridge, MA: Harvard University Center for International Affairs.

30. Valerie Bunce. 1999. *Subversive Institutions: The Design and Destruction of Socialism and the State*. Cambridge: Cambridge University Press.

31. Shaheen Mozaffar and James R. Scarritt. 1999. 'Why territorial autonomy is not a viable option for managing ethnic conflict in African plural societies.' *Nationalism and Ethnic Politics* 5.

32. Michael Hechter. 1992. 'The dynamics of secession.' *Acta Sociologica* 35 (4): 267–283; Ian S. Lustik, Dan Miodownik, and Roy J. Eidelson. 2004. 'Secessionism in multicultural states: Does sharing power prevent or encourage it?' *American Political Science Review* 98 (2): 209–229.

33. Dawn Brancati. 2006. 'Decentralization: Fueling the fire or dampening the flames of ethnic conflict and secessionism?' *International Organization* 60 (3): 651–685; Dawn Brancati. 2007. *Design over Conflict: Managing Ethnic Conflict and Secessionism through Decentralization*. Cambridge: Cambridge University Press.

34. Jonathan Rodden. 2004. 'Comparative federalism and decentralization: On meaning and measurement.' *Comparative Politics* 36 (4): 481.

35. U. Panizza. 1999. 'On the determinants of fiscal centralization: Theory and evidence.' *Journal of Public Economics* 74 (1): 97–139.

36. Dan Stegarescu. 2005. 'Public sector decentralisation: Measurement concepts and recent international trends.' *Fiscal Studies* 26 (3): 301–333.

37. R. A. Nickson. 1995. *Local Government in Latin America*. Boulder, CO: Lynne Reinner.

38. Dawn Brancati. 2006. 'Decentralization: Fueling the fire or dampening the flames of ethnic conflict and secessionism?' *International Organization* 60 (3): 651–685.

39. J. Rodden. 2004. 'Comparative federalism and decentralization: On meaning and measurement.' *Comparative Politics* 36 (4): 481.

40. For a discussion, see Daniel Elazar. 1994. *Federal Systems of the World: A Handbook of Federal, Confederal and Autonomy Arrangements*. Essex: Longman.

41. Ronald L. Watts. 1999. *Comparing Federal Systems*, 2nd ed. Kingston, Canada: McGill-Queen's University Press; Michael Burgess. 1993. 'Federalism and federation: A reappraisal.' In Michael Burgess and Alain-G. Gagnon (Eds.), *Comparative Federalism and Federation*. London: Harvester Wheatsheaf; Peter King. 1982. *Federalism and Federation*. London: Croom Helm.

42. William Riker. 1964. *Federalism: Origin, Operation, Significance*. Boston: Little, Brown, p. 11.

43. Samuel C. Patterson and Anthony Mughan. Eds. 1999. *Senates: Bicameralism in the Contemporary World*. Columbus: Ohio State University Press; George Tsebelis and Jeannette Money. 1997. *Bicameralism*. Cambridge: Cambridge University Press.

44. Alfred Stephan. 1999. 'Federalism and democracy: Beyond the U.S. model.' *Journal of Democracy* 10 (4): 19–34.

45. C. Souza. 2002. 'Brazil: The prospects of a center-constraining federation in a fragmented polity.' *Publius: The Journal of Federalism* 32 (2): 23–48; Scott Mainwaring. 1997. 'Multipartism, robust federalism, and presidentialism in Brazil.' In Scott Mainwaring and Matthew Soberg Shugart (Eds.), *Presidentialism and Democracy in Latin America*. Cambridge: Cambridge University Press.

46. Barry Ames. 2001. *The Deadlock of Democracy in Brazil*. Ann Arbor: University of Michigan Press; Leslie Bethell. 2000. 'Politics in Brazil: From elections without democracy to democracy without citizenship.' *Daedalus* 129 (2): 1–27.

47. Gordon P. Means. 2005. 'Malaysia.' In Ann L. Griffiths (Ed.), *Handbook of Federal Countries, 2005*. Montreal: Forum of Federations/McGill University Press.

48. Alastair McAuley. Ed. 1991. *Soviet Federalism: Nationalism and Economic Decentralization*. Leicester: Leicester University Press; Elizabeth Pascal. 2003. *Defining Russian Federalism*. London: Praeger.

49. G. P. Herd. 'Russia: Systemic transformation or federal collapse?' *Journal of Peace Research* 36 (3): 259–269.

50. D. Bahry. 2005. 'The new federalism and the paradoxes of regional sovereignty in Russia.' *Comparative Politics* 37 (2): 127.

51. Michael S. De Vries. 2000. 'The rise and fall of decentralization: A comparative analysis of arguments and practices in European countries.' *European Journal of Political Research* 38: 193–224; Ed C. Page. 1991. *Localism and Centralism in Europe: The Political and Legal Bases of Local Self-Government*. Oxford: Oxford University Press.

52. Carl A. Trocki. 2006. *Singapore: Wealth, Power and the Culture of Control*. New York: Routledge; Diane K. Mauzy and R. S. Milne. 2002. *Singapore Politics under the People's Action Party*. New York: Routledge.

53. 'Hybrid' unions can also been termed 'semifederal' or 'decentralized unions' (Watts), but 'hybrid' seems a better term to capture the characteristics of this mixed category.

54. Andrew Gamble. 2006. 'The constitutional revolution in the United Kingdom.' *Publius: The Journal of Federalism* 36 (1): 19–35.

55. Ronald L. Watts. 1999. *Comparing Federal Systems*, 2nd ed. Kingston, Canada: McGill-Queen's University Press, chapter 1.

56. John Geering and Strom C. Thacker. 2004. 'Political institutions and corruption: The role of unitarism and parliamentarism.' *British Journal of Political Science* 34: 295–330.

57. Daniel J. Elazar. Ed. 1991. *Federal Systems of the World: A Handbook of Federal, Confederal and Autonomy Arrangements.* Detroit: Gale Research; Ronald L. Watts. 1999. *Comparing Federal Systems*, 2nd ed. Kingston, Canada: McGill-Queen's University Press, chapter 1; Ann L. Griffiths. Ed. 2005. *Handbook of Federal Countries, 2005.* Montreal: Forum of Federations/McGill University Press.

58. See Aaron Schneider. 2003. 'Decentralization: Conceptualization and measurement.' *Studies in Comparative International Development* 38 (3): 32–56.

59. Ronald L. Watts. 1999. *The Spending Power in Federal Systems: A Comparative Study.* Kingston, Canada: Institute of Intergovernmental Relations, Queens University.

60. Monty G. Marshall and Ted Robert Gurr. 2006. *Peace and Conflict 2005.* Baltimore: University of Maryland CIDCM.

61. Akhtar Hossain. 2000. 'Anatomy of hartal politics in Bangladesh.' *Asian Survey* 40 (3): 508–529; Stanley A. Kochanek. 2000. 'Governance, patronage politics, and democratic transition in Bangladesh.' *Asian Survey* 40 (3): 530–550.

62. Jalal Alamgir. 2007. 'Bangladesh: Democracy saved or sunk?' *Foreign Policy.*

63. The Fund for Peace. 2006. 'Failed States Index Scores 2006.' www.fundforpeace. org

64. Louise Tillin. 2007. 'United in diversity? Asymmetry in Indian federalism.' *Publius: The Journal of Federalism* 37 (1): 45–67.

65. Aseema Sinha. 2005. *The Regional Roots of Development Politics in India: A Divided Leviathan.* Bloomington: University of Indiana Press.

66. H. M. Rajashekara. 1997. 'The nature of Indian federalism: A critique.' *Asian Survey* 37 (3): 245–253.

67. M. P. Singh and D. V. Verney. 2003. 'Challenges to India's centralized parliamentary federalism.' *Publius: The Journal of Federalism* 33 (4): 1–20; P. Chhibber and G. Murali. 2006. 'Duvergerian dynamics in the Indian states – Federalism and the number of parties in the state assembly elections.' *Party Politics* 12 (1): 5–34.

68. Ashutosh Varshney. 2003. *Ethnic Conflict and Civic Life: Hindus and Muslims in India.* New Haven, CT: Yale University Press; Monty G. Marshall and Ted Robert Gurr. 2006. *Peace and Conflict 2005.* Baltimore: University of Maryland CIDCM.

69. B. Currie. 1997. 'Multiple identities in a single state: Indian federalism in comparative perspective.' *Journal of Commonwealth & Comparative Politics* 35 (1): 125–126; M. P. Singh and D. V. Verney. 2003. 'Challenges to India's centralized parliamentary federalism.' *Publius: The Journal of Federalism* 33 (4): 1–20.

70. Peter Ronald deSouza. 2003. 'The struggle for local government: Indian democracy's new phase.' *Publius: The Journal of Federalism* 33 (4): 99–118.

71. Raghabendra Chattopadhyay and Esther Duflo. 2004. 'Women as policy makers: Evidence from a randomized policy experiment in India.' *Econometrica* 72 (5): 1409–1443.

72. J. P. Jain. 1997. 'The Gram Sabha: Gateway to grassroots democracy.' *Journal of Rural Development* 16: 557–573.

73. A. Rashid. 2005. 'The politics of administrative decentralization in Bangladesh.' *Canadian Journal of Development Studies* 26 (4): 781–798.

Chapter 8: The Fourth Estate

1. For a bibliographic guide to the literature on the media and development, see Clement E. Asante. *Press Freedom and Development: A Research Guide and Selected Bibliography*. Westport, CT: Greenwood Press. For a discussion of how alternative theories have evolved in the normative debate see H. Shah. 1996. 'Modernization, marginalization and emancipation: Toward a normative model of journalism and national development.' *Communication Theory* 6 (2); Denis McQuail. 2001. *Political Communication Theory*. London: Sage.

2. Amartya Sen. 1999. *Development as Freedom*. New York: Anchor Books.

3. Goran Hyden, Michael Leslie, and Folu F. Ogundimu. Eds. 2002. *Media and Democracy in Africa*. Uppsala: Nordiska Afrikainstitutet.

4. Amartya Sen. 1999. 'Democracy as a universal value.' *Journal of Democracy* 10: 3.

5. Amartya Sen. 1999. *Development as Freedom*. New York: Anchor Books; Timothy Besley and Robin Burgess. 2001. 'Political agency, government responsiveness and the role of the media.' *European Economic Review* 45 (4–6): 629–640.

6. James D. Wolfenson. 1999. 'Voices of the poor.' *Washington Post,* 10 November 1999, A39.

7. Alicia Adsera, Carlos Boix, and Mark Payne. 2003. 'Are you being served? Political accountability and governmental performance.' *Journal of Law, Economics and Organization* 19: 445–490; S. K. Chowdhury. 2004. 'The effect of democracy and press freedom on corruption: An empirical test.' *Economics Letters* 85 (1): 93–101; A. Brunetti and B. Weder. 2003. 'A free press is bad news for corruption.' *Journal of Public Economics* 87 (7–8): 1801–1824.

8. Barry James. Ed. 2006. *Media Development and Poverty Eradication*. Paris: UNESCO; Roumeen Islam. 2003. *Do More Transparent Governments Govern Better?* Washington, DC: World Bank.

9. D. Anable. 2006. 'The role of Georgia's media – and Western aid – in the Rose Revolution.' *Harvard International Journal of Press – Politics* 11 (3): 7–43.

10. Michael McFaul. 2005. 'Transitions from post-communism.' *Journal of Democracy* 16 (3): 5–19.

11. For an earlier comparison of media access and press freedom, see Pippa Norris. 2004. 'Global political communication.' In Frank Esser and Barbara Pfetsch (Eds.), *Comparing Political Communication: Theories, Cases and Challenges*. Cambridge: Cambridge University Press, pp. 115–150.

12. See, for example, Arendt Lijphart. 1999. *Patterns of Democracy*. New Haven, CT: Yale University Press.

13. Alasdair Roberts. 2006. *Blacked Out: Government Secrecy in the Information Age*. Cambridge: Cambridge University Press. For details about the legislation on freedom of information passed in different countries, see http://www.freedominfo.org/

14. Roumeen Islam. Ed. 2002. *The Right to Tell: The Role of Mass Media in Economic Development*. Washington, DC: World Bank; Roumeen Islam. 2003. *Do More Transparent Governments Govern Better?* Washington, DC: World Bank.

15. Pippa Norris. 2000. *A Virtuous Circle: Political Communications in Post-Industrial Societies.* Cambridge: Cambridge University Press; Pippa Norris. 2001. *Digital Divide.* Cambridge: Cambridge University Press.

16. For the classics in this account see Daniel Lerner. 1958. *The Passing of Traditional Society.* Glencoe, IL: The Free Press; Lucian W. Pye. 1963. *Communications and Political Development.* Princeton, NJ: Princeton University Press; Seymour Martin Lipset. 1959. 'Some social prerequisites of democracy: Economic development and political legitimacy.' *American Political Science Review* 53: 69–105; Donald J. McCrone and Charles F. Cnudde. 1967. 'Toward a communication theory of democratic political development: A causal model.' *American Political Science Review* 61 (1): 72–79.

17. Daniel Lerner. 1958. *The Passing of Traditional Society.* Glencoe, IL: The Free Press, p. 60.

18. Samuel Huntington. 1993. *The Third Wave.* Norman: The University of Oklahoma Press.

19. For a discussion of the criticisms of the older literature and heated debates about the role of the media in development that arose in the late 1970s and early 1980s see Hamid Mowlana. 1985. *International Flow of Information: A Global Report and Analysis.* Paris: UNESCO; Annabelle Sreberny-Mohammadi et al. 1984. *Foreign News in the Media: International Reporting in Twenty-Nine Countries.* Reports and Papers on Mass Communication, 93. Paris: UNESCO; Robert L. Stevenson and Donald Lewis Shaw. Eds. 1984. *Foreign News and the New World Information Order.* Ames: Iowa State University Press; K. Kyloon Hur. 1984. 'A critical analysis of international news flow research.' *Critical Studies in Mass Communication* 1: 365–378; William Preston, Edward S. Herman, and Herbert I. Schiller. 1989. *Hope and Folly: The United States and UNESCO 1945–1985.* Minneapolis: University of Minnesota Press.

20. See Pippa Norris. 2000. *A Virtuous Circle.* Cambridge: Cambridge University Press.

21. George A. Donohue, Philip Tichenor, et al. 1995. 'A guard dog perspective on the role of the media.' *Journal of Communication* 45 (2): 115–128.

22. Renate Kocher. 1986. 'Bloodhounds or missionaries: Role definitions of German and British journalists.' *European Journal of Communication* 1: 43–64.

23. A. Brunetti and B. Weder. 2003. 'A free press is bad news for corruption.' *Journal of Public Economics* 87 (7–8): 1801–1824; S. K. Chowdhury. 2004. 'The effect of democracy and press freedom on corruption: An empirical test.' *Economics Letters* 85 (1): 93–101; D. Fell. 2005. 'Political and media liberalization and political corruption in Taiwan.' *China Quarterly* 18 (4): 875–893.

24. Leonard R. Sussman. 2001. *Press Freedom in Our Genes.* Reston, VA: World Press Freedom Committee.

25. See, for example, the International Federation of Journalists. http://www.ifj.org/; and the Human Rights Watch. http://www.hrw.org/

26. See, for example, cases documented by the Index on Censorship. http://www.indexoncensorship.org/; the World Press Freedom Council. www.wpfc.org; and the International Press Institute. http://www.freemedia.at. See also Louis Edward Inglehart. 1998. *Press and Speech Freedoms in the World, from Antiquity until 1998: A Chronology.* Westport, CT: Greenwood Press.

27. See Shanthi Kalathil and Taylor C. Boas. 2001. *The Internet and State Control in Authoritarian Regimes: China, Cuba and the Counterrevolution.* Global Policy

Program No. 21. Washington, DC: Carnegie Endowment for International Peace; Leonard R. Sussman. 2000. 'Censor Dot Gov: The Internet and press freedom.' *Press Freedom Survey 2000.* Washington, DC: Freedom House. www. freedomhouse.com

28. See, for example, the International Federation of Journalists. http://www.ifj.org/; and the Human Rights Watch. http://www.hrw.org/

29. See Peter Dahlgren and Colin Sparks. 1995. *Communication and Citizenship.* London: Routledge; Peter Dahlgren. 1995. *Television and the Public Sphere.* London: Sage.

30. Arthur Lupia and Mathew D. McCubbins. 1998. *The Democratic Dilemma.* Cambridge: Cambridge University Press.

31. ACE Project. http://www.aceproject.org/main/english/me/meao1b.htm

32. See, for example, the Report by the Organization for Security and Cooperation in Europe on the October 2000 parliamentary elections in Belarus. http://www. osce.org/odihr/documents/reports/election_reports/by/bel200fin.pdf

33. P. Andriantsoa, N. Andriasendrarivony, S. Haggblade, B. Minten, M. Rakotojaona, F. Rakotovoavy, and H. S. Razafinimanana. 2005. 'Media proliferation and democratic transition in Africa: The case of Madagascar.' *World Development* 33 (11): 1939–1957.

34. See Jeremy Tunstall and Michael Palmer. 1991. *Media Moguls.* London: Routledge; Anthony Smith. 1991. *The Age of Behemoths: The Globalization of Mass Media Firms.* New York: Priority Press; Alfonso Sanchez-Tabernero. 1993. *Media Concentration in Europe: Commercial Enterprises and the Public Interest.* London: John Libbey.

35. Ben Bagdikian. 1997. *The Media Monopoly.* Boston: Beacon Press; Leo Bogart. 1995. *Commercial Culture.* New Brunswick, NJ: Transaction. Robert McChesney. 1999. *Rich Media, Poor Democracy: Communication Politics in Dubious Times.* Urbana: University of Illinois Press; Robert G. Picard. 1988. *Press Concentration and Monopoly: New Perspectives on Newspaper Ownership and Operation.* Norwood, NJ: Ablex.

36. S. Hughes and C. Lawson. 2005. 'The barriers to media opening in Latin America.' *Political Communication* 22 (1): 9–25.

37. Timothy Besley and Robin Burgess. 2001. 'Political agency, government responsiveness and the role of the media.' *European Economic Review* 45 (4–6): 629–640. See also Timothy Besley, Robin Burgess, and Andrea Prat. 2003. *The Right to Know: Information and the Media.* Ed. Roumeen Islam. Washington, DC: World Bank.

38. For more details, see Freedom House. 2007. *Global Press Freedom 2007.* www. freedomhouse.org

39. Roumeen Islam. 2003. *Do More Transparent Governments Govern Better?* Washington, DC: World Bank.

40. David Collier and Robert Adcock. 1999. 'Democracy and dichotomies: A pragmatic approach to choices about concepts.' *Annual Review of Political Science* 1: 537–565.

41. Christopher Clague, Suzanne Gleason, and Stephen Knack. 2001. 'Determinants of lasting democracy in poor countries: Culture, development and institutions.' *Annals of the American Academy of Social Sciences* 573: 16–41.

42. Alberto Alesina, Arnaud Devleeschauwer, William Easterly, Sergio Kurlat, and Romain Wacziarg. 2003. 'Fractionalization.' *Journal of Economic Growth* 8: 155–194. For details see www.stanford.edu/~wacziarg/papersum.html

43. Robert A. Dahl and E. R. Tufte. 1973. *Size and Democracy*. Stanford, CA: Stanford University Press; Robert A. Dahl. 1998. *On Democracy*. New Haven, CT: Yale University Press; Alberto Alesina and Enrico Spolaore. 2003. *The Size of Nations*. Cambridge, MA: MIT Press.

44. Michael McFaul. 2005. 'Transitions from postcommunism.' *Journal of Democracy* 16: 5–19; Valerie Bunch and Sharon l. Wolchik. 2006. 'International diffusion and post-Communist electoral revolutions.' *Communist and Post-Communist Studies* 39 (3): 283–304; Mark R. Beissinger. 2006. 'Promoting democracy: Is exporting revolution a constructive strategy?' *Dissent Magazine* Winter.

45. Henry E. Hale. 2005. 'Regime cycles – democracy, autocracy, and revolution in post-Soviet Eurasia.' *World Politics* 58 (1): 133.

46. Valerie Bunce. 2003. 'Rethinking recent democratization: Lessons from the post-communist experience.' *World Politics* 55; Stephen E. Hanson. 2001. 'Defining democratic consolidation.' In Richard D. Anderson Jr., M. Steven Fish, Stephen E. Hanson, and Philip G. Roeder (Eds.), *Postcommunism and the Theory of Democracy*. Princeton, NJ: Princeton University Press; Henry E. Hale. 2005. 'Regime cycles – democracy, autocracy, and revolution in post-Soviet Eurasia.' *World Politics* 58 (1): 133; Charles H. Fairbanks Jr. 2007. 'Revolution reconsidered.' *Journal of Democracy* 18 (1): 42–57.

47. http://www.osce.org/documents/odihr/2005/03/4355_en.pdf

48. Committee for the Protection of Journalists. www.cpj.org

49. F. Hill and K. Jones. 2006. 'Fear of democracy or revolution: The reaction to Andijon.' *Washington Quarterly* 29 (3): 111.

50. Amnesty International. 2005. *Uzbekistan: Lifting the Siege on the Truth about Andizhan* (AI Index: EUR 62/021/2005); Amnesty International. 2006. *Uzbekistan-Andizhan – Impunity Must Not Prevail*. http://web.amnesty.org/library/Index/ENGEUR620102006

51. OSCE. 2005. 'Coverage of the events and governmental handling of the press during the Andijan crisis in Uzbekistan: Observations and recommendations.' In *Freedom and Responsibility: Representative on Freedom of the Media*. Vienna: OSCE. http://www.osce.org/fom

52. Committee for the Protection of Journalists. www.cpj.org

53. Sarah Birch. 1997. 'Ukraine: The perils of majoritarianism in a new democracy.' In Andrew Reynolds and Ben Reilly (Eds.), *The International IDEA Handbook of Electoral System Design*. Stockholm: International Institute for Democracy and Electoral Assistance; Sarah Birch and Andrew Wilson. 1999. 'The Ukrainian parliamentary elections of 1998.' *Electoral Studies* 18 (2): 276–282; Sarah Birch. 1998. 'Electoral reform in Ukraine: The 1988 parliamentary elections.' *Representation* 35 (2/3): 146–154.

54. Sarah Birch and Andrew Wilson. 1999. 'The Ukrainian parliamentary elections of 1998.' *Electoral Studies* 18 (2): 276–282.

55. The Organization for Security and Cooperation in Europe (OSCE). *International Election Observation Mission*. http://www.osce.org/odihr-elections/14667.html

56. Gerhard Simon. 2006. 'An orange-tinged revolution – the Ukrainian path to democracy.' *Russian Politics and Law* 44 (2): 5–27; P. D'Anieri. 2005. 'What has changed in Ukrainian politics? Assessing the implications of the Orange Revolution.' *Problems of Post-Communism* 52 (5): 82–91; Robert K. Christensen, Edward R. Rakhimkulov, and Charles R. Wise. 2005. 'The Ukrainian Orange Revolution brought more than a new president: What kind of democracy will the

institutional changes bring?' *Communist and Post-Communist Studies* 38 (2): 207–230; Charles Fairbanks Jr. 2007. 'Revolution reconsidered.' *Journal of Democracy* 18 (1): 42–56.

Chapter 9: What Works? Lessons for Public Policy

1. Arend Lijphart. 1969. 'Consociational democracy.' *World Politics* 21: 207–225; Arend Lijphart. 1975. *The Politics of Accommodation: Pluralism and Democracy in the Netherlands.* Berkeley: University of California Press; Arend Lijphart. 1999. *Patterns of Democracy: Government Forms and Performance in 36 Countries.* New Haven, CT: Yale University Press.

2. See, for example, V. K. Nanayakkara. 2006. 'From dominion to republican status: Dilemmas of constitution making in Sri Lanka.' *Public Administration and Development* 26 (5): 425–437; Andrew Reynolds. Ed. 2002. *The Architecture of Democracy: Constitutional Design, Conflict Management and Democracy.* Oxford: Oxford University Press.

3. See Rudy B. Andweg. 2000. 'Consociational democracy.' *Annual Review of Politics* 3: 509–536. For an early and influential critique, see Brian Barry. 1975. 'Review article: Political accommodation and consociational democracy.' *British Journal of Political Science* 5 (4): 194.

4. Donald L. Horowitz. 1985. *Ethnic Groups in Conflict.* Berkeley: University of California Press; S. G. Simonsen. 2005. 'Addressing ethnic divisions in post-conflict institution-building: Lessons from recent cases.' *Security Dialogue* 36 (3): 297–318.

5. For a discussion of the pros and cons of case study methods, see Alexander L. George and Andrew Bennett. 2004. *Case Studies and Theory Development.* Cambridge, MA: MIT Press.

6. Ulrich Schneckener. 2002. 'Making power-sharing work: Lessons from successes and failures in ethnic conflict regulation.' *Journal of Peace Research* 39 (2): 203–228.

7. Anna Morawiec Mansfield. 'Ethnic but equal: The quest for a new democratic order in Bosnia and Herzegovina.' *Columbia Law Review* 103: 2015–2020; Roland Paris. 2004. *At War's End: Building Peace after Civil Conflict.* Cambridge: Cambridge University Press, chapter 6.

8. For a discussion, see Roland Paris. 2005. *At War's End: Building Peace after Civil Conflict.* Cambridge: Cambridge University Press; Paul Collier and Nicholas Sambanis. Eds. 2005. *Understanding Civil War.* Washington, DC: World Bank; Michael W. Doyle and Nicholas Sambanis. 2006. *Making War and Building Peace.* Princeton, NJ: Princeton University Press.

9. Rene Lemarchand. 2007. 'Consociationalism and power sharing in Africa: Rwanda, Burundi, and the Democratic Republic of the Congo.' *African Affairs* 106 (422): 1–20. For an alternative interpretation, see also D. P. Sullivan. 2005. 'The missing pillars: A look at the failure of peace in Burundi through the lens of Arend Lijphart's theory of consociational democracy.' *Journal of Modern African Studies* 43 (1): 75–95.

10. G. Vuckovic. 1997. *Ethnic Cleavages and Conflict: The Sources of National Cohesion and Disintegration. The Case of Yugoslavia.* Aldershot, England: Ashgate.

11. Henry Brady and David Collier. 2004. *Rethinking Social Inquiry: Diverse Tools, Shared Standards.* New York: Rowman & Littlefield.

12. Thomas Carothers. 1999. *Aiding Democracy Abroad: The Learning Curve.* Washington, DC: The Carnegie Institute for International Peace; Thomas Carothers. 2004. *Critical Mission: Essays on Democracy Promotion.* Washington, DC: The Carnegie Endowment for International Peace.

13. R. Young. 2003. 'European approaches to democracy assistance: Learning the right lessons?' *Third World Quarterly* 24 (1): 127–138; Edwards R. McMahon and Scott H. Baker. 2006. *Piecing a Democratic Quilt? Regional Organizations and Universal Norms.* Bloomfield, CT: Kumarian Press.

14. Steven E. Finkel, Anibal Perez-Linan, and Mitchell A. Seligson with Dinorah Azpuru. 2005. *Effects of U.S. Foreign Assistance on Democracy Building: Results from a Cross-National Quantitative Study.* Washington, DC: USAID.

15. Jonathan Monten. 2005. 'The roots of the Bush Doctrine: Power, nationalism, and democracy promotion in U.S. strategy.' *International Security* 29 (4): 112–156.

16. Thomas Carothers. 1999. *Aiding Democracy Abroad: The Learning Curve.* Washington, DC: Carnegie Endowment for International Peace; Peter Burnell. Ed. 2000. *Democracy Assistance: International Co-Operation for Democratization.* London: Frank Cass; Thomas Carothers. 2004. *Critical Mission: Essays on Democracy Promotion.* Washington, DC: Carnegie Endowment for International Peace.

17. Hans Peter Schmitz. 2004. 'Domestic and transnational perspectives on democratization.' *International Studies Review* 6: 403–426.

18. Ramesh Thakur and Edwards Newman. Eds. 2000. *New Millennium, New Perspectives: The United Nations, Security and Governance.* New York: UN University Press; Edward Neuman and Roland Rich. Eds. 2004. *The UN Role in Promoting Democracy: Between Ideals and Reality.* New York: UN University Press.

19. Steven E. Finkel, Anibal Perez-Linan, and Mitchell A. Seligson. 2005. *Effects of U.S. Foreign Assistance on Democracy Building.* Nashville: USAID/Vanderbilt University.

20. For case studies, see Joroen de Zeeuw and Krishna Kumar. 2006. *Promoting Democracy in Postconflict Societies.* Boulder, CO: Lynne Reinner; Ted Piccone and Richard Youngs. Eds. 2006. *Strategies for Democratic Change: Assessing the Global Response.* Washington, DC: Democracy Coalition Project.

21. Zachary Elkins, Tom Ginsburg, and James Melton. 2007. 'The lifespan of written constitutions.' For more details of this research project, see http://netfiles.uiuc.edu/zelkins/constitutions

22. Joseph M. Colomer. Ed. 2004. *Handbook of Electoral System Choice.* Basingstoke: Palgrave Macmillan; Michael Gallagher and Paul Mitchell. Eds. 2006. *The Politics of Electoral Systems.* Oxford: Oxford University Press.

23. Zachary Elkins, Tom Ginsburg, and James Melton. 2007. 'The lifespan of written constitutions.' For more details of this research project, see http://netfiles.uiuc.edu/zelkins/constitutions

24. Paul Collier and Nicholas Sambanis. Eds. 2005. *Understanding Civil War.* Washington, DC: World Bank.

25. William I. Zartman. 1995. *Elusive Peace: Negotiating an End to Civil Wars 1995–1996.* Washington, DC: Brookings Institution; Caroline Hartzell, Matthew Hoddie, and Donald Rothchild. 2001. 'Stabilizing the peace after civil war: An investigation of some key variables.' *International Organization* 55 (1): 183–208; Donald Rothchild. 2002. 'Settlement terms and post-agreement stability.' In Stephen Stedman, Donald Rothchild, and Elizabeth Cousens (Eds.), *Ending Civil Wars.* Boulder,

CO: Lynne Reinner; Paul Collier and Nicholas Sambanis. Eds. 2005. *Understanding Civil War: Evidence and Analysis.* Volume 1. Washington, DC: World Bank.

26. Robert H. Wagner. 1993. 'The causes of peace.' In Roy Licklider (Ed.), *Stopping the Killing.* New York: New York University Press; Patrick M. Regan. 2002. 'Third party interventions and the duration of intrastate conflict.' *Journal of Conflict Resolution* 46 (1): 55–73.

27. Oliver Ramsbotham, Tom Woodhouse, and Hugh Miall. 2006. *Contemporary Conflict Resolution,* 2nd ed. Cambridge: Polity Press.

28. Helga Malmin Binningsb. 2005. *Consociational Democracy and Post-Conflict Peace: Will Power-Sharing Institutions Increase the Probability of Lasting Peace after Civil War?* Paper presented at the Norwegian National Political Science Conference, January.

29. Possible reasons which have been suggested to explain the failure of the Iraqi constitutional settlement include the slow pace of the program of social and economic reconstruction, inadequate humanitarian assistance and budgetary support, the role of the United States military occupation and the size of the stabilization force, the lack of multilateral support and the unwillingness of the international community to become engaged, the role of neighboring states and ongoing conflict in the region, the limited timetable for reconstruction and for constitutional debate, or, even earlier, the historical legacy of colonial rule and the drawing of national boundaries. For a discussion and comparison of the Iraq situation with earlier cases of US state-building and postwar reconstruction, see James F. Dobbins. 2003. 'America's role in nation-building: From Germany to Iraq.' *Survival* 45 (4): 87.

30. See, for example, Toby Dodge. 2007. 'The causes of US failure in Iraq.' *Survival* 49 (1): 85; Jack Snyder. 2000. *From Voting to Violence: Democratization and Nationalist Conflict.* New York: W. W. Norton; Edward D. Mansfield and Jack Snyder. 2007. *Electing to Fight: Why Emerging Democracies Go to War.* Cambridge, MA: MIT Press.

31. Dawn Brancati. 2004. 'Can federalism stabilize Iraq?' *Washington Quarterly* 27 (2): 7–21.

32. United Nations. 2006. *The Millennium Development Goals Report 2006.* New York: United Nations. http://www.un.org/millenniumgoals/

33. World Bank. 2004. *Human Development Report.* Washington, DC: World Bank.

34. Andreas Schedler. Ed. 2006. *Electoral Authoritarianism: The Dynamics of Unfree Competition.* Boulder, CO: Lynne Reinner.

35. Arch Puddington. 2007. 'The pushback against democracy.' *Journal of Democracy* 18 (2): 125–137.

Select Bibliography

Acemoglu, Daron, and James A. Robinson. 2000. 'Why did the West extend the franchise? Democracy, inequality and growth in historical perspective.' *Quarterly Journal of Economics* 115 (4): 1167–1199.

Acemoglu, Daron, and James A. Robinson. 2001. 'A theory of political transitions.' *American Economic Review* 91 (4): 938–963.

Acemoglu, Daron, and James A. Robinson. 2006. *Economic Origins of Dictatorship and Democracy*. Cambridge: Cambridge University Press.

Adcock, Robert, and David Collier. 2001. 'Measurement validity: A shared standard for qualitative and quantitative research.' *American Political Science Review* 95 (3): 529–546.

Alesina, Alberto, Arnaud Devleeschauwer, William Easterly, Sergio Kurlat, and Romain Wacziarg. 2003. 'Fractionalization.' *Journal of Economic Growth* 8: 155–194.

Alesina, Alberto, and Eliana La Ferrara. 2005. 'Ethnic diversity and economic performance.' *Journal of Economic Literature* 43 (3): 762–800.

Alesina, Alberto, and Enrico Spolaore. 2003. *The Size of Nations*. Cambridge, MA: MIT Press.

Allison, Graham T., and R. P. Beschel. 1992. 'Can the United States promote democracy?' *Political Science Quarterly* 107 (1): 81–98.

Almond, Gabriel A., and Sidney Verba. 1963. *The Civic Culture: Political Attitudes and Democracy in Five Nations*. Princeton, NJ: Princeton University Press.

Almond, Gabriel A., and Sidney Verba. Eds. 1980. *The Civic Culture Revisited*. Boston: Little, Brown.

Alvarez, Michael, José Antonio Cheibub, Fernando Limongi, and Adam Przeworski. 1996. 'Classifying political regimes.' *Studies in International Comparative Development* 31: 3–36.

Ames, Barry. 2001. *The Deadlock of Democracy in Brazil*. Ann Arbor: University of Michigan Press.

Anckar, D., and C. Anckar. 2000. 'Democracies without parties.' *Comparative Political Studies* 33 (2): 225–247.

Anderson, Christopher J. 1995. *Blaming the Government: Citizens and the Economy in Five European Democracies*. Armonk, NY: M. E. Sharpe.

Anderson, Christopher J., and Christine A. Guillory. 1997. 'Political institutions and satisfaction with democracy.' *American Political Science Review* 91 (1): 66–81.

Andweg, Rudy B. 2000. 'Consociational democracy.' *Annual Review of Politics* 3: 509–536.

Arat, Zehra. 1988. 'Democracy and economic development: Modernization theory revisited.' *Comparative Politics* 21: 21–36.

Armingeon, Klaus. 2002. 'The effects of negotiation democracy: A comparative analysis.' *European Journal of Political Research* 41: 81.

Armony, Ariel C., and Hector E. Schamis. 2005. 'Babel in democratization studies.' *Journal of Democracy* 16 (4): 113–128.

Banducci, Susan A., Todd Donovan, and Jeffrey A. Karp. 2004. 'Minority representation, empowerment, and participation.' *Journal of Politics* 66 (2): 534–556.

Banks, Arthur S. 2000. *Cross-Polity Time-Series Database*. Binghamton: State University of New York-Binghamton. www.databanks.sitehosting.net

Barnes, Samuel, and Max Kaase. 1979. *Political Action: Mass Participation in Five Western Democracies*. Beverley Hills, CA: Sage.

Barnes, Samuel, and Janos Simon. Eds. 1998. *The Post-Communist Citizen*. Budapest, Hungary: Erasmus Foundation.

Baron, Stephen, John Field, and Tom Schuller. Eds. 2000. *Social Capital: Critical Perspectives*. Oxford: Oxford University Press.

Barro, Robert J. 1996. 'Democracy and growth.' *Journal of Economic Growth* 1 (1): 1–27.

Barro, Robert J. 1997. *Determinants of Economic Growth: A Cross-Country Empirical Study*. Cambridge, MA: MIT Press.

Barro, Robert J. 1999. 'Determinants of democracy.' *Journal of Political Economy* 107 (6): 158–183.

Barry, Brian. 1975. 'Review article: Political accommodation and consociational democracy.' *British Journal of Political Science* 5 (4): 194.

Bartolini, Stephano, and Peter Mair. 1990. *Identity, Competition, and Electoral Availability: The Stabilization of European Electorates, 1885–1985*. Cambridge: Cambridge University Press.

Baum, Matthew A., and David A. Lake. 2003. 'The political economy of growth: Democracy and human capital.' *American Journal of Political Science* 47 (2): 333–347.

Beck, Nathaniel. 2001. 'Time-series/cross-section data: What have we learned in the past few years?' *Annual Review of Political Science* 4: 271–293.

Beck, Nathaniel, and Jonathan Katz. 1996. 'Nuisance vs. substance: Specifying and estimating time-series cross-sectional models.' In J. Freeman (Ed.), *Political Analysis*. Ann Arbor: University of Michigan Press.

Beck, Nathaniel, Jonathan Katz, and Richard Tucker. 1998. 'Taking time seriously: Time-series-cross-section analysis with a binary dependent variable.' *American Journal of Political Science* 42 (4): 1260–1288.

Beetham, David. 1994. *Defining and Measuring Democracy*. London: Sage.

Beetham, David. 2001. *International IDEA Handbook of Democracy Assessment*. New York: Kluwer.

Bell, Daniel. 1999. *The Coming of Post-Industrial Society: A Venture in Social Forecasting*. New York: Basic Books.

Bendix, Reinhard. 1978. *Kings or People: Power and the Mandate to Rule*. Berkeley: University of California Press.

Benoit, Kenneth. 2001. 'District magnitude, electoral formula, and the number of parties.' *European Journal of Political Research* 39 (2): 203–224.

Benoit, Kenneth. 2002. 'The endogeneity problem in electoral studies: A critical reexamination of Duverger's mechanical effect.' *Electoral Studies* 21 (1): 35–46.

Benoit, Kenneth. 2007. 'Electoral laws as political consequences: Explaining the origins and change of electoral institutions.' *Annual Review of Political Science* 10: 363–390.

Berelson, Bernard R., Paul F. Lazarsfeld, and W. N. McPhee. 1954. *Voting*. Chicago: University of Chicago Press.

Berglund, Sten, and Jan A. Dellenbrant. 1994. *The New Democracies in Eastern Europe: Party Systems and Political Cleavages*. Aldershot, England: Edward Elgar.

Berg-Schlosser, Dietrich, and Gisèle De Meur. 1994. 'Conditions of democracy in interwar Europe: A Boolean test of major hypotheses.' *Comparative Politics* 26 (3): 253–280.

Bermeo, Nancy. 2002. 'The import of institutions.' *Journal of Democracy* 13 (12): 96–110.

Bermeo, Nancy. 2003. *Ordinary People in Extraordinary Times: The Citizenry and the Breakdown of Democracy*. Princeton, NJ: Princeton University Press.

Bernhard, Michael, Christopher Reenock, and Timothy Nordstrom. 2004. 'The legacy of Western overseas colonialism on democratic survival.' *International Studies Quarterly* 48 (1): 225–250.

Bielasiak, Jack. 2002. 'The institutionalization of electoral and party systems in postcommunist states.' *Comparative Politics* 34 (2): 189.

Birch, Sarah. 1998. 'Electoral reform in Ukraine: The 1988 parliamentary elections.' *Representation* 35 (2/3): 146–154.

Birch, Sarah. 2002. *Electoral Systems and Political Transformation in Post-Communist Europe*. New York: Palgrave.

Birch, Sarah, Frances Millard, Marina Popescu, and Kieran Williams. 2002. *Embodying Democracy: Electoral System Design in Post-Communist Europe*. New York: Palgrave.

Birch, Sarah, and Andrew Wilson. 1999. 'The Ukrainian parliamentary elections of 1998.' *Electoral Studies* 18 (2): 276–282.

Bird, Richard M., and François Vaillancourt. Eds. 1999. *Fiscal Decentralization in Developing Countries*. Cambridge: Cambridge University Press.

Birnir, Johanna Kristín. 2007. *Ethnicity and Electoral Politics*. New York: Cambridge University Press.

Blais, André, and Agnieszka Dobrzynska. 1998. 'Turnout in electoral democracies.' *European Journal of Political Research* 33 (2): 239–261.

Blais, André. 1988. 'The classification of electoral systems.' *European Journal of Political Research* 16: 99–110.

Blais, André. 2000. *To Vote or Not to Vote? The Merits and Limits of Rational Choice Theory*. Pittsburgh: University of Pittsburgh Press.

Blais, André, and R. Kenneth Carty. 1990. 'Does proportional representation foster voter turnout?' *European Journal of Political Research* 18 (2): 167–181.

Blais, André, and R. Kenneth Carty. 1991. 'The psychological impact of electoral laws – measuring Duverger's elusive factor.' *British Journal of Political Science* 21 (1): 79–93.

Blais, André, Louis Massicote, and Agnieszka Dobrzynska. 1997. 'Direct presidential elections: A world summary.' *Electoral Studies* 16 (4): 441–455.

Blais, André, Louis Massicote, and A. Yoshinaka. 2001. 'Deciding who has the right to vote: A comparative analysis of election laws.' *Electoral Studies* 20 (1): 41–62.

Blanton, Shannon L. 2000. 'Promoting human rights and democracy in the developing world: U.S. rhetoric versus U.S. arms exports.' *American Journal of Political Science* 44 (1): 123–131.

Bogdanor, Vernon, and David Butler. Eds. 1983. *Democracy and Elections*. Cambridge: Cambridge University Press.

Boix, Carles. 1999. 'Setting the rules of the game: The choice of electoral systems in advanced democracies.' *American Political Science Review* 93 (3): 609–624.

Boix, Carles. 2003. *Democracy and Redistribution*. Cambridge: Cambridge University Press.

Bollen, Kenneth A. 1979. 'Political democracy and the timing of development.' *American Sociological Review* 44: 572–587.

Bollen, Kenneth A. 1980. 'Issues in the comparative measurement of political democracy.' *American Sociological Review* 45: 370–390.

Bollen, Kenneth A. 1983. 'World system position, dependency, and democracy: The cross-national evidence.' *American Sociological Review* 48: 468–479.

Bollen, Kenneth A. 1991. 'Political democracy: Conceptual and measurement traps.' In Alex Inkeles (Ed.), *On Measuring Democracy: Its Consequences and Concomitants*. New Brunswick, NJ: Transaction.

Bollen, Kenneth A. 1993. 'Liberal democracy: Validity and method factors in cross-national measures.' *American Journal of Political Science* 37: 1207–1230.

Bollen, Kenneth A., and Robert W. Jackman. 1985. 'Political democracy and the size distribution of income.' *American Sociological Review* 50: 438–458.

Bollen, Kenneth A., and Robert W. Jackman. 1989. 'Democracy, stability and dichotomies.' *American Sociological Review* 54: 612–621.

Bollen, Kenneth A., and Robert W. Jackman. 1995. 'Income inequality and democratization revisited: Comment on Muller.' *American Sociological Review* 60: 983–989.

Bollen, Kenneth A., and Pamela Paxton. 2000. 'Subjective measures of liberal democracy.' *Comparative Political Studies* 33 (1): 58–86.

Boone, P. 1996. 'Politics and the effectiveness of foreign aid.' *European Economic Review* 40: 289–329.

Bourdieu, Pierre. 1970. *Reproduction in Education, Culture and Society*. London: Sage.

Brady, Henry, and David Collier. 2004. *Rethinking Social Inquiry: Diverse Tools, Shared Standards*. New York: Rowman & Littlefield.

Brancati, Dawn. 2006. 'Decentralization: Fueling the fire or dampening the flames of ethnic conflict and secessionism?' *International Organization* 60 (3): 651–685.

Brancati, Dawn. 2007. *Design over Conflict: Managing Ethnic Conflict and Secessionism through Decentralization*. Cambridge: Cambridge University Press.

Bratton, Michael, and Nicholas van de Walle. 1997. *Democratic Experiments in Africa*. Cambridge: Cambridge University Press.

Brautigam, Deborah. 1992. 'Governance, economy, and foreign aid.' *Studies in Comparative International Development* 27 (3): 325.

Brautigam, Deborah. 2000. *Aid Dependence and Governance*. Stockholm: Almqvist and Wiksell International.

Brenner, Y. S., Hartmut Kaelble, and Mark Thomas. Eds. 1991. *Income Distribution in Historical Perspective*. Cambridge: Cambridge University Press.

Brown, Michael E. Ed. 2001. *Nationalism and Ethnic Conflict*. Cambridge, MA: MIT Press.

Brunk, Gregory C., Gregory A. Caldeira, and Michael S. Lewis-Beck. 1987. 'Capitalism, socialism, and democracy: An empirical inquiry.' *European Journal of Political Research* 15: 459–470.

Bueno de Mesquita, Bruce, and Hilton Root. 2000. *Governing for Prosperity*. New Haven, CT: Yale University Press.

Bueno de Mesquita, Bruce, Alastar Smith, Randolph M. Siverson, and James D. Morrow. 2003. *The Logic of Political Survival*. Cambridge, MA: MIT Press.

Bunch, Valerie, and Sharon l. Wolchik. 2006. 'International diffusion and post-Communist electoral revolutions.' *Communist and Post-Communist Studies* 39 (3): 283–304.

Burkhart, Ross E., and Michael S. Lewis-Beck. 1994. 'Comparative democracy: The economic development thesis.' *American Political Science Review* 88: 903–910.

Burnell, Peter. Ed. 2000. *Democracy Assistance: International Co-Operation for Democratization*. London: Frank Cass.

Burnside, Craig, and David Dollar. 2000. 'Aid, policies, and growth.' *American Economic Review* 90 (4): 847–868.

Byman, Daniel L. 2002. *Keeping the Peace: Lasting Solutions to Ethnic Conflict*. Baltimore: Johns Hopkins University Press.

Cain, Bruce E., Russell J. Dalton, and Susan E. Scarrow. 2004. *Democracy Transformed? Expanding Political Opportunities in Advanced Industrial Democracies*. Oxford: Oxford University Press.

Campbell, Colin, and M. J. Wyszimirski. Eds. 1991. *Executive Leadership in Anglo-American Systems*. Pittsburgh: University of Pittsburgh Press.

Caplan, Richard D. 2005. *International Governance of War-Torn Territories: Rule and Reconstruction*. Oxford/New York: Oxford University Press.

Caraway, Teri L. 2004. 'Inclusion and democratization: Class, gender, race, and the extension of suffrage.' *Comparative Politics* 36 (4): 443–460.

Cardoso, Fernando Henrique, and Enzo Faletto. 1979. *Dependency and Development in Latin America*. Berkeley: University of California Press.

Carothers, Thomas. 1999. *Aiding Democracy Abroad*. Washington, DC: Carnegie Endowment for International Peace.

Carothers, Thomas. 2002. 'The end of the transition paradigm.' *Journal of Democracy* 13: 5–21.

Carothers, Thomas. 2004. *Critical Mission: Essays on Democracy Promotion*. Washington, DC: Carnegie Endowment for International Peace.

Carothers, Thomas, and Marina Ottaway. Eds. 2005. *Uncharted Journey: Promoting Democracy in the Middle East*. Washington, DC: Carnegie Endowment for International Peace.

Chandra, Kanchan. 2001. 'Ethnic bargains, group instability, and social choice theory.' *Politics & Society* 29 (3): 337–362.

Chandra, Kanchan. 2004. *Why Ethnic Parties Succeed: Patronage and Ethnic Headcounts in India*. Cambridge: Cambridge University Press.

Chandra, Kanchan. 2005. 'Ethnic Parties and Democratic Stability.' *Perspectives on Politics* 3 (2): 235–252.

Chase-Dunn, Christopher. 1975. 'The effects of international economic dependence on development and inequality: A cross-national study.' *American Sociological Review* 40: 720–738.

Cheibub, José. 2002. 'Minority governments, deadlock situations, and the survival of presidential democracies.' *Comparative Political Studies* 35 (3).

Cheibub, José. 2002. 'Presidentialism and democratic performance.' In Andrew Reynolds (Ed.), *Constitutional Design: Institutional Design, Conflict Management, and Democracy in the Late Twentieth Century*. Oxford: Oxford University Press.

Cheibub, José. 2007. *Presidentialism, Parliamentarism, and Democracy*. Cambridge: Cambridge University Press.

Cheibub, José, and Jennifer Gandhi. 2004. 'Classifying political regimes: A six-fold measure of democracies and dictatorships.' *Presented at the American Political Science Association Annual Meeting*. Chicago, September 2–5.

Cheibub, José, and Fernando Limongi. 2002. 'Democratic institutions and regime survival: Parliamentary and presidential democracies reconsidered.' *Annual Review of Political Science* 5: 151.

Cheibub, José, Adam Przeworski, and S. M. Saiegh. 2004. 'Government coalitions and legislative success under presidentialism and parliamentarism.' *British Journal of Political Science* 34: 565.

Chirot, Daniel. 1981. 'Changing fashions in the study of the social causes of economic and political change.' In J. F. Short (Ed.), *The State of Sociology: Problems and Prospects*. London: Sage.

Chirot, Daniel. 2001. 'A clash of civilizations or of paradigms? Theorizing progress and social change.' *International Sociology* 16 (3): 341–360.

Chua, Amy. 2003. *World on Fire: How Exporting Free Market Democracy Breeds Ethnic Hatred and Global Instability*. New York: Doubleday.

Cingranelli, David L., and Thomas E. Pasquarello. 1985. 'Human rights practices and the distribution of U.S. foreign aid to Latin America.' *American Journal of Political Science* 29 (3): 539–563.

Clague, Christopher, Suzanne Gleason, and Stephen Knack. 2001. 'Determinants of lasting democracy in poor countries: Culture, development, and institutions.' *Annals of the American Academy of Political and Social Science* 573: 16–41.

Clarke, Harold D., Alan Kornberg, C. McIntyre, P. Bauer-Kaase, and Max Kaase. 1999. 'The effect of economic priorities on the measurement of value change: New experimental evidence.' *American Political Science Review* 93 (3): 637–647.

Coakley, John. Ed. 1993. *The Territorial Management of Ethnic Conflict*. London: Frank Cass.

Cohen, Frank. 1997. 'Proportional versus majoritarian ethnic conflict management in democracies.' *Comparative Political Studies* 30 (5).

Collier, David, and Robert Adcock. 1999. 'Democracy and dichotomies: A pragmatic approach to choices about concepts.' *Annual Review of Political Science* 1: 537–565.

Collier, Paul, and Nicholas Sambanis. Eds. 2005. *Understanding Civil War*. Washington, DC: World Bank.

Collier, Ruth Berins. 1999. *Paths toward Democracy: Working Class and Elites in Western Europe and South America*. Cambridge: Cambridge University Press.

Colomer, Joseph M. Ed. 2004. *Handbook of Electoral System Choice*. New York: Palgrave Macmillan.

Cooper, Andrew F., and Thomas Legler. 2007. *Intervention without Intervening? The OAS Defense and Promotion of Democracy in the Americas*. New York: Palgrave Macmillan.

Coppedge, Michael. 1999. 'Thickening thin concepts and theories: Combining large N and small in comparative politics.' *Comparative Politics* 31 (4): 465–476.

Coppedge, Michael, and Wolfgang Reinicke. 1990. 'A scale of polyarchy.' *Studies in Comparative and International Development* 25 (1): 51–72.

Coppedge, Michael, and Wolfgang Reinicke. 1991. 'Measuring polyarchy.' In Alex Inkeles (Ed.), *On Measuring Democracy*. New Brunswick, NJ: Transaction.

Coulter, Philip B. 1975. *Social Mobilization and Democracy: A Macro-Quantitative Analysis of Global and Regional Models*. Lexington, KY: Lexington Books.

Cox, Gary. 1997. *Making Votes Count*. Cambridge: Cambridge University Press.

Crawford, Gordon. 1997. 'Foreign aid and political conditionality: Issues of effectiveness and consistency.' *Democratization* 4 (3): 69–108.

Creevey, Lucy, Paul Ngomo, and Richard Vergroff. 2005. 'Party politics and different paths to democratic transitions – a comparison of Benin and Senegal.' *Party Politics* 11 (4): 471–493.

Cutright, Phillips. 1963. 'National political development: Measurement and analysis.' *American Sociological Review* 28: 253–264.

Daalder, Hans. 1974. 'The consociational democracy theme.' *World Politics* 26: 604–621.

Dahl, Robert A. 1971. *Polyarchy: Participation and Opposition*. New Haven, CT: Yale University Press.

Dahl, Robert A. 1989. *Democracy and Its Critics*. New Haven, CT: Yale University Press.

Dahl, Robert A. 1998. *On Democracy*. New Haven, CT: Yale University Press.

Dalton, Russell, and Martin P. Wattenberg. Eds. 2000. *Parties without Partisans: Political Change in Advanced Industrial Democracies*. Oxford: Oxford University Press.

Dashti-Gibson, Jaleh, Patricia Davis, and Benjamin Radcliff. 1997. 'On the determinants of the success of economic sanctions: An empirical analysis.' *American Journal of Political Science* 41 (2): 608–618.

Database of Political Institutions. 2005. http://www.worldbank.org/research/bios/pkeefer.htm

Davidson, Chandler, and Bernard Grofman. Eds. 1994. *Quiet Revolution in the South: The Impact of the Voting Rights Act 1965–1990*. Princeton, NJ: Princeton University Press.

De Vries, Michael S. 2000. 'The rise and fall of decentralization: A comparative analysis of arguments and practices in European countries.' *European Journal of Political Research* 38: 193–224.

Decalo, Samuel. 1997. 'Benin: First of the new democracies.' In John F. Clarke and David E. Gardiner (Eds.), *Political Reform in Francophone Africa*, pp. 41–61. Boulder, CO: Westview Press.

Della Porta, Donnatella. 1999. *Corrupt Exchanges*. New York: Aldine de Gruyter.

Della Porta, Donnatella, and Yves Meny. 1996. *Democracy and Corruption in Europe*. New York: Pinter.

Denters, Bas, and Lawrence Rose. Eds. 2005. *Comparing Local Governance: Trends and Developments*. London: Palgrave/Macmillan.

Deutsch, Karl W. 1964. 'Social mobilization and political development.' *American Political Science Review* 55: 493–514.

Deutscher, Irwin. 2002. *Accommodating Diversity: National Policies That Prevent Conflict*. Lanham, MD: Lexington Books.

Di Palma, Guiseppe. 1990. *To Craft Democracies: An Essay on Democratic Transitions*. Berkeley: University of California Press.

Diamond, Larry. 1992. 'Economic development and democracy reconsidered.' *American Behavioral Scientist* 35: 450–499.

Diamond, Larry. 1992. 'Economic development and democracy reconsidered.' In Gary Marks and Larry Diamond (Eds.), *Reexamining Democracy*, pp. 93–139. Newbury Park, CA: Sage.

Diamond, Larry. 1996. *Developing Democracy: Toward Consolidation*. Baltimore: Johns Hopkins University Press.

Diamond, Larry. 2002. 'Thinking about hybrid regimes.' *Journal of Democracy* 13 (2): 21–35.

Diamond, Larry, and Richard Gunther. 2001. *Political Parties and Democracy*. Baltimore: Johns Hopkins University Press.

Diamond, Larry, Mark Plattner, and Daniel Brumberg. Eds. 2003. *Islam and Democracy in the Middle East*. Baltimore: Johns Hopkins University Press.

Doig, Alan. 2000. *Corruption and Democratization*. London: Frank Cass.

Dollar, David, and Lant Pritchett. 1998. *Assessing Aid: What Works, What Doesn't, and Why*. New York: Oxford University Press.

Dominguez, Jorge, and Michael Shifter. Eds. 2003. *Constructing Democratic Governance in Latin America*. 2nd ed. Baltimore: Johns Hopkins University Press.

Doorenspleet, Renske. 1997. 'Political democracy: A cross-national quantitative analysis of modernization and dependency theories.' *Acta Politica* 32: 349–374.

Doorenspleet, Renske. 2000. 'Reassessing the three waves of democratization.' *World Politics* 52: 384–406.

Doorenspleet, Renske. 2002. 'Development, class and democracy.' In G. Hyden and O. Elgstrom (Eds.), *Development and Democracy*. London: Routledge.

Doorenspleet, Renske. 2005. *Democratic Transitions: Exploring the Structural Sources during the Fourth Wave*. Boulder, CO: Lynne Rienner.

Doyle, Michael W., and Nicholas Sambanis. 2006. *Making War and Building Peace*. Princeton, NJ: Princeton University Press.

Easterly, William, and R. Levine. 1997. 'Africa's growth tragedy: Policies and ethnic divisions.' *Quarterly Journal of Economics* 111 (4): 1203–1250.

Ehtisham, Ahmad. Ed. 2002. *Fiscal Decentralization*. London: Routledge.

Elazar, Daniel. 1994. *Federal Systems of the World: A Handbook of Federal, Confederal and Autonomy Arrangements* Essex, England: Longman.

Elkins, Zachary. 2000. 'Gradations of democracy? Empirical tests of alternative conceptualizations.' *American Journal of Political Science* 44 (2): 293–300.

Elkins, Zachary, and John Sides. 2007. 'Can institutions build unity in multiethnic states?' *American Political Science Review* 101 (4): 1–16.

Elkit, Jorgen, and Palle Svensson. 1997. 'What makes elections free and fair?' *Journal of Democracy* 8 (3): 32–46.

Erk, Jan. 2006. 'Does federalism really matter?' *Comparative Politics* 39 (1): 103.

Esposito, John L. Ed. 1997. *Political Islam: Revolution, Radicalism or Reform?* Boulder, CO: Lynne Reinner.

Esposito, John L., and John O. Voll. 1996. *Islam and Democracy*. Oxford: Oxford University Press.

Fearon, James D., and David D. Laitin. 1996. 'Explaining interethnic cooperation.' *American Political Science Review* 90 (4): 715–735.

Fearon, James D., and David D. Laitin. 2003. 'Ethnicity, insurgency, and civil war.' *American Political Science Review* 97 (1): 75–90.

Feng, Yi. 1997. 'Democracy, political stability and economic growth.' *British Journal of Political Science* 27: 391–418.

Feng, Yi. 2003. *Democracy, Governance and Economic Performance*. Cambridge, MA: MIT Press.

Feng, Yi, and I. Gizelis. 2002. 'Building political consensus and distributing resources: A trade-off or compatible choice?' *Economic Development and Cultural Change* 51 (1): 217–236.

Feng, Yi, and P. J. Zak. 1999. 'Determinants of democratic transitions.' *Journal of Conflict Resolution* 43 (2): 162–177.

Finkel, Steven E., Anibal Perez-Linan, and Mitchell A. Seligson with Dinorah Azpuru. 2005. *Effects of U.S. Foreign Assistance on Democracy Building: Results from a Cross-National Quantitative Study*. Washington, DC: USAID.

Fish, M. Stephen. 2006. 'Stronger legislatures, stronger democracies.' *Journal of Democracy* 17 (1): 5–20.

Foley, Michael, and Bob Edwards. 1998. 'Beyond Tocqueville: Civil society and social capital in comparative perspective.' *American Behavioral Scientist* 42 (1): 5–20.

Foweraker, Joe, and Roman Krznaric. 2000. 'Measuring liberal democratic performance: An empirical and conceptual critique.' *Political Studies* 48: 759–787.

Fox, Jonathan. 2001. 'Two civilizations and ethnic conflict: Islam and the West.' *Journal of Peace Research* 38 (4): 459–472.

Freedom House. *Democracy's Century*. http://www.freedomhouse.org/reports/century.html

Freedom House. *Freedom in the World*. www.freedomhouse.org (various years).

Friedman, Milton. 1958. 'Foreign economic aid: Means and objectives.' *Yale Review* 47 (4): 500–516.

Frye, Timothy. 1997. 'A politics of institutional choice: Post-communist presidencies.' *Comparative Political Studies* 30: 523.

Fukuyama, Francis. 1995. *Trust: The Social Virtues and the Creation of Prosperity*. New York: Free Press.

Gagnon, Alain-G., and James Tully. Eds. 2001. *Multinational Democracies*. Cambridge: Cambridge University Press.

Gallagher, Michael, and Paul Mitchell. Eds. 2005. *The Politics of Electoral Systems*. Oxford: Oxford University Press.

Gasiorowski, Mark J. 1995. 'Economic crisis and political regime change: An event history analysis.' *American Political Science Review* 89 (4): 882–897.

Gasiorowski, Mark J., and Timothy J. Power. 1997. 'Institutional design and democratic consolidation in the Third World.' *Comparative Political Studies* 30 (2): 123–155.

Gasiorowski, Mark J., and Timothy J. Power. 1998. 'The structural determinants of democratic consolidation.' *Comparative Political Studies* 31: 740–771.

Gastil, Raymond D. 1991. 'The comparative survey of freedom: Experiences and suggestions.' In A. Inkeles (Ed.), *On Measuring Democracy*. New Brunswick, NJ: Transaction.

Gastil, Raymond D. 1979. *Freedom in the World: Political Rights and Civil Liberties*. Washington, DC: Freedom House.

Geddes, Barbara. 2003. *Paradigms and Sand Castles: Theory Building and Research Design in Comparative Politics*. Ann Arbor: University of Michigan Press.

Geering, John, and Strom C. Thacker. 2004. 'Political institutions and corruption: The role of unitarism and parliamentarism.' *British Journal of Political Science* 34: 295–330.

George, Alexander L., and Andrew Bennett. 2004. *Case Studies and Theory Development*. Cambridge, MA: MIT Press.

Gerges, Fawaz A. 1999. *America and Political Islam: Clash of Cultures or Clash of Interests?* Cambridge: Cambridge University Press.

Gleditsch, Kristian, and Michael D. Ward. 1997. 'Double take: A re-examination of democracy and autocracy in modern polities.' *Journal of Conflict Resolution* 41: 361–383.

Gleditsch, Kristian, and Michael D. Ward. 2000. 'War and peace in space and time: The role of democratization.' *International Studies Quarterly* 44 (1): 1–29.

Gleditsch, Kristian Skrede, and Michael D. Ward. 2006. 'Diffusion and the international context of democratization.' *International Organization* 60: 911–933.

Golder, Matthew. 2004. *Codebook: Democratic Electoral Systems around the World 1945–2000.* http://homepages.nyuedu/~mrg217

Golder, Matthew. 2005. 'Democratic electoral systems around the world, 1946–2000.' *Electoral Studies* 24 (2): 103–121.

Goldsmith, Michael. 2002. 'Central control over local government: A Western European comparison.' *Local Government Studies* 28 (3): 91.

Gonick, Lev S., and Robert M. Rosh. 1988. 'The structural constraints of the world-economy on national political development.' *Comparative Political Studies* 21: 171–199.

Gray, Mark, and Miki Caul. 2000. 'Declining voter turnout in advanced industrialized democracies, 1950 to 1997.' *Comparative Political Studies* 33 (9): 1091–1122.

Griffiths, Ann L. Ed. 2005. *Handbook of Federal Countries, 2005.* Montreal: Forum of Federations/McGill University Press.

Grindle, Merilee. 2004. 'Good enough governance: Poverty reduction and reform in developing countries.' *Governance* 17 (4): 525–548.

Grossman, Herschel I. 1991. 'A general equilibrium theory of insurrections.' *American Economic Review* 81: 912–921.

Grossman, Herschel I. 1992. 'Foreign aid and insurrection.' *Defense Economics* 3: 275–288.

Grugel, Jean. 1999. *Democracy without Borders: Transnationalisation and Conditionality in New Democracies.* London: Routledge.

Guelke, Adrian. Ed. 2004. *Democracy and Ethnic Conflict.* New York: Palgrave.

Gunther, Richard, Jose Ramon Montero, and Joan J. Linz. 2002. *Political Parties: Old Concepts and New Challenges.* Oxford: Oxford University Press.

Gurr, Ted Robert. 1970. *Why Men Rebel.* Princeton, NJ: Princeton University Press.

Gurr, Ted Robert. 1974. 'Persistence and change in political systems.' *American Political Science Review* 74: 1482–1504.

Gurr, Ted Robert. Ed. 1980. *Handbook of Political Conflict.* New York: Free Press.

Gurr, Ted Robert. 2000. *Peoples versus States: Minorities at Risk in the New Century.* Washington, DC: US Institute for Peace Press.

Gurr, Ted Robert. 2000. 'Ethnic conflict on the wane.' *Foreign Affairs* 79 (3): 52–64.

Gurr, Ted Robert, Keith Jaggers, and Will H. Moore. 1990. 'Transformation of the Western state: The growth of democracy, autocracy and state power since 1800.' *Studies in Comparative International Development* 25 (1): 84.

Gurr, Ted Robert, Keith Jaggers, and Will H. Moore. 1991. 'The transformation of the Western state: The growth of democracy, autocracy and state power since 1800.' In Alex Inkeles (Ed.), *On Measuring Democracy.* New Brunswick, NJ: Transaction.

Gurr, Ted Robert, Monty G. Marshall, and Deepa Khosla. 2007. *Peace and Conflict 2007.* College Park: University of Maryland/CIDCM.

Hadenius, Alex. 1997. *Democracy's Victory and Crisis*. Cambridge: Cambridge University Press.

Hadenius. Axel. 1992. *Democracy and Development*. Cambridge: Cambridge University Press.

Haggard, Stephen, and R. R. Kaufman. 1995. *The Political Economy of Democratic Transitions*. Princeton, NJ: Princeton University Press.

Hagopian, Frances, and Scott Mainwaring. Eds. 2005. *The Third Wave of Democratization in Latin America: Advances and Setbacks*. Cambridge: Cambridge University Press.

Hale, Henry E. 2004. 'Divided we stand: Institutional sources of ethno-federal state survival and collapse.' *World Politics* 56: 165–193.

Halperin, Morton H., Joseph T. Siegle, and Michael M. Weinstein. 2005. *The Democracy Advantage: How Democracies Promote Prosperity and Peace*. New York: Routledge.

Handley, Lisa. 2005. 'Comparative redistricting practices.' Paper presented at the annual meeting of the American Political Science Association, Washington, DC.

Hannan, Michael T., and Glenn R. Carroll. 1981. 'Dynamics of formal political structure: An event-history analysis.' *American Sociological Review* 46: 19–35.

Harrison, Lawrence E., and Samuel P. Huntington. Eds. 2000. *Culture Matters*. New York: Basic Books.

Hartzell, Caroline A., and Matthew Hoddie. 2007. *Crafting Peace: Power Sharing and Negotiated Settlements of Civil Wars*. Philadelphia: Pennsylvania State University Press.

Hechter, Michael. 1992. 'The dynamics of secession.' *Acta Sociologica* 35 (4): 267–283.

Heidenheimer, Arnold. Ed. 2002. *Political Corruption: Concepts and Contexts*. New Brunswick, NJ: Transaction.

Held, David. 1987. *Models of Democracy*. Stanford, CA: Stanford University Press.

Helliwell, John F. 1994. 'Empirical linkages between democracy and economic growth.' *British Journal of Political Science* 24 (2): 225–248.

Henderson, Errol A., and Richard Tucker. 2001. 'Clear and present strangers: The clash of civilizations and international politics.' *International Studies Quarterly* 45 (2): 317–338.

Hibbing, John R., and Elizabeth Theiss-Morse. 2003. *Stealth Democracy: Americans' Beliefs about How Government Should Work*. Cambridge: Cambridge University Press.

Horowitz, Donald L. 1985. *Ethnic Groups in Conflict*. Berkeley: University of California Press.

Horowitz, Donald L. 1991. *A Democratic South Africa? Constitutional Engineering in a Divided Society*. Berkeley: University of California Press.

Horowitz, Donald L. 2003. 'Electoral systems: A primer for decision-makers.' *Journal of Democracy* 14 (4).

Horowitz, Donald L. 2003. *The Deadly Ethnic Riot*. Berkeley: University of California Press.

Hossain, Akhtar. 2000. 'Anatomy of hartal politics in Bangladesh.' *Asian Survey* 40 (3): 508–529.

Hsiao, Cheng M. 1986. *Analysis of Panel Data*. Cambridge: Cambridge University Press.

Huber, Evelyne, Dietrich Rueschmeyer, and John D. Stephens. 1993. 'The impact of economic development on democracy.' *Journal of Economic Perspectives* 7 (3): 71–85.

Humphreys, M. 2005. 'Natural resources, conflict, and conflict resolution – uncovering the mechanisms.' *Journal of Conflict Resolution* 49 (4): 508–537.

Hunter, Shireen T. 1998. *The Future of Islam and the West: Clash of Civilizations or Peaceful Coexistence?* Westport, CT: Praeger.

Huntington, Samuel P. 1991. *The Third Wave: Democratization in the Late Twentieth Century.* Norman: University of Oklahoma Press.

Huntington, Samuel P. 1996. *The Clash of Civilizations and the Remaking of World Order.* New York: Simon & Schuster.

Huntington, Samuel P. 1997. 'The clash of civilizations: A response.' *Millenium – Journal of International Studies* 26 (1): 141–142.

Inglehart, Ronald. 1977. *The Silent Revolution: Changing Values and Political Styles among Western Publics.* Princeton, NJ: Princeton University Press.

Inglehart, Ronald. 1988. 'The renaissance of political culture.' *American Political Science Review* 82: 1203–1230.

Inglehart, Ronald. 1990. *Culture Shift in Advanced Industrial Society.* Princeton, NJ: Princeton University Press.

Inglehart, Ronald. 1997. *Modernization and Post-Modernization: Cultural, Economic and Political Change in 43 Societies.* Princeton, NJ: Princeton University Press.

Inglehart, Ronald. 2003. 'How solid is mass support for democracy and how do we measure it?' *PS: Political Science and Politics* 36 (1): 51–57.

Inglehart, Ronald. Ed. 2003. *Islam, Gender, Culture, and Democracy.* Ontario: De Sitter.

Inglehart, Ronald, and Paul Abramson. 1999. 'Measuring post-materialism.' *American Political Science Review* 93 (3): 665–677.

Inglehart, Ronald, and Wayne E. Baker. 2000. 'Modernization, globalization and the persistence of tradition: Empirical evidence from 65 societies.' *American Sociological Review* 65: 19–55.

Inglehart, Ronald, and Pippa Norris. 2003. 'Muslims and the West: A clash of civilizations?' *Foreign Policy* 135: 63–70.

Inglehart, Ronald, and Christopher Welzel. 2003. 'Political culture and democracy: Analyzing cross-level linkages.' *Comparative Politics* 36 (1): 61.

Inglehart, Ronald, and Christopher Welzel. 2005. *Modernization, Cultural Change, and Democracy: The Human Development Sequence.* Cambridge: Cambridge University Press.

Inkeles, Alex. Ed. 1991. *On Measuring Democracy: Its Consequences and Concomitants.* New Brunswick, NJ: Transaction.

International IDEA State of Democracy Project. www.idea.int

Isham, Jonathan, Daniel Kaufmann, and Lant Pritchett. 1997. 'Civil liberties, democracy, and the performance of government projects.' *World Bank Economic Review* 11 (2): 219–242.

Jackman, Robert W. 1973. 'On the relation of economic development and democratic performance.' *American Journal of Political Science* 17: 611–621.

Jackman, Robert W., and Ross A. Miller. 1995. 'Voter turnout in industrial democracies during the 1980s.' *Comparative Political Studies* 27: 467–492.

Jaggers, Keith, and Ted Gurr. 1995. 'Tracking democracy's third wave with the Polity III data.' *Journal of Peace Research* 32: 469–482.

Jarstad, Anna, and Timothy D. Sisk. Eds. 2007. *From War to Democracy*. Cambridge: Cambridge University Press.

Jelen, Ted Gerard, and Clyde Wilcox. Eds. 2002. *Religion and Politics in Comparative Perspective*. Cambridge: Cambridge University Press.

Jensen, N., and L. Wantchekon. 2004. 'Resource wealth and political regimes in Africa.' *Comparative Political Studies* 37: 816–841.

Jeong, Ho-Won. 2005. *Peace-Building in Post-Conflict Societies*. Boulder, CO: Lynne Reinner.

Jesse, Neal G., and Kristen P. Williams. 2005. *Identity and Institutions: Conflict Reduction in Divided Societies*. Albany: State University of New York Press.

Jones, Mark P. 1995. *Electoral Laws and the Survival of Presidential Democracies*. Notre Dame, IN: University of Notre Dame Press.

Kabuli, Niaz Faizi. 1994. *Democracy According to Islam*. Pittsburgh: Dorrance.

Kaiser, Andre, Matthias Lehnert, Bernhard Miller, and Ulrich Sieberer. 2002. 'The democratic quality of institutional regimes: A conceptual framework.' *Political Studies* 50: 313–331.

Karl, Terry L. 1991. 'Dilemmas of democratization in Latin America.' In D. A. Rustow and K. P. Erickson (Eds.), *Comparative Political Dynamics: Global Research Perspectives*, pp. 163–191. New York: Harper Collins.

Karl, Terry L. 1997. *The Paradox of Plenty: Oil Booms and Petro-States*. Berkeley: University of California Press.

Kasza, Gregory. 1996. 'War and comparative politics.' *Comparative Politics* 28 (3): 355–373.

Katz, Richard S. 1997. *Democracy and Elections*. New York: Oxford University Press.

Kaufman, Stuart J. 2001. *Modern Hatreds: The Symbolic Politics of Ethnic War*. Ithaca, NY: Cornell University Press.

Kaufmann, Chaim. 1996. 'Possible and impossible solutions to ethnic civil wars.' *International Security* 20 (4): 136–175.

Kaufmann, Daniel, Aart Kraay, and Massimo Mastruzzi. 2003. *Governance Matters III: Governance Indicators 1996–2002*. Washington, DC: World Bank. http://www.worldbank.org/wbi/governance/pubs/govmatters3.html

Kaufmann, Daniel, Aart Kraay, and Massimo Mastruzzi. 2006. *Governance Matters V: Governance Indicators for 1996–2005*. Washington, DC: World Bank. www.worldbank.org

Kaufmann, Daniel, Aart Kraay, and Massimo Mastruzzi. 2007. *Governance Matters VI: Aggregate and Individual Governance Indicators, 1996–2006*. Washington, DC: World Bank. www.worldbank.org

Kaufmann, Daniel, and Pablo Zoido-Lobatón. 1999. *Governance Matters*. Washington, DC: World Bank. http://www.worldbank.org/wbi/governance/pubs/govmatters.htm

Keck, Margaret E., and Kathryn Sikkink, 1998. *Activists beyond Borders – Advocacy Networks in International Politics*. Ithaca, NY: Cornell University Press.

Keefer, Philip. 2005. *Database of Political Institutions, 2004*. Washington, DC: World Bank.

Kitschelt, Herbert. 1992. 'Political regime change: Structure and process-driven explanations.' *American Political Science Review* 86: 1028–1034.

Klingemann, Hans-Dieter, and Dieter Fuchs. 1995. *Citizens and the State*. Oxford: Oxford University Press.

Kloti, U. 'Consensual government in a heterogeneous polity.' *West European Politics* 24 (2): 19–25.

Knack, Stephen. 2001. 'Aid dependence and the quality of governance.' *Southern Economic Journal* 68 (2): 310–329.

Knack, Stephen. 2004. 'Does foreign aid promote democracy?' *International Studies Quarterly* 48 (1): 251–266.

Knack, Stephen, and Philip Keefer. 1995. 'Institutions and economic performance: Cross-country tests using alternative institutional measures.' *Economics and Politics* 7 (4): 207–227.

Kochanek, Stanley A. 2000. 'Governance, patronage politics, and democratic transition in Bangladesh.' *Asian Survey* 40 (3): 530–550.

Kornai, János, Bo Rothstein, and Susan Rose-Ackerman. Eds. 2004. *Creating Social Trust in Post-Socialist Transitions*. New York: Palgrave Macmillan.

Kosack, Stephen. 2003. 'Effective aid: How democracy allows development aid to improve the quality of life.' *World Development* 31 (1): 1–22.

Kreisi, Hans, et al. 1995. *New Social Movements in Western Europe: A Comparative Analysis*. Minneapolis: University of Minnesota Press.

Krieckhaus, J. 2004. 'The regime debate revisited: A sensitivity analysis of democracy's economic effect.' *British Journal of Political Science* 34 (4): 635–655.

Laakso, Marku, and Rein Taagepera. 1979. 'The "effective" number of parties: A measure with application to Western Europe.' *Comparative Political Studies* 12: 3–28.

LeDuc, Lawrence, Richard G. Niemi, and Pippa Norris. Eds. 2002. *Comparing Democracies 2: Elections and Voting in Global Perspective*. London: Sage.

Lehmbruch, Gerhard. 1967. *Proporzdemokratie. Politisches System und politische Kultur in der Schweiz und Osterreich*. Tubingen: Mohr.

Lerner, David. 1958. *The Passing of Traditional Society*. Glencoe, IL: The Free Press.

Levitsky, Stephen. 2003. 'Autocracy by democratic rules: The dynamics of competitive authoritarianism in the post–cold war era.' Paper presented at the Conference, 'Mapping the Great Zone: Clientelism and the Boundary between Democratic and Democratizing.' Columbia University, April 4–5.

Levitsky, Steven, and Lucan A. Way. 2002. 'The rise of competitive authoritarianism.' *Journal of Democracy* 13 (2): 51–65.

Lewis, Arthur W. 1965. *Politics in West Africa*. London: Allen & Unwin.

Lewis, Bernard. 2002. *What Went Wrong? Western Impact and Middle Eastern Response*. New York: Oxford University Press.

Li, Richard P. Y., and William R. Thompson. 1975. 'The "coup contagion" hypothesis.' *Journal of Conflict Resolution* 19: 63–88.

Lijphart, Arend. 1969. 'Consociational democracy.' *World Politics* 21: 207–225.

Lijphart, Arend. 1975. *The Politics of Accommodation: Pluralism and Democracy in the Netherlands*. Berkeley: University of California Press.

Lijphart, Arend. 1977. *Democracy in Plural Societies: A Comparative Exploration*. New Haven, CT: Yale University Press.

Lijphart, Arend. 1984. *Democracies*. New Haven, CT: Yale University Press.

Lijphart, Arend. 1991. 'Constitutional choices for new democracies.' *Journal of Democracy* 2: 72–84.

Lijphart, Arend. 1994. *Electoral Systems and Party Systems: A Study of Twenty-Seven Democracies, 1945–1990*. Oxford: Oxford University Press.

Lijphart, Arend. Ed. 1996. *Presidential v. Parliamentary Government*. Oxford: Oxford University Press.

Lijphart, Arend. 1997. 'Unequal participation: Democracies' unresolved dilemma.' *American Political Science Review* 91: 1–14.

Lijphart, Arend. 1999. *Patterns of Democracy: Government Forms and Performance in 36 Countries*. New Haven, CT: Yale University Press.

Lijphart, Arend. 2002. 'Negotiation democracy versus consensus democracy: Parallel conclusions and recommendations.' *European Journal of Political Research* 41 (1): 107–113.

Lijphart, Arend. 2004. 'Constitutional design for divided societies.' *Journal of Democracy* 15 (2): 96–109.

Lijphart, Arend. 2008. *Thinking about Democracy: Power Sharing and Majority Rule in Theory and Practice*. New York: Routledge.

Linder, Wolf, and Andre Baechtiger. 2005. 'What drives democratization in Asia and Africa?' *European Journal of Political Research* 44: 861–880.

Linz, Juan J., and Alfred Stepan. 1978. *The Breakdown of Democratic Regimes*. Baltimore: Johns Hopkins University Press.

Linz, Juan J., and Alfred Stepan. 1996. *Problems of Democratic Transition and Consolidation: Southern Europe, South America and Post-Communist Europe*. Baltimore: Johns Hopkins University Press.

Linz, Juan J., and Arturo Valenzuela. Eds. 1994. *The Failure of Presidential Democracy*. Baltimore: Johns Hopkins University Press.

Lipset, Seymour Martin. 1959. 'Some social requisites of democracy: Economic development and political legitimacy.' *American Political Science Review* 53: 69–105.

Lipset, Seymour Martin. 1960. *Political Man: The Social Basis of Politics*. New York: Doubleday.

Lipset, Seymour Martin. 1994. 'The social requisites of democracy revisited.' *American Sociological Review* 59: 1–22.

Lipset, Seymour Martin. 1995. 'Economic development.' In *The Encyclopedia of Democracy*. London: Routledge.

Lipset, Seymour Martin, and Jason M. Lakin. 2004. *The Democratic Century*. Norman: University of Oklahoma Press.

Lipset, Seymour Martin, Kyoung-Ryung Seong, and John Charles Torres. 1993. 'A comparative analysis of the social requisites of democracy.' *International Social Science Journal* 45 (2): 154–175.

Lublin, David. 1997. *The Paradox of Representation: Racial Gerrymandering and Minority Interests*. Princeton, NJ: Princeton University Press.

Lustik, Ian S., Dan Miodownik, and Roy J. Eidelson. 2004. 'Secessionism in multicultural states: Does sharing power prevent or encourage it?' *American Political Science Review* 98 (2): 209–229.

Mainwaring, Scott. 1993. 'Presidentialism, multipartism, and democracy: The difficult combination.' *Comparative Political Studies* 26 (2): 198–228.

Mainwaring, Scott, Guillermo O'Donnell, and J. Samuel Valenzuela. Eds. 1992. *Issues in Democratic Consolidation: The New South American Democracies in Comparative Perspective*. Notre Dame, IN: University of Notre Dame Press.

Mainwaring, Scott, and Matthew Soberg Shugart. 1997. *Presidentialism and Democracy in Latin America*. Cambridge: Cambridge University Press.

Mair, Peter. 2001. 'Party membership in twenty European democracies 1980–2000.' *Party Politics* 7 (1): 5–22.

Malloy, James M., and Mitchell A. Seligson. Eds. *Authoritarians and Democrats: Regime Transition in Latin America*. Pittsburgh: University of Pittsburgh Press.

Manor, James. 1999. *The Political Economy of Democratic Decentralization*. Washington, DC: World Bank.

Manor, James. 2007. *Aid That Works: Successful Development in Fragile States*. Washington, DC: World Bank.

Mansfield, Edward D., and Jack Snyder. 2007. *Electing to Fight: Why Emerging Democracies Go to War*. Cambridge, MA: MIT Press.

Maren, Michael. 1997. *The Road to Hell: The Ravaging Effects of Foreign Aid and International Charity*. New York: Free Press.

Marshall, Monty G., and Ted Robert Gurr. 2006. *Peace and Conflict 2005*. Baltimore: University of Maryland/CIDCM.

Marshall, Monty G., Ted Robert Gurr, Christian Davenport, and Keith Jaggers. 2002. 'Polity IV, 1800–1999: Comments on Munck and Verkuilen.' *Comparative Political Studies* 35 (1): 40–45.

Marshall, Monty G., and Keith Jaggers. 2002. *Polity IV Project: Political Regime Characteristics and Transitions, 1800–2002*: Dataset Users' Manual. University of Maryland. http://www.bsos.umd.edu/cidcm/polity/

McAdam, Doug, John D. McCarthy, and Mayer N. Zeld. 1996. *Comparative Perspectives on Social Movements*. Cambridge: Cambridge University Press.

McCormick, James M., and Neil Mitchell. 1988. 'Is U.S. aid really linked to human rights in Latin America?' *American Journal of Political Science* 32 (1): 231–239.

McCrone, Donald J., and Charles F. Cnudde. 1967. 'Toward a communications theory of democratic political development: A causal model.' *American Political Science Review* 61: 72–79.

McDonald, Michael P., and Samuel L. Popkin. 2001. 'The myth of the vanishing voter.' *American Political Science Review* 95 (4): 963–974.

McRae, Kenneth. Ed. 1974. *Consociational Democracy: Conflict Accommodation in Segmented Societies*. Toronto: McClelland and Stewart.

Meernik, James, Eric L. Krueger, and Stephen C. Poe. 1998. 'Testing models of U.S. foreign policy: Foreign aid during and after the Cold War.' *Journal of Politics* 60: 63–85.

Middleton, John. Ed. 2005. *World Monarchies and Dynasties*. New York: Sharpe Reference.

Midlarsky, Manus I. Ed. 1997. *Inequality, Democracy and Economic Development*. Cambridge: Cambridge University Press.

Midlarsky, Manus I. 1998. 'Democracy and Islam: Implications for civilizational conflict and the democratic process.' *International Studies Quarterly* 42 (3): 485–511.

Milner, Henry. 2002. *Civic Literacy: How Informed Citizens Make Democracy Work*. Hanover, NH: University Press of New England.

Minorities at Risk database. http://www.cidcm.umd.edu/inscr/mar/

Monten, Jonathan. 2005. 'The roots of the Bush doctrine: Power, nationalism and democracy promotion in U.S. strategy.' *International Security* 29 (4): 112–156.

Moore, Barrington. 1966. *Social Origins of Dictatorship and Democracy*. Boston: Beacon Press.

Moore, Mick. 1998. 'Death without taxes: Democracy, state capacity, and aid dependence in the fourth world.' In G. White and M. Robinson (Eds.), *Towards a Democratic Developmental State*. Oxford: Oxford University Press.

Morlino, Leonardo. 1998. *Democracy between Consolidation and Crisis: Parties, Groups, and Citizens in Southern Europe*. New York: Oxford University Press.

Most, Benjamin A., and Harvey Starr. 1980. 'Diffusion, reinforcement, geopolitics, and the spread of war.' *American Political Science Review* 74: 932–946.

Mozaffar, Shaheen, James R. Scarritt, and Glen Galaich. 2003. 'Electoral institutions, ethnopolitical cleavages, and party systems in Africa's emerging democracies.' *American Political Science Review* 97: 379–390.

Muller, Edward N. 1988. 'Democracy, economic development, and income inequality.' *American Sociological Review* 53 (2): 50–68.

Muller, Edward N. 1995. 'Economic determinants of democracy.' *American Sociological Review* 60 (4): 966–982.

Muller, Edward N. 1995. 'Income inequality and democratization: Reply to Bollen and Jackman.' *American Sociological Review* 60 (4): 990–996.

Muller, Edward N., and Mitch A. Seligson. 1994. 'Civic culture and democracy: The question of causal relationships.' *American Political Science Review* 88: 635–652.

Munck, Geraldo L. 2001. 'The regime question: Theory building in democratic societies.' *World Politics* 54: 119–144.

Munck, Geraldo L., and Jay Verkuilen. 2002. 'Conceptualizing and measuring democracy: Evaluating alternative indices.' *Comparative Political Studies* 35 (1): 5–34.

Munck, Geraldo L., and Jay Verkuilen. 2002. 'Generating better data: A response to discussants.' *Comparative Political Studies* 35 (1): 52–57.

Murphy, Craig N. 2006. *The United Nations Development Programme: A Better Way?* Cambridge: Cambridge University Press.

Neubauer, Deane E. 1967. 'Some conditions of democracy.' *American Political Science Review* 61: 1002–1009.

Neuman, Edward, and Roland Rich. Eds. 2004. *The UN Role in Promoting Democracy: Between Ideals and Reality*. New York/Tokyo: UN University Press.

Noel, Sid. Ed. 2005. *From Power Sharing to Democracy: Post-Conflict Institutions in Ethnically Divided Societies*. Montreal: McGill-Queen's University Press.

Norris, Pippa. 2000. *A Virtuous Circle*. Cambridge: Cambridge University Press.

Norris, Pippa. 2001. *Digital Divide*. Cambridge: Cambridge University Press.

Norris, Pippa. 2002. *Democratic Phoenix: Reinventing Political Activism*. Cambridge: Cambridge University Press.

Norris, Pippa. 2004. *Electoral Engineering*. Cambridge: Cambridge University Press.

Norris, Pippa. Ed. 1998. *Critical Citizens: Global Support for Democratic Government*. New York: Oxford University Press.

Norris, Pippa, and Ronald Inglehart. 2004. *Sacred and Secular*. Cambridge: Cambridge University Press.

North, Douglass C. 1990. *Institutions, Institutional Change, and Economic Performance*. Cambridge: Cambridge University Press.

North, Douglass C. 2005. *Understanding the Process of Economic Change*. Princeton, NJ: Princeton University Press.

O'Donnell, Guillermo. 1979. *Modernization and Bureaucratic-Authoritarianism Studies in South American Politics*. Berkeley: Institute of International Studies, University of California.

O'Donnell, Guillermo. 2004. Ed. *The Quality of Democracy: Theory and Applications*. Notre Dame, IN: University of Notre Dame Press.

O'Donnell, Guillermo, and Phillippe Schmitter. 1986. *Transitions from Authoritarian Rule: Tentative Conclusions about Uncertain Transitions*. Baltimore: Johns Hopkins University Press.

O'Loughlin, J., et al. 1998. 'The diffusion of democracy, 1946–1994.' *Annals of the Association of American Geographers* 88: 545–574.

Olsen, Mancur E. 1968. 'Multivariate analysis of national political development.' *American Sociological Review* 33: 699–712.

Ottaway, Marina, and Thomas Carothers. Eds. 2000. *Funding Virtue: Civil Society Aid and Democracy Promotion*. Washington, DC: Brookings Institution.

Page, Ed C. 1991. *Localism and Centralism in Europe*. Oxford: Oxford University Press.

Page, Ed C., and Michael Goldsmith. 1987. *Central and Local Government Relations*. London: Sage.

Paxton, Pamela. 2000. 'Women's suffrage in the measurement of democracy: Problems of operationalization.' *Studies in Comparative International Development* 35 (3): 92–111.

Paxton, Pamela. 2002. 'Social capital and democracy: An interdependent relationship.' *American Sociological Review* 67 (2): 254–277.

Paxton, Pamela, Kenneth A. Bollen, Deborah M. Lee, and Hyo Joung Kim. 2003. 'A half century of suffrage: New data and a comparative analysis.' *Studies in Comparative International Development* 38 (1): 93–122.

Pérez-Liñán, Aníbal. 2001. 'Neo-institutional accounts of voter turnout: Moving beyond industrial democracies.' *Electoral Studies* 20 (2): 281–297.

Persson, Torsten, and Guido Tabellini. 2003. *The Economic Effects of Constitutions*. Cambridge, MA: MIT Press.

Petersen, Roger. 2002. *Understanding Ethnic Violence: Fear, Hatred and Resentment in Twentieth-Century Eastern Europe*. Cambridge: Cambridge University Press.

Pevehouse, Jon C. 2002. 'Democracy from the outside-in? International organizations and democratization.' *International Organization* 56 (3): 515.

Pevehouse, Jon C. 2002. 'With a little help from my friends? Regional organizations and the consolidation of democracy.' *American Journal of Political Science* 46 (3): 611–626.

Pevehouse, Jon C. 2004. *Democracy from Above: Regional Organizations and Democratization*. Cambridge: Cambridge University Press.

Pharr, Susan, and Robert Putnam. Eds. 2000. *Disaffected Democracies: What's Troubling the Trilateral Countries?* Princeton, NJ: Princeton University Press.

Piccone, Ted, and Richard Youngs. Eds. 2006. *Strategies for Democratic Change: Assessing the Global Response*. Washington, DC: The Democracy Coalition.

Pintor, Rafael Lopez, and Maria Gratschew. *Voter Turnout since 1945: A Global Report*. Stockholm: International IDEA. www.idea.int

Posner, Daniel. 2004. 'Measuring ethnic fractionalization in Africa.' *American Journal of Political Science* 48 (4): 849–863.

Posner, Daniel. 2005. *Institutions and Ethnic Politics in Africa*. Cambridge: Cambridge University Press.

Posner, Daniel. 2004. 'The political salience of cultural difference: Why Chewas and Tumbukas are allies in Zambia and adversaries in Malawi.' *American Political Science Review* 98 (4): 529–546.

Potter, Daniel, et al. Eds. 1997. *Democratization*. Cambridge: Polity Press.

Powell, G. Bingham. 1982. *Contemporary Democracies*. New Haven, CT: Yale University Press.

Powell, G. Bingham. 1986. 'American turnout in comparative perspective.' *American Political Science Review* 80: 17–43.

Powell, G. Bingham. 2000. *Elections as Instruments of Democracy*. New Haven, CT: Yale University Press.

Pridham, Geoffrey. Ed. 1995. *Transitions to Democracy: Comparative Perspectives from Southern Europe, Latin America and Eastern Europe*. Brookfield, VT, and Aldershot, England: Dartmouth Publishing Group.

Pridham, Geoffrey, and Tatu Vanhanen. Eds. 1994. *Democratization in Eastern Europe: Domestic and International Perspectives*. London: Routledge.

Prudhomme, Remy. 1995. 'The dangers of decentralization.' *World Bank Research Observer* 10 (2): 201–220.

Przeworski, Adam. 1991. *Democracy and the Market: Political and Economic Reforms in Eastern Europe and Latin America*. Cambridge: Cambridge University Press.

Przeworski, Adam. 1999. 'Minimalist conception of democracy: A defense.' In Ian Shapiro and Casiano Hacker-Cordon (Eds.), *Democracy's Value*. Cambridge: Cambridge University Press.

Przeworski, Adam, Michael Alvarez, José Antonio Cheibub, and Fernando Limongi. 1996. 'What makes democracies endure?' *Journal of Democracy* 7 (1): 39–55.

Przeworski, Adam, Michael E. Alvarez, José Antonio Cheibub, and Fernando Limongi. 2000. *Democracy and Development: Political Institutions and Well-Being in the World, 1950–1990*. Cambridge: Cambridge University Press.

Przeworski, Adam, and Fernando Limongi. 1993. 'Political regimes and economic growth.' *Journal of Economic Perspectives* 7 (3): 51–69.

Przeworski, Adam, and Fernando Limongi. 1997. 'Modernization: Theories and facts.' *World Politics* 49: 155–183.

Putnam, Robert D. 1993. *Making Democracy Work: Civic Traditions in Modern Italy*. Princeton, NJ: Princeton University Press.

Putnam, Robert D. 2000. *Bowling Alone*. New York: Simon & Schuster.

Putnam, Robert. Ed. 2002. *Democracy in Flux*. Oxford: Oxford University Press.

Putnam, Robert D., and Lewis Feldstein. 2003. *Better Together: Restoring the American Community*. New York: Simon & Schuster.

Reilly, Ben. 2001. *Democracy in Divided Societies: Electoral Engineering for Conflict Management*. Cambridge: Cambridge University Press.

Reilly, Ben, and Andrew Reynolds. 1998. *Electoral Systems and Conflict in Divided Societies*. Washington, DC: National Academy Press.

Remmer, Karen L. 1996. 'The sustainability of political democracy.' *Comparative Political Studies* 296: 611–634.

Reynolds, Andrew. Ed. 2002. *The Architecture of Democracy: Constitutional Design, Conflict Management and Democracy*. Oxford: Oxford University Press.

Reynolds, Andrew. 2005. 'Reserved seats in national legislatures.' *Legislative Studies Quarterly* 30 (2): 301–310.

Reynolds, Andrew. 2007. 'Minority MPs in national legislatures: Existing research and data gaps.' Minority Rights Group International/UNDP. http://www.minorityrights.org/?lid=674?

Reynolds, Andrew, and Ben Reilly. 1997. *The International IDEA Handbook of Electoral System Design*. Stockholm: International Institute for Democracy and Electoral Assistance.

Riker, William H. 1964. *Federalism: Origins, Operations, Significance*. Boston: Little, Brown.

Rodden, Jonathan. 2004. 'Comparative federalism and decentralization: On meaning and measurement.' *Comparative Politics* 36 (4): 481.

Roeder, Philip, and Donald Rothschild. 2005. *Sustainable Peace: Power and Democracy after Civil Wars*. Ithaca, NY: Cornell University Press.

Rose, Richard. 2001. *The International Encyclopedia of Elections*. Washington, DC: CQ Press.

Rose-Ackerman, Susan. 1999. *Corruption and Government: Causes, Consequences and Reform*. Cambridge: Cambridge University Press.

Ross, M. L. 2001. 'Does oil hinder democracy?' *World Politics* 53: 325–361.

Ross, M. L. 2004. 'How do natural resources influence civil war? Evidence from thirteen cases.' *International Organization* 58 (1): 35–67.

Rostow, Walt W. 1952. *The Process of Economic Growth*. New York: W. W. Norton.

Rostow, Walt W. 1960. *The Stages of Economic Growth*. Cambridge: Cambridge University Press.

Rothchild, Donald. 1997. *Managing Ethnic Conflict in Africa: Pressures and Incentives for Cooperation*. Washington, DC: Brookings Institution.

Rucht, Dieter, Ruud Koopmans, and F. Niedhart. 1998. *Acts of Dissent: New Developments in the Study of Protest*. Berlin: Sigma Edition.

Rueschemeyer, Dietrich. 1991. 'Different methods, contradictory results? Research on development and democracy.' *International Journal of Comparative Sociology* 32 (1–2): 9–38.

Rueschemeyer, Dietrich, Evelyne H. Stephens, and John D. Stephens. 1992. *Capitalist Development and Democracy*. Cambridge: Polity Press.

Russett, Bruce M., John R. O'Neal, and Michael Cox. 2000. 'Clash of civilizations, or realism and liberalism déjà vu? Some evidence.' *Journal of Peace Research* 37 (5): 583–608.

Rustow, Dankwart. 1970. 'Transitions to democracy: Toward a dynamic model.' *Comparative Politics* 2: 337–363.

Sartori, Giovani. 1987. *The Theory of Democracy Revisited*. Chatham: Chatham House.

Sartori, Giovanni. 1994. *Comparative Constitutional Engineering: An Inquiry into Structures, Incentives, and Outcomes*. New York: Columbia University Press.

Scarritt, James R., and Shaheen Mozaffar. 1999. 'The specification of ethnic cleavages and ethnopolitical groups for the analysis of democratic competition in contemporary Africa.' *Nationalism and Ethnic Politics* 5: 82–117.

Schattschneider, Elmer Eric. 1942. *Party Government*. New York: Holt, Rinehart & Winston.

Schedler, Andreas. Ed. 2005. *Electoral Authoritarianism: The Dynamics of Unfree Competition*. Boulder, CO: Lynne Reinner.

Scherrer, Christian P. 2002. *Structural Prevention of Ethnic Violence*. New York: Palgrave Macmillan.

Schmitz, Hans Peter. 2004. 'Domestic and transnational perspectives on democratization.' *International Studies Review* 6: 403–426.

Schneckener, Ulrich. 2002. 'Making power-sharing work: Lessons from successes and failures in ethnic conflict regulation.' *Journal of Peace Research* 39 (2): 203–228.

Schneckner, Ulrich, and Stefan Wolff. Eds. 2004. *Managing and Settling Ethnic Conflicts: Perspectives on Successes and Failures in Europe, Africa and Asia*. London: C. Hurst.

Schneider, Aaron. 2003. 'Decentralization: Conceptualization and measurement.' *Studies in Comparative International Development* 38 (3): 32–56.

Schneider, Gerald, Thomas Plumper, and Steffen Baumann. 2000. 'Bringing Putnam to the European regions: On the relevance of social capital for economic growth.' *European Urban and Regional Studies* 7 (4): 307–317.

Schofer, Evan, and Marion Fourcade-Gourinchas. 2001. 'The structural contexts of civic engagement: Voluntary association membership in comparative perspective.' *American Sociological Review* 66 (6): 806–828.

Scholdan, Bettina. 2000. 'Democratization and electoral engineering in post-ethnic conflict societies.' *Javnost* 7 (1).

Schugart, Mathew Soberg, and John M. Carey. 1992. *Presidents and Assemblies: Constitutional Design and Electoral Dynamics*. Cambridge: Cambridge University Press.

Schumpeter, Joseph A. 1947. *Capitalism, Socialism, and Democracy*. 2nd ed. New York: Harper.

Seligson, Mitchell. A. 2002. 'The renaissance of political culture or the renaissance of the ecological fallacy?' *Comparative Politics* 34 (3): 273.

Sen, Amartya. 1999. *Development as Freedom*. New York: Knopf.

Shadid, Anthony. 2001. *Legacy of the Prophet: Despots, Democrats, and the New Politics of Islam*. Boulder, CO: Westview Press.

Shin, Doh C. 1994. 'On the Third Wave of democratization: A synthesis and evaluation of recent theory and research.' *World Politics* 47: 135–170.

Shugart, Matthew, and Martin Wattenberg. Eds. 2001. *Mixed-Member Electoral Systems*. New York: Oxford University Press.

Siegle, Joseph T., Michael M. Weinstein, and Morton H. Halperin. 2004. 'Why democracies excel.' *Foreign Affairs* 83 (5): 57–72.

Simonsen, S. G. 2005. 'Addressing ethnic divisions in post-conflict institution-building: Lessons from recent cases.' *Security Dialogue* 36 (3): 297–318.

Sirowy, Larry, and Alex Inkeles. 1990. 'The effects of democracy on economic growth and inequality: A review.' *Studies in Comparative International Development* 25 (2): 126–157.

Sisk, Timothy. 1996. *Power-Sharing and International Mediation in Ethnic Conflicts*. Washington, DC: US Institute of Peace.

Sisk, Timothy, and Andrew Reynolds. Eds. 1998. *Elections and Conflict Management in Africa*. Washington, DC: US Institute of Peace.

Smith, Peter. 2005. *Democracy in Latin America: Political Change in Comparative Perspective*. New York: Oxford University Press.

Snyder, David, and Edward L. Kick. 1979. 'Structural position in the world system and economic growth, 1955–1970: A multiple-network analysis of transnational interactions.' *American Journal of Sociology* 84: 1096–1126.

Snyder, Jack. 2000. *From Voting to Violence: Democratization and Nationalist Conflict*. New York: W. W. Norton.

Snyder, Richard. 2006. 'Does lootable wealth breed disorder? A political economy of extraction framework.' *Comparative Political Studies* 39 (8): 943–968.

Starr, Harvey, and Christina Lindborg. 2003. 'Democratic dominoes: Diffusion approaches to the spread of democracy in the international system.' *Journal of Conflict Resolution* 35 (2): 356–381.

Stegarescu, Dan. 2005. 'Public sector decentralisation: Measurement concepts and recent international trends.' *Fiscal Studies* 26 (3): 301–333.

Steiner, Jurg. 1974. *Amicable Agreement versus Majority Rule: Conflict Resolution in Switzerland*. Chapel Hill: University of North Carolina Press.

Stepan, Alfred. 1986. 'Paths toward redemocratization: Theoretical and comparative considerations.' In Guillermo O'Donnell, Phillippe Schmitter, and Laurence White-head (Eds.), *Transitions from Authoritarian Rule*, Vol. III, pp. 64–84. Baltimore: Johns Hopkins University Press.

Stepan, Alfred. 1999. 'Federalism and democracy: Beyond the U.S. model.' *Journal of Democracy* 10 (4): 19–34.

Stepan, Alfred, and Cindy Skach. 1993. 'Constitutional frameworks and democratic consolidation: Parliamentarism and presidentialism.' *World Politics* 46 (1): 1–22.

Stimson, James A. 1985. 'Regression in time and space: A statistical essay.' *American Journal of Political Science* 29 (9): 14–947.

Svensson, Jakob. 1999. 'Aid, growth and democracy.' *Economics & Politics* 11: 275–297.

Taagepera, Rein, and Matthew Shugart. 1989. *Seats and Votes: The Effects and Determinants of Electoral Systems*. New Haven, CT: Yale University Press.

Taras, Raymond, and Rajat Ganguly. 1998. *Understanding Ethnic Conflict*. New York: Longman.

Transparency International. Annual. *The Corruption Perception Index*. http://www.transparency.org/surveys/index.html#cpi

Transparency International. Annual. *Global Corruption Barometer*. http://www.transparency.org/

Treisman, Daniel. 2007. *The Architecture of Government: Rethinking Political Decentralization*. Cambridge: Cambridge University Press.

Tsebelis, George. 2002. *Veto Players: How Political Institutions Work*. Princeton, NJ: Princeton University Press.

Tull, Denis M., and Andreas Mehler. 2005. 'The hidden costs of power-sharing: Reproducing insurgent violence in Africa.' *African Affairs* 104: 375–398.

UNDP. 2004. *Arab Human Development Report 2004*. New York: UNDP/Oxford University Press.

Vanhanen, Tatu. 1990. *The Process of Democratization: A Comparative Study of 147 States: 1980–88*. New York: Crane Russak.

Vanhanen, Tatu. 1997. *Prospects for Democracy: A Study of 172 Countries*. New York: Routledge.

Vanhanen, Tatu. 2000. 'A new dataset for measuring democracy, 1810–1998.' *Journal of Peace Research* 37 (2): 251–265.

Varshney, Ashutosh. 2003. *Ethnic Conflict and Civic Life: Hindus and Muslims in India*. New Haven, CT: Yale University Press.

Verba, Sidney, and Norman Nie. 1972. *Participation in America: Political Democracy and Social Equality*. New York: Harper & Row.

Verba, Sidney, Kay Schlozman, and Henry E. Brady. 1995. *Voice and Equality: Civic Voluntarism in American Politics*. Cambridge, MA: Harvard University Press.

Verba, Sidney, Norman Nie, and Jae-on Kim. 1978. *Participation and Political Equality: A Seven-Nation Comparison*. Cambridge: Cambridge University Press.

Wallerstein, Peter, and Margareta Sollenberg. 1997. 'Armed conflicts, conflict termination, and peace agreements, 1989–96.' *Journal of Peace Research* 34 (3): 339–358.

Walter, Barbara, and Jack Snyder. Eds. 1999. *Civil Wars, Insecurity and Intervention*. New York: Columbia University Press.

Watts, Ronald L. 1999. *Comparing Federal Systems*. 2nd ed. Kingston, Canada: McGill-Queen's University Press.

Watts, Ronald L. 2006. *Models of Federal Power-Sharing*. Washington, DC: National Democratic Institute.

Webb, Paul, David Farrell, and Ian Holliday. Eds. *Political Parties in Advanced Industrial Democracies*. Oxford: Oxford University Press.

Weiss, Thomas G., David P. Forsythe, and Roger A. Coate. 2004. *United Nations and Changing World Politics*. Boulder, CO: Westview Press.

Weller, Marc, and Stefan Wolff. Eds. 2005. *Autonomy, Self-Governance and Conflict Resolution: Innovative Approaches to Institutional Design in Divided Societies*. London/New York: Routledge.

Welzel, Christopher, Ronald Inglehart, and Hans-Dieter Klingemann. 2003. 'The theory of human development: A cross-cultural analysis.' *European Journal of Political Research* 42 (3): 341–379.

Whitehead, Laurence. 1986. 'International aspects of democratization.' In Guillermo O'Donnell, Phillippe Schmitter, and Laurence Whitehead (Eds.), *Transitions from Authoritarian Rule: Comparative Perspectives*, pp. 3–46. Baltimore: Johns Hopkins University Press.

Wibbels, Erik. 2005. *Federalism and the Market: Intergovernmental Conflict and Economic Reform in the Developing World*. Cambridge: Cambridge University Press.

Wilson, Sven E., and Daniel M. Butler. 2007. 'A lot more to do: The sensitivity of time-series cross-section analyses to simple alternative specifications.' *Political Analysis* 15: 101–123.

Wolff, Stefan. 2003. *Disputed Territories: The Transnational Dynamics of Ethnic Conflict Settlement*. New York: Berghahn Books.

World Bank. 1999. 'Can corruption be measured? Bank offers diagnostic tools to measure and combat corruption in member countries.' http://www.worldbank.org/wbi/governance/pubs/measurecor.htm

World Bank Governance Indicators. Annual. http://www.worldbank.org/wbi/governance

Zakaria, Fareed. 1997. 'The rise of illiberal democracy.' *Foreign Affairs* 76 (6): 22–41.

Zakaria, Fareed. 2003. *The Future of Freedom: Illiberal Democracy at Home and Abroad*. New York: W. W. Norton.

Zielonka, Jan. Ed. 2001. *Democratic Consolidation in Eastern Europe*. Oxford: Oxford University Press.

Index

administrative decentralization, 164–165
  scaled degrees of, 170–171
adult suffrage
  within democracy, 66–67
  in Saudi Arabia, for women, 67
  in South Africa, 67
  in Switzerland, for women, 67
Afghanistan
  constitutional arrangements in, 30
  electoral system in, 29
  Wolesi Jirga, 112
Africa, sub-Saharan. *See also* African Union;
    Angola; Benin; Burundi; Congo, Republic
    of; Equatorial Guinea; Ghana; Lesotho;
    Mali; Mauritius; Namibia; Nigeria;
    Senegal; South Africa; Sudan; Togo;
    Zimbabwe
  ethnic conflicts in, 13
  regional diffusion in, 18
*African Charter on Democracy, Elections, and
    Governance,* 17
African Charter on Human and People's
    Rights, 186
African National Congress, 64
African Union, 15, 216
  *African Charter on Democracy, Elections,
    and Governance* endorsement by, 17
  regional diffusion through, 17–18
Algeria, 19
alternative vote electoral system, 29, 110
Alvarez, Michael, 81
American Convention on Human Rights, 186
Amnesty International, 6, 216
Angola, 19
Arab League, 216
Argentina, 10
Armingeon, Klaus, 3
Arroyo, Gloria, 144
al-Assad, Bashar, 138

al-Assad, Hafez, 138
associated statehood, 170
Association of Southeast Asian Nations, 216
Atlas Narodov Mira, 51
  ELF index and, 51
Austria, 38
  Freiheitliche Partei Osterreichs in, 110
autocracies, electoral, 57, 115
  definition of, 8
  Togo as, 6–10
  traditional v., 57–58
autocracies, traditional, 57–58
  electoral v., 57–58
Awami League (Bangladesh), 181, 183

Baath Party (Iraq), 109
Bangladesh, 180–181
  Awami League in, 181, 183
  Bangladesh National Party in, 181, 183
  centralized government in, 183–184
  Emergency Power Ordinance in, 181
  federal structure of, 183–184
  independence for, 181
  Jatiya Party in, 183
Bangladesh National Party, 181, 183
Banks, Arthur S., 149
Belgium, 38
  constitutional reforms in, 39
  ethnic identity in, 50
  federal constitution in, 167–168
  Vlaams Blok Party in, 110
Benin, 9–10
  Cauri Forces for an Emerging Benin in, 10
  constitutional rules within, 19–20
  economic development as political factor in,
    12
  electoral system changes in, 9, 19
  ethnic divisions in, 13–14
  ethno-religious groups in, 13–14